Equal Pay – Law and Practice

Equal Pay – Law and Practice

Michael Duggan

Published by
Jordan Publishing Limited
21 St Thomas Street, Bristol BS1 6JS

British Library Cataloguing-in-Publication Data

A catalogue record for this book is available from the British Library.

ISBN 978 1 84661 088 2

Typeset by Letterpart Ltd, Reigate, Surrey

Printed in Great Britain by Antony Rowe Limited, Chippenham, Wilts

This book is dedicated to my wife, Michelle Duggan, my mother, Kathleen Duggan and also to my sisters, Ann, Clare and Trish, sister-in-law, Susan, nieces, Charlotte, Abigail, Isla and Josie – all of whom, in my view, demonstrate the true meaning of equal value!

PREFACE

The Equal Pay Act 1970 has laid on the statute book since 1975, its importance and impact largely unrecognised, despite several trips to the House of Lords, until the beginning of this century. The Employment Tribunal cases, now cutting a swathe through the country, have exposed the unequal pay structures throughout the public sector, which is likely to cost Local Authorities and Health Trusts many millions of pounds. The fact that discriminatory pay practices are historical is no excuse; as Mummery LJ stated in *Bainbridge*, 'it would be most unattractive if the employer who turned a blind eye was in a better position on justification' (see [2008] IRLR 776 at para 159).

The current litigation makes it clear that all employers must have an eye to their pay practices and ensure that they are not discriminatory, preferably by putting into place a JES. It is hoped that this book will assist employment lawyers and HR professionals who are advising both employers and employees on the nuances of this difficult area of law.

Given the pace of this area it is inevitable that there will be a number of important cases over the life of this book. The reader is therefore referred to the Littleton Chambers website which will contain periodic update on developments in equal pay legislation and new case-law at www.littletonchambers.com/Employment-Law-Bullettins.aspx.

I would like to thank John Bowers QC, Naomi Ellenbogen and Katherine Apps for their comments on the first draft of this book; they are both very experienced practitioners in this area.

The Publishers and I would also like to express our thanks to the Equality and Human Rights Commission for permission to reproduce EHRC materials in the text and Appendices.

My publisher, Mary Kenny has been extremely patient and helpful despite the date for publication being put back and I am grateful to Kiran Goss, Cheryl Prophet and Kate Hather for their hard work on the proofs.

As ever, my heartfelt thanks go to Francis, Andrew and Thomas who have grown up with a father who spends too much time in his study, having completed this, my tenth book.

The law is as stated as at 1 November 2008.

Michael Duggan
Littleton Chambers

CONTENTS

TABLE OF STATUTES

References are to paragraph numbers.

TABLE OF STATUTORY INSTRUMENTS

References are to paragraph numbers.

TABLE OF CASES

References are to paragraph numbers.

TABLE OF EUROPEAN LEGISLATION

References are to paragraph numbers.

TABLE OF ABBREVIATIONS

CEEP	European Centre for Enterprises with Public Participation and Services of General Interest
DDA 1995	Disability Discrimination Act 1995
DDP	dismissal and disciplinary procedure
DDR	German Democratic Republic
EA 2002	Employment Act 2002
EA Regs 2004	Employment Act 2002 (Dispute Resolution) Regulations 2004, SI 2004/752
EAT	Employment Appeal Tribunal
ECJ	European Court of Justice
EHRC	Equality and Human Rights Commission
EOC	Equal Opportunities Commission
EqPA 1970	Equal Pay Act 1970
ERA 1996	Employment Rights Act 1996
ETUC	European Trade Union Confederation
EWC	expected week of childbirth
GMF	genuine material factor
GPs	Grievance procedures
ICR	Industrial Cases Report
IRLR	Industrial Relations Law Reports
JARs	Job Analysis Reports
JES	job evaluation study
MAPLE Regs 1999	The Maternity and Parental Leave etc Regulations 1999, SI 1999/3312
NJC	National Joint Council
OML	ordinary maternity leave
PTW Regs 2000	Part-time Workers (Prevention of Less Favourable Treatment) Regulations 2000, SI 2000/1551
RRA 1976	Race Relations Act 1976
RVI	Royal Victoria Infirmary
SDA 1975	Sex Discrimination Act 1975
SERPS	State Earnings Related Pensions Scheme
SMP	Statutory Maternity Pay
TULR(C)A 1992	Trade Union and Labour Relations (Consolidation) Act 1992
TUPE	Transfer of Undertakings (Protection of Employment) Regulations 2006, SI 2006/246

UNICE   Union of Industrial and Employers' Confederations of Europe

Chapter 1

INTRODUCTION

HISTORY

1.1   The Equal Pay Act 1970 (EqPA 1970) came into force on 29 December 1975 at the same time as the Sex Discrimination Act 1975 (SDA 1975). It received Royal Assent on 29 May 1970 but its implementation was delayed so that employers could prepare by voluntarily removing discrimination from their pay scales before legislation actually required them to do so. The EqPA 1970 was produced as a schedule to the SDA 1975. The Acts are to be read together as a code though their provisions are mutually exclusive (see below at **2.43-2.52**). Complaints may be brought under both Acts in the alternative or in combination, with the EqPA 1970 covering contractual terms and SDA 1975 covering non-contractual benefits.

1.2   Despite the laudatory aims of the EqPA 1970 it has been slow in achieving its objectives and the evidence is that there are still substantial inequalities in pay levels between men and women. In 1970, the gender pay gap stood at 35%, with men earning significantly more than women both in full and part-time employment. Since then, significant strides have been made to narrow this gap and, in 2008, the Trade Union Congress produced a report suggesting that the full-time gender pay gap is currently 17.2%, while the part-time gap is 35.6%. The Government's official figures produced by Annual Survey of Hours and Earnings for the National Office of Statistics reveal a more favourable position. They show that the median hourly pay gap between women and men across all industry sectors and positions is continuing to show signs of narrowing and stands at 12.6% – a 5% improvement on 1997. Nevertheless, it is apparent that the gender pay gap remains. The factors behind these disparities in pay are no doubt due to complex and multiple reasons, some of them historical, such as perceptions of 'the breadwinner' being male and the segregation of women into more poorly paid 'women's jobs' and consequent depression of women's pay. The fact that part-time work has historically been less well paid and more female dominated has also played a part.

1.3   There have been a number of amendments to the EqPA 1970 and the implementation of statutory instruments which are intended to make it easier to bring an equal pay claim, as well as a number of seminal European Court of Justice (ECJ) cases which have a fundamental effect upon the timing of claims. In particular:

- In *Defrenne v Sabena (No 2)* [1976] ICR 547 the ECJ ruled that Art 141 of the EC Treaty 'is directly applicable and may thus give rise to individual rights which the courts must protect'. Thus it is important to consider the considerable EC jurisprudence when assessing the rights that arise under the EqPA 1970 (see **2.1–2.30** in relation to the application of EEC law).

- On 1 January 1984 there were major amendments to the EqPA 1970 to bring in the right to claim equal pay for work of equal value. It was predicted that these provisions would see a move towards disparities between pay being eradicated. As noted, this has not happened, though many years later there has been a massive escalation of cases as seen in the equal pay claims sweeping the public sector at present.

- The decision of the ECJ in *Barber v GRE Assurance* [1990] IRLR 240 that equality is required, under Art 141, in relation to levels of pension benefits/contributions had changed the map so far as pensions law is concerned. Because of its fundamental impact, the ECJ stated that the effect of its decision is to only apply from 17 May 1990.

- The Equal Pay (Questions and Replies) Order 2003, SI 2003/722 came into force on 6 April 2003. This Order was derived from the EqPA 1970, s 7B which was introduced by the Employment Act 2002 (EA 2002), s 42. This questionnaire procedure is designed to make it easier for an employee to establish whether she has a case and is an important tool for the potential claimant.

- The Equal Pay Act 1970 (Amendment) Regulations 2003, SI 2003/1656 made changes with effect from 19 July 2003 to the time-limits in which a claim may be made and the extent to which an Employment Tribunal can award arrears of pay. The changes came about as a result of the rulings of the ECJ in *Levez v TH Jennings (Harlow Pools) Ltd* [1999] IRLR 36 and *Preston v Wolverhampton Healthcare NHS Trust; Fletcher v Midland Bank plc* [2000] IRLR 506.

- The Equal Pay Act 1970 (Amendment) Regulations 2004, SI 2004/2352 set out procedures to be followed where a Tribunal is considering a claim of equal value as well as making amendments to EqPA 1970, s 2A. These changes came about as a result of the ECJ judgment in *EC Commission v United Kingdom of Great Britain and Northern Ireland* [1982] IRLR 333, ICR 578 that the UK had failed to implement the principles of equality with regard to work of equal value.

- The procedures relating to equal pay are now to be found in the Employment Tribunals (Constitution and Rules of Procedure) Regulations 2004, SI 2004/1861, in particular Sch 6 deals with equal value claims.

1.4 The recent legislation involving Health Trusts and Local Authorities have given rise to a number of important decisions in the Employment Appeal Tribunal (EAT) and the Court of Appeal which are covered in detail in this book. There are a number of cases which remain due to be heard in the EAT and readers should check the Littleton Chambers website at www. littletonchambers.com/Employment-Law-Bullettins.aspx for updates to this book.

REVIEWING PAY SYSTEMS – EQUAL OPPORTUNITY POLICIES: FROM LIP SERVICE TO ACTION

1.5 The Equal Opportunities Commission (EOC – now the Equality and Human Rights Commission (EHRC)) has a simple checklist in order to decide whether an employer is an equal opportunities employer when it comes to equal pay, which may be considered as an initial employment 'health check'.

		Yes	No
•	Does your organisation have a stated policy on equal pay?	☐	☐
•	Has the equal pay policy been communicated to employees and recognised trade unions?	☐	☐
•	Has responsibility for the implementation of the policy been clearly assigned?	☐	☐
•	Have you carried out an equal pay review comparing the pay of men and women doing equal work, in line with the EOC's (now EHRC's) Code of Practice?	☐	☐
•	Does your organisation use a single job evaluation scheme covering all employees that has been designed and implement so as not to discriminate on grounds of sex?	☐	☐

The above are very basic questions and if the employer cannot answer 'Yes' to all five questions it is necessary to immediately implement procedures by way of putting into place a policy and, more importantly, by considering whether a workforce job evaluation study (JES) should be carried out. A JES is fundamental since it will provide a defence to an equal value claim as set out below. This is considered in more detail in Chapters 8 and 15. .

AVOIDING CLAIMS – THE CODE OF PRACTICE AND OTHER AIDS

An equal opportunities policy

1.6 The first stage is the necessity for an equal opportunities policy. The EOC (now the EHRC) has a suggested policy which is contained at Section

Three of the Code of Practice on Equal Pay. The policy contained in the Code is quite simply an expression of sentiment rather than detail – but it is to be noted that statements of intent are pointless if they are not put into practice (cf *Balgobin v Tower Hamlets LBC* [1987] ICR 829 – a case on race relations policies).

'A model equal pay policy

We are committed to the principle of equal pay for all our employees. We aim to eliminate any sex bias in our pay systems.

We understand that equal pay between men and women is a legal right under both domestic and European law.

It is in the interest of the organisation to ensure that we have a fair and just pay system. It is important that employees have confidence in the process of eliminating sex bias and we are therefore committed to working in partnership with the recognised trade unions. As good business practice we are committed to working with trade union/employee representatives to take action to ensure that we provide equal pay.

We believe that in eliminating sex bias in our pay system we are sending a positive message to our staff and customers. It makes good business sense to have a fair, transparent reward system and it helps us to control costs. We recognise that avoiding unfair discrimination will improve morale and enhance efficiency.

Our objectives are to:

- Eliminate any unfair, unjust or unlawful practices that impact on pay
- Take appropriate remedial action.

We will:

- Implement an equal pay review in line with EOC (now the EHRC) guidance for all current staff and starting pay for new staff (including those on maternity leave, career breaks, or non-standard contracts)
- Plan and implement actions in partnership with trade union/employee representatives
- Provide training and guidance for those involved in determining pay
- Inform employees of how these practices work and how their own pay is determined
- Respond to grievances on equal pay as a priority
- In conjunction with trade union/employee representatives, monitor pay statistics annually.'

The above policy is more aspirational than anything and the practical detail of what must be done by an employer seeking to ensure equality and avoid an equal pay claim is covered further in this book.

1.7   The aim of this book is to consider the various stages of an equal pay claim from persons covered, comparator, like work, work rated as equivalent and work of equal value through to the material factor defence. The text focuses on what we can learn from the case-law with suggestions as to bringing or defending a claim. Given that the EqPA 1970 is essentially based upon discriminatory treatment, Chapter 10 considers this in some detail. It will be seen that despite the fact the Act has been around for over 30 years there are still considerable problems of interpretation and application. Specialist areas such as maternity, pensions, part-time workers and the Transfer of Undertakings (Protection of Employment) Regulations 2006, SI 2006/246 (TUPE) will be considered whilst Chapters 15–18 consider the procedures that employers may adopt to achieve equality as well as the procedures in the Tribunals. It is necessary to commence with a consideration of the impact of EC law and the dichotomy between the EqPA 1970 and the SDA 1975.

Chapter 2

EUROPEAN AND UK LEGISLATION

THE ACT AND EUROPE

2.1 Given the direct effect of Art 141 of the EC Treaty, that Article and the provisions of the relevant Directives must be taken into account in construing equal pay rights. It will be seen that, in some respects, the Article and European Court of Justice case-law is wider than the UK legislation; in particular in relation to comparator issues and common employment. The European case-law does not require the identification of a comparator but envisages the possibility of discrimination based upon statistical evidence (*Grundy v British Airways* [2008] IRLR 74) and the existence of a comparator may not be necessary in relation to challenges to state legislation (see *Allonby Accrington and Rossendale College* [2004] IRLR 224). Community law also envisages comparison with a comparator in the 'same service' who works for another employer (*South Ayrshire Council v Morton* [2002] IRLR 256, ICR 966). It remains to be seen how far these developments will impact but it has been stated by the ECJ that Community Law will prevail where domestic law is less favourable (*Barber v Guardian Royal Exchange Assurance Group* [1990] IRLR 240, ICR 616). Indeed, increasingly equal pay cases are becoming flashpoints for deciding difficult issues of constitutional and European law.

2.2 It is necessary to consider Art 141 (formerly Art 119) of the EC Treaty, the Equal Pay Directive (75/117/EC), the Burden of Proof Directive (97/80/EC) as well as other associated Directives, such as the Equal Treatment Directive (76/207/EC), the Part Time Workers Directive (97/81/EC) and the Framework Directive (2000/78/EC). There is a Consolidating Directive which codifies a number of the Directives (see 2006/54/EC) and which will apply from 15 September 2009, though governments had a duty to ensure that it was put into effect by 15 September 2008.

2.3 It is not intended to give a detailed exposition of the application of European law in this text but it is necessary to have the general principles in mind when considering equal pay since the ECJ cases adopt a wider approach and EC law may provide a remedy where there is none under the EqPA 1970. Ever since the European Communities Act 1972 came into force EC law can have direct effect (s 2(1)).

2.4 Given that the EqPA 1970 and the Sex Discrimination Act 1975 (SDA 1975) are intended to comply with European measures it is necessary to construe UK law so that it is in conformity with EC law. In cases involving purely private parties, the Tribunal must interpret the EqPA 1970 consistently with EC law in so far as it is 'possible' to do so (see *Unison v Brennan* [2008] IRLR 492). This principle permits words to be 'read in' or 'read out' of a statute (see *Alabaster* at **12.28** for example), but it has limits; it does not permit a Tribunal to go against a 'fundamental feature' of the legislation.

2.5   In cases involving public employers, it also becomes relevant that Art 141 has direct effect. This obliges courts to disapply national legislation where there is an inconsistency. Article 141 has been held to have 'horizontal direct effect' which means that it confers rights directly on private parties in cases against purely private parties. It is an unresolved question whether this horizontal direct effect obliges national tribunals to disapply legislation where it is not possible to interpret it consistently (as in cases involving state entities) but it is likely that the courts will be sympathetic to this argument.

2.6   Article 141 of the EC Treaty provides:

'1 Each Member State shall ensure that the principle of equal pay for male and female workers for equal work or work of equal value is applied.

2 For the purpose of this Article, "pay" means the ordinary basic or minimum wage or salary and any other consideration, whether in cash or in kind, which the worker receives directly or indirectly, in respect of his employment, from his employer.

Equal pay without discrimination based on sex means:

(a)   that pay for the same work at piece rates shall be calculated on the basis of the same unit of measurement;
(b)   that pay for work at time rates shall be the same for the same job.

3 The Council, acting in accordance with the procedure referred to in Article 251, and after consulting the Economic and Social Committee, shall adopt measures to ensure the application of the principle of equal opportunities and equal treatment of men and women in matters of employment and occupation, including the principle of equal pay for equal work or work of equal value.

4 With a view to ensuring full equality in practice between men and women in working life, the principle of equal treatment shall not prevent any Member State from maintaining or adopting measures providing for specific advantages in order to make it easier for the under-represented sex to pursue a vocational activity or to prevent or compensate for disadvantages in professional careers.'

2.7   Article 141 was previously Art 119 and was explained in *Defrenne v Sabena (No 2)* [1976] ICR 547 as follows:

'8. Article 119 [141] pursues a double aim.

9. First, in the light of the different stages of the development of social legislation in the various member states, the aim of article 119 is to avoid a situation in which

undertakings established in states which have actually implemented the principle of equal pay suffer a competitive disadvantage in intra-community competition as compared with undertakings established in states which have not yet eliminated discrimination against women workers as regards pay.

10. Secondly, this provision forms part of the social objectives of the community, which is not merely an economic union, but is at the same time intended, by common action, to ensure social progress and seek the constant improvement of the living and working conditions of their peoples, as is emphasised by the preamble to the Treaty.'

2.8 The social objectives of Art 141 are to be carried through to the EqPA 1970 and a party may seek to apply Art 141 in the courts if there is a lacunae in the UK legislation. Given that the EqPA 1970 only covers contractual terms it will be necessary to consider the provisions of the Equal Pay Directive, the Equal Treatment Directive (and see now the Consolidating Directive) and SDA 1975 to consider whether UK law provides a remedy (see *Alabaster* at **12.21** and *Hoyland* at **12.35**). *Defrenne* confirmed that Art 141 will have direct effect with regard to direct discrimination. It will also have direct effect with regard to indirect discrimination (*Bilka-Kaufaus GmbH v Weber Von Hartz* [1987] ICR 110).

2.9 It has been held that the Equal Pay Directive does not create an alternative cause of action (*Worringham v Lloyds Bank Ltd* [1981] ICR 558) nor does it alter the scope of Art 141, but it is designed to facilitate the practical application of equal pay outlined in the Article (*Jenkins v Kingsgate (Clothing Productions) Ltd* [1981] IRLR 228). Similarly, the Equal Treatment Directive may be relied upon to interpret national legislation. Claims brought under Art 141 will be able to rely on Directives to enunciate the principles contained in Art 141; ie national Courts should interpret the domestic legislation in the context of the wording and purpose of the Directives (see *Von Colson and Kamann v Land Nordrhein-Westfalen* [1984] ECR 1891). The Directive therefore has indirect effect and there are numerous examples of the courts interpreting domestic law to reconcile it with EU law (*Chessington World of Adventures Ltd v Reed* [1998] ICR 97; *Webb v EMO Air Cargo (UK) Ltd* [1993] ICR 175) by even reading words into the legislation (*Pickstone and others v Freemans plc* [1988] ICR 697; *Litster and others v Forth Dry Dock and Engineering Co Ltd (in receivership) and another* [1989] ICR 341). Where the legislation is clear, changes will have to be implemented by changes to domestic legislation (see the recent changes to the SDA 1975 as a result of *Equal Opportunities Commission v Secretary of State for Trade and Industry* [2007] IRLR 327). The individual may not be able to bring a claim against another private party based upon the direct effect of a Directive. It is apparent, however, that the individual may have the right to bring a claim against the state where Directives have direct effect (*Francovich & Bonifaci v Italy* [1995] ICR 722, [1992] IRLR 84). A claim may be brought against the state or an emanation of the state, examples being *Foster v British Gas plc* [1990] IRLR 353, *Marshall v Southampton and South West*

Hampshire Area Health Authority [1986] IRLR 140. The latter case is of particular relevance given the number of equal pay cases in the public sector at present.

2.10 Where UK law does not provide a remedy but this is provided by EC law, then the procedural rules of the EqPA 1970 will be applied to determine time-limits and limitation periods, though the UK provisions have themselves been found to be in breach of EC law and required modification (see Chapter 18). As already noted, the community standard will prevail (*Barber v Guardian Royal Exchange Assurance Group* [1990] IRLR 240, ICR 616). It will only be if domestic law provides no remedy (*Blaik v The Post Office* [1994] IRLR 280) that reliance on Art 141 can arise. So, for example, the fact that the EqPA 1970 excludes non-contractual benefits does not mean that there is no remedy, as a claim can be brought under SDA 1975 (see **2.43-2.52**).

2.11 The following issues indicate that, in important respects, there will be a distinction between the approach under the UK legislation and EC law:

- It was stated in *Defrenne v Sabena (No 2)* [1976] ICR 547 that the prohibition on discrimination extends to collective agreements as well as private contracts (see the position with regard to collective agreements set out at **2.63-2.69**).

- It was also stated in *Defrenne* that 'among the forms of direct discrimination which may be identified solely by reference to the criteria laid down by article 119 must be included in particular those which have their origin in legislative provisions or in collective labour agreements and which may be detected on the basis of a purely legal analysis of the situation'. This statement appeared to negate the necessity for a comparator in certain cases, and this has been held to be the position (see Chapter 5). Under the EqPA 1970 the orthodox principle is that a comparator will always be needed.

- Article 141 has been relied upon to extend the possibility of comparisons where the EqPA 1970, s 1(6) is more restrictive (see *Lawrence v Regent Office Care Ltd* [2002] IRLR 822; *Allonby v Accrington & Rossendale College* [2004] IRLR 244 and see Chapter 5).

- Under the statutory grievance procedures there is a the requirement to name a comparator by way of a grievance as set out in *Highland Council v TGWU* [2008] IRLR 272 and *Cannop v Highland Council* [2008] IRLR 634 though the scope of this rule has been disputed by Elias P more recently in the case of *Suffolk Mental Health Partnership NHS Trust v Hurst and Others* UKEAT/0332/08/RN, [2009] IRLR 12. It is arguable that this requirement, if the former two cases are correct, infringes EC law in terms of providing an effective remedy. In *van Schijndel and van Veen v Stichting Pensioenfonds Voor Fysiotherapeuten* [1995] ECR I-4705, [1996] All ER (EC) 259 the ECJ stated that 'each case which raises the question whether a national procedural provision renders application of Community Law impossible or excessively difficult must be analysed by reference to the role of that provision in the procedure, its progress and its special features, viewed as a whole, before the various national instances' (see Chapter 17).

- There is an issue whether the ECJ jurisprudence requires objective justification in all cases where a woman is doing work of equal value to a man (*Brunnhofer v Bank der österreichischen Postsparkasse* (Case 381/99), [2001] IRLR 571) or whether the correct approach is that objective justification is only required where there is discrimination (see Chapter 10).

THE DIRECTIVES

2.12 Whilst the original Art 119 came into effect in 1957 it was not for some considerable time before further positive steps came to be taken to implement the effect of the Article. Important Directives were adopted as a result of the Social Action Programme in 1974 which had aspired to a positive programme to achieve equality between men and women in the labour market. The three Directives were:

- Directive 75/117/EEC, of 10 February 1974, on the approximation of the laws of the member states relating to the application of the principle of equal pay for men and women – the Equal Pay Directive;

- Directive 76/207/EEC, of 9 February 1976, on the implementation of the principle of equal treatment for men and women as regards access to employment, vocational training and promotion, and working conditions – the Equal Treatment Directive; and

- Directive 79/7/EEC, of 19 December 1978, on the progressive implementation of the principle of equal treatment for men and women in matters of social security.
  There was a further Directive in relation to occupational schemes for social security in 1986 being Directive 86/378/EEC, of 24 July 1986, on the implementation of the principle of equal treatment for men and women in occupational social security schemes. This Directive enshrines the principle of equal treatment in relation to occupational pension and other schemes. It was amended by Directive 96/97/EEC to take into account the *Barber* judgment (see Chapter 13).

2.13 In 1986 there was also a Directive, of 11 December 1986, relating to the self-employed, the 'Council Directive on the application of the principle of equal treatment between men and women engaged in an activity, including agriculture, in a self-employed capacity, and on the protection of self-employed women during pregnancy and motherhood'.

2.14   The 1989 Social Action Programme (COM(89) 568, 29 November 1989) led to Directive 92/85/EC, dated 19 October 1992, on the introduction of measures to encourage improvements in the safety and health at work of pregnant workers and workers who have recently given birth or are breastfeeding (tenth individual Directive within the meaning of Art 16(1) of Directive 89/391/EEC). Then in 1996 there was Directive 96/34/EC of 3 June 1996 on the framework agreement on parental leave concluded by the Union of Industrial and Employers' Confederations of Europe (UNICE – now called Business Europe), the European Centre for Enterprises with Public Participation and Services of General Interest (CEEP) and the European Trade Union Confederation (ETUC). Directive 97/81/EC, of 15 December 1997, concerning the Framework Agreement on part-time work concluded by UNICE, CEEP and the ETUC established a framework for equality of treatment of part-time workers in comparison to full-time workers. The above Directives all had an impact on the issue of equal pay. For example, in relation to maternity leave and pay it was noted in *Hoyland v Asda Stores Ltd* [2005] IRLR 438 that the case involved 'another chapter in the history of attempts to obtain for pregnant workers the same remuneration, while absent on maternity leave, as they would receive if they were attending at work'. The impact of EC law and the dichotomy between equal treatment and equal pay was considered in some detail in that case.

2.15   A further Directive, 97/80/EC on the burden of proof in cases of discrimination based on sex was dated 15 December 1997. This Directive has had an important impact on the burden of proof in equal pay cases as will be seen at **10.7-10.16**.

2.16   These Directives are considered at the appropriate places in the text. It is, however, important to note that Directives 75/117, 76/207, 86/378 and 97/80 (as well as their amending Directives) are all repealed with effect from 15 August 2009 by Directive 2006/54/EC of the European Parliament and of the Council of 5 July 2006 on the implementation of the principle of equal opportunities and equal treatment of men and women in matters of employment and occupation (the Consolidating Directive). Member states had a duty to implement the substantive parts of this Consolidating Directive by 15 August 2008 in so far as it had not already been implemented. This Directive aims to provide a statement of the ECJ case-law and is referred to at the appropriate parts of this text. The preamble to this Directive provides a useful summary of the development of the law in this area and is worth reading.

The Equal Pay Directive, 75/117/EEC

2.17   The Articles of this Directive sought to flesh out the principle of equal pay. By Art 1, the principle 'means, for the same work or for work to which equal value is attributed, the elimination of all discrimination on grounds of sex with regard to all aspects and conditions of remuneration. In particular, where a job classification system is used for determining pay, it must be based on the same criteria for both men and women and so drawn up as to exclude any discrimination on grounds of sex'. The principle of equal pay for work of equal value was thus clearly stated, both in relation to criterion for deciding pay and all aspects of remuneration. It is to be noted that the Equal Pay Directive does not expressly refer to direct or indirect discrimination, though the Consolidating Directive 2006/54/EC makes it plain that the concepts apply to equal pay.

2.18   Article 4 required that measures be taken to ensure equality of treatment for pay in relation to 'collective agreements, wage scales, wage agreements or individual contracts of employment which are contrary to the principle of equal pay shall be, or may be declared, null and void or may be amended'. The position with regard to collective agreements in UK law is not an easy one and is considered further at **2.63-2.69**. Member states are under a duty to ensure 'that effective means are available to take care that this principle is observed'. This lack of effective means has led to findings against the UK in several ECJ judgments with corresponding amending legislation.

2.19   The European Commission has produced a useful, though slightly out of date Memorandum on Equal Pay for Work of Equal Value (COM(94) 6 final, 23 June 1994) which has also produced a Code of Practice on the Implementation of Equal Pay for Work of Equal Value for Women and Men (COM(96) 336 final, 17 July 1996). These are both available on the EC website.

The Equal Treatment Directive, 76/207/EEC

2.20   We shall see in the next section that there is a dichotomy between 'equal treatment' and 'equal pay' in UK law; the former being covered by the SDA 1975 and the latter by the EqPA 1970. There is a similar distinction in EC law, which on occasion is of real significance; for example the classification of maternity pay as coming under the Equal Pay Directive has enabled the ECJ to decide that differential treatment of women on maternity leave is possible so far as their pay is concerned (see *Gillespie and others* (Case C-342/93), [1996] IRLR 214 and Chapter 12).

2.21   Articles 1–11 (including 8a–e which were inserted by Directive 2002/73/EC) aim to 'to put into effect in the Member States the principle of equal treatment for men and women as regards access to employment, including promotion, and to vocational training and as regards working conditions and, on the conditions referred to in paragraph 2, social security' (Art 1). Article 2 was substituted by Art 1.2 of Directive 2002/73/EC. It provides definitions of discrimination and harassment, the definitions of the former being:

- direct discrimination: where one person is treated less favourably on grounds of sex than another is, has been or would be treated in a comparable situation;

- indirect discrimination: where an apparently neutral provision, criterion, or practice would put persons of one sex at a particular disadvantage compared with persons of the other sex, unless that provision, criterion or practice is objectively justified by a legitimate aim, and the means of achieving that aim are appropriate and necessary.

2.22 Less favourable treatment of a woman relating to pregnancy or maternity leave within the meaning of Directive 92/85/EEC constitutes discrimination within the meaning of the Directive. Article 3 provides that there will be no discrimination in relation to:

(a) conditions for access to employment, to self-employment or to occupation, including selection criteria and recruitment conditions, whatever the branch of activity and at all levels of the professional hierarchy, including promotion;

(b) access to all types and to all levels of vocational guidance, vocational training, advanced vocational training and retraining, including practical work experience;

(c) employment and working conditions, including dismissals, as well as pay as provided for in Directive 75/117/EEC;

(d) membership of, and involvement in, an organisation of workers or employers, or any organisation whose members carry on a particular profession, including the benefits provided for by such organisations.

2.23 Article 8b encourages dialogue regarding equal treatment, providing that:

> '8b.3 Member States shall, in accordance with national law, collective agreements or practice, encourage employers to promote equal treatment for men and women in the workplace in a planned and systematic way.
> 8b.4 To this end, employers should be encouraged to provide at appropriate regular intervals employees and/or their representatives with appropriate information on equal treatment for men and women in the undertaking.'

2.24 This book is concerned with equal pay but, as stated, it is necessary to bear in mind the dichotomy between equal pay and equal treatment.

The Consolidating Directive, 2006/54/EC

2.25 This Directive is of some importance in relation to the developing jurisprudence on equality since equal pay, equal treatment, occupational benefits and the burden of proof are all now in one Directive, which may be seen as a more comprehensive 'code'. Of particular note, is that the Consolidating Directive contains definitions of direct and indirect discrimination which are imported into equal pay.

2.26 The detail of Directive 2006/54/EC is set out where appropriate in the text. The detailed preamble (which runs to 41 paragraphs) usefully sets out the EC view of where the current law stands. The Directive is stated, by Art 1, to ensure equal opportunities and treatment in relation to:

(a) access to employment, including promotion, and to vocational training;

(b) working conditions, including pay;

(c) occupational social security schemes.

2.27 Article 2 inter alia contains the following definitions as being applicable:

'(a) "direct discrimination": where one person is treated less favourably on grounds of sex than another is, has been or would be treated in a comparable situation;

(b) "indirect discrimination": where an apparently neutral provision, criterion or practice would put persons of one sex at a particular disadvantage compared with persons of the other sex, unless that provision, criterion or practice is objectively justified by a legitimate aim, and the means of achieving that aim are appropriate and necessary;

. . .

(e) "pay": the ordinary basic or minimum wage or salary and any other consideration, whether in cash or in kind, which the worker receives directly or indirectly, in respect of his/her employment from his/her employer;

(f) "occupational social security schemes": schemes not governed by Council Directive 79/7/EEC of 19 December 1978 on the progressive implementation of the principle of equal treatment for men and women in matters of social security whose purpose is to provide workers, whether employees or self-employed, in an undertaking or group of undertakings, area of economic activity, occupational sector or group of sectors with benefits intended to supplement the benefits provided by statutory social security schemes or to replace them, whether membership of such schemes is compulsory or optional.'

2.28 Chapter 1, Equal Pay, contains provision in relation to equal pay as follows:

'Article 4 Prohibition of discrimination

For the same work or for work to which equal value is attributed, direct and indirect discrimination on grounds of sex with regard to all aspects and conditions of remuneration shall be eliminated.

In particular, where a job classification system is used for determining pay, it shall be based on the same criteria for both men and women and so drawn up as to exclude any discrimination on grounds of sex.'

The definitions above of direct and indirect discrimination will apply.

2.29 Chapter 2 contains detailed provision relating to social security schemes (Arts 2–13) and Chapter 3 covers equal treatment (Articles 14–16). There are provisions for remedy and enforcement including Art 19 on Burden of Proof. Articles 20–22 contain details to promote dialogue, including like provisions to those which were founding Art 8b of the Equal Treatment Directive. Further detailed provisions relating to equality, enforcement and implementation take up Arts 23–36.

2.30 It is necessary to consider the above EC provisions at every stage of this textbook, together with the extensive European jurisprudence when considering UK law.

THE EQUAL PAY ACT 1970 – AN OVERVIEW

2.31 The EqPA 1970, as amended, consists of 16 sections which set out the framework for equality in relation to the terms of the employment contract. The Act deals with sex related discrimination relating to pay and other terms of the contract of employment. Discrimination on grounds, such as age, disability, race, sexual orientation or religious discrimination may be challengeable under other statutes, regulations or EC legislation (see **2.55-2.62** for a brief consideration).

2.32 The EqPA 1970, s 1 imports an equality clause into the contract of employment in relation to pay and all other contractual terms. By s 1(2) where the woman carries out like work, work rated as equivalent or work of equal value then the woman's contract shall be modified so as to be not less favourable and the contract shall be deemed to include an equality clause. Section 1(3) provides a defence where the reason for the disparate treatment is genuinely due to a material factor which is not the difference of sex.

2.33 The Act applies to pay given in consideration for 'work'. It will normally be obvious that the pay has been in relation to work, though there has been an issue as to whether, for example, attendance at a union organised conference is work (see *Manor Bakeries Ltd v Nazir* [1996] IRLR 604).

2.34 Comparison is to be made with a man in the same employment and, by s 1(6), men shall be treated as in the same employment with a woman if they are men employed by her employer or any associated employer at the same establishment or at establishments in Great Britain which include that one and at which common terms and conditions of employment are observed either generally or for employees of the relevant classes. It is for the claimant to choose the comparator but if an atypical comparator is chosen there may be a s 1(3) defence where the difference is not sex based. In some circumstances Art 141 may be relied upon where there is no comparator or no male employee in common employment but there is a single source of employment terms.

2.35 The Act applies to employees and workers since s 1(6)(a) provides that 'employed' means employed under a contract of service or of apprenticeship or a contract personally to execute any work or labour. It also applies to Crown and government department employees, members of the armed forces, House of Lords and House of Commons staff and trainees, statutory office other than political office including the police where the employment is in Great Britain (see ss 1(6A)–(13)).

2.36 By the EqPA 1970, s 2(1) claims relating to the contravention of a term modified or included by virtue of an equality clause, including a claim for arrears of remuneration or damages in respect of the contravention, may be presented by way of a complaint to an employment tribunal. The employer may make an application (s 1(1A)) or it may be made by a Minister (s 1(2)). Given that proceedings may be commenced in the county court as contractual claims, there is provision so that where it appears that the claim may more conveniently be disposed of separately by an employment tribunal, the court may strike it out or direct it to be referred to the Employment Tribunal or refer it on the application of a party (s 2(3)).

2.37 Section 2(4) provides that proceedings must be instituted by the qualifying date. Section 2ZA provides for the qualifying date as being:

- in a standard case, 6 months from the date of the last day on which the woman was employed;

- in a stable employment case, 6 months from the day that the stable employment relationship ended. 'Stable employment' is the period during which a stable employment relationship is in force notwithstanding that the period includes any time after the ending of a contract of employment when no further contract of employment is in force. The effect of this is considered in Chapter 18;

- in a concealment case, 6 months from the date when the woman discovered, or could with reasonable diligence have discovered, the qualifying fact;

- in a disability case, counting from the standard, stable relationship or concealment date 6 months after the date on which the woman ceased to have a disability; and

- the qualifying date will be the latest of the dates referred to above.

2.38 In proceedings for breach of the equality clause, by s 2(5), any payment by way of arrears of remuneration or damages, is limited to arrears under s 2ZB, which provides that in a standard case, the arrears date is the date falling 6 years before the day on which the proceedings were instituted, or in a disability or concealment case, the date of the contravention. By s 2ZC, subject to provisions as to fraud or errors induced by the employer, the period in Scotland is 5 years.

2.39 Section 2A contains detailed provisions for the determination of equal pay for work of equal value cases which are considered at Chapter 9.

2.40 Section 5 relates to agricultural workers orders which have a separate scheme, s 6 excludes pensions, since there are specific provisions, whilst s 7A applies the EqPA 1970 to the armed forces.

2.41 By s 7B, provision has been made for a questionnaire procedure under which the person who considers that she may have a complaint may serve a questionnaire, with a view to helping her to decide whether to institute proceedings and to formulate and present her case in the most effective manner. The complainant may question the employer on any matter considered to be relevant. The types of questions that may be asked are considered at paragraphs **10.17-10.22** and in Chapter 11 on the Genuine Material Factor (GMF) defence.

2.42 The Regulations, relating to equal value, questionnaires and to Tribunal procedures, which are complimentary to the above statutory provisions are considered in the text of the book.

Interaction between EqPA 1970 and SDA 1975

2.43 The dichotomy between the Equal Pay Directive and Equal Treatment Directive has been considered above. There is a similar, stark, distinction between the EqPA 1970 and the SDA 1975. It has been said that the EqPA 1970 and the SDA 1975 are separate enactments which must be construed separately. This was stated in one of the early cases under the Act, *Durrant v North Yorkshire Health Authority & Secretary of State for Social Services* [1979] IRLR 401, though it must be said that this separation has occasionally become hazy, for example in considering concepts of direct and indirect discrimination (see Chapter 10). The Employment Appeal Tribunal (EAT) confirmed in *Peake v Automotive Products Ltd* [1977] IRLR 105, ICR 480 that the two Acts are mutually exclusive. The employer in this case had operated a rule for about 30 years that all female employees stopped work at 4.25 am but the men were not able to leave until 4.30 pm. A male employee complained that the rule discriminated against him. The Tribunal dismissed the claim but failed to consider the applicability of the EqPA 1970. The EAT held that the complaint did not relate to the payment of money or a matter regulated by the contract of employment so that the EqPA 1970 did not apply. Phillips J stated:

> '(a) If the less favourable treatment relates to the payment of money which is regulated by a contract of employment, only the Equal Pay Act can apply.

(b) If the employee is treated less favourably than an employee of the other sex who is doing the same or broadly similar work, or whose work has been given an equal value under job evaluation, and the less favourable treatment relates to some matter which is regulated by the contract of employment of either of them, only the Equal Pay Act can apply.

(c) If the less favourable treatment relates to a matter which is not included in a contract (either expressly or by virtue of the Equal Pay Act), only the Sex Discrimination Act can apply.

(d) If the less favourable treatment relates to a matter (other than the payment of money) in a contract, and the comparison is with workers who are not doing the same or broadly similar work, or work which has been given an equal value under job evaluation, only the Sex Discrimination Act can apply.

(e) If the complaint relates to a matter (other than the payment of money) which is regulated by an employee's contract of employment, but is based on an allegation that an employee of the other sex would be treated more favourably in similar circumstances (ie it does not relate to the actual treatment of an existing employee of the other sex), only the Sex Discrimination Act can apply. (See: A Guide to the Sex Discrimination Act 1975)

Accordingly, the Industrial Tribunal should first have considered whether Mr Peake had a valid claim under the Equal Pay Act 1970, and it is necessary for us to do so. If the less favourable treatment of which he complained related only to the payment of money he could have no claim under the Sex Discrimination Act 1975.'

It was considered that the rule in question was part of an administrative arrangement for the running of the factory rather than something that was incorporated into the contract. (Note that the Court of Appeal overruled the case but effectively on the basis that the acts were de minimis.)

2.44   A case where it was held that the EqPA 1970 must apply was *Meeks v National Union of Agricultural Workers* [1976] IRLR 198 where the EAT held that discrimination on the grounds of wage rates was not unlawful under the SDA 1975 and that no claim could lie under the EqPA 1970 unless there was a comparator. The claimant was paid less as a part-time worker but there was no claim as all of the secretarial staff were women. The EAT stated:

'Presumably the reason why a provision for the payment of money under a contract of employment was excluded from the scope of the Sex Discrimination Act was that it was envisaged by Parliament that such matters should be dealt with exclusively under the Equal Pay Act.'

It should be noted that the case demonstrates the effect of the SDA 1975, s 8(3) (see **2.46** below). There were in fact potential remedies under the SDA 1975 (cf *Home Office v Holmes* [1984] IRLR 299) and note the position with regard to part-time workers at Chapter 14.

2.45   By the SDA 1975, s 6(1) it is unlawful to discriminate against a woman in (a) the arrangements that the employer makes for the purpose of determining who should be offered that employment, or (b) in the terms on which he offers her that employment. The SDA 1975, s 6(2) provides that it is unlawful for an employer to discriminate in employment 'in the way he affords her access to opportunities for promotion, transfer or training, or any other benefits, facilities or services, or by refusing or deliberately omitting to afford her access to them'. However, s 6(6) provides:

> 'Subsection (2) does not apply to benefits consisting of the payment of money where the provision of those benefits is regulated by the woman's contract of employment.'

2.46   The SDA 1975, s 8(2) provides that the EqPA 1970 does not apply in determining for the purposes of the SDA 1975, s 6(1)(b) the terms on which employment is offered. However, by s 8(3):

> 'Where a person offers a woman employment on certain terms, and if she accepted the offer then, by virtue of an equality clause, any of those terms would fall to be modified, or any additional term would fall to be included, the offer shall be taken to contravene section 6(1)(b).'

Nevertheless, where a person offers a woman employment on certain terms, and s 8(3) would apply but for the fact that, on her acceptance of the offer, the EqPA 1970, s 1(3) would prevent the equality clause from operating, then by s 8(4) the offer shall be taken not to contravene s 6(1)(b). This convoluted provision simply means that if an offer is made where there would, on the face of it, be a breach of the EqPA 1970 but the material factor defence would apply, then the offer will not amount to a breach of the SDA 1975, s 6(1)(b).

2.47   Further, by s 8(5) an act does not contravene s 6(2) if (a) it contravenes a term modified or included by virtue of an equality clause, or (b) it would contravene such a term but for the fact that the equality clause is prevented from operating by the EqPA 1970, s 1(3). Again, the GMF defence operates to prevent there being a breach of the SDA 1975.

2.48   The effect of these somewhat convoluted provisions are that:

- s 6(1)(b) applies to discrimination in relation to the terms on which employment is offered and, by s 8(2) the EqPA 1970 is not applicable;

- by s 8(3) this will remain the position if the offer was accepted and would breach the EqPA 1970;

- however, if the employer can show that the material factor defence would apply then, by s 8(4), the offer shall not be regarded as being in breach of s 6(1)(b);

- the same approach is taken in relation to occupational pension schemes (see s 6(4)).

2.49 Where there are *contractual terms* which are operated in a manner which is discriminatory then the EqPA 1970 will apply (s 6(6)). Where the terms are non-contractual then any claim must be under the SDA 1975. The test is whether the terms are regulated by the woman's contract of employment; if so, the EqPA 1970 applies.

2.50 The latter distinction is illustrated by *Hoyland v Asda Stores Ltd* [2005] IRLR 438 (see **12.35** for full facts) which considered the distinction between a discretionary bonus, which is not contractual remuneration, and pay. Lord Johnston in the Court of Session stated:

> '[14] In seeking to resolve this matter we consider that the important word in section 6(6) is "regulated". While we recognise that the word "discretionary" is used by the employer in referring to the bonus scheme, that can be construed as relating only to the amount being paid in any one year and we recognise that the Tribunal found, as a matter of fact, that every employee received a bonus. **We have no doubt that that entitlement, if it be such in law, arose out of the contract of employment and is regulated by it in the sense that but for the existence of the contract of employment the bonus would not be paid and it is therefore being paid as a consequence of its very existence. It does not seem to us to be necessary for section 6(6) to have any application in a given situation that the entitlement in question should be part of the formal contract of employment.** This conclusion reflects the dichotomy between equal pay and equal treatment, and avoids an employer being exposed to double jeopardy.
>
> [15] We are therefore in no doubt that the Employment Tribunal and the Employment Appeal Tribunal reached the correct decision in construing the arrangements for bonus payments in respect of the appellant as falling within the terms of section 6(6) and thus excluding any claim for sex discrimination under the 1975 Act.
>
> [16] We confess to be surprised that the issue of whether there was any discrimination at all was not taken before the lower Tribunals having regard to the fact that it appears that a man claiming paternity leave is in precisely the same position as a woman claiming maternity leave. It may be that some distinction is sought to be drawn because in the female's case pregnancy requires her to leave her employment temporarily, while a father, or potential father, has an option.
>
> [17] Be that as it may, we recognise that we cannot determine this matter and if we had been in favour of the appellant's position we would have remitted the matter back for a further hearing before an Employment Tribunal on the issue of discrimination in principle.
>
> [18] However, in the circumstances, for the reasons we have given the appeal will be dismissed and the order of the Employment Appeal Tribunal, itself supporting the order of the Employment Tribunal, will be endorsed.' **(emphasis added)**

The difficulty with the dicta highlighted in bold is that it could be said that the employee would not have obtained any bonus but for the contract of employment so that it arises out of the contract. However, where there is a bonus which is genuinely discretionary and expressed not to be part of the contract then the EqPA 1970 is not likely to apply. In some cases it will be prudent to claim both under the SDA 1975 and the EqPA 1970 to ensure that any claim is in time.

2.51 The legislation may be mutually exclusive but in *Shields v E Coombes (Holdings) Ltd* [1978] ICR 1159, IRLR 263, it was stated by Orr LJ that it should be construed 'as a harmonious whole' and Lord Denning MR commented:

> 'The English statutes are plainly designed so as to implement the Treaty of Rome and the Directives issued by the Council. They are the Sex Discrimination Act 1975, to which is scheduled the Equal Pay Act 1970, as amended. All came into force on 29.12.75. They must all be taken together. But the task of construing them is like fitting together a jig-saw puzzle. The pieces are all jumbled up together, in two boxes. One is labelled the Sex Discrimination Act 1975. The other, the Equal Pay Act 1970. You pick up a piece from one box and try to fit it in. It does not. So you try a piece from the other box. That does not fit either. In despair you take a look at the picture by the makers. It is the Guide issued by the Home Office. Mr Lester recommended especially paragraph 3.18, which he says will show the distinction between the two Acts. Even that will not make you jump with joy. You will not find the missing pieces unless you are very discriminating.'

2.52 The importation of the concepts of direct and indirect discrimination into equal pay continues to blur the distinction but there are clearly still demarcation lines. The UK courts and tribunals will be likely to follow the definitions in the Consolidating Directive, which gives a degree of uniformity to the relevant concepts.

OTHER CLAIMS

2.53 As well as claims under the EqPA 1970, there may be a number of other grounds on which it may be claimed that there has been discrimination in relation to pay and other terms. Claimants will need to bear in mind the following possible claims.

Age discrimination under the Employment Equality (Age) Regulations 2006, SI 2006/1031

2.54 These Regulations came into force on 1 October 2006. They outlaw direct and indirect discrimination on the grounds of age though there is a defence if the employer can show that the discriminatory treatment or provision, criterion or practice is a 'proportionate means of achieving a legitimate aim' so that direct discrimination can be justified. There is not space to consider these Regulations in detail and the reader is referred to S Cheetham

Age Discrimination, the New Law (Jordans). It should be noted, however, that there is a specific exception in reg 32 for the award of benefits based upon length of service for the first 5 years. After that the employer will only be able to justify a differential award of benefits based upon length of service where the use of such criterion 'fulfils a business need of his undertaking (for example by encouraging the loyalty or motivation, or rewarding the experience of some or all of his workers)'. This should be compared with the cases on the GMF relating to experience, etc (see **11.27**). The female employee who has taken time out to have children and returned to the workforce is likely to have difficulties in arguing differential treatment in relation to the provision of benefits because of this Regulation; query whether she would fare any better under the EqPA 1970 where the claim is put on this basis.

Race discrimination under the Race Relations Act 1976

2.55 A claim for differential treatment in relation to the provision of contractual benefits may be brought under the Race Relations Act 1976 (RRA 1976) where it is alleged that there has been direct or indirect discrimination on one of the grounds proscribed under the Act; ie colour, race, nationality or ethnic or national origins. Although, equal pay does not jump out as an issue under the RRA 1976, it has been noted by the Commission for Racial Equality in its *Factfile, Employment and Ethnicity*, March 2006, that in 2004, ethnic minority workers earned an average of £7.50 per hour, compared with £8.00 per hour for workers from white backgrounds. This gap has been increasing since 1998. Overall, ethnic minority women earned about £0.70 per hour more than white women; this was because a larger proportion of white women tended to work part time, which does not pay as well as full-time work. However, pay differences between men and women in some of the industries where ethnic minority women worked were large; an example being personal service occupations in the health sector. On average, white men were paid higher hourly rates than men from ethnic minorities – a difference of about £1.80 per hour in spring 2004. Indian men were paid about the same as white men, but Pakistani and Bangladeshi men were paid about £3.00 per hour less, on average. In the context of race, it will be necessary for the worker to claim direct or indirect discrimination under the RRA 1976 and to apply this legislation. There have been a number of cases where the Tribunals have found indirect discrimination in pay grading or practices: see *Sougrin v Haringey Health Authority* [1991] IRLR 447; *Wakeman v Quick Corporation* [1999] IRLR 424.

Discrimination against part-time workers under the Part-Time (Prevention of Less Favourable Treatment) Regulations 2000, SI 2000/1551

2.56 This is considered in Chapter 14.

Discrimination against fixed-term employees under the Fixed-Term Employees (Prevention of Less Favourable Treatment) Regulations 2002, SI 2002/2034

2.57 This is considered in Chapter 14.

Discrimination in relation to pensions

2.58 This is considered in Chapter 13.

Sex discrimination and victimisation

2.59 It has already been noted that there is a dichotomy between contractual claims under the EqPA 1970 and the provision of non-contractual benefits under the SDA 1975. This book is concerned with the former but it should be noted that there may be claims for direct or indirect discrimination under the SDA 1975 relating to the provision of non-contractual or discretionary benefits, for example in relation to matters such as promotion which will have an indirect effect upon remuneration. There may also be discrimination on the grounds of pregnancy or maternity where the employee is subjected to a detriment for this reason but, again, there is a distinction between pay and other unequal treatment (see Chapter 12). It is important to note that consideration should first be given to whether the claim is under the EqPA 1970 or the SDA 1975 and, in the case of doubt, it may be that a claim should be commenced under both.

2.60 It should also be noted that the victimisation provisions of the SDA 1975 apply in the equal pay context. The SDA 1975, s 4 provides that a person discriminates against another 'if he treats the person victimised less favourably than in those circumstances he treats or would treat other persons, and does so by reason that the person victimised' has brought proceedings, given evidence or otherwise done anything by reference to the EqPA 1970 (and the SDA 1975, the Social Security Act 1989 or the Pensions Act 1995). The other anti-discrimination legislation contains similar provisions. Thus, less favourable treatment because the claimant has pursued a claim of equal pay will be victimisation.

2.61 The scope of these provisions were recently considered by the Court of Appeal in *Allen v GMB* [2008] EWCA Civ 810, [2008] IRLR 690. During the course of negotiations with Middlesbrough, the union, GMB, compromised claims in a manner that led to the claimants alleging that the union had discriminated against them by reason of the terms on which the union had compromised claims for equal pay to their disadvantage. In *GMB v Allen* [2007] IRLR 752 the EAT rejected arguments which the Tribunal had accepted that the union had discriminated and victimised the claimants. On appeal the Court of Appeal (*Allen v GMB* [2008] EWCA Civ 810,) held that the Tribunal had been correct and its judgment was reinstated. Under the 'single status' Agreement a job evaluation scheme (JES) was carried out and new terms and conditions were agreed with effect from 1 April 2005. The union wanted to ensure that those who had been the victims of past discrimination be compensated but at the same time that a measure of pay protection was provided for those who would lose out. The Court of Appeal stated that it was beyond dispute that the union decided to give priority to those who needed pay protection and to achieving equality and better pay for the future rather than to maximising claims for past unequal pay. The deal done between the union and the Council provided the White Book women (see **10.32** for an explanation of the different local authority 'Books') with some compensation for the historical inequalities (in the region of 25% of the full value of successful equal pay claims) but did not provide the Purple Book women with any such compensation, the Council having apparently taken the view that their equal pay claims were without merit. These women claimed that the union had directly or indirectly discriminated or had victimised them in the way that they had prioritised pay protection. The indirect discrimination claims succeeded. The union had engaged in a potentially discriminatory practice by agreeing to a low back pay settlement in order to release more money for pay protection. The disadvantaged group were predominately women and the union had failed to justify the practices. The question was whether the means were proportionate to the attainment of a legitimate aim. However, the claimants were kept in the dark about the means adopted and could not make a fully informed choice as they were not informed of the sacrifice they were making. The claimants had been victimised as the union refused to do anything further for them when they instructed solicitors.

2.62 Maurice Kay LJ referred to the provision, criterion or practice (PCP) found by the Tribunal, as being that the union 'applied a practice of agreeing to a low back pay settlement for Mrs Spayne and doing nothing for the APTLC workers in order to leave as much money as possible for the pay line in the future and pay protection where necessary'. On that basis he stated that he 'would characterise the PCP as the deal that was done with Middlesbrough as a result of that policy. It fell to the Union to justify it'. The aims to avoid privatisations, avoid job losses, avoid cuts in hours, avoid or minimise losers and, in so far as losers were inevitable, to get the best possible pay protection were all legitimate but the means were not a proportionate way of achieving a legitimate aim. The union was not 'free to procure the acceptance or acquiescence of those members by a marked economy of truth in what it says and writes to them'. The Tribunal had been entitled to find that the means were disproportionate to the achievement of the overall aim or aims. The decision on indirect discrimination was restored. The above case is of some importance in showing that those who compromise claims may be liable themselves for sex discrimination or victimisation if they do not take into account the interests of the different gender groups.

COLLECTIVE AGREEMENTS AND ARRANGEMENTS

2.63   The Equal Pay Directive, Art 3, included collective agreements within its scope. The Consolidating Directive now contains provisions in Art 23 as follows:

'Article 23 Compliance

Member States shall take all necessary measures to ensure that:

(a)   any laws, regulations and administrative provisions contrary to the principle of equal treatment are abolished;

(b)   provisions contrary to the principle of equal treatment in individual or collective contracts or agreements, internal rules of undertakings or rules governing the independent occupations and professions and workers' and employers' organisations or any other arrangements shall be, or may be, declared null and void or are amended;

(c)   occupational social security schemes containing such provisions may not be approved or extended by administrative measures.'

2.64   The EqPA 1970 originally contained provisions in ss 3 and 4 with regard to collective bargaining and wage structures. It will be seen that employers have sought to rely on collective bargaining as a defence, under s 1(3) to a claim under the Act. If the collective agreement is indirectly discriminatory then Art 141 may be relied upon (*Kowalska v Freie und Hansestadt Hamburg* (Case 33/89), [1990] IRLR 447; *Nimz v Freie und Hansestadt Hamburg* (Case C-184/89), [1991] IRLR 222) and it is clear from *Enderby v Frenchay Health Authority* [1993] IRLR 591, that, under domestic legislation a collective agreement that itself is discriminatory will not provide a s 1(3) defence; see *William Ball Ltd v Wood* EAT/89/01, and see Chapter 10. The sections in the EqPA 1970 were repealed (save s 5 which deals with agricultural wages orders) so that claims under the EqPA 1970 are individual claims.

2.65   By the SDA 1975, s 77 (amended by the SDA 1986, s 6(1)) any discriminatory provisions in a collective agreement will be void and a party will not be able to rely upon such terms (s 77(2)). It had been held that s 77 breached the Equal Treatment Directive as it applied only to contracts in *EC Commission v United Kingdom* (Case 165/82), [1984] IRLR 29, [1984] ICR 192 so that there was no mechanism for challenging discriminatory collective agreements, since the latter do not normally have contractual status (see Trade Union and Labour Relations (Consolidation) Act 1992 (TULR(C)A 1992), ss 178 and 179). The SDA 1986, s 6 applied s 77 to collective agreements, whether or not they are legally enforceable.

2.66   The Trade Union Reform and Employment Rights Act 1993, s 32, which came into force on 30 November 1993, introduced a new s 4A into the SDA 1986, s 6. This provides that a complaint may be presented to an employment tribunal that a term or rule is void if the claimant has reason to believe that the term or rule may at some future time have effect in relation to him and the collective agreement is void. By s 4(4D) when an employment tribunal finds that a complaint presented to it under s 4(4A) is well-founded the tribunal shall make an order declaring that the term or rule is void. The provisions apply to employees and to persons who genuinely and actively are seeking to become employees of an employer who is party to a suspect collective agreement.

2.67 The remedy is thus for a declaration that the collective agreement is void. The EAT in *(1) Unison and (2) GMB v (1) Brennan and (2) Sunderland City Council* UKEAT/0589/07/MAA, [2008] IRLR 492 noted that an individual with an equal pay claim may make such an application, as to find otherwise would breach the EC principle of effectiveness and equivalence.

2.68 In relation to pay structures, s 5 gives the Central Arbitration Committee's jurisdiction to revise an Agricultural Wages Order where the order contains a provision which applies to men or women only. Where the Order does discriminate the discrimination must be removed unless one of the exceptions in the EqPA 1970, s 6 applies. The woman's rate of pay is to be increased to the comparable man's rate and, if there is no comparator, to the lowest man's rate in the Order.

2.69 There is thus scope to challenge collective agreements under UK law though the claimant will have to demonstrate an interest as set out above.

Chapter 3

PERSONS COVERED BY THE EQUAL PAY ACT 1970

3.1   It is necessary to consider the following:

(1)   employment within the meaning of the Equal Pay Act 1970 (EqPA 1970), s 1(6);

(2)   the armed forces;

(3)   Crown employment;

(4)   House of Commons and House of Lords staff;

(5)   illegal employment;

(6)   office holders;

(7)   overseas employment;

(8)   permissible discrimination (exceptions to EqPA 1970).

EMPLOYMENT WITHIN THE MEANING OF EQPA 1970, S 1(6)

3.2   The EqPA 1970 applies where a woman 'is employed' under a contract. For the purposes, of s 1 '"employed" means employed under a contract of service or of apprenticeship or a contract personally to execute any work or labour, and related expressions shall be construed accordingly'.

3.3   The definition of employment is wider than employment under the Employment Rights Act 1996 since it includes a contract personally to execute work or labour which covers persons who would normally be regarded as self-employed. In *Quinnen v Hovells* [1984] IRLR 227 the similar provision in the SDA 1975, s 82 was considered. A self-employed salesman of fancy goods in a department store engaged self-employed assistants on a commission basis at busy times. Two women acted as sales staff and the claimant, a man, operated an engraving machine for customers. The two women were better paid than he was, and his engagement was terminated after 4 weeks. The EAT held that the claimant was engaged in personal work or labour. It stated that:

> 'The concept of a contract for the personal engagement of work or labour lying outside the scope of a master-servant relationship is a wide and flexible one, intended by Parliament to be interpreted as such. Its application to particular circumstances will depend very much upon the facts of each case as and when they arise.'

3.4 The definition 'contract personally to execute any work or labour' has been considered in many cases under the SDA 1975 and other provisions with the same wording: see *Hugh-Jones v St John's Cambridge* [1979] ICR 848, EAT; *Tanna v Post Office* [1981] ICR 374, EAT; *Mirror Group Newspapers Ltd v Gunning* [1986] IRLR 27, ICR 145; *Loughran v Northern Ireland Housing Executive* [1998] IRLR 593, ICR 828, HL; *Sheehan v Post Office Counters Ltd* [1999] ICR 734; *Percy v Church of Scotland Board of National Mission* [2005] UKHL 73, [2006] IRLR 195. Where there is no obligation to perform any personal work or services the individual will not come within the EqPA 1970 (*Mingeley v Pennock & Ivory (t/a Amber Cars)* [2004] EWCA Civ 328, [2004] IRLR 373 – a Race Relations Act 1976 claim). The fact that self-employed persons are required by European law to be covered was confirmed by the ECJ in *Allonby v Accrington and Rossendale College* (Case C-256/01), [2004] IRLR 224 at paras 67–68.

THE ARMED FORCES

3.5 Section 7A was incorporated into the EqPA 1970 in 1997. At the same time s 1(9) which excluded the armed forces was repealed. The effect of the section is that the Act shall apply to service in the armed forces in the same manner as it applies to employment by a private person. Claims may be presented to an Employment Tribunal (s 7A(3)). However, by s 7A(5) no complaint may be presented unless the claimant has made a complaint to an officer under the service redress procedures applicable to her and submitted the complaint to the Defence Council under the procedures and the Defence Council has made a determination in relation to the complaint. There are detailed provisions as to when a complaint may be presented in s 7AA and as to how far back damages may be claimed in s 7AB. See further, the Equal Pay (Complaints to Employment Tribunals) (Armed Forces) Regulations 1997, SI 1997/2162.

CROWN EMPLOYMENT

3.6 By the EqPA 1970, s 1(8), the Act applies to: (a) service for purposes of a Minister of the Crown or government department, other than service of a person holding a statutory office, or (b) service on behalf of the Crown for the purposes of a person holding a statutory office or purposes of a statutory body, as it applies to employment by a private person, as if references to a contract of employment included references to the terms of service. Statutory body is defined by s 1(10). Crown employees are therefore covered and are deemed to be working under a contract of service.

3.7   The section equates employment in the civil and public service with private employment whilst at the same time stating that the holder of a public office will be excluded. The position with regard to public office has been considered in a number of cases. In *Stevenson v Lord Advocate* 1999 SLT 382, Lord Kirkwood expressed the view that a sheriff may be a worker within Art 141, though the case was decided on appeal without reference to the issue. The Northern Ireland Court of Appeal considered the position in *Perceval-Price v Department of Economic Development* [2000] IRLR 380. Three female office holders of permanent full-time posts in the industrial and social security tribunals in Northern Ireland claimed discrimination in relation to pension rights under legislation which was the same in content as the EqPA 1970 and the SDA 1975. They were statutory office holders who were specifically excluded from the domestic legislation. The Tribunal found that the claims could be brought under Art 141 and this was upheld by the Northern Ireland Court of Appeal. It was held that the chairmen were workers in employment within the meaning of EC law and were therefore entitled to bring claims.

3.8   The criteria for the application of Art 39, free movement of workers, had been established in *Lawrie-Blum v Land Baden-Würtenberg* [1987] ICR 483 as being the existence of an employment relationship regardless of the nature of that relationship and purpose. In *Perceval-Price*, Sir Robert Carswell LCJ did not see any compelling reason why the term worker should have a narrower meaning in the context of equality of pay and opportunity than it did with free movement of workers. Judges 'are not free agents to work as and when they choose, as are self-employed persons. Their office accordingly partakes of some of the characteristics of employment, as servants of the State, even though as office-holders they do not come within the definition of employment in domestic law'. The Northern Ireland Court of Appeal interpreted the legislation based upon the supremacy of Community law. Section 1(6A) now expressly brings such office holders within the EqPA 1970 (see below).

HOUSE OF COMMONS AND HOUSE OF LORDS STAFF

3.9   These staff are covered by the EqPA 1970, s 1(10A), (House of Commons) and s 1(10B), (House of Lords). An equality clause will be implied into the relevant member of House of Commons staff contract or the relevant member of House of Lords staff contract, which has the same meaning as in the Employment Rights Act 1996, ss 194 and 195.

ILLEGAL EMPLOYMENT

3.10 Where the contract of employment is illegal then a claim cannot be brought under the EqPA 1970. Claims of discrimination are not contract based so that the courts have been rather more lax in the application of the doctrine (see *Leighton v Michael and Charalambous* [1996] IRLR 67, [1995] ICR 1091; *Hall v Woolston Hall Leisure Ltd* [2000] IRLR 578 and for the latest approach to the test of illegality see *Enfield Technical Services Ltd v Payne* [2007] IRLR 840).

OFFICE HOLDERS

3.11 By the EqPA 1970, s 1(6A) the Act applies to:

'(a) the holding of an office or post to which persons are appointed to discharge functions personally under the direction of another person, and in respect of which they are entitled to remuneration, or

(b) any office or post to which appointments are made by (or on the recommendation of or subject to the approval of) a Minister of the Crown, a government department, the National Assembly for Wales or any part of the Scottish Administration,

as it applies to employment by a private person, and shall so apply as if references to a contract of employment included references to the terms of appointment, and as if references to the employer included references to the person responsible for paying any remuneration that a holder of the office or post is entitled to in respect of the office or post.'

3.12 Section 1(6B)(a) provides that a person is to be regarded as discharging her functions under the direction of another person if that other person is entitled to direct her as to when and where she discharges those functions but, by s 1(6B)(b) is not to be regarded as entitled to remuneration merely because she is entitled to payments in respect of expenses incurred by her in carrying out the functions of the office or post, or by way of compensation for the loss of income or benefits she would or might have received from any person had she not been carrying out the functions of the office or post. However, by s 1(6C) 'office or post' does not include a political office, and appointment to an office or post does not include election to an office or post. The position with regard to political office is covered by s 1A which lists political offices for the purpose of s 1(6C)(a).

OVERSEAS EMPLOYMENT

3.13 The EqPA 1970, s 1(1) refers to a woman 'employed at an establishment in Great Britain'. Section 1(2) provides that 'Great Britain' includes such of the territorial waters of the UK as are adjacent to Great Britain. Overseas employment is thus excluded.

3.14 The test is where the employee is based as the EqPA 1970 applies only to employment which is at an establishment in Great Britain. The SDA 1975, s 10 contains the definition of employment at an establishment for the purposes of both the SDA 1975 and the EqPA 1970. It is apparent from s 10(4) that everyone must have a base as it states that where work is not done at an establishment it shall be treated for the relevant purposes as done at the establishment from which it is done or at the establishment with which it has the closest connection. By s 10(1) employment is at an establishment in Great Britain if the employee does his work wholly or partly in Great Britain, or the employee does his work wholly outside Great Britain and s 10(1A) applies.

3.15 Section 10(1A) applies if (a) the employer has a place of business at an establishment in Great Britain, (b) the work is for the purposes of the business carried on at that establishment, and (c) the employee is ordinarily resident in Great Britain at the time when he applies for or is offered the employment, or at any time during the course of the employment.

3.16 There is provision for employment on board a ship, aircraft or hovercraft (s 10(2), (3)) and in relation to exploration of the sea bed (s 10(5)–(7)). In such cases if the tests contained in the subsections are satisfied the employee will be deemed to be home based. The issue of an employee working on a German registered ferry which plied between Sheerness and Flushing was considered in *Haughton v Olau Line (UK) Ltd* [1986] IRLR 465, [1986] ICR 357. It was argued that the 'establishment' was the employer's premises at Sheerness. The Court of Appeal held that the section excluded those who mainly or wholly worked outside Great Britain, unless it was on a British registered ship, aircraft or hovercraft operated by a party that had its principal business or was ordinarily resident in Great Britain. The work was done mainly outside territorial waters on a non-British registered ship so that there was no jurisdiction.

3.17 It is a question of fact and degree whether an establishment is to be treated as a separate establishment or not (see the approaches taken in other contexts in *Secretary of State for Employment and Productivity v Vic Hallam Ltd* (1969) 5 ITR 108; *Barley v Amey Roadstone Corpn Ltd (Nos 1 & 2)* [1977] IRLR 299, [1978] ICR 190).

3.18 There is also provision under s 10(8) for contract workers.

PERMISSIBLE DISCRIMINATION (EXCEPTIONS TO THE EQPA 1970)

3.19 There are three areas in the EqPA 1970 where it is permissible for an employer to continue to discriminate. The EqPA 1970, s 6 provides that the equality clause shall not operate in relation to terms:

- affected by compliance with the laws regulating the employment of women;

- affording special treatment to women in connection with pregnancy or childbirth (see Chapter 12); and

- relating to a person's membership of, or rights under, an occupational pension scheme, being terms in relation to which, by reason only of any provision made by or under, the Pensions Act 1995, ss 62–64 (equal treatment), an equal treatment rule would not operate if the terms were included in the scheme (see Chapter 13).

Chapter 4

THE EQUALITY CLAUSE

4.1   The Equal Pay Act 1970 achieves its object by implying an equality clause into contracts of employment where there will otherwise be a breach of the Act. Section 1(1) provides that:

> 'If the terms of a contract under which a woman is employed at an establishment in Great Britain do not include (directly or by reference to a collective agreement or otherwise) an equality clause they shall be deemed to include one.'

4.2   Where the woman is employed on like work, work rated as equivalent or work of equal value and any term of the woman's contract is or becomes less favourable then the contract of the woman shall be treated as 'modified' so as not to be less favourable. Alternatively, if at any time the woman's contract does not include a term corresponding to a term benefiting a man included in the contract under which he is employed, the woman's contract shall be treated as including such a term.

4.3   Where the woman is paid less than a man or is subject to inferior contract terms then the contract will be treated as modified so that she will be entitled to the same pay or contractual terms.

4.4   The equality clause only applies by comparing the claimant's terms to that of her comparator so that the right to equal pay is only concerned with considering whether the woman is entitled to the same terms and not whether the claimant is entitled to greater or proportionate terms. This is illustrated by *Pointon v University of Sussex* [1979] IRLR 119. The claimant was a university lecturer who was paid £4,403 at point 5 on the salary scale. The comparator was appointed as a lecturer on scale 5 but was only paid £4,190. The claimant asserted that she should have been paid on a higher scale to that of the man as she was older and better qualified. The Court of Appeal held that the claim could not succeed as there was no term in her contract that was less favourable than the equivalent term in the comparator's contract.

4.5   Where the claimant can show that her work is of greater value than a higher paid comparator the woman will be entitled to equal pay. This was the position in *Murphy v Bord Telecom Eirean* [1988] IRLR 267 in which it was held by the European Court of Justice (ECJ) that the principle of equal pay for work of equal value does not allow for workers of one sex to be paid less where the work that they are carrying out is of greater value than the comparators. It noted that:

'To adopt a contrary interpretation would be tantamount to rendering the principle of equal pay ineffective and nugatory.'

4.6   The legislation is aimed at removing inequalities that are based upon sex discrimination so that the equality clause will not be implied where there are valid *non-discriminatory* reasons which justify any differential treatment. Where there is apparent discriminatory treatment it will be necessary for the employer to objectively justify such treatment under s 1(3) by demonstrating that there is a genuine material factor (GMF) other than related to sex which explains and justifies the differential (see Chapter 11).

4.7   The equality clause, then, will strike out a term that is less favourable and substitute the more favourable term which is contained in the comparator's contract of employment or import an equivalent term if one is not contained in the contract. The equality clause will eradicate the less favourable treatment between the claimant and the comparator so that it may not necessarily be all terms which are different that will be struck out, modified or imported. In *Electrolux Ltd v Hutchinson* [1977] ICR 252, Phillips J gave an example of how this would work:

> 'Suppose the men are by contract bound to work on a Sunday morning shift one week in three, but the women are not. In our judgment the mere existence of that obligation does not remove the case from S.1(4). The material question is whether what they do on Sunday in pursuit or performance of that obligation is different from what the women do during the week. If in such a case the basic rate payable to the men, unlike that payable to the women, reflects some additional element attributable to the obligation to work on Sundays, or at nights (over and above any shift or Sunday shift premium payable) that fact can be reflected by the way in which the equality clause is applied under S.1(2)(a)(1). In other words, it can be applied not to produce equality but so that the woman is not treated less favourably. In applying the man's rate to the woman's it may be discounted for this purpose.'

In other words, the additional element which is paid to reflect the Sunday work can be separated out and the claimant would otherwise be entitled to the same basic salary as the comparator. This may be of some significance where men are paid a bonus or an allowance for additional duties, inclement weather working or unsocial hours. This element of remuneration may be separated out in considering whether there is equal work for equal value. This is illustrated by *Stadt Lengerich v Helmig* [1995] IRLR 216, [1996] ICR 35. Collective agreements provided that the employees were only entitled to overtime payments for full-time or part-time employees for time worked beyond the ordinary working time laid down by the agreements, which in all cases amounted to full-time hours. This meant that part-time workers were not entitled to overtime for the hours they worked above their part-time hours but only to overtime when they had exceeded the full time hours. It was contended that this was a breach of Art 141 of the EC Treaty. The overall pay of full-time employees was not higher than that of part-time employees in respect of the same number of hours worked. As the ECJ noted:

'A part-time employee whose contractual working hours are 18 receives, if he works 19 hours, the same overall pay as a full-time employee who works 19 hours. Part-time employees also receive the same overall pay as full-time employees if they work more than the normal working hours fixed by the collective agreements because on doing so they become entitled to overtime supplements.'

4.8 It is necessary to consider *each separate term* of the contract of employment; employers cannot argue that the *total package* is overall the same so that there is no breach of the Act if there are inequalities in relation to particular terms. The House of Lords rejected the argument that less favourable terms could be balanced by more favourable terms in the contract in *Hayward v Cammell Laird Shipbuilders Ltd* [1988] IRLR 257, ICR 464. The claimant, a canteen assistant, compared herself with a painter, a joiner and an insulation engineer, who were paid approximately £30 a week more. The employer argued that other terms relating to sick pay, meals allowances and breaks as well as 2 days' extra holiday meant that she benefited overall by in excess of £11 when compared to her comparators. It was argued that 'pay' under Art 141 was an overall term. The House of Lords held that 'term' under the Act meant that each term had to be considered separately if it had sufficient content to make it possible to compare with a similar provision in the comparators' contracts. The provision related to basic pay was a term in its own right and not part of a term embracing all contractual entitlements. Terms should then be compared individually. Lord Mackay LC stated:

'When elimination of all discrimination on grounds of sex is to be applied to all aspects and conditions of remuneration I consider this requires each of these aspects to be considered and discrimination existing in any aspect to be eliminated irrespective of the other aspects.'

Lord Goff stated:

'If I look at the words used, and give them their natural and ordinary meaning, they mean quite simply that one looks at the man's contract and at the woman's contract, and if one finds in the man's contract a term benefiting him which is not included in the woman's contract, then that term is treated as included in hers. On this simple and literal approach, the words "benefiting that man" mean precisely what they say – that the term must be one which is beneficial to him, as opposed to being burdensome. So if, for example, the man's contract contains a term that he is to be provided with the use of a car, and the woman's contract does not include such a term, then her contract is to be treated as including such a term.'

4.9 The House of Lords were of the view that the proper construction of the word 'term' in the Act meant that a woman was entitled to equal treatment in relation to each individual term under the contract. The House of Lords considered the 'leap-frogging' argument that was raised by the employer; namely that if the woman had one term improved under her contract, regardless of the other more favourable provisions, then the man would be able to point to those more favourable provisions and claim parity. The House of Lords considered whether s 1(3) may be used as a defence. Lord Mackay did not think s 1(3) could be used in such a case whilst Lord Goff thought that the defence may be available in appropriate circumstances. The other Law Lords agreed with both speeches. It was not, however, necessary for the House to decide the point. The principle that one has to look at each term of the contract accords with the ECJ decision in *Barber v Guardian Royal Exchange Assurance Group* [1990] IRLR 240, ICR 616, in which it was stated, in answer to the third question that:

> 'The application of the principle of equal pay must be ensured in respect of each element of remuneration and not only on the basis of a comprehensive assessment of the consideration paid to workers.' (see also *Jorgensen v Forerningen* [2000] IRLR 726)

It should be noted that claimants cannot pick and choose the most beneficial terms from different employees in order to achieve terms and conditions which will be overall better than those of the male counterparts (*Redcar and Cleveland BC v Degnan* [2005] IRLR 179).

4.10 In *Redcar and Cleveland BC v Degnan* [2005] IRLR 179 the Employment Appeal Tribunal stated that it is not possible to make comparisons by reference to subdivisions of remuneration. In that case it was not possible to make subdivisions in respect of pay for attendance allowances and bonuses where the claimants and comparators were on work rated as equivalent rather than considering the overall hourly rate.

4.11 It is a central principle of the EqPA 1970 that where there is a term which is less favourable to the woman then she is entitled, under the equality clause to have her contract upgraded to that of the comparator rather than for the term to be downgraded. Once the entitlement arises, the term cannot be downgraded even where the comparator no longer remains in employment, so that in *Sorbie v Trust House Forte Hotels Ltd* [1977] ICR 55, it was held that the contract remained modified though the man immediately moved out of employment.

Chapter 5

THE COMPARATOR

5.1   The general principle is that a claimant cannot succeed under the EqPA 1970 unless she can point to an actual comparator. This principle has, however, been subject to a recent exception and it will be of interest to see whether this inroad will be carried further.

5.2   The comparator will have to be of the opposite sex (see *Collins v Wilkin Chapman* EAT/945/93 but cf *A v Chief Constable of the West Yorkshire Police* [2002] EWCA Civ 1584, [2003] IRLR 32, ICR 161).

5.3   In considering this issue, the EqPA 1970, s 1(6) must be taken into account. This provides:

> '. . . men shall be treated as in the same employment with a woman if they are men employed by her employer or any associated employer at the same establishment or at establishments in Great Britain which include that one and at which common terms and conditions of employment are observed either generally or for employees of the relevant classes.'

It is for the claimant to select the comparator of her choice. The Employment Tribunal cannot select the comparator, contrary to the claimant's choice. This was made clear in *Ainsworth v Glass Tubes & Components Ltd* [1977] IRLR 74, ICR 347 where the Tribunal chose a different comparator from that of the claimant then dismissed the claim. The claimant wished the comparator to be an inspector working alongside her whereas the Tribunal chose an inspector working at a different time. This was an obvious misdirection.

5.4   However, the claimant must be careful about the comparator that is chosen since the Tribunal can only modify the term of the contract and award higher pay based upon the earnings of the comparator. Thus, in *Evesham v North Hertfordshire Health Authority & Another* [2000] IRLR 257, [2000] ICR 612 the claimant, a female speech therapist, claimed equal pay with a male senior clinical psychologist. The claimant named a comparator who was on the lowest point of the incremental scale and the claimant's work was found to be of equal value but the claimant sought to be placed on a higher point on the scale due to length of service and experience. The Court of Appeal held that the entitlement to be paid no less favourably than the comparator meant only that the claimant should mirror the comparator on the incremental pay scale. Roch LJ stated that:

'... neither the obligation to modify terms in the applicant's contract or the obligation to include a term found in the comparator's contract in the applicant's contract requires the employer to modify a term or to include a term so that the term in the applicant's contract becomes more favourable than the term in the comparator's contract. What is to be achieved is equality of treatment by the employer of the applicant and the comparator whom the applicant has chosen.'

Thus, although the men earned more than the women in this case the women should have identified more experienced comparators who were higher on the pay scale. It should be noted that if there was not a senior comparator who worked for the particular health authority it may have been possible to identify one working for another authority on the basis of the EqPA 1970, s 1(6) or Art 141 (see *Scullard* at **5.25** and *Lawrence* at **5.41**).

5.5   The EAT held in *Bainbridge v Redcar and Cleveland Borough Council (No 2)* [2007] IRLR 494 that each claim against a comparator is, in effect, a separate claim so that the principle of res judicata would not apply to prevent an employee from bringing a fresh claim against a different comparator where a claim had already been adjudicated against a different comparator. The EAT stated at paras 125–126 that:

'In our view these separate claims are distinct causes of action. It is not accurate to say that each breach of the equality clause is the same breach of contract. It is a breach of the same term but committed in different ways. *Conquer v Boot* shows that you cannot seek to dissect what is in substance a single promise into a series of separate obligations and treat them all distinctly. The analysis in fact is closely linked to the principle in *Henderson v Henderson*. All aspects of the single promise must be considered together. It would be an abuse to run the litigation in any other way. But the promise to pay the same as man A is not the same as the promise to pay the same as man B. The second claim is not simply a reframing of the original cause of action ... in our view the evidence in the two cases would be quite different, the breach may occur at a different time – for example, man B may be employed much later than man A – and the limitation periods would not necessarily then be the same. This is one contractual term, but it potentially contains a number of contractual promises, and the employer is obliged to honour each.'

The Court of Appeal upheld the EAT on this issue. It stated that the doctrines of res judicata, merger and election did not operate to prevent such claims so that the Tribunal had not erred in law in refusing to strike out equal value claims for the same pay period covered by work rated as equivalent claims (see **11.59** et seq for more detail about this case).

5.6   It is necessary that the comparator be of the opposite sex (see *Collins v Wilkin Chapman* EAT/945/93). The comparator may, however, be a predecessor in employment to the claimant where there is no male comparator in employment. It may also be possible in limited circumstances to rely on Art 141 so that there is no requirement to name a comparator. The comparator cannot be a successor as the case of *Walton Centre v Neurology & Neurosurgery NHS Trust v Bewley* [2008] IRLR 588 has recently made clear (see **5.9**).

5.7   The ECJ held that there was no need for contemporaneous employment in *McCarthys Ltd v Smith* [1980] ICR 672. The claimant was employed as a stockroom manageress at £50 a week in a job which had previously been carried out by a man for £60 a week. The Court of Appeal took the view that a strict interpretation of the EqPA 1970 meant that the work had to be contemporaneous but referred the case to the ECJ for a ruling under Art 119 (now Art 141). The ECJ held that that the principle that men and women should receive equal pay for equal work, enshrined in Art 119 of the EEC Treaty, is not confined to situations in which men and women are contemporaneously doing equal work for the same employer. This principle was followed by the Court of Appeal (see [1980] IRLR 209, [1980] ICR 672). Further, in *Albion Shipping Agency v Arnold* [1981] IRLR 525, [1982] ICR 22 the EAT stated that the ruling could be given effect whether the claim is treated as coming under Art 119 alone or under the EqPA 1970 as impliedly amended by Art 119.

5.8   This principle was clearly illustrated by *Kells v Pilkington plc* EAT/1435/00. The claimant worked as a research assistant from 1989 to 20 August 1999. She brought a claim on 10 November 1999 for, inter alia, breach of the EqPA 1970. She compared herself to comparators who had been employed more than 6 years previously, between 1990 and 1993 and between 1989 and 1991. The EAT held that she was entitled to make such a comparison and that any difficulties in time were of fact not law.

5.9   It was held in *Diocese of Hallam Trustee v Connaughton* [1996] ICR 860, IRLR 505 that a female employee could claim equal pay with a more highly paid successor. The EAT relied on the interpretation of Art 119 (now Art 141) in holding that the claimant could claim in respect of her employment between January 1990 and September 1994 (notice being given to take effect from April 1994) by comparing herself with a man who commenced employment in January 1995 at a salary well in excess of what the claimant had been paid. This position was reviewed in *Walton Centre for Neurology and Neurosurgery NHS Trust v Bewley* [2008] IRLR 588. The claimant was employed as a senior health care assistant/nursing assistant. She brought a claim under the EqPA 1970 and Art 141 claiming work of equal value prior to 1 October 2004 and that she had not been paid as much as a comparator for work rated as equivalent thereafter. An issue arose as to whether she could make a claim for a period when she had been employed but her comparators had not. The Employment Judge held that he was bound by *Hallam* to find that the claimant could compare herself with a successor. The EAT held that the EqPA 1970 could not be applied to comparisons with a successor. The statute envisages comparison with someone employed at the same time as the claimant. Comparison with a successor could only be permitted if it was required by Art 141. This Article has direct effect only in those areas where the court can apply its provisions by reference to the criteria that those provisions themselves lay down, without national or Community measures being required.

5.10 Elias J noted that the rationale behind this was that, in order for an equal pay claim to get off the ground, there had to be a concrete appraisal of work actually performed. The EAT noted that in *McCarthys Ltd v Smith* [1980] IRLR 210 and *Coloroll Pension Trustees Ltd v Russell* [1994] IRLR 586 it was held that a predecessor would provide a basis for a concrete appraisal whilst at the same time rejecting the possibility of a hypothetical comparator. The logic of the argument that a successor may be used is that the law should allow comparison with a hypothetical comparator since the existence of a successor is no more than a fortuitous event which provides a peg to justify the legal comparison. The comparison requires asking what would have happened in the past, namely, what would the successor have been paid if he had been employed at the same time as the claimant, as opposed to the question in *McCarthys,* which was what the predecessor had actually been paid at the time of the termination of his contract. Comparison with a successor does not enable the concrete appraisal that the ECJ has emphasised is the bedrock of the application of Art 141. It does not provide the secure factual premise which enables the determination of the proper and precise extent of the past, and necessarily hypothetical, discrimination. Elias J stated at paragraphs 55–56:

> 'It seems to me that there are two problems in particular with the comparison which demonstrate its speculative nature. The first is the assumption that if the male successor is now receiving higher pay then he would have done so in the past. That is not, it seems to me, necessarily a safe prediction at all. It may well depend upon who is fixing the values of the job at any particular time. It may be an easy inference to draw where the successor is employed on like work with the claimant, but it seems to me that it is far more difficult where it is work of equal value or work rated as equivalent which is being compared. The valuation of jobs is not a science and the assumption that values attached to a post now would necessarily have been conferred in an identical way in the past is by no means a safe one.
>
> The second premise is that the current differential would have been maintained in the past. That, or some such similar assumption, must be made in order to make any realistic assessment of the hypothetical historical effect of present discrimination. This is not to say that some rough and ready calculation could not be made, and some inferences may be more defensible than others.'

5.11 Thus the whole basis of the EqPA 1970 prevents comparison with a successor.

5.12 The third situation is where the claimant may make a claim without a named comparator, whether preceding or contemporaneous by relying on Art 141. This may be the position in relation to pension claims where the claimant is denied access solely because she is part time. The comparison in such a case may be with a group of workers eligible for pension benefits under the pension scheme (see Chapter 13). The other area where it may not be possible to find an appropriate comparator is in relation to maternity or pregnancy (as to which see Chapter 12 and in particular *Alabaster* at **12.21-12.30**).

5.13 Given that it is for the claimant to identify a comparator this raises two issues. What is the position if there is a 'token man' carrying out the same work as the claimant? The House of Lords made it clear in *Pickstone and Others v Freeman plc* [1988] IRLR 357, [1988] ICR 697 that the fact that there is a man who is carrying out the same work will not preclude a claim being brought. The claimants were 'warehouse operatives' and compared themselves with 'checker warehouse operatives' who earned £4.22 per week more. The House of Lords held that the claimants were entitled to compare themselves with these comparators even though there were men who were carrying out like work, for the purpose of arguing that the work was of equal value to the chosen comparators.

5.14 A token man doing the same work will not preclude the claimant from choosing another comparator but does the comparator chosen actually have to be representative? In *Thomas and Others v National Coal Board* [1987] ICR 757 the EAT held that a group of women were entitled to claim equal pay with a man who was the 'odd one out' in a protected position. It was not necessary for a representative comparator to be chosen and *Dance v Dorothy Perkins Ltd* [1978] ICR 760 was not followed in this respect.

5.15 The Northern Ireland Court of Appeal questioned whether an anomalous comparator could be chosen in *McPherson v Rathgael Centre for Children and Young People* [1991] IRLR 206 but did not need to decide the point. It is submitted that a claimant would not be precluded from choosing such a comparator but this is a risky option since the GMF defence may apply.

5.16 There is a risk that choosing the wrong comparator may lead to the case failing or claim being limited to that of the comparator's employment contract. The claimant can name as many comparators as she wishes and in some circumstances it may be that the cautious approach is to name a number of comparators of varying grades or jobs. This may particularly be the approach to take in a claim of equal pay for work of equal value because the expert will have to carry out a job evaluation and it may not be until this is carried out that the claimant can make her assertion of parity. It is to be noted that in a number of well-known cases the claimants compared themselves to several different jobs (*Hayward* – canteen cook with painters, insulation engineers and joiners; *Enderby* – speech therapists with male senior pharmacists and clinical psychologists). Naming several comparators may lead to a better prospect of success but on the other hand there is a danger of abuse where the claimant sets out her claim too widely. In *Leverton v Clwyd County Council* [1989] IRLR 28, ICR 33 Lord Bridge stated that:

> 'The larger the number of comparators whose jobs have to be evaluated, the more elaborate and expensive the process is likely to be. Here, as already mentioned, the appellant spread her net very widely by claiming equality with eleven comparators . . . that Industrial Tribunals should, so far as possible, be alert to prevent abuse of the equal value claims procedure by applicants who cast their net over too wide a spread of comparators. To take an extreme case, an applicant who claimed equality with A who earns £X and also with B who earns £2X could

hardly complain if an Industrial Tribunal concluded that her claim of equality with A itself demonstrated that there were no reasonable grounds for her claim of equality with B.'

5.17 It may be possible for the claimant to name classes of comparators rather than individuals and the Tribunal may then select the most relevant individuals from such classes. This approach was taken in Tribunal case, *Vaughan v Kraft Foods Ltd* COIT/814/95 where the claimant named a class of male production supervisors and the Tribunal stated that 'we have confined ourselves to those males who, from the evidence, seem to us most obviously relevant and valid for the purpose of Mrs Vaughan's claim' and picked out three male comparators.

5.18 The use of the disclosure and questionnaire procedure may be used to assist the claimant in identifying a comparator (see *Clywd County Council v Leverton* [1985] IRLR 197; see **10.17**).

5.19 A claim may be brought by a man who will, obviously, rely on a female comparator. It was held by the Court of Session in *South Ayrshire Council v Milligan* [2003] IRLR 153 that a claimant, a male primary school head teacher, could make a claim on a contingent basis where a female primary school head teacher who was not earning more would do so if a claim that she was bringing, in which she compared herself to male secondary school head teachers, succeeded. The proceedings were stayed pending the outcome of the female comparator's claim. To prevent such a claim would be in breach of the right of equality of pay under Art 141, since the man otherwise would suffer prejudice if he could not bring the claim until after the comparator's case was resolved as the 2-year limitation period would (as it was then), at that time, apply with regard to arrears of pay under the EqPA 1970, s 2(5).

COMMON TERMS AND CONDITIONS

5.20 The claimant may be able to compare herself with a comparator who:

- is employed by her employer at the same establishment;

- is employed by any associated employer at the same establishment;

- is employed by the employer or an associated employer at establishments in Great Britain which include that one and at which *common terms and conditions of employment* are observed either generally or for employees of the relevant classes; and

- is, under Art 141, employed in the 'same service' by different employers.

The same establishment

5.21   Where the claimant and comparator are employed at the same workplace there should not be a difficulty. In *Lawson and Others v Britfish Ltd* [1987] ICR 726, [1988] IRLR 53 a Tribunal had held that the claim could not be brought where it found that common terms and conditions were not observed between the claimant and comparators at the same establishment. The claimants were process workers who sought to compare themselves with a male handyman at the same establishment. The EAT held that the Tribunal had erred in law. The phrase 'and at which common terms and conditions of employment are observed' in the EqPA 1970, s 1(6) does not relate to employment at the same establishment. It relates to other establishments outside the establishment at which the applicant is employed. Once it is found that the applicants and the comparator are employed at the same establishment, whether there are common terms and conditions does not arise.

Associated employer

5.22   The wording of the EqPA 1970, s 1(6) provides that a woman may compare herself with a man employed by an associated employer at the same establishment though the two employers *do not have common terms and conditions* in relation to employees in the same class as the claimant and the comparator.

5.23   The EqPA 1970, s 1(6)(c) provides that:

'. . . two employers are to be treated as associated if one is a company of which the other (directly or indirectly) has control or if both are companies of which a third person (directly or indirectly) has control.'

5.24   The definition of 'associated employer' is the same as that which is adopted for the purpose of continuity of employment under the Employment Rights Act 1996. It is necessary for one employer to be *a company* of which the other has control so that there could not be a comparison between a claimant at the Fair Employment Agency and a comparator at the Equal Opportunities Commission of Northern Ireland since the two were statutory bodies rather than companies (see *Hasley v Fair Employment Agency* [1989] IRLR 106).

5.25   The position was considered in *Scullard v Knowles and Another* [1996] ICR 399, IRLR 344, where a female claimant was employed by the Southern Regional Council for Education and Training as director and manager of a further education unit. There were 12 units in Great Britain which were mostly attached to advisory councils. All of the other unit managers were men and received higher salaries for the same or similar work. The claimant alleged that she was entitled to the same pay as the male unit managers. It was argued that the regional councils were under the control of the Department of Education and were thus associated. This was rejected by the Tribunal but on appeal the EAT held that the Tribunal had erred in law. The definition of associated employers excluded a comparison between work at establishments where the two employers were not companies, notwithstanding that the employers were subject to direct or indirect control of a third party and observed common terms and conditions. The Act referred to associated 'companies'. The EAT contrasted Art 141 which envisaged a wider class of comparators as made clear by *Defrenne v Sabena (No 2)* [1976] ICR 547, in which it was stated that Art 119 (now Art 141) covered 'cases in which men and women receive unequal pay for equal work which is carried out in the *same establishment or service,* whether private or public'. The ECJ drew no distinction between work carried out for limited companies or other employers that were not incorporated.

5.26   The EAT stated that:

> 'The crucial question for the purposes of Article 119 [now Art 141] is, therefore, whether the applicant and the male unit managers of the other councils were employed "in the same establishment or service". The industrial tribunal did not ask or answer that question. To the extent that that is a wider class of comparators than is contained in S.1(6) EqP Act 1970, S.1(6), which is confined to an "associated employer", is displaced and must yield to the paramount force of Article 119 [now Art 141]. On this aspect of the claim it will be relevant for the industrial tribunal to examine factual areas which have not so far been explored, namely, whether the regional councils, even though none is a company, were directly or indirectly controlled by a third party – the directorate – the extent and nature of control and whether they constitute the "same establishment or service". For that purpose, it will also be relevant to consider whether common terms and conditions of employment were observed in the regional advisory councils for the relevant class of employees.'

The EAT referred to *Hasley* as supporting their view of Art 141.

Common terms and conditions at different establishments

5.27   A claimant may also compare herself to a comparator at a different establishment where the comparator is employed by the same employer or an associated employer and at which common terms and conditions of employment are observed either generally or for employees of the relevant classes. These provisions have given rise to a considerable amount of case-law. It is necessary that there be common terms and conditions at both workplaces. The scope of the provision was considered in detail in *Leverton v Clwyd County Council* [1989] IRLR 28, ICR 33. The claimant and her comparators were employed by Clwyd County Council *at different establishments* under terms which were contained in the conditions of service of the National Joint Council (NJC) for Local Authorities' Administrative, Professional, Technical and Clerical Services (the 'Purple Book'). This set pay scales for each of the categories of work from caretaking and supervisory duties through to clerical and administrative. The claimant was a nursery nurse in scale 1 whilst the comparators were in scales 3 and 4. The claimant worked less hours a week (32.5 as against 37/39) and had 70 days holiday compared to 20. It was argued that these differences meant that the claimant could not be in the same employment. A majority of the Court of Appeal held that for 'common terms and conditions' to apply their terms had to be broadly similar and this was not the position because of hours of work and holidays.

5.28   May LJ, however, dissented. He held that the requirement that common terms and conditions apply meant no more than that the terms of the claimant and the terms of the comparators were not dependent upon the establishment at which each are employed but are observed either generally or for employees of the relevant class; that is, the class of which the claimant was an employee and the class of which the comparator was a member regardless of their place of employment.

5.29   The House of Lords reversed the Court of Appeal, agreeing with the reasoning of May LJ. Where the claimants and comparators work at different establishments, in order to bring a claim it must be shown that she is employed on common terms and conditions and this concept contemplates terms and conditions which are governed by the same Collective Agreement. Where both the claimant and the comparators were employed by the same local authority under terms and conditions which were set by the NJC, the claimant was employed on common terms and conditions notwithstanding that there were significant differences in the hours of work and holiday.

5.30   Lord Bridge stated that:

> '. . . the language of the subsection is clear and unambiguous. It poses the question whether the terms and conditions of employment "observed" at two or more establishments (at which the relevant woman and the relevant men are employed) are "common", being terms and conditions of employment observed "either generally or for employees of the relevant classes". The concept of common terms and conditions of employment observed generally at different establishments necessarily contemplates terms and conditions applicable to a wide range of employee whose individual terms will vary greatly inter se. On the construction of the subsection adopted by the majority below the phrase "observed either generally or for employees of the relevant classes" is given no content. Terms and conditions of employment governed by the same collective agreement seem to me to represent the paradigm though not necessarily the only example, of the common terms and conditions of employment contemplated by the subsection.'

If there was any ambiguity in the EqPA 1970, s 1(6), his Lordship would have rejected any contrary construction on the ground that it frustrated rather than served the manifest purpose of the Act, to eliminate differences between the terms of the woman's contract and that of any man doing like work, work rated as equivalent or equal value. To hold otherwise would mean that it was necessary to prove an undefined substratum of similarity between the particular terms of her contract and his as the basis of her entitlement to eliminate any discriminatory differences between those terms.

5.31   It is important to note that there are limitations to this principle, which is why common terms and conditions of employment have to be observed. Lord Bridge explained this clearly by way of examples:

> 'On the construction of S.1(6) which I would adopt there is a sensible and rational explanation for the limitation of equality claims as between men and women employed at different establishments to establishments at which common terms and conditions of employment are observed. There may be perfectly good geographical or historical reasons why a single employer should operate essentially different employment regimes at different establishments. In such cases the limitation imposed by S.1(6) will operate to defeat claims under S.1 as between men and women at the different establishments. I take two examples by way of illustration. A single employer has two establishments, one in London and one in Newcastle. The rates of pay earned by persons of both sexes for the same work are substantially higher in London than in Newcastle. Looking at either the London establishment or the Newcastle establishment in isolation there is no sex discrimination. If the women in Newcastle could invoke S.1 of the Act of 1970 to achieve equality with the men in London this would eliminate a differential in earnings which is due not to sex but to geography. S.1(6) prevents them from doing so. An employer operates factory A where he has a long-standing collective agreement with the ABC union. The same employer takes over a company operating factory X and becomes an "associated employer" of the persons working there. The previous owner of factory X had a long-standing collective agreement with the XYZ union which the new employer continues to operate. The two collective agreements have produced quite different structures governing pay and other terms and conditions of employment at the two factories. Here again S.1(6) will operate to prevent women in factory A claiming equality with men in factory X and vice versa. These examples are not, of course, intended to be exhaustive. So long as industrial tribunals direct themselves correctly in law to make the appropriate broad comparison, it will always be a question of fact for them, in any particular case, to decide whether, as between two different establishments, "common terms and conditions of employment are observed either generally or for employees of the relevant classes". Here the majority of the industrial tribunal misdirected themselves in law and their conclusion on this point cannot be supported.'

The House of Lords overturned the Court of Appeal but it is noteworthy that it was held that there was a GMF which provided a defence (see **11.29**).

5.32   The House of Lords only had to consider the position where the employees were governed by the same collective agreement; the Purple Book. Where the comparator is subject to a different agreement there is no problem if the comparator works in the same establishment. Where the comparator works in a different establishment the statement of Lord Bridge that the terms and conditions had to be applicable to 'all the employees at the relevant establishments, or to a particular class or classes of employees to which both the man and the woman belong' would appear to defeat a claim if there were different collective agreements at different establishments. It was apparent that this was not the approach of May LJ in the Court of Appeal, which judgment was approved in the House of Lords, as he referred to the terms and conditions of each group. This would mean that if the nursery nurses were employed on the same conditions at the different establishments and the same applied to the comparators at whichever establishment they were employed, then common terms and conditions would apply.

5.33 The position was considered in *British Coal Corporation v Smith and Others* [1996] ICR 515; IRLR 404. Some 1,286 claimants were employed as canteen workers and cleaners at 47 different establishments. They claimed work of equal value with 150 surface mineworkers and clerical staff. Many of the claimants worked in different establishments to their comparators. The Tribunal adopted what it called a common-sense approach and held that it was necessary for the claimants to be governed at the different locations by common terms and conditions and the class or comparators at the locations to also be governed by common terms and conditions but there was no need for commonality or uniformity between each of the sets of terms and conditions. The Tribunal noted that there were regional variations but that the mineworkers were in the same employment. The EAT upheld the decision but this was overturned by the Court of Appeal. The House of Lords reinstated the Tribunal's judgment.

5.34 It held that the Tribunal was correct to find that the canteen workers and cleaners were in the same employment as the comparators at the different establishments and it was entitled to find that local differences relating to bonuses and fuel allowances did not negate the centralised industry-wide nature of the terms and conditions. Lord Slynn noted that it was plain and agreed that the woman does not have to show that she shares common terms and conditions with her comparator, either in the sense that all the terms are the same, since necessarily his terms must be different in some respect if she is to show a breach of the equality clause, or in regard to terms other than that said to constitute the discrimination. His Lordship stated that what has to be shown:

' . . . is that the male comparators at other establishments and at her establishment share common terms and conditions. If there are no such men at the applicant's place of work then it has to be shown that like terms and conditions would apply if men were employed there in the particular jobs concerned.'

5.35 It is apparent from the case that there may be common terms and conditions provided that, on a broad common-sense basis, common terms are observed in each group across the establishments, even though the claimants/comparators are subject to different Collective Agreements. The Tribunal, quoted by Lord Slynn in the House of Lords, put it well:

'What in our view is necessary is commonality, uniformity of employment which can be satisfied if the class to which the applicant belongs is governed – at the relevant locations – by common terms and conditions and if the class to which her comparator(s) belong – at those same locations – is governed by common terms and conditions; without there being necessity for commonality or uniformity between each set of terms and conditions.'

5.36 The scope of the rulings in the above two cases was considered in *South Tyneside Metropolitan Borough Council v Anderson* [2007] IRLR 715, ICR 1581. The claimants were a group of female support staff who were employed by the local education authority as cooks or cleaners. The terms of employment were set out in the White Book. They compared themselves inter alia to drivers, a street cleaner, a painter, a refuse collector and a foreman, who were on the same scale point but, by reason of top-up payments which were found to be a sham or unjustified, the men were paid more. By the time of the appeal to the Court of Appeal the case concerned only those who had been employed on the recommendation of a governing body of a community school. The engagement of such staff was governed by the School Standards and Framework Act 1998, Sch 16, paras 20 and 21 and its successor provisions contained in the School Staffing (England) Regulations 2003, SI 2003/1963. It was agreed to substitute as a respondent an employee, Ms Irving, who was employed as a learning support assistant. Her male comparator was a road sweeper on the same point of the White Book scale. Under the legislation it was for the school governing body to recommend the staff and terms and conditions, including remuneration, to the local authority. The Employment Tribunal, upheld by the EAT, had held that bonuses paid to male comparators were a sham or were not justified. In the Court of Appeal the issue was whether the women and comparators were employed by the same employer at different establishments at which common terms and conditions were observed. The Court of Appeal held that it was clear from *British Coal Corporation v Smith* that 'common' as applied to terms and conditions of employment meant sufficiently similar to a broad comparison to be made, which was a matter of factual judgment for the Tribunal. The Tribunal had not erred in finding that the *British Coal* test was met as the issue was concluded by the application of s 1(6) since Ms Irving, a learning support assistant, was employed by the same employer at a separate establishment at which common terms and conditions were observed for employees of the relevant classes.

5.37 Sedley LJ considered an argument based upon the dicta of Lord Slynn in *British Coal* that if there are no men at the applicant's place of work on common terms and conditions 'then it has to be shown that like terms and conditions would apply if men were employed there in the particular jobs concerned'. It was argued that the statutory arrangements rendered the argument there were common terms and conditions untenable since the arrangements meant that the governing bodies decided the terms and the claimants had to prove they would agree to such common terms. However, Sedley LJ stated that it had to be borne in mind that the claimants in the *British Coal* case were:

'... seeking to compare themselves with miners and other staff who were employed on the terms of different collective agreements. In the absence of common terms and conditions, a way needed to be found of ascertaining whether, if they were to have been employed under the same roof, the women and the men would have had common terms and conditions: hence Lord Slynn's formula. Had they all been employed by British Coal in different establishments but on common terms and conditions, the need for a hypothetical answer would not have arisen.'

5.38 In the present case it was sufficient that the claimants and comparators were employed by the same employer, albeit at different establishments, on different terms and conditions. However, the Court of Appeal did go on to consider the argument that it was necessary for the claimant to establish that her terms and conditions and those of a street cleaner hypothetically employed by the local authority at the school would be broadly similar. Sedley LJ held that they would be as they would be on Grade 1 of the White Book scale. The Court of Appeal considered that the margins of discretion which were stated to be vested in the governing body were 'largely illusory'. It was fanciful to suppose that a governing body could select and bind the local authority to an inappropriate grade for a new member of the school's staff. There would ordinarily be a known pay grade which it would be both unrealistic and arguably perverse for governors to seek to depart from.

5.39 The EAT in *Barclays Bank plc v James* [1990] IRLR 90, IRC 333 relied on Lord Bridge's dictum in *Leverton* that:

> 'The concept of common terms and conditions observed generally at different establishments contemplates terms and conditions applicable to a wide range of employees whose individual terms will vary greatly *inter se* . . . Terms and conditions of employment governed by the same collective agreement seem to me to represent the paradigm, though not necessarily the only example, of the common terms and conditions of employment contemplated by the subsection.'

It is apparent that the concept should be construed as widely as possible.

The same service

5.40 Article 141 of the EC Treaty may be relied upon in identifying the appropriate comparator. This is apparent from cases in which Art 141 has been directly relied upon. Thus, in *McCarthys Ltd v Smith* [1980] ICR 672 the ECJ stated that:

> 'Among the forms of discrimination which may be thus judicially identified, the Court mentioned in particular cases where men and women receive unequal pay for equal work carried out in the same establishment or service.'

5.41 The test of the same 'service' on the face of it appears to be substantially wider than that of establishment since a number of different employers may provide a private or public unified or national service. This issue was considered in *Lawrence and Others v Regent Office Care and Others* [2002] IRLR 822, [2003] ICR 1092. The claimants brought equal value claims against contractors who had employed the claimants on inferior terms when North Yorkshire Council had put its school meals and cleaning services out to tender. The claimants had been formerly employed by the Council. They argued that unless they could compare themselves with employees who remained employed by the County Council they would lose the fruits of earlier litigation (the claim is related to equal value claims which eventually succeeded in *Ratcliffe v North Yorkshire County Council*, see **11.102**). This issue which therefore arose was whether the claimant could compare herself to a male comparator who was employed by a former employer of the claimant. The Tribunal dismissed the claim as the employer which it was alleged was discriminating was not in control of the wages of the claimants and comparators.

5.42   The claimants sought to rely on Art 141 before the EAT. It was argued that the Article was wide enough to enable employees to compare themselves with County Council staff. The claimants relied on *Scullard* in which Art 141 had been used to expand the application of the Act. The EAT dismissed the appeal and the Court of Appeal referred the case to the ECJ. The ECJ ruled as follows:

> 'A situation such as that in the main proceedings, in which the differences identified in the pay conditions of workers of different sex performing equal work or work of equal value cannot be attributed to a single source, does not come within the scope of Article 141(1) EC.'

5.43   It was not possible in *Lawrence* to argue that there was a single source as:

> 'The argument that the services provided by the council itself and those provided for it are ultimately funded from the same source is one which I consider forthwith to be untenable. Authorities purchase goods and services on a large scale. The council cannot be obliged, when contracting out specified services, to impose on the suppliers concerned a requirement that the terms and conditions of employment for women whom they employ must be the same as those of male workers who perform equivalent work for the council. A fortiori, this argument cannot be used to oblige the present employers to continue to bring the working conditions of women whom they employ into line with those of men performing equivalent work for the council.'

The claimants and comparators worked for different employers. The work which the claimants performed was identical to that which some of them had carried out before the transfer to outside contractors. The work had already been recognised as of equal value to the chosen comparators at a time before the competitive tendering. Whilst there was nothing in Art 141 to suggest it was limited to situations where the claimants and comparators worked for the same employer where the differences that were identified in the pay conditions cannot be attributed *to a single source* there is no single body that is responsible for the inequality *and which could restore equal treatment* so that the workers could not be compared. The words in italics set out the limitation and reason for the test.

5.44   It appears from the judgment that the ECJ assumed that employment by a single employer was a sufficient condition to be able to compare under Art 141 and that the single source test would only be necessary where there were different employers. However, in *Robertson v Department for the Environment, Food and Rural Affairs* [2005] IRLR 363 the Court of Appeal stated that the 'single source' test was of general application and was not restricted to cases where the claimants and comparators worked for different employers. The fact of common employment was not necessary or sufficient as the approach of EC law is to locate the single source with the body responsible for setting the terms and conditions. Since in this case the responsibility for negotiating terms and conditions had been delegated to individual government departments there was no single source to which differences in pay could be attributed so that male civil servants working in DEFRA could not compare themselves to females in DETR. Such cross-departmental comparison was not possible since, though the civil servants were technically all working for the Crown, there was no single source.

5.45 A good example of the application of the single source test is the decision in *South Ayrshire Council v Morton* [2002] ICR 956, IRLR 256. A large number of primary school head teachers brought claims claiming equal pay with secondary school head teachers. The claimant was employed by South Ayrshire Council and was chosen as one of the test cases. She compared herself with three men, one of whom worked for the Highland Council. It was accepted that the education authorities were not associated employers but argued that s 1(6) was not compatible with Art 141. The salary scales were set by the Scottish Joint Negotiating Committee, which was a quasi autonomous body controlled by the Secretary of State. Each education authority was autonomous with regard to its employees but in reality there was little scope to depart from pay set by the Committee. The Tribunal held that the education authorities had sufficient community of interest for the whole structure of education to be regarded as a 'service'. The EAT upheld the Tribunal's decision. The Scottish Court of Session held that, on the facts, a female primary school head teacher could cite a male secondary school head teacher employed by a different local authority as a comparator under Art 141. The Court referred to *Defrenne v Sabena* [1976] ICR 547 where it had stated:

> '21. Among the forms of direct discrimination which may be identified solely by reference to the criteria laid down by Article 119 [now Art 141] must be included in particular those which have their origin in legislative provisions or in collective labour agreements and which may be detected on the basis of a purely legal analysis of the situation.
>
> 22. This applies even more in cases where men and women receive unequal pay for equal work carried out in the same establishment or service, whether public or private.'

In this case, the Court of Session agreed with the claimant that:

> ' . . . the question whether there was an establishment or service under paragraph 22 of the Defrenne decision did not arise because the comparator was admissible under paragraph 21 by reason of the statutory nature of the collective bargaining that the SJNC mechanism involved.'

5.46 The terms negotiated by the Committee under statutory authority and government control consisted of a collective agreement as envisaged in *Defrenne.* Lord Gill stated:

' . . . it is logical and reasonable to suggest that in a uniform statutory regime governing pay and conditions in the public sector of education, comparisons may be made across the boundaries of the authorities that are statutorily obliged to give effect to it. We conclude therefore that a comparator employed by another education authority is admissible in this case . . .'

5.47 The Court of Session went on to state that the Tribunal had reached the right conclusion that the public sector of education constituted a service though it did not need to decide this given the above reasoning:

' . . . the material considerations are that the applicant and her comparators are in the same branch of public service and are subject to a uniform system of national pay and conditions set by a statutory body whose decision is binding on their employers. It seems reasonable to us to refer to them as being engaged in the same service.'

5.48 More recently, in *Allonby v Accrington and Rossendale College and Others* [2004] IRLR 224 a female lecturer claimed equal pay, comparing herself to a male lecturer. She had been employed by the college but her contract was terminated and she was immediately engaged through an employment agency on terms which were far less favourable. The employer's occupational pension scheme was restricted to those under employment contracts. The ECJ held, in relation to the contract of employment, that the claimant was not entitled to rely on Art 141 using the male teacher still employed by the school. The differences in pay could not be attributed to a single source. However, in relation to the occupational pension scheme, which derived from state legislation and which restricted membership to teachers under contracts of employment, the claimant could rely on statistical evidence to show that the scheme was contrary to Art 141 as it discriminated against female workers. Where the provision was disapplied under Art 141 the consequences applied to both the state and public authorities and the employer. The ECJ drew a distinction between rules on pay that derive from national law and those that do not. Where the claimant challenges the discriminatory effect of a pension scheme derived from legislation there is no need to point to a male comparator and statistical evidence can be relied upon (cf *Coloroll Pension Trustees Ltd v Russell* on occupational pension schemes where a comparator is needed). The ECJ ruled as follows in *Allonby*:

'1. In circumstances such as those of the main proceedings, Article 141(1) EC must be interpreted as meaning that a woman whose contract of employment with an undertaking has not been renewed and who is immediately made available to her previous employer through another undertaking to provide the same services is not entitled to rely, vis-à-vis the intermediary undertaking, on the principle of equal pay, using as a basis for comparison the remuneration received for equal work or work of the same value by a man employed by the woman's previous employer.

2. Article 141(1) EC must be interpreted as meaning that a woman in circumstances such as those of the main proceedings is not entitled to rely on the principle of equal pay in order to secure entitlement to membership of an

occupational pension scheme for teachers set up by State legislation of which only teachers with a contract of employment may become members, using as a basis for comparison the remuneration, including such a right of membership, received for equal work or work of the same value by a man employed by the woman's previous employer.

3. In the absence of any objective justification, the requirement, imposed by State legislation, of being employed under a contract of employment as a precondition for membership of a pension scheme for teachers is not applicable where it is shown that, among the teachers who are workers within the meaning of Article 141(1) EC and fulfil all the other conditions for membership, a much lower percentage of women than of men is able to fulfil that condition. The formal classification of a self-employed person under national law does not change the fact that a person must be classified as a worker within the meaning of that article if his independence is merely notional.

4. Article 141(1) EC must be interpreted as meaning that, where State legislation is at issue, the applicability of that provision vis-à-vis an undertaking is not subject to the condition that the worker concerned can be compared with a worker of the other sex who is or has been employed by the same employer and who has received higher pay for equal work or work of equal value.'

5.49   The above cases shows the importance of identifying a single source for the determination of pay where the claimant and comparator are employed by difference parties (*Lawrence* was followed in *Board of Governors of Blessed Edward Jones High School v Rawlinson* EAT/0776/02 DM and cf *Dolphin v Hartlepool Borough Council; South Tyneside Metropolitan Borough Council v Middleton* UKEAT/0559/05/LA; UKEAT/0684/05/ZT.)

5.50   The Court of Appeal considered the 'single source' issue in relation to the NHS in *Armstrong and Others v Newcastle Upon Tyne Hospital Trust* [2006] IRLR 124. Female ancillary workers were employed in three hospitals run by an NHS Trust and sought to compare themselves with male ancillary workers at a fourth hospital. In 1985 the Newcastle Health Authority put out its domestic work to tender as a result of which the domestic staff lost its bonuses whilst the porters retained their bonuses. The domestic staff and porters remained in the Newcastle Health Authority's employment until 1991 when responsibility for the four hospitals was divided between two new Trusts, the Royal Victoria Infirmary (RVI) and Freeman, which in 1998 merged to become the Newcastle NHS Hospital Trust. Domestic workers brought equal pay claims against the Trust, arguing that their work was of equal value to the male porters at the RVI. An issue arose whether the claimants who were not employed at the RVI could compare themselves with male staff at that hospital. The Tribunal held that s 1(6) did not apply since the bonus agreements were subject to collective negotiation on a departmental basis. The claims could not come within Art 141 since there were 'essentially different employment regimes' and it could not be said that the differences in pay were attributable to a single source. The Court of Appeal held that the Tribunal had been correct to find there were no common terms and conditions of employment. It was not enough for the claimants to show that they had the same employer as their comparators. They must show that the employer was also the body responsible for setting the terms of both groups of employees.

5.51 It should be noted that the claimants in *Lawrence* would now be able to rely on TUPE to argue that the equality clause had modified their contracts and that this clause had been transferred over (See *Kells v Pilkington plc* EAT/1435/00).

SUMMARY OF THE POSITION

5.52 The following is offered as a summary of the principles, extracted from the above case-law:

• The claimant may chose the comparator, who must be of the opposite sex, though an atypical/anomalous comparator may lead to a GMF defence, and the Tribunal can only make a finding or award by reference to the chosen comparator.

• There is no need for contemporaneous employment so that a predecessor may be chosen as a comparator but a successor cannot be chosen.

• The comparator may be at the same establishment as the employer or an associated employer, being a company of which one or the other has direct or indirect control or which are both under the control of a third person.

• If the comparator is not at the same establishment but the employer or an associated employer observes common terms and conditions for employees generally or for employees of the relevant classes there will be a valid comparator. Where the class of claimant and the class of comparator are governed by different collective agreements but they are the same in relation to each class of job at the different establishments then there may be a valid comparator. If there are no men at the claimant's establishment it has to be shown that, if there had been, like terms would have applied.

• The comparator may be one employed by a different employer where the claimant and comparator are in the same service and the employment terms emanate from a single source. As is apparent from the above cases this area of law is still in a state of development.

Chapter 6

PAY

GENERAL

6.1   Section 1(2) of the EqPA 1970 provides that:

> 'An equality clause is a provision which relates to terms (whether concerned with pay or not) of a contract under which a woman is employed . . .'

The Act, thus, does not just deal with pay but applies to all contractual terms and conditions in the contract of employment. This will include access to benefits such as, for example, social facilities, terms concerning holiday entitlement, access to overtime and other such benefits.

6.2   It should be borne in mind that non-contractual terms will be covered by the SDA 1975 so that such matters as discretionary bonuses will be covered by the equal treatment provisions (see **2.43-2.50**). The issue of bonuses may be an area of particular importance in the private sector, such as bonus claims in the City, and it is necessary to consider with some care whether there is an EqPA 1970 or SDA 1975 claim, based upon the nature of the contractual or discretionary arrangements.

6.3   Article 141 of the EC Treaty also contains a definition of pay, as follows:

> 'For the purpose of this Article, "pay" means the ordinary basic or minimum wage or salary and any other consideration, whether in cash or in kind, which the worker receives directly or indirectly, in respect of his employment, from his employer.'

The Article is narrower than the EqPA 1970 in that it covers monetary pay terms but does not cover non-pay terms such as holiday entitlement. It is, however, broader in that it covers non-contractual pay such a discretionary bonus. The pay must arise directly or indirectly as a result of employment so that payments under social security schemes will be excluded (*Defrenne v Belgian State* [1971] ECR 445). However, provided that the payment is related to employment the courts have interpreted the definition of pay extremely widely so that it covers payments made during or after employment (*Garland v British Rail Engineering* [1982] ICR 420), fringe benefits, severance payments, occupational pensions and redundancy payments.

6.4   Where domestic law is less favourable then the Community provisions will take precedence (*Barber v Guardian Royal Exchange Assurance Group* (Case C-262/88), [1990] IRLR 240, ICR 616). An Employment Tribunal will hear the claim under the EqPA 1970 and approach the case based on the broader definition of pay under Art 141 so that the procedural requirements of the Act will have to be complied with (including time-limits) but the substantive Community law will apply (*Biggs v Somerset County Council* [1996] IRLR 203, ICR 364). However, where there is a remedy, such as a claim under the SDA 1975 in relation to discretionary bonuses, the proper route will be to bring a claim under that provision rather than arguing that the EqPA 1970 is amended or supplemented by Art 141.

6.5   It should also be noted that, under Art 141, there can be no set off as between different benefits, so that, for example, in *Jämställdhetsombudsmannen v Örebro Läns Landsting* [2000] IRLR 421 an inconvenient hours supplement was not to be taken into account in calculating monthly salary. Swedish midwives who received lower monthly salaries than a clinical technician, but who received an inconvenient hours supplement and reduction in weekly working hours on account of their working shifts, were entitled to claim without the latter being taken into account.

6.6   The Employment Appeal Tribunal (EAT) made it clear in *Redcar and Cleveland Borough Council v Degnan* [2005] IRLR 179 that the concept of equal pay does not permit comparison by reference to subdivisions of remuneration. The claimants and comparators were paid the same basic rates but there was a difference in the rates for attendance allowances and bonuses. The Employment Tribunal considered the terms for bonuses and allowances separately from the hourly rate. The EAT held that it was not possible to make this subdivision.

6.7   There is a large body of case-law which considers what does or does not amount to pay. In some cases the definition is considered under the EqPA 1970, in others under Art 141. It is submitted that it does not in practical terms make any difference whether the claim is under the EqPA 1970 or Art 141 definition of pay as where the disputed matter is identified as pay then the Tribunal will consider the claim in any event.

A-Z OF PAY

6.8   The following have been considered in the case-law.

Additional payments

6.9   It was held in *EC Commission v Belgium* (Case C-173/91) [1991] IRLR 404 that an additional monthly payment which was made to employees over 60 who had been made redundant provided that they remained entitled to unemployment benefit was pay for the purposes of Art 141.

Allowances

6.10 An allowance which is paid to compensate for loss of salary whilst on a training course has been held to be pay within Art 141. In *Arbeiterwohlfahrt der Stadt Berlin Ev v Bötel* [1992] IRLR 423 and *Kuratorium für Dialyse und Nierentransplantation Ev v Lewark* [1996] IRLR 637 payments made to staff workplace committees who had attended training courses as part of their duties was pay as it arose from the contract of employment.

6.11 In *Davies v Neath Port Talbot County Borough Council* [1999] IRLR 769 a female part-time worker took time off to attend a union health and safety course which was full time. She was paid her normal contractual hours rather than for the time spent attending the course. The EAT held that the attendance on the course was related to the employment relationship and constituted work for the purpose of Art 141. A female part-time employee was therefore entitled to receive the allowance calculated by the time actually spent attending the course. The EAT declined to follow the earlier decision of *Manor Bakeries Ltd v Nazir* [1996] IRLR 604, which held that attendance on a trade union course was not work. Tribunals are likely to hold in the future that an allowance paid for attending such a course is pay for work done.

Bonuses

6.12 Payment of a bonus under the contract of employment is almost certainly pay as it relates to work that has been carried out. The issue here that is likely to arise is whether the bonus is discretionary and comes under the EqPA 1970 provisions or under the SDA 1975 (see **2.43** and *Hoyland v ASDA Stores Ltd* [2005] IRLR 438). A genuinely discretionary bonus may lead to a claim under the SDA 1975 but if the bonus is regulated by the contract of employment then it is an EqPA 1970 situation.

6.13 A voluntary Christmas bonus paid to staff as an incentive for work to be carried out in the future or as a reward for loyalty was held to be pay in *Lewen v Denda* [2000] IRLR 67, ICR 648. The bonus was granted to employees who were in active employment but a female worker was not paid because she was on parental leave at the time. It was argued that Art 141 was breached as more women than men were likely to take leave. The ECJ stated that the reason for which an employer pays a benefit is of little importance provided that the benefit is granted in connection with employment. It followed that a Christmas bonus of the kind at issue, even if paid on a voluntary basis and even if paid mainly or exclusively as an incentive for future work or loyalty to the undertaking or both, constituted pay within the meaning of Art 119 of the Treaty. However, the ECJ stated that a worker who exercises a statutory right to take parenting leave, which carries with it a parenting allowance paid by the state, is in a special situation, which cannot be assimilated to that of a man or woman at work since such leave involves suspension of the contract of employment and, therefore, of the respective obligations of the employer and the worker. The refusal to pay a woman on parenting leave a bonus as an exceptional allowance given voluntarily by an employer at Christmas does not therefore constitute discrimination within the meaning of Art 119 where the award of that allowance is subject only to the condition that the worker is in active employment when it is awarded. The ECJ noted that the position would be different if the bonus was retroactive pay for work performed in the course of the year in which the bonus is awarded (see also *GUS Home Shopping Ltd v Green & McClaughlin* [2001] IRLR 75).

Bursaries, grants, scholarships etc

6.14   Such payments may not be made as salary and not be pay under the EqPA 1970 but there will be a claim for disparate treatment under the SDA 1975 (see *Ms C Fletcher and Others v NHS Pensions Agency/Student Grants Unit and The Secretary of State for Health* [2005] IRLR 689 in which it was held that a bursary was a facility within the meaning of the SDA 1975, s 14).

Employee participation schemes

6.15   There may be a number of ways in which the employee is given incentive benefits, such as share ownership plans or other financial participation schemes. These are likely to be pay if they are regulated by the contract of employment and linked to performance under the contract.

Fringe benefits

6.16   Where a fringe benefit is referable to employment then it will be regarded as pay (see *Garland v British Rail Engineering* [1982] IRLR 111).

Increases

6.17   Where there are automatic increases in pay levels, based, for example, upon seniority, then the increases will constitute pay and will give rise to claims under the EqPA 1970 where there is a contractual right. There may also be a claim for age discrimination. A distinction needs to be drawn here between contractual increases and discretionary increases which are given as part of a promotion or an assessment of skill or potential/appraisals. The latter are likely to raise issues of equal treatment so that the provisions of the SDA 1975 and the Equal Treatment Directive are applicable. Where a pay progression is effectively automatic, as in *Nimz v Freie und Hansestadt Hamburg* [1991] IRLR 222, the salary will be pay for the purposes of Art 141. In *Nimz* the claimant had to work 12 years before she was automatically upgraded because she worked part time, whereas an employee who worked for three-quarters of the full-time hours would be upgraded after 6 years (90% of public service administrators working less than three-quarters of the normal working hours for full-time employees were women whereas only 55% of full-time administrators in the public service were women). The ECJ held that the increases were pay and there was a right to claim under equal pay legislation.

6.18 The case may be contrasted with *Gerster v Freistaat Bayern* [1997] IRLR 699, [1998] ICR 327. The claimant worked part time. The rules governing the civil service provided that employees were entitled to be considered for promotion but periods during which the hours worked were one-half to two-thirds only counted at a rate of two-thirds, whilst two-thirds and above hours counted in full. The employer was only prepared to consider the claimant on the basis that her part-time work counted for two-third's service. It was alleged that this was contrary to Art 141 and the Equal Treatment Directive (76/207/EC). The ECJ held that the employee was seeking to be placed on a list of eligible candidates and progression to a higher grade and higher salary was a possibility rather than a right. Promotion depended on a number of factors so that inclusion on the list of eligible candidates was a precursor to such promotion. The claim related to equal treatment and therefore came within the scope of the Equal Treatment Directive (76/207/EC) rather than to equal pay.

Injury to feelings

6.19 See non-monetary benefits.

Job shares

6.20 The ECJ considered the position with regard to job shares in *Hill & Stapleton v Revenue Commissioners and Another* [1998] IRLR 466. It was held that the claimants were able to rely on Art 141 where the pay progression was less favourable to workers who were job sharing than to full-time workers.

Maternity pay

6.21 Maternity pay is pay under Art 141. However, the equality clause does not operate in relation to terms of the contract of employment which afford a woman special treatment in connection with pregnancy or childbirth (EqPA 1970, s 6 and see Chapter 12). A man cannot complain of additional payments made to a woman during maternity whilst a female can complain of extra paternity benefits that are accorded to a man. It was held that a payment to women to compensate for the fact that they were unable to access certain benefits whilst they were on maternity leave counted as pay in *Abdoulaye v Régie Nationale des Usines Renault SA* (Case C-218/98) [2001] ICR 527. A female employee received a lump sum on commencement of maternity leave but new fathers were not paid an equivalent lump sum allowance. Since the benefit paid by an employer to a female employee when she goes on maternity leave was based on the employment relationship, it constituted pay within the meaning of Art 141 and the Equal Pay Directive 75/117/EC. While such a payment was not made periodically and not indexed on salary, its characteristics did not alter its nature of pay within the meaning of Art 141. Whilst the sum did amount to pay, the payment was not precluded by Art 141 where that payment was designed to offset the occupational disadvantages inherent in taking maternity leave.

6.22   Where a woman is paid less than her full pay whilst on maternity leave or is not paid benefits, the position as to whether there is a valid claim is likely to depend on whether the claim is of equal treatment or equal pay, as to which see Chapter 12.

National service and parental leave

6.23   Since the principle of equal pay and contractual benefits relates to comparable situations, the equality principle will not be breached where it is not possible to compare males and females in comparable situations. It was held in *Österreichischer Gewerkschaftsbund, Gewerkshaschaft der Privatang-estellten v Wirtschaftskammer Österreich* (Case C-220/02) [2004] All ER (D) 03 (Jun) that there was no breach of Art 141 and the Equal Pay Directive (75/117/EC) where parental leave was not taken into account in calculating termination payments but national service was taken into account. The types of leave differed so it was not possible to make a comparison.

Non-monetary benefits

6.24   Since the concept of pay connotes a tangible benefit, whether or not expressed in monetary terms, it cannot include non-economic loss, such as injury to feelings (*Council of the City of Newcastle upon Tyne v Allan* [2005] IRLR 504).

Nursery places

6.25   It was held in *Lommers v Minister van Landbouw, Natuurbeheer en Visserij* (Case C-476/99) [2002] IRLR 430 that the provision of nursery places was a matter that was covered by the Equal Treatment Directive (76/207/EC) rather than as pay under Art 141. Subsidised nursery places were made available to female employees but to male employees only in the case of an emergency. A male employee's request for a place to be reserved for his unborn child was refused. It was held that the provision was a lawful and proportional derogation from the duty to provide equal treatment in view of Art 2(4) of the Equal Treatment Directive (76/207/EC), which permits a derogation from the principle of equal treatment where an employer institutes a positive-action programme designed to remove inequalities affecting a particular sex's opportunities in the workplace. On the application of Art 141, the court stated that:

> ' . . . the fixing of certain working conditions may have pecuniary consequences is not sufficient to bring such conditions within the scope of Article [141] of the EC Treaty, which is a provision based on the close connection existing between the nature of the work done and the amount of pay . . .'

Pension benefits

6.26 This is considered in detail in Chapter 13 but it is useful to set out a summary of the cases on pay at this stage.

6.27 Payments made by employers to occupational pension schemes are pay under Art 141. In *Worringham and Humphreys v Lloyds Bank Ltd* [1979] IRLR 440 (CA), [1981] ICR 558, IRLR 178 the ECJ stated that:

> 'Sums such as those in question which are included in the calculation of the gross salary payable to the employee and which directly determine the calculation of other advantages linked to the salary, such as redundancy payments, unemployment benefits, family allowances and credit facilities, form part of the worker's pay within the meaning of the second paragraph of Article 119 of the Treaty even if they are immediately deducted by the employer and paid to a pension fund on behalf of the employee. This applies a fortiori where those sums are refunded in certain circumstances and subject to certain deductions to the employee as being repayable to him if he ceases to belong to the contractual retirement benefits scheme under which they were deducted.'

6.28 The impact of the EqPA 1970 cannot be understated, when the ECJ gave its decision in *Barber v Guardian Royal Exchange Assurance* [1990] ICR 616, IRLR 240 that pensions paid under an occupational pension scheme are pay for the purposes of Art 141 and subject to the principles of equal pay. However, where the claim is in relation to the level of pension benefits individuals cannot claim in relation to periods of service up to and including 17 May 1990, the date of the *Barber* judgment, unless proceedings had already been instituted. This does not apply to denial of access to the scheme. This temporal limitation was starkly illustrated by *Quirk v Burton Hospitals NHS Trust* [2002] EWCA Civ 149 in which it was held that it was not objectionable for men retiring under 55 to receive benefits calculated only from 17 May 1990 even though women retiring before 60 received pension benefits by reference to all their pensionable service.

6.29 The ECJ confirmed in *Barber* that the pension will come within Art 141 whether the scheme is contracted in or contracted out. This was confirmed in *Maroni v Firma Collo GmbH* [1994] IRLR 130.

6.30 It is necessary to differentiate between access to a pension scheme and level of benefits. In *Bilka-Kaufhaus v Karin Weber von Hartz* [1986] IRLR 317, [1987] ICR 110 it was held that a worker's entitlement to join an occupational pension scheme fell within the scope of the right to equal pay. Thus exclusion of part-time workers from a scheme was in breach of Art 141 if it affected a greater number of women than men and the exclusion would have to be objectively justified.

6.31 In *Bestuur Van Het Algemeen Burgerlijk Pensioenfonds v Beune* [1995] IRLR 103 the test was stated to be whether the pension is paid to the worker by reference to employment and, since occupational pensions are linked with employment, this will be covered by Art 141.

6.32   *Dietz v Stichting Thuiszorg Rotterdam* [1996] IRLR 692 held that the right to a retirement pension was indissolubly linked to the right to join a pension scheme.

6.33   Importantly, it was confirmed in *Vroege v NCIV Instituut voor Volkshuisvesting BV and Stichting Pensioenfonds NCIV* [1995] ICR 635 that the loss of benefits where access has been refused can be calculated back to since 8 April 1976 when the ECJ first held in *Defrenne v Sabena* [1976] ECR 455 that Art 119 (now Art 141) has direct effect (see Chapter 18 further on time-limits).

6.34   Survivors pensions also come within the scope of Art 141 (see *Ten Oever v Stichting Bedrijfspensioenfonds voor het Glazenwassers- en Schoonmaakbedrijf* [1993] IRLR 601).

6.35   The position with regard to public sector pension schemes, where employees are members of a statutory scheme rather than an occupational pension scheme was considered in *Griffin v London Pensions Fund Authority* [1993] ICR 564, IRLR 248. The EAT concluded that there is a line between those benefits outlined in *Defrenne v Belgian State* which are not pay within Art 141 but are social security payments, and pension benefits which do come within the scope of Art 141 because they come within the circumstances of *Barber v Guardian Royal Exchange*. The EAT stated that the line was a narrow one but the determinative difference was that in *Defrenne* the scheme was a statutory scheme of application to a general category of workers and governed by exhaustive rules leaving the employers no discretion at all. The *Griffin* decision does not sit well with *Bestuur Van Het Algemeen Burgerlijk Pensioenfonds v Beune* [1995] IRLR 103 in which benefits paid under a Dutch civil service pension scheme were held by the ECJ to come within the definition of pay. The ECJ stated that the scheme was pay. Although the fact that the scheme was statutory was a strong indication that the benefits were social security benefits, the pension concerned only a particular category of workers, it was directly related to the period of service and its amount was calculated by reference to the civil servant's last salary. This meant that it was entirely comparable with that paid by a private employer. The ECJ accepted that the entire Dutch civil service was a category of employee. The decision, in effect, accepts the reasoning of the Advocate General in *Liefting v Academisch Ziekenhuis bij de Universiteit van Amsterdam* [1984] ECR 3225 which had been relied on by the employee in the *Griffin* case but which had not found its way into the reasoning of the ECJ in *Liefting*. The arguments which the EAT had felt constrained to adopt in *Griffin* and which were against the EAT's own inclinations were thus disposed of. It is submitted that the *Griffin* case should not be followed. The employment connection is the most important if not decisive criterion in deciding whether the pension benefit is pay under Art 141 (see also *Griesmar v Ministre de l'Economie des Finances et de l'Industrie* (C-366/99), unreported).

6.36 Members of a pension scheme are entitled to be offered the opportunity to acquire extra benefits by additional voluntary contributions (AVCs), which are credited to a special fund separate from the main pension fund. In *Coloroll Pension Trustees v Russell and Others* [1994] IRLR 586, [1995] ICR 179 the ECJ held that AVCs do not come within Art 141 as they are made on a purely voluntary basis and the pension scheme simply provides an administrative framework for them.

6.37 The *Coloroll Pension Trustees v Russell and Others* [1994] IRLR 586, [1995] ICR 179 case also held that contributions paid by *employees* must be the same regardless of sex. In the case of final salary schemes the employer's contributions are likely to be higher for female employees since actuarial factors, which are used to determine how much money will be required to fund the scheme, will take into account the fact that women tend to live longer than men so that the cost of providing the retirement pension will be greater. The ECJ held that it was possible to apply sex-based actuarial assumptions though this meant that men who opted for early retirement would receive a lower pension and lower reversionary pensions would be payable to men's wives.

6.38 It was held in *Neath v Hugh Steeper Ltd* [1995] ICR 158 that where a male employee retired early so that he had a choice of waiting for the pension, with the option to convert part into a lump sum that was immediately payable, or transferring the pension rights to another scheme, the fact that the transfer value would be lower than that of women in the same circumstances did not bring Art 141 into play since the transfer benefit and lump sum options were not pay. The funding arrangements for the final salary scheme were not part of the consideration that the employee received and so were outside Art 141. The ECJ considered *Barber v Guardian Royal Exchange Assurance Group* and stated that:

> 'The assumption underlying this approach is that the employer commits himself, albeit unilaterally, to pay his employees defined benefits or to grant them specific advantages and that the employees in turn expect the employer to pay them those benefits or provide them with those advantages. Anything that is not a consequence of that commitment and does not therefore come within the corresponding expectations of the employees falls outside the concept of pay.'

It concluded:

> 'In contributory schemes, funding is provided through the contributions made by the employees and those made by the employers. The contributions made by the employees are an element of their pay, since they are deducted directly from an employee's salary, which by definition is pay (see the judgment in Case C-69/80 *Worringham and Humphreys v Lloyds Bank Ltd*). The amount of those contributions must therefore be the same for all employees, male and female, which is indeed so in the present case. This is not so in the case of the employer's contributions which ensure the adequacy of the funds necessary to cover the cost of the pensions promised, so securing their payment in the future, that being the substance of the employer's commitment.

It follows that, unlike periodic payment of pensions, inequality of employers' contributions paid under funded defined-benefit schemes, which is due to the use of actuarial factors differing according to sex, is not struck at by Article 119.'

6.39 Where employees are paid the same salary it will *not* be contrary to Art 141 or the Equal Treatment Directive for the employer to make compulsory deductions from mens' salaries as contributions to a widow's pension fund provided in an occupational pension scheme (*Newstead v (1) Dept of Transport and (2) HM Treasury (Case 192/85)* [1988] IRLR 66, ICR 332). The scheme involved deductions of contributions from gross pay and was not therefore a disparity in pay (cf *Worringham* where the amounts that were paid were taken back as additional contributions; and cf *Hammersmith & Queen Charlotte's Special Health Authority v Cato* [1987] IRLR 483, [1988] ICR 132).

Redundancy

6.40 The ECJ ruled in *Barber v Guardian Royal Exchange* [1990] ICR 616, IRLR 240 that a redundancy payment is pay within Art 141. The first question asked on the reference was:

'When a group of employees are made compulsorily redundant by their employer . . . and receive benefits in connection with that redundancy, are all those benefits "pay" within the meaning of Article 119 of the EEC Treaty and the Equal Pay Directive, or do they fall within the Equal Treatment Directive, or neither?'

The ECJ responded that benefits paid by an employer in connection with redundancy are pay and a statutory redundancy payment is pay for this purpose.

6.41 Contractual redundancy payments are pay under Art 141 (see *Hammersmith and Queen Charlotte's Special Health Authority v Cato* [1987] IRLR 483, [1988] ICR 132 and *McKechnie v UBM Building Supplies (Southern) Ltd* [1991] IRLR 283).

Severance payments

6.42 The issue here is whether a payment in lieu of notice is pay for the purpose of Art 141. The issue was considered by the Court of Appeal in *Clark v Secretary of State for Employment* [1996] IRLR 578, [1997] ICR 64. The court considered that statutory notice payments to be made by the Secretary of State could be pay under Art 141, though the employee failed for other reasons. Neill LJ stated that he considered damages for wrongful dismissal to be pay within the meaning of Art 141.

6.43 In *Kowalska v Freie und Hansestadt Hamburg* [1990] IRLR 447, [1992] ICR 29 a collective agreement restricted severance payments to full-time workers. It was held that the severance payment was pay as such payments constituted a form of deferred remuneration to which the worker was entitled by virtue of the employment but which was paid at the time of termination of employment. The claimants were entitled to be paid on a pro rata basis according to the hours they worked.

6.44 Termination payments which were graduated according to length of service, based on past loyalty to the employer but which took into account military service were pay within Art 141, though on the facts of the case the claimant did not succeed in claiming a breach of Art 141 when absences due to parental leave were not taken into account (*Österreichischer Gewerkschafts-bund, Gewerkshaschaft der Privatangestellten v Wirtschaftskammer Österreich* (Case C-220/02), [2004] All ER (D) 03 (Jun)).

Sick pay

6.45 Sick pay is regarded as pay under Art 141. This will include statutory sick pay and statutory maternity pay (see *Rinner-Kühn v FWW Spezial--Gebäudereinigung GmbH & Co KG* [1989] IRLR 493).

Social security payments

6.46 See *Griffin v London pensions Fund Authority* [1993] ICR 564, IRLR 248 above. Where payments are made under a compulsory statutory scheme under which employers have no discretion this may be regarded as a social security payment rather than pay. See *Bestuur van Het Algemeen Burgerlijk Pensioenfonds v Beune* [1995] IRLR 103 for consideration of when a payment falls under a social security scheme and is covered by Directive 79/7 or is pay under Art 141.

Travel facilities

6.47 Travel facilities which are extended to staff after retirement have been held to be pay under Art 141 (see *Garland v British Rail Engineering* [1982] IRLR 111).

Unfair dismissal compensation

6.48 The EAT in *Mediguard Services Ltd v Thame* [1994] ICR 751, [1994] IRLR 504 stated that:

> 'It seems to us quite clear that compensation for unfair dismissal is consideration received by the former employee, albeit indirectly, from his former employer in respect of his employment.'

There was no sensible distinction to be drawn between a redundancy payment and compensation for unfair dismissal. The EAT stated that:

> 'Compensation for unfair dismissal is no different in principle from damages for wrongful dismissal. It could not be suggested that damages for failure to give

proper contractual notice were not "pay": the damages are, essentially, the monies due under the contract which the employee has been deprived of earning as such by reason of the dismissal; so, also, in the case of unfair dismissal compensation.'

6.49   The ECJ confirmed that this was the position in *R v Secretary of State for Employment ex p Seymour-Smith* [1999] ICR 447, [1999] IRLR 253. Unfair dismissal compensation is designed to give an employee what would have been earned if the employer had not unfairly terminated employment so that it fell within the definition of pay. The basic award referred directly to the remuneration which the employee would have received had she not been dismissed. The compensatory award covered the loss sustained as a result of the dismissal, including any expenses reasonably incurred in consequence thereof and, subject to certain conditions, the loss of any benefit which the claimant might reasonably be expected to have gained but for the dismissal. However, the conditions relating to eligibility for reinstatement or re-engagement were concerned with working conditions and, as such, fell within the provisions of the Equal Treatment Directive (76/207/EC).

Chapter 7

LIKE WORK

7.1 By the EqPA 1970, s 1(2)(a) an equality clause will be deemed:

'where the woman is employed on like work with a man in the same employment—

(i) if (apart from the equality clause) any term of the woman's contract is or becomes less favourable to the woman than a term of a similar kind in the contract under which that man is employed, that term of the woman's contract shall be treated as so modified as not to be less favourable, and

(ii) if (apart from the equality clause) at any time the woman's contract does not include a term corresponding to a term benefiting that man included in the contract under which he is employed, the woman's contract shall be treated as including such a term . . .'

FURTHER DEFINITION

7.2 The EqPA 1970, s 1(4) further clarifies the meaning of 'like work' stating that:

'A woman is to be regarded as employed on like work with men if, but only if, her work and theirs is of the same or a broadly similar nature, and the differences (if any) between the things she does and the things they do are not of practical importance in relation to terms and condition of employment; and accordingly in comparing her work with theirs regard shall be had to the frequency or otherwise with which any such differences occur in practice as well as to the nature and extent of the differences.'

7.3 Section 1(4) dictates the approach to be taken to 'like work':

(a) The woman will be regarded on like work if the work is the 'same or of a broadly similar nature' to that of the work of the comparator. The section applies a broad brush approach to the meaning of like work.

(b) The section goes on to state that differences which are not of practical importance in relation to terms and conditions will not prevent the work being 'like work'. In other words, if the differences are of 'practical importance' the work will not be like work.

(c)   The section enjoins one to have regard to the factual reality of the comparison rather than just the terms and conditions of the contract so that one must have regard to the frequency, nature and extent of any differences.

7.4   The question of whether the work is of a 'broadly similar nature' should be considered separately from the issue of whether the differences are of 'practical importance'. This was made clear in *Waddington v Leicester Council for Voluntary Service* [1977] ICR 266. The claimant was employed as a community worker and paid on a national salary scale for social workers. She set up an adventure playground and a man was appointed play leader. His pay was based on a negotiated scale for youth leaders and community centre wardens and was higher than the claimants. The Tribunal decided that the man did not do like work since the claimant had additional duties and responsibilities. The EAT held that the Tribunal had failed to adopt the correct approach, stating:

> 'In previous cases the Appeal Tribunal has approved a two-stage approach to S.1(4). First, looking at it generally, is the work which she does and the work which he does of the same or a broadly similar nature? And secondly, if so, are the differences between the things she does and the things he does of practical importance in relation to terms and conditions of employment? The Industrial Tribunal here ran the two stages together.'

7.5   The two-stage approach was restated in *Baker v Rochdale Health Authority* EAT/295/91. In *Morgan v Middlesbrough Borough Council* EAT/0375/04, the EAT explained how s 1(4) works in practice at para 7:

> ' . . . the test in section 1(4) in practice in most cases involves the tribunal in a two-stage inquiry. First, is the work of the same, or, if not, of a broadly similar nature? Secondly, if on a general consideration of the type of work involved and the skill and knowledge required to do it, the answer is that the work is of a broadly similar nature, it is then necessary to go on and consider the detail and inquire whether the differences between the work being compared are of practical importance in relation to terms and conditions of employment. At both stages a minute examination of detail and trivial differences not likely in the real world to be reflected in the terms and conditions of employment ought to be avoided. Furthermore, in considering the second question a difference between duties the man and woman being compared are contractually required to perform is relevant only insofar as it results in an actual difference in what is done in practice: it is the actual activities involved in the individual's job not the notional paper obligations that are important in ascertaining any relevant differences. In these two stages of the inquiry under section 1(4) the legal burden of proving that she is employed on like work with a man rests on the woman claimant, but if the first question is answered in her favour a practical and evidential burden of showing differences of practical importance rests upon the employers. It is only if she does manage to establish that the two questions are to be answered in her favour so that she is employed on like work with a man, that the third question on her Equal Pay Act claim arises under section 1(3), namely whether the employer can then prove that any variation between her contract and that of the male comparator is genuinely due to a material difference (other than the difference of sex) between her case and

his: see in particular *Shields v. E Coomes Holdings Limited* [1978] ICR 1159, especially per Bridge L J at 1179E to 1180D.'

SAME OR BROADLY SIMILAR WORK

7.6   The first stage is to consider whether the work is the same or broadly similar. The Tribunal will consider whether, as a matter of fact, the work that is carried out is similar on a broad basis. In *Capper Pass Ltd v Lawton* [1977] ICR 83 the claimant worked as a cook, on a 40-hour week and prepared a choice of three lunches for 10–20 directors and guests. The comparator, a male assistant chef worked a 40-hour week with five and a half hours overtime and one weekend in three, helping to prepare 350 meals in two sittings at breakfast, lunch and tea. The Tribunal held that the claimant did like work and the EAT dismissed an appeal. Phillips J stated:

> 'It is clear from the terms of the subsection that the work need not be of the same nature in order to be like work. It is enough if it is of a similar nature. Indeed, it need only be broadly similar. In such cases where the work is of a broadly similar nature (and not of the same nature) there will necessarily be differences between the work done by the woman and the work done by the man. It seems clear to us that the definition requires the industrial tribunal to bring, to the solution of the question whether work is of a broadly similar nature, a broad judgment. Because, in such cases, there will be such differences of one sort or another it would be possible in almost every case, by too pedantic an approach, to say that the work was not of a like nature despite the similarity of what was done and the similar kinds of skill and knowledge required to do it. That would be wrong.
>
> The intention, we think, is clearly that the industrial tribunal should not be required to undertake too minute an examination, or be constrained to find that work is not like work merely because of insubstantial differences . . .'

7.7   The first question, whether the work is broadly similar can be answered by a consideration of the type of work involved and of the skill and knowledge required to do it without any minute examination of the detail of the differences between the work done by the man and the work done by the woman. If the work is of a broadly similar nature it is then necessary to go on and consider the detail. Kilner Brown J stated in *Dorothy Perkins Ltd v Dance and Others* [1977] IRLR 226 that 'it is vitally important to reiterate . . . that it is no part of a tribunal's duty to get involved in fiddling detail or pernickety examination of differences which set against the broad picture fade into significance'.

7.8   It is necessary to consider the whole job so that parts of the work cannot be separated out and equality argued in relation to the duties that are similar (*Maidment and Hardacre v Cooper & Co (Birmingham) Ltd* [1978] IRLR 462). It may, however, be possible to exclude part of the job where it is separate and distinct. For example, when comparing two cleaners, one male and one female, both of whom do identical work during the week, it might be right to ignore the fact the man comes in on Saturdays just to cut the grass. In *Doncaster Education Authority v Gill* EAT/568/89 the claimant was Head of Business Studies. The comparator had been employed at another school in the same education authority and the issue was whether the Tribunal was right in treating as severable from his activities as Head of the Business Studies department the activities that the comparator performed as House Master or Assistant House Master. The EAT stated that for there to be severability, it was essential that there should be discernible separate activities, which requirement was satisfied in the case.

DIFFERENCES OF PRACTICAL IMPORTANCE

7.9   Having decided that there was broadly similar work the Tribunal must consider whether there are differences of practical importance. Phillips J noted in *Capper Pass Ltd v Lawton* [1977] ICR 83 that if:

> ' . . . the work is of a broadly similar nature, it is then necessary to go on to consider the detail and to enquire whether the differences between the work being compared are of "practical importance in relation to terms and conditions of employment". In answering that question the industrial tribunal will be guided by the concluding words of the subsection. But again, it seems to us, trivial differences, or differences not likely in the real world to be reflected in the terms and conditions of employment, ought to be disregarded. In other words, once it is determined that work is of a broadly similar nature it should be regarded as being like work unless the differences are plainly of a kind which the industrial tribunal in its experience would expect to find reflected in the terms and conditions of employment. This last point requires to be emphasised. There seems to be a tendency, apparent in some of the decisions of industrial tribunals cited to us, and in some of the arguments upon the hearing of this appeal, to weigh up the differences by reference to such questions as whether one type of work or another is or is not suitable for women, or is the kind of work which women can do, or whether the differences are prescribed by the Act. The only differences which will prevent work which is of a broadly similar nature from being "like work" are differences which in practice will be reflected in the terms and conditions of employment.'

7.10   The above provides useful general guidance. Section 1(4) states that one must consider the frequency, nature and extent of the differences. The actual differences become of importance at this second stage. In *Shields Ltd v E Coomes (Holdings) Ltd* [1978] ICR 1159 the respondent, bookmakers, employed two female counter hands in 81 of their 90 shops. In the other nine it employed one female counter hand and one male, because it considered that customers could be troublesome and the males were employed to deter trouble. The females were paid £0.92 whilst the males were paid £1.06. The Tribunal held that the man's security role was a difference of practical importance so that they did not do like work. The EAT allowed the employee's appeal and an appeal by the employer to the Court of Appeal failed. The Court of Appeal held that the claimant and comparators did like work so that it was necessary to consider whether the differences were of practical importance. The security role was not such a difference to the extent that it warranted a difference in pay. The man and the woman worked alongside each other doing the same work and each had their own way of dealing with awkward customers and may be subject to abuse or unpleasant behaviour. Lord Denning MR stated:

> 'The one difference of any significance between them was that the man filled a protective role. He was a watchdog ready to bark and scare off intruders. This difference, when taken with the others, amounted to differences which the majority of the industrial tribunal found were "real and existing and of practical importance". Accepting this finding, I do not think these differences could or did affect the "rate for the job". Both the woman and the man worked alongside one another hour after hour doing precisely the same work. She should, therefore, receive the same hourly rate as he. It is rather like the difference between a barman and a barmaid. They do the same work as one another in serving drinks. Each has his or her own way of dealing with awkward customers. Each is subject to the same risk of abuse or unpleasantness. But, whichever way each adopts in dealing with awkward customers, the job as of each, as a job, is of equivalent rating.'

The potential security role was also not a material difference under s 1(3).

7.11 Tribunals should, at this stage, look closely at the detail in considering whether there are differences of practical importance. In *Adamson & Hatchett Ltd v Cartlidge* EAT/126/77 the claimant worked for a manufacturer of heavy engineering components for North Sea Oil rigs which were produced to order on a production line. Both involved 'consumables buying' of shelf items such as protective clothing, office furniture and tool room and welding spares and also 'production buying' of materials. The claimant was a consumables buyer and she refused to take over or extend to production buying or extend her duties to a new branch at Reddish when the senior buyer left. A new buyer, who was appointed at Reddish, did both forms of work so that her job was redundant. She lodged a claim for equal pay with the new buyer or the predecessor, senior buyer. The claim in relation to the senior buyer failed, based on experience, seniority and knowledge but succeeded in relation to the new buyer on the basis that they did broadly similar work. The EAT held that the Tribunal had taken into account factors such as seniority and job label which were inadmissible, without asking and answering the question whether there were differences of practical importance. It stated:

> 'What then are the questions which the Tribunal has to ask itself when it has made its findings of fact, and in what order? In our judgment these:
>
> Is the woman's work the same as the men's, or of a broadly similar nature? The terminology requires a "broad brush" approach.
>
> Are there any differences? You have to go beyond the "broad brush" approach and look at the detail. What you have got to look at is what the woman does and what the men do, not the labels on their jobs nor their seniority, status or experience, but what they actually do, and the skills and knowledge involved in doing it.

> How often do they do something different, are the differences big or small, are
> they differences in the kind of thing that is done? Again you have got to look
> closely at the detail of what the differences are and look at it in the context of what
> their work involves.'

The Tribunal failed to consider all the detail and to inquire whether the
differences between the work being compared were of practical importance in
relation to the terms and conditions of employment.

7.12 The Tribunal may ask itself whether the differences are such that they
would put the two employees into a different category if a job evaluation study
(JES) was carried out. In *British Leyland (UK) Ltd v Powell* [1978] IRLR 57, a
case where the claimant and comparators were drivers, the only difference was
that the claimant could not drive outside the employer's premises on the public
highway due to a union demarcation agreement. The EAT in that case stated
that:

> ' . . . it would not, we think, be out of the place to see whether the differences
> (which ex hypothesi are not sufficient to make the work not of the same or of a
> broadly similar nature) are such as to put the two employments into different
> grades or categories, in an evaluation study.'

7.13 It should be noted that it is not just the contractual obligations as
stipulated in the terms and conditions of the contract of employment which are
relevant; consideration should be given to whether the obligations are *actually
performed*. In *Electrolux Ltd v Hutchinson and Others* [1997] ICR 252 the
claimants were graded as 01 assembly workers. Men doing similar work were
graded more highly and paid at a higher hourly rate. The men were
contractually obliged to transfer between jobs and work overtime, night shifts
and Sundays but the Tribunal and EAT, nevertheless, held that the claimants
did 'like work'. A relevant consideration was the frequency with which duties
were carried out. It stated that 'it must be shown that as well as being obliged to
do additional, different duties the men in fact do so to some significant extent'
(see also *Redland Roof Tiles Ltd v Harper* [1977] ICR 349).

7.14 It should be noted that factors which may be of relevance to the issue of
whether there are differences of practical importance to the comparator's job
will not be relevant to the question of whether there are material differences
under s 1(3); so, for example, seniority may not be a difference of practical
importance under s 1(4) for the purpose of 'like work' but be a genuine material
difference under s 1(3).

7.15 The cases illustrate a range of factors that may be considered in deciding
whether the differences are of 'practical importance'.

A-Z of factors that may amount to differences of practical importance

Additional duties

7.16 As illustrated by *Electrolux Ltd v Hutchinson and Others* [1997] ICR 252 it will be necessary for the additional duties to be carried out on a sufficiently frequent basis for such differences to be of practical importance.

Experience and skill

7.17 This was considered in *Stevenson v Rentokil Ltd* EAT/192/1978. The claimant worked as a package supervisor, dealing with stock worth £500,000 and the job involved responsibility for cleanliness, safety and discipline as well as sampling checks. The comparator supervised the processing department which produced approximately £13m worth a year and which job involved handling toxic materials as well as loading and unloading packages and sampling for quality control. The Tribunal held that there were differences of practical importance as the claimant's job did not involve anything like the same element of risk, skill, experience or knowledge. The EAT upheld the decision, stating:

> 'I think they thought it was of significance that Mrs Stevenson was not involved to anything like the same extent in either the risk or in the carrying out of a function requiring his skill and experience and knowledge.'

Flexibility

7.18 Where there is flexibility in the man's work but not in the woman's this may be a difference of practical importance. However, the fact that men work weekends or have been asked to work flexibly may not lead to such an inference where men could be compensated for the weekend work separately or where women have not been asked to work flexibly. The criterion of flexibility needs to be considered carefully as it may disguise systematic unfairness. In *Handels-OG Kontorfunktionaererernes Forbund i Danmark v Dansk Arbejdsgiverforening (acting for Danfoss)* [1989] IRLR 532, [1991] ICR 74 women were subject to the terms of a collective agreement which provided for a uniform basic wage based on pay grades which depended on job classification. Employers could increase wages under the agreement based on factors, including seniority, vocational training and flexibility. The statistical evidence showed that women were paid an average of 6.85% less than men in the same grades. On referral to the ECJ one of the questions asked was:

> 'Is it contrary to the Equal Pay Directive to pay a higher wage to male workers carrying out the same work or work of equal value as female workers, exclusively on the basis of subjective criteria, such as the greater flexibility of a (male) employee?'

7.19   The ECJ held that 'flexibility', in the sense of quality of work is sex neutral. However, if it is used in a general way to justify lower pay to female employees there is no scope to justify its use since it is inconceivable that women generally perform lower quality work than men. Where it is used in the sense of adaptability to varying work schedules or places of work it will be for the employer to justify the use of such a criteria by showing that flexibility is of importance for the carrying out of specific duties entrusted to the employee, women have not been excluded and the criterion can be justified for each woman.

Physical effort

7.20   Where a man does work which involves physical strength and effort which a woman is unable to provide the woman will not be employed on 'like work'. An employer must not assume that the woman is unable carry out work involving physical strength but each woman should be assessed individually, taking into account her strength and experience. In *Noble and Others v David Gold & Son (Holdings) Ltd* [1980] ICR 543 three women worked with other women and men in a warehouse, the women doing the lighter work. When the lighter work declined six of eight of the women were made redundant and three complained of unfair dismissal as well as under the SDA 1975 and the EqPA 1970, on the basis that they had been dismissed for claiming rights under these Acts. The EAT considered the distinction between light and heavy work to be a relevant factor in deciding whether the selection for redundancy was based upon the work being different. The Court of Appeal held that there was evidence to justify the conclusion that there was heavier work which the women were not capable of carrying out. Lord Denning stated that:

> 'The men were mainly doing the heavier work of unloading, carrying and lifting the pallets on to the benches, which the women could not do. The women were doing the lighter work, namely, the sorting and arranging of the packages on the benches. They were not doing any of the lifting at all: because they were not physically capable of carrying these heavy weights.'

Lawton LJ noted that:

> 'Whether a woman applicant for a job can physically do it must be a matter of judgment for the employer, and he should base his judgment on his own assessment of the candidate, based upon her physique and his experience of what other women doing that kind of job have been able to do. What he must not do is to assume that all women are incapable of doing a particular job.'

7.21   The frequency of the heavier work may be of relevance so that where the work is carried out infrequently it is possible that it does not amount to a difference of practical importance.

Qualifications

7.22 It was held in *Angestelltenbetriebsrat v Wiener Gebietskrankenkasse* [1999] IRLR 804, [2000] ICR 1134 that where men and women carry out the same work but are recruited on the basis of different training and qualifications and can be asked to perform different tasks, then the two groups may not be engaged on 'like work'. The workers were employed as psychotherapists but there were two groups being those who had trained first as graduate psychologists and those who had first completed their general practitioner training as doctors. The ECJ stated that 'two groups of persons who have received different professional training and who, because of the different scope of the qualifications resulting from that training, on the basis of which they were recruited, are called on to perform different tasks or duties, cannot be regarded as being in a comparable situation'.

Responsibility

7.23 Where the comparator exercises greater responsibility than the claimant this may amount to a difference of practical importance. In *Eaton Ltd v Nuttall* [1977] ICR 272, [1977] IRLR 71, [1977] 3 All ER 1131 a female scheduler claimed equal pay with a male scheduler. Any error by the comparator was more serious as he dealt with 1,200 items at between £5 and £1,000 whereas the claimant dealt with 2,400 items at £2.50 each. The Tribunal held that there was like work but the EAT reversed the decision. Phillips J stated that:

> 'The sort of situation where we think that the existence of a factor such as responsibility, in the case of one only of two persons whose work is being compared, might truly be decisive is where it can be seen to put one into a different grade from the other. For example, suppose two book-keepers working side by side doing, so far as actions were concerned, almost identical work, where on an examination of the importance of the work done it could be seen that one was a senior book-keeper and another a junior book-keeper. Such distinctions between two employees are often easy to spot in practice but difficult to distinguish only in the terms of what each of them does. That is the sort of case where we think the existence of the factor of responsibility might be crucial.'

See also *Waddington* above, and *Peskett v Robinsons Ltd* [1976] IRLR 134 (man's job as buyer more responsible); *Ford v R Weston (Chemists) Ltd* (1977) 12 ITR 369 (dispensary – 'the deputy's job is one thing and the manager's or director's job is another thing'); *De Brito v Standard Chartered Bank* [1978] ICR 650 (trainee on same general work and women who were very experienced and trained him).

Seniority

7.24 Seniority may go hand in hand with experience but it is apparent from the cases that 'since seniority goes hand in hand with experience which generally places a worker in a better position to carry out his duties, it is permissible for the employer to reward it without the need to establish the importance which it takes on for the performance of the specific duties to be entrusted to the worker' (*Handels-OG Kontorfunktionaerernes Forbund i Danmark v Dansk Arbejdsgiverforening (acting for Danfoss)* [1989] IRLR 532, [1991] ICR 74). See further the cases on objective justification at **10.76** et seq.

Skill

7.25 It was held in *Brodie and Another v Startrite Engineering Co* [1976] IRLR 101 that there were differences of practical importance where the claimant and comparator were working alongside each other but the male comparator was able to obtain the correct drill and set his machine then submit the first machined component to the charge hand for approval and, thereafter, to machine the rest. The comparator sharpened his own drills, replaced broken drills and corrected minor mechanical faults that may develop. All of the aforesaid tasks were done by the charge hand for the claimants. The comparator operated the same three drilling machines as the claimants but, in addition, he was also called upon to operate a pulley balancing machine. The comparator's ability to obtain the appropriate jig and drill and set his own machine, coupled with the fact that he was able to sharpen and replace drills and carry out minor repairs meant that he carried through each job entirely on his own, thereby relieving the charge hand of responsibility so that the jobs were different on account of skill.

Time of work

7.26 This will normally be regarded as irrelevant. In *Dugdale and Others v Kraft Foods Ltd* [1977] ICR 48 female quality controllers worked on two shifts whilst male quality controllers worked on three shifts involving night and Sunday work. The men were given a larger shift allowance. The EAT held that the mere fact that the work of the men and the women was done at different times was not a difference of practical importance justifying different pay. Phillips J stated that:

> 'Where the work done is the same, and the only difference is the time at which it is done, the men will be compensated for the extra burden of working at night or on Sundays by the shift payment or premium. There seems to be no reason why the women should not have equality of treatment in respect of the basic wage, or in respect of the day shift payment, if any.'

7.27 A similar approach was taken in *National Coal Board v Sherwin & Spruce* [1978] ICR 700, IRLR 122. The claimants, who were canteen workers on the day shift, compared themselves with a male canteen worker on the night shift, who was paid a higher basic rate and given concessionary coal. He did some cleaning work and had responsibility for the till but the EAT held that the fact that he worked at night did not itself mean that the work was not like work as the disadvantage of night work did not need to be compensated over and above a shift premium. The fact that there are different duties because of night work 'need to be considered with care, and what must be avoided is the practice of praying in aid the time at which the work is done to support a conclusion that the man and the woman are not employed on like work albeit that what they do is substantially the same or even identical'. There may be cases where the job is different because it is night work where 'a different time has changed the nature of what is done'. The latter case should be compared with *Thomas and Others v National Coal Board* [1987] ICR 757 where the fact that the comparators were unsupervised at night was something that was reflected in the terms and conditions.

Vocational training

7.28 One of the factors argued in *Handels-OG Kontorfunktionaerernes Forbund I Danmark v Dansk Arbejdsgiverforening (acting for Danfoss)* [1989] IRLR 532, [1991] ICR 74 which could lead to justifiable pay differences was vocational training. The ECJ stated that as regards vocational training:

> '... it cannot be ruled out that it may act to the detriment of female workers insofar as they have fewer opportunities to obtain vocational training which is as advanced as that of male workers, or that they use those opportunities to a lesser extent. However ... the employer may justify rewarding specific vocational training by demonstrating that that training is of importance for the performance of the specific duties entrusted to the worker.'

If the criterion systematically discriminates against women it will be necessary to show that the training improves the performance of employees in relation to the duties that are carried out.

Work environment

7.29 Where the claimant compares herself with a man who works in different adverse conditions this may amount to a difference of practical importance, as in *Wood and Others v Tootalk Ltd Strines Printing Co* COIT/516/51 where the women worked in a warehouse and the men in conditions that were open to the weather, doing harder dirtier work at the commencement of the production process (see also *McLuskie v Haddow Aird & Crerer Ltd* COIT SCOIT/200/76; *Pearce v Matbey Printed Products Ltd* COIT/1516/83).

CHECKLIST FOR LIKE WORK

7.30 The following is a summary checklist to consider whether there is like work between the claimant and a comparator:

Stage 1: Is the work the same of or a broadly similar nature?

- What is the type of work involved and the skill and knowledge required to do it on a broad brush basis without any minute examination of the duties?

- Are there parts of the job which are distinct and separate and which should be considered separately?

- Is the work similar on a broad brush basis?

Stage 2: Are there differences of practical importance in relation to the things that the claimant and comparator do?

- Are the differences reflected in the contractual terms?

- Consider the alleged differences in detail looking at the work that is actually carried out.

- Do apparently different contractual terms result in a difference in practice?

- Are the differences trivial?

- What is the nature, frequency and extent of the differences?

- Would the differences, for example, result in a different grade under a JES?

- Consider the various factors as exemplified in the case-law:
  - Additional duties: are they carried out with sufficient frequency to be a difference of practical importance?
  - Experience and skill: What degree of risk, skill, experience and knowledge is actually required?
  - Flexibility: Is this a cloak for discrimination or is it used in the sense of 'adaptability' where there may be a genuine difference of practical importance?
  - Physical effort: Has this been considered on an individual basis? Is there genuine heavier work which the woman could not carry out?
  - Qualifications: Does the difference in the qualifications mean that the comparator is called on to carry out different work?
  - Responsibility: Is there genuinely greater responsibility on the part of the comparator in terms of risk, result of error or impact of the job?
  - Seniority: Is this a cloak for discrimination or does it go hand in hand with experience?
  - Skill: Are there differences of practical importance in the skilled tasks that the claimant and comparator perform?
  - Time of work: Does it make any difference whether there is shift work or is this a supervision/responsibility issue? Are the comparators separately compensated when they work shifts/nights?
  - Vocational training: Is the comparator rewarded because of vocational training that he has undergone? Does this disguise systematic discrimination?

–   Work environment: Are there genuinely different work conditions such as dirtier work or outside work in adverse conditions?

Whilst the above may amount to differences of practical importance it may be necessary to consider whether there is systematic discrimination based, for example, on assumptions about 'women's work' etc.

Chapter 8

WORK RATED AS EQUIVALENT

8.1   By the EqPA 1970, s 1(2)(b) an equality clause will be deemed:

'where the woman is employed on work rated as equivalent with that of a man in the same employment—

(i)   if (apart from the equality clause) any term of the woman's contract determined by the rating of the work is or becomes less favourable to the woman than a term of a similar kind in the contract under which that man is employed, that term of the woman's contract shall be treated as so modified as not to be less favourable, and

(ii)   if (apart from the equality clause) at any time the woman's contract does not include a term corresponding to a term benefiting that man included in the contract under which he is employed and determined by the rating of the work, the woman's contract shall be treated as including such a term.'

FURTHER DEFINITION

8.2   The EqPA 1970, s 1(5) contains further definition of work that is rated as equivalent:

'A woman is to be regarded as employed on work rated as equivalent with that of any men if, but only if, her job and their job have been given an equal value, *or her job has been given a higher value,* in terms of the demand made on a worker under various headings (for instance effort, skill, decision), on a study undertaken with a view to evaluating in those terms the jobs to be done by all or any of the employees in an undertaking or group of undertakings, or would have been given an equal value but for the evaluation being made on a system setting different values for men and women on the same demand under any heading.'

The words above in italics were added by the Court of Appeal in *Redcar and Cleveland Borough Council v Bainbridge (No 1)* [2007] IRLR 984. The question arose whether a claimant could base her comparison on a man who had been placed in a lower grade by the JES but who had in fact received more pay. The Employment Appeal Tribunal (EAT) held that she could (see [2007] IRLR 91). On appeal, the Court of Appeal held that the Employment Tribunal was correct to hold that the claimants were entitled to make claims in relation to comparators on a lower band but who received more pay. It was appropriate to adopt a purposive interpretation to the legislation and read s 1(5) with the above words in italics added.

8.3   Where a JES has been carried out which shows that the work is rated as equivalent to that of a man, then the woman will be entitled to equal pay. However, it was held in *Bainbridge v Redcar & Cleveland Borough Council (No 2)* [2007] IRLR 494 that employees whose jobs were rated as equivalent under a JES which came into effect on 1 April 2004 did not have the right to rely upon that JES to seek compensation going back up to 6 years (assuming their jobs and those of their chosen comparators had not changed in any material way in that period). The language of s 1(2)(b) was clear, that it was simply wrong to say that somebody, who had a claim for the period prior to the JES coming into effect, was so rated prior to that date. It was held to be an impossible construction to say that someone whose job was rated as equivalent with her comparator under a JES from a particular date, was so rated prior to that date. All that can be said is that if precisely the same JES had been carried out earlier, they would have been so rated. Thus it is clear that a JES is not retrospective.

8.4   It is apparent that a rating under a JES is not the same as finding that the two jobs are necessarily of equal value. There are two elements: the evaluation of jobs and the fixing of grade boundaries. The EAT noted that it is not uncommon for jobs to be fitted into grades where there may be real distinctions in the value of the jobs. Pay scales may embrace a wide class of jobs even though the value of the jobs at the higher end may be significantly higher than the those lower down.

8.5   The judgment of the EAT was considered and upheld by the Court of Appeal at paras 267–285. Mummery LJ considered the logic of this argument as follows:

> 'As for the "logic" of retroactive effect, it is, in our view, to overlook that schemes have no force whatsoever before they are agreed and to overlook also that bands and brackets can and do change from one JES to another; it is also to regard the treatment of RAE cases as different from the treatment afforded to "like work" or "equal value" cases under section 1(2)(a) and 1(2)(c) respectively. In fact, each of the three cases is treated identically. Under whichever heading a claimant has applied, she is, if successful, entitled to recover in respect of such parts of the past period of up to six years before she instituted her claim in relation to which the type of equality which she has successfully asserted is either proved or conceded to have existed. Thus if, in year 10, she institutes a claim, later upheld in year 12, which is based upon "like work" being proved as between her job and that of her comparator under section 1(2)(a) as at year 10, she will be able, looking to the 6 years prior to the institution of her claim, to recover for the inequality over such parts of years 4 to 10 and also of years 11 and 12 during which she can demonstrate that the condition which she has asserted – "like work" – obtained. So also, correspondingly, as to a claim raised under section 1(2)(c) – equal value – but so also, again, if, in year 10, she is able correspondingly to establish, as to periods even prior to the institution of her claims, that the assertion upon which she has relied – that she and her comparator were RAE under one and the same JES – was made good.'

8.6   The test as to whether the JES can be relied on is strict. It was stated by the EAT in *Department for the Environment, Food and Rural Affairs v Robertson* UKEAT/0273/03/DM that it is will be necessary in considering a JES to address the questions raised in *Eaton Ltd v Nuttall* [1977] ICR 272, namely whether there was a study which 'satisfied the test of being thorough in analysis and capable of impartial application' or one such as to enable arrival 'at the position of a particular employee at a particular point in a particular salary grade'. If this cannot be done in relation to the particular claimant then the JES cannot be relied upon.

8.7   The EqPA 1970, s 1(5) gives some guidance on the nature of a JES. It is necessary for the claimant to show that:

(a)   the jobs have been rated as of equal value in terms of the demands made on the worker under various heads, such as effort, skill and decision, with a view to evaluating in those terms the jobs to be done by all of any of the employees in an undertaking or group of undertakings, or

(b)   would have been given an equal value but for different values being given to men and women, ie that the values that were applied were inherently discriminatory.

JES AS A DEFENCE

8.8   Where there is a valid JES which has been accepted then this may be a defence to a claim for equal pay for work of equal value. This is considered in more detail at **9.25**.

Objectivity

8.9   A JES is meant to provide a fair and rational basis for evaluating a range of jobs and evaluating pay on as objective a basis as is possible. It has, however, been recognised that there will be an element of subjectivity when comparing the demands of one job with another (*Dibro Ltd v Hore and Others* [1990] ICR 370).

8.10   The JES must aim to ensure that the criteria which are applied in valuing the job are as objective as possible. This point was made in *Rummler v Dato-Druck GmbH* [1987] IRLR 32. The employer's classification graded jobs using criteria such as knowledge required, concentration, effort, exertion and responsibility. The claimant's job was Grade III, which covered jobs requiring medium and sometimes high muscular effort, Grade II being slight to medium and Grade IV medium or, on occasion, high exertion, especially of the kind entailed by machine-dependent work. The claimant thought she should be Grade IV as she was required to pack parcels of over 20 kg in weight. The employer argued it should be Grade II. The ECJ held that the Directive 75/117/EC did not preclude the use of criteria such as muscular effort or exertion or the degree of physically heavy work if an objective amount of strength is required, provided that the system as a whole precludes all discrimination on grounds of sex by taking account also of other criteria. If a job classification system is not to be discriminatory overall, then, insofar as the nature of the tasks to be done allow this, criteria should be used which can measure particular aptitude on the part of employees of both sexes. Referring to *Rummler*, in *Bromley and Others v H & J Quick Ltd* [1988] IRLR 249, [1988] ICR 623, Dillon LJ stated:

> 'As there are no universally accepted external criteria available for measuring how much of a factor or quality is involved in a particular job or for measuring what relative weights ought to be attached to different factors or qualities involved, to differing extents, in various jobs, every attempt at job evaluation will inevitably at some stages involve value judgments, which are inherently to some extent subjective. Although it is clear from the decision of the European Court in *Rummler v Dato Druck* [1987] IRLR 32 that the consideration of any job, and of the qualities required to perform that job, under a job evaluation study must be objective and the approach of English law to the construction of s.1(5) appears to be in line with the European law approach, within measure there may be subjective elements in an objective process.'

Analytical and non-analytical JES

8.11   The leading case in considering the nature of JESs is *Eaton Ltd v Nuttall* [1977] ICR 272 in which a production scheduler claimed equal pay with a male production scheduler in the same department on the basis of like work. The EAT had remitted the case on 'like work' for a rehearing. During the course of the hearing in the EAT it became apparent that a valid JES under s 1(5) may have been carried out and the EAT stated that it would be open to the parties to rely on this at the remitted hearing. Guidelines were given by the EAT to determine the validity of a JES. Phillips J stated:

> 'It seems to us that subsection (5) can only apply to what may be called a valid evaluation study. By that, we mean a study satisfying the test of being thorough in analysis and capable of impartial application. It should be possible by applying the study to arrive at the position of a particular employee at a particular point in a particular salary grade without taking other matters into account except those unconnected with the nature of the work. It will be in order to take into account such matters as merit or seniority, etc, but any matters concerning the work (eg responsibility) one would expect to find taken care of in the evaluation study. One which does not satisfy that test, and requires the management to make a subjective judgment concerning the nature of the work before the employee can be fitted into the appropriate place in the appropriate salary grade, would seem to us not to be a valid study for the purpose of subsection (5).'

The principal methods of JES

8.12 The most common types of JES were set out in *Eaton* who referred to the ACAS Guide No 1, though it should be noted that variants of these evaluations may be acceptable (*Hayward v Cammell Laird Shipbuilders Ltd* [1988] IRLR 257; [1988] ICR 464)

Job ranking

8.13 This is commonly thought to be the simplest method. Each job is considered as a whole and is then given a ranking in relation to all other jobs. A ranking table is then drawn up and the ranked jobs grouped into grades. Pay levels can then be fixed for each grade. *This is non-analytical.*

Paired comparisons

8.14 This is also a simple method. Each job is compared as a whole with each other job in turn and points (0, 1 or 2) awarded according to whether its overall importance is judged to be less than, equal to or more than the other. Points awarded for each job are then totalled and a ranking order produced. *This is non-analytical.*

Job classification

8.15 This is similar to ranking except that it starts from the opposite end; the grading structure is established first and individual jobs fitted into it. A broad description of each grade is drawn up and individual jobs considered typical of each grade are selected as 'benchmarks'. The other jobs are then compared with these benchmarks and the general description and placed in their appropriate grade. *This is non-analytical.*

Points assessment

8.16 This is the most common system in use. It is an analytical method, which, instead of comparing whole jobs, breaks down each job into a number of factors – for example, skills, responsibility, physical and mental requirements and working conditions. Each of these factors may be analysed further. Points are awarded for each factor according to a predetermined scale and the total points decide a job's place in the ranking order. Usually, the factors are weighted so that, for example, more or less weight may be given to hard physical conditions or to a high degree of skill. *This is an analytical assessment.*

Factor comparison

8.17 This is also an analytical method, employing the same principles as points assessment but using only a limited number of factors, such as skill, responsibility and working conditions. A number of 'key' jobs are selected because their wage rates are generally agreed to be 'fair'. The proportion of the total wage attributable to each factor is then decided and a scale produced showing the rate for each factor of each key job. The other jobs are then compared with this scale, factor by factor, so that a rate is finally obtained for each factor of each job. The total pay for each job is reached by adding together the rates for its individual factors. *This is an analytical assessment.*

8.18   If the evaluation is not analytical then it will not satisfy the requirements of s 1(5). The Court of Appeal considered the position in *Bromley and Others v H & J Quick Ltd* [1988] IRLR 249, [1988] ICR 623. The employer had 820 employees, of whom 189 were women. Some women claimed that they were not paid equal pay so the employer undertook a JES which awarded the claimants a lower value than those of their male co-workers. The claimants brought a claim for equal pay and, at a preliminary hearing, it was argued that the JES did not bar a claim as it did not comply with the requirements set out in s 1(5) and was therefore invalid. It was also argued that the JES was discriminatory.

8.19   The employers had commissioned a firm of management consultants, Inbucon, to carry out a JES. The method chosen by the consultants was 'direct consensus' which involved establishing joint panels of management and employees, including women. The panels chose representative jobs and produced job descriptions of those jobs under six factors. They then ranked the jobs by means of paired comparison, ie by looking at the job descriptions as a whole for two jobs and determining which of the two jobs as a whole was more valuable. Benchmark jobs were then selected from the representative jobs and paired comparisons of those jobs made both on a whole job basis and by factor. Multiple regression analysis was then used to determine the percentage contribution made by each factor and to draw up a factor plan. Grade boundaries were then decided. The next step was to permit the panel to change the ranking of the benchmark jobs on a 'felt fair' basis, ie in accordance with the general level of expectation as to the value of the jobs. The remainder of the representative jobs were then slotted into the order of ranking. The remaining jobs, which included the jobs of the appellants and of three of their four comparators, were slotted in. No written job descriptions for these jobs were produced and the slotting in was done by management on an assessment of the whole job in each case, without regard to the factors chosen.

8.20   An appeals mechanism was provided for those objecting to their grading. Two of the appellants brought appeals and their jobs were considered under the factor headings. However, none of the comparators' jobs were subject to appeal. The Tribunal held that there was no reasonable ground for determining that the work was of equal value in light of the JES. The EAT held that it was not necessary for the JES to be analytical but the Court of Appeal allowed the appeal. The use of the word 'analytical' was not a gloss on the statutory provisions. It indicated conveniently the general nature of what is required by the section, viz that the jobs of each worker covered by the study must have been valued in terms of the demand made on the worker under various headings. It is not enough that benchmark jobs have been evaluated on a factor demand basis if the jobs of the applicants and their comparators were not. The jobs of the appellants and their comparators were slotted into the structure on a 'whole job' basis and no comparison was made by reference to the selected factors between the demands made on the individual workers under the selected headings. The JES did not therefore comply with s 1(5).

8.21 It appears from the speech of Woolf LJ that selection of benchmark jobs will be acceptable provided that the jobs grouped together are not materially different. He stated:

> 'In order to comply with s.1(5), employers can identify a group of jobs which when evaluated under the headings have no material difference. Then one of that group of jobs can be evaluated under headings and slotted into the rank in the appropriate position having taken into account the factor value and that job can then represent the other jobs within the group. If, however, a system of choosing a representative job for a group of jobs is adopted, then in relation to a job which has not been evaluated under headings it will be open to an employee to contend that his or her job is materially different from the alleged representative job and, if this is the case, the study will not comply with s.1(5).'

8.22 It is apparent from the above case that whole job comparisons risk merely replicating the status quo and perpetuating discrimination. The Court of Appeal recognised that there will always be an element of subjectivity but that it is the duty of the person carrying out the study and the Tribunal to scrutinise the JES to ensure that discrimination is not inadvertently retained (see the dicta from Dillon LJ at **8.10** above). Dillon LJ stated:

> ' . . . it is for the employer to explain how any job evaluation study worked and what was taken into account at each stage.
>
> In practice, where there has been a job evaluation study and there is evidence from the employer as to how that study was carried out, the applicant is likely to point to particular matters as indicating, or possibly indicating, that the system involved direct or indirect sex discrimination. Natural justice will then require that the employer be given an opportunity of explaining these matters. It will be for the Industrial Tribunal to decide, at the end of the hearing, on the evidence whether or not they are satisfied that there are no reasonable grounds for determining that the evaluation made in the study was made on a system which discriminated on grounds of sex, and the Tribunal's decision can only be challenged on *Edwards v Bairstow* grounds on appeal.
>
> In the present case, the appellants' submission that in the grading of various benchmark jobs certain staff jobs which had higher factor scores than certain manual jobs were placed in lower grades than the manual jobs would have afforded reasonable grounds for determining that the study had been made on a discriminatory system. However, that point was not open to the appellants as it had never been suggested before the Industrial Tribunal.'

8.23 See also *Paterson v London Borough of Islington* UKEAT/0347/03/DA where the JES was defective as the assessment had departed from the agreed rules by assessing one of the jobs based upon locally assessed jobs when only nationally assessed jobs should have been used. A failure to properly implement the scheme may make it ineffective to any defence to an equal value claim (see *Diageo plc v Thomson* EATS/0064/03.

8.24   The JES may be invalid where it is itself tainted by discriminatory assumptions. It was held in *Rummler v Dato-Druck GmbH* [1987] IRLR 32 that a scheme is not discriminatory merely because some of its characteristics are more commonly found among men – provided that the factors are representative of the tasks done by both sexes – but if it fails to take into account a demand (ie caring) that is an important part of the job it may be indirectly discriminatory. It does not matter that there is no intention to discriminate.

Translating the JES into grades

8.25   A JES will ascribe points to each job based upon the criteria that has been applied. It will then be necessary for the employer to convert the scores into grades or salary bands. The actual salary may be affected by the width of the banding or how the grades work. Nevertheless, it is possible to place the scores into bands. In *Springboard Sunderland Trust v Robson* [1992] ICR 554, IRLR 261 the claimant was a team leader and claimed equal pay with an induction officer. She claimed her job had been rated as equivalent. The comparator had been rated on education at level 5 and the claimant at 4. Level 5 related to 'ability to carry out work requiring good practical knowledge of accountancy, technical work, etc. This will include qualifications shown in the attached schedule' but no such qualification appeared to be necessary. Level 4 related to 'ability to write letters and reports on various subjects or do more complex calculations or prepare simple statistical statements'. The difference in grading in this category produced a 10-point score difference in the JES as 45 points were allocated to level 4 and 55 points to level 5. With regard to supervisory responsibility, the comparator was placed at level 3, whilst the claimant was at level 2, which produced an 8 point difference. The result was that the claimant scored 410 whilst the comparator scored 428 points.

8.26   Jobs with between 360 and 409 points constituted salary grade 3 whilst jobs with between 410 and 449 points constituted salary grade 4. The employer failed to pay the claimant a level 4 salary and she brought a claim. The Tribunal decided that the work was rated as equivalent on the ground that the banding had to be taken into account and the EAT held that the work was rated as equivalent because the process of converting points to grade provided for under the scheme had the result of placing the jobs in the same grade. The EAT stated that:

> '. . . it is necessary to have regard to the full results of the job evaluation scheme to see whether or not one can say whether a study undertaken under a job evaluation scheme gives an equal value to the two jobs in question, and that includes the allocation of a scale at the foot of the score sheets.'

8.27 See also *England v Bromley London Borough Council* [1978] ICR 1 where the employer had added 5 points to take account of work pressures to the two comparators' scores so that they were not rated as equivalent. The EAT refused to interfere with the job evaluation by deleting the special factors that would have made the scores equal.

Employees covered by the JES

8.28 The JES will only bind the classes of employees who are covered by the evaluation, so, for example a JES which related to National Health ancillary workers in Great Britain could not prevent an equal pay claim by similar workers in the NHS in Northern Ireland (*McAuley and Others v Eastern Health and Social Services Board* [1991] IRLR 467). The JES had not been undertaken for the employees employed by the Northern Ireland Health Boards.

Effect of the JES

Acceptance

8.29 As will be seen, it will be difficult for a JES to be carried out without the co-operation of both parties. Once a JES has been carried out it will be necessary for it to be *accepted as a valid study before it will be treated as a JES under s 1(5)*. This means that if a JES is not accepted a claimant will be unable to rely on the study to claim equal pay, even if the claimant has been graded the same or higher. In *Arnold v Beecham Group* [1982] IRLR 307 a catering supervisor claimed equal pay with a vending supervisor. The employers carried out a job evaluation exercise as a result of which the claimant was graded 1 and the comparator graded 2. Agreement could not be reached with the scheme and it was not implemented. A new evaluation was undertaken in 1980 but on the basis that 'either side could reject the scheme at the end of the road' and in May 1980 there was a meeting to consider the report at which the committee confirmed its belief in the JES, arranged to draw up grade boundaries, to publish the results to staff and hear individual appeals. Both were then graded as grade 2. Objections were raised to the scheme but the employees' counter proposals were not accepted so that the 1980 JES was never implemented and a pay settlement was based on the earlier scheme so that the earlier grades applied. An equal pay application based upon the 1980 JES was dismissed on the basis that the JES has not been accepted so that it was not possible to make conclusions based on the terms of the JES.

8.30 The EAT held that, on the facts, the employers and the unions had accepted the JES and it was irrelevant that they had decided not to use it in their negotiations. The EAT followed earlier cases, including *Greene v Broxtowe District Council* [1977] IRLR 34 and *Hebbes v Rank Precision Industries* [1978] ICR 489, stating that 'there is no complete job evaluation study falling within s 1(5) of the Act unless and until it has been accepted or adopted by employers and employees as regulating their relationship'. The EAT concluded that:

' . . . however carefully a study is undertaken and conducted there is always a substantial risk that the results may offend common sense and be unacceptable to those whose relationship it is designed to regulate. It therefore seems to us to accord with industrial common sense if there is not a complete study unless and until those whose relationship is to be regulated by it have accepted it as a study. It is perfectly possible to accept the validity of a study at a stage substantially before it is implemented by being used as the basis of the payment of remuneration. It is not the stage of implementing the study which makes it complete, it is the stage at which it is accepted as a study . . . If the law were that for the purposes of the Act of 1970 the study was to be treated as effective even though employers and employees had rejected it as a valid study, it would in our view discourage employers and employees from entering into such studies. In our view, that would be contrary to the best interests of good industrial relations and is not a conclusion which we would reach in the absence of clear authority.'

In this case the parties accepted the validity of the study subject to any adjustments following upon the appeals. The parties were therefore taken to have accepted the JES. It has been questioned whether the narrow approach in *Arnold* is consistent with EC law.

Rejection by one party

8.31 One party may not be happy with the results of a JES. The employer may wish to maintain differentials between jobs which the JES has found to be of equal value. The employees and representatives may take the view that the JES is flawed because it has found jobs not to be of equal value where they were asserting that they were. In such a case one party or other may refuse to accept a JES. The effect of this was considered in *Dibro Ltd v Hore and Others* [1990] ICR 370 where it was held that the employer could rely on the result of a JES that had been jointly commissioned after a claim for equal value had been lodged. Where the JES was analytical and valid under s 1(5) its results may be admitted to show that the comparator's jobs were unequal in value. The JES may therefore be taken account of by a Tribunal in any claim that is brought to accept or reject the claim for equal value.

Valid but not implemented

8.32 Where there is a valid JES but is has not been implemented, it was held by the House of Lords in *O'Brien and Others v Sim-Chem Ltd* [1980] IRLR 373, ICR 573 that a claim may be brought under s 1(2)(b). An evaluated pay structure was not implemented because of the Government's new pay policy. Lord Russell stated:

'Once a job evaluation study has been undertaken and has resulted in a conclusion that the job of the woman has been evaluated under S.1(5) as of equal value with the job of the man, then the comparison of the respective terms of their contracts of employment is made feasible and a decision can be made (subject of course to S.1(3)) whether "modification" under (b)(i) or "treatment" under (b)(ii) is called for by the equality clause. I would expect that at that stage when comparison becomes first feasible, and discrimination can first be detected, that the provisions of paragraph (b) would be intended to bite, and bite at once. Comparison of terms and conditions of employment must be at the heart of the legislation: and I cannot imagine any reason why Parliament should postpone to a later stage the operation of paragraph (b).'

Disputing the results

8.33 A woman may have received a lower rating under the JES. There is likely to be a procedure for her to challenge the results. The Guidance that was given by the EOC (now the EHRC), is helpful (see below). A Tribunal should not substitute its own assessment of a JES unless it can be shown that it is discriminatory or there has been a mistake in the evaluation process. In *Greene v Broxtowe District Council* [1977] IRLR 34, [1977] ICR 241 a JES was carried out in relation to six part-time female rent collectors which recommended no variation in rates of pay between the part-time employees and full-time male rent collectors. The Tribunal found that neither the employer or employees accepted the totality of the JES so that it considered whether there was a claim based on 'like work' with full-time male rent collectors. The EAT held that there had been a properly constituted evaluation process so that:

> 'It seems to us therefore that where there has been a properly constituted evaluation study the industrial tribunal is bound by the terms of that subsection to act upon the conclusions and the content of the evaluation study. This can only be challenged, in our view, if it can be shown that there is a fundamental error in the evaluation study, or where, to use words otherwise used in other cases, there is a plain error on the face of the record.'

8.34 The grounds for challenge are very limited. The JES may be challenged if it is based on discriminatory assumptions so that a woman should be able to claim equal pay if she can show that but for the inequality of treatment the JES would have graded her as equal or of greater value (*Murphy and Others v Bord Telecom Eireann* [1988] ICR 445).

8.35 See further under 'Work of equal value' at **9.69** and **9.73**.

Carrying out a valid JES: practical issues

8.36 The former Equal Opportunities Commission (EOC), now the EHRC, produced an Equal Pay Review Kit, together with six sets of Guidance Notes, which should be the starting point in carrying out a JES. They may now be found on the Equality and Human Rights Commission (EHRC) website and consist of the following:

Equal Pay Review Kit – Guidance Notes

- Guidance Note 1: The Legal Framework

- Guidance Note 2: Data Required for Pay Review

- Guidance Note 3: Statistical Analyses

- Guidance Note 4: Job Evaluation Schemes Free of Sex Bias

- Guidance Note 5: Estimating Equal Value

- Guidance Note 6: Reviewing Your Payment Systems, Policies and Practices

ACAS has also recently produced a booklet entitled 'Job Evaluation: Considerations and Risks' (see www.acas.org.uk/CHttpHandler. ashx?id=922&p=0).

8.37 The practical guidance contained in the rest of this chapter is very much based upon the recommendations of the Equal Opportunities Commission (now EHRC) and ACAS.

REASONS TO HAVE A JES

8.38 The most expensive and time-consuming claim that may be made is a claim for work of equal value, which will involve expert evidence. However, where a JES has been carried out, this may be conclusive and the Employment Tribunal may dismiss an equal value claim. If the employer uses an analytical JES the employer needs to be able to show that the scheme has been designed and implemented in such a way that it does not discriminate on grounds of sex. It will be seen that a JES which attributes different values to the jobs of the claimant and comparators will be the best possible defence, provided that the JES is valid. Employers should therefore be encouraged to carry out a JES if they have not already done so. Where a JES has been carried out it may need to be checked to ensure that there is no inherent discrimination, particularly where it lacks transparency or employees/trade unions were not involved in the process. It may be necessary to consider whether there should be involvement under the Information and Consultation of Employees Regulations 2004, SI 2004/3426 in any event.

8.39 The EOC (now the EHRC) recommend a five-stage process in carrying out or reviewing a JES:

STEP 1	Deciding the scope of the review and identifying the data required
STEP 2	Identifying where men and women are doing equal work
STEP 3	Collecting and comparing pay data to identify any significant equal pay gaps
STEP 4	Establishing the causes of any significant pay gaps and deciding whether these are free from discrimination

STEP 5 Developing an Equal Pay Action Plan or reviewing and monitoring

This is considered further below. However, it is first necessary to consider the nature of a JES that will be acceptable under the Act.

TYPES OF JES

8.40 The legal implications of this are considered above at **8.11-8.24.** It has been noted above that there are two basic types of JES, known as 'non-analytical' and 'analytical'.

Non-analytical schemes

8.41 The defining feature of non-analytical schemes is that whole jobs are compared with each other *without any attempt to break down and analyse jobs under their various demands or components.*

• These types of schemes are particularly prone to sex discrimination because where whole jobs are being compared (rather than scores on components of jobs) judgments made by the evaluators can have little objective basis other than the traditional value of the job.

• The rationale of such schemes is to reproduce in a systematic way a hierarchy of jobs, which approximates to the 'felt-fair' ranking of these jobs in the minds of the people working in the organisation.

• Examples of non-analytical schemes include job ranking and paired comparisons, which consist almost entirely of drawing up a list of jobs in rank order (the 'felt-fair' order for the organisation). Such schemes are not a barrier to an individual taking an equal pay claim.

8.42 In many industries the sex of the jobholder has been a factor contributing to the traditional place of the job within the ranking system. Removing this sex discrimination is a break with tradition for which there is no provision in job evaluation procedures based on the 'felt fair' order. According to the EOC (now the EHRC), strongly ingrained attitudes still exist about what work is appropriate to each sex:

> 'These attitudes can lead to acceptance of a grading and pay structure based unthinkingly on current and/or past practice, which can undermine equality of treatment. Unless steps are taken to prevent it, non-analytical job evaluation schemes can maintain a situation in which the jobs most frequently performed by women are regarded as having less value than those mostly performed by men.'

Examples of this would arise in situations where the job titles listed at **8.58** (taken from the EOC,(now the EHRC)) were applied to workers of different sexes who are in fact doing essentially the same work. Another example could be where a 'male' job which has become deskilled through technological change is still regarded as skilled, even though in the process it has become equivalent to 'female' jobs which are regarded as semi or unskilled (see *Bromley v H & J Quick* [1988] IRLR 456 at **8.18**). Employers should be discouraged from adopting the above approach as it will not assist by providing any form of defence in any event.

Analytical schemes

8.43   An analytical scheme will avoid sex discrimination in the grading of jobs. There are several points at which a bias related to the sex of the jobholder can be built into the job evaluating procedure of this kind of 'analytical' scheme. When this occurs, such a scheme would be discriminatory and, in these circumstances, would not debar a worker from proceeding with an equal value claim. Care is therefore needed to ensure that sex discrimination does not occur. In analytical schemes which subdivide jobs into factors and aggregate the factor scores, the 'felt fair' order of jobs is frequently used as a checking mechanism (eg by using paired comparisons on benchmark jobs as a cross-check with the points scheme rankings). *It is important to avoid re-introducing potential sex bias at this checking stage in an analytical scheme as this in itself is not an analytical process.*

Discriminatory JES

8.44   The EqPA 1970 states that a scheme will be discriminatory if it is made on a system which discriminates on grounds of sex where a difference or coincidence between values set by that system on different demands under the same or different headings is not justifiable, irrespective of the sex of the person on whom these demands are made. This means, for example, that a woman may argue that instead of 'mental concentration' (in her job) being awarded fewer points than 'physical effort' (in a man's job), it should have received the same or more points. Similarly, she may argue that the 'physical effort' (in his job) has been overrated compared with the skill her job requires for 'manual dexterity'. Even where she has received the same or more points than a man under a particular heading, she may still argue that the demands of her job under this heading have been underrated. In addition a study will be discriminatory if it fails to include, or properly take into account, a demand (eg caring demands in a job involving looking after sick or elderly people such as nursing) that is an important element in the woman's job. A study will also be discriminatory if it gives an unjustifiably heavy weighting to factors that are more typical of the man's job. See Appendix 7 which lists job functions that are often overlooked.

DEVISING A SCHEME

8.45   A number of issues need to be considered in setting up a JES:

(a)   Who should be included in the scheme?

(b)   Steering groups

(c)   Computerised job evaluation

(d)   Job descriptions and job analysis and the pay structure

(e)   Factors, weighting, grading, ranking and benchmarks

(f)   Red circling

(g)   Revising scores: practical questions

Who should be included in the scheme?

8.46   Excluding groups of jobs from a JES may perpetuate sex bias, especially if the groups excluded are composed predominantly of workers of one sex. Discrimination in the grading and pay of the jobs of female employees in many organisations has occurred or been perpetuated by their separation into a different grading structure based on a different JES, or none at all. Incorporating them within the same JES as the male jobs, provided that the JES is not discriminatory, will assist in achieving equal pay for equal work.

8.47   Groups of workers should only be excluded from a scheme for justifiable and non-discriminatory reasons. Employers and trade unions should appreciate that problems can be created if *bargaining units* are used as the sole basis for the scope of jobs to be covered, since this can often be discriminatory. Claims for equal pay for work of equal value can be brought where separate schemes or collective bargaining arrangements are used to justify differences in pay between the sexes, or where members of one sex are left out of a JES with the effect that the spirit of equal pay legislation is frustrated.

Steering groups

8.48   All JESs are based on the exercise of judgment. Steering groups or project teams overseeing the design and implementation of a scheme are the main way in which employees and staff representatives are involved with exercising judgment. These groups are aimed at ensuring that participation takes place on a structured, equitable, representative, and clearly understood basis. They also contribute to employees' perceptions of the schemes acceptability and help to foster a sense of ownership in the participants. It is recognised good practice in job evaluation to include in these groups a representative sample of people from the spread of jobs covered by a scheme. A fair representation of women in all job evaluation groups and discussions is strongly recommended as a means of reducing the probability of sex bias.

8.49   The EOC (now the EHRC) note that there may be a number of overseeing groups in a job evaluation exercise. These can include:

- a steering group/project team responsible for the determination of policy issues;

- an evaluation panel which undertakes the evaluations;

- an appeals committee which handles appeals against the results of the original evaluations;

- a maintenance panel which assesses the impact of changes in job content, evaluates new jobs that did not previously exist, and periodically reviews the overall operation of the scheme.

In some, although not all, evaluation exercises there will also be one or more groups of people responsible for collecting information on job content, analysing the information, and writing job descriptions. If a scheme is computerised there may well be fewer panels than those detailed above.

8.50   In addition to any other training, members of all the overseeing groups should receive training in how sex bias in job evaluation can arise and they should understand how their actions and decisions can produce such discrimination. The EOC (now the EHRC) state that research has shown that, in general, chairs of committees and especially of job evaluation groups can be very influential in determining the outcome of the groups' considerations. It is therefore important that the chairs of all groups concerned with a JES should be selected not just for their knowledge of job evaluation and their acceptability to the various parties involved, but also because they are unbiased and concerned to ensure the procedures do not result in discrimination against jobs performed by women.

8.51   Regular progress reports on the job evaluation process should be given to keep all employees fully in touch with developments. This will help detect problems as early as possible and avoid disputes over scheme results.

8.52   It is important that minutes and record systems are kept so that they can be made available in the event of appeals and, if necessary, at Employment Tribunal hearings should sex discrimination be alleged.

Computerised job evaluation

8.53   Increasingly, the process of job evaluation is being computerised so that, for example, information on jobs is inputted onto computers in the form of answers to pre-formulated questions and a score for the job is then given. Schemes that are computerised are often quicker to implement and they are not inherently discriminatory. However, any computerised system will reflect the nature of the information it analyses. Therefore, it is important that computerised schemes gather comprehensive information about jobs and are based on factors that are non-discriminatory. The EOC (now the EHRC) also recommend that at the benchmarking stage, an evaluation of the benchmark jobs should be made using both the computerised scheme and written job descriptions or completed job questionnaires. A comparison of the two exercises should then be undertaken to check for sex bias.

Job descriptions and job analysis and the pay structure

8.54 Job descriptions written to an agreed format enable the jobs to be assessed according to a common standard. The EOC (now the EHRC) recommend that forms or guidance notes should be provided to those who are writing job descriptions containing a comprehensive list of elements, which are in the jobs to be assessed. This will help to avoid the possibility of unconscious bias coming into the evaluations at the job description stage (see Appendix 5).

8.55 The EOC (now the EHRC) recommend that job descriptions contain at least the following information:

- job title;

- relationships at work (e g the kind and degree of supervision received; the kind and degree of supervision given; the nature and extent of co-operation with other workers);

- a short summary of the primary functions of the job;

- a description of specific duties of the job showing approximate percentage of time spent on each and the extent of discretion or responsibility in relation to each; and

- the job requirements listed under the headings used for the subsequent job evaluation procedure (e g skill, responsibility, mental effort, physical effort).

8.56 If sub-factors are to be used in the job evaluation procedure, these should also be indicated at the job description stage. Where the format for preparing job descriptions differs significantly from the above, careful attention should be paid to whether the omissions or the additions are likely to result in aspects of jobs more commonly performed by women being underrated relative to other aspects of the spectrum of jobs.

8.57 The preparation of the job description involves at least three people: the employee who does the job or a representative employee, that person's supervisor or manager, and the job analyst or person responsible for the procedures. Close involvement of employees in the preparation of descriptions of their own jobs will benefit from their detailed knowledge of the job, and help to ensure that important aspects of it are not overlooked. Involvement of the manager or supervisor is essential because of their responsibility for stating what is required of the job. The job analyst is important at this stage in detecting any bias against a fair description of women's jobs and advising the manager accordingly.

Job titles

8.58 There is a long history of using different titles for the jobs of men and women who are doing essentially the same work. This has frequently also denoted a status difference, reflected in a pay difference which is based on sex discrimination and not on the content of the work done. Job titles which are applied predominantly to one sex and which have a counterpart applied to the other sex should be carefully examined. If they do not reflect a genuine difference in the nature of the work done they should be changed and the same title applied to both jobs. Examples of such job titles, which can result in discrimination in pay, are listed below (taken from the EOC (now the EHRC)).

Male Job Title	**Female Job Title**
Salesman	Shop Assistant
Assistant Manager	Manager's Assistant
Technician	Operator
Office Manager	Typing Supervisor
Tailor	Seamstress
Personal Assistant	Secretary
Administrator	Secretary
Chef	Cook

It is, of course, recognised that in some circumstances these different job titles are applied to jobs, which are in fact different. Sex discrimination occurs where these titles are applied to the same job and result in different status or pay levels.

The pay structure

8.59 Most pay structures are complex, usually consisting of basic pay and a number of other elements. Changes in *grading* as a result of a job evaluation exercise should reflect all elements of the enumeration package. Relevant questions here are:

- How many women have moved to a higher grade but not a higher salary?

- How many women have moved to a higher grade but receive less in terms of bonus and monetary and non-monetary benefits than men on the same grade?

- Have steps been agreed to eliminate the pay differential for equivalently rated jobs? If not, can the differences be clearly justified by non-sex based reasons?

Not all pay structures are based on grades. Where pay is directly linked to the evaluation result then it is important to check there is a perceptible difference in job size.

Factors, weighting, grading, ranking and benchmarks

8.60 An analytical scheme requires some form of scoring process. This is generally carried out by scoring 'factors' (ie particular functions or skills) which may be weighted and then classified by grades or ranking. The scores may be double checked by looking at benchmark jobs. There is a *risk* that discriminatory assumptions infiltrate each stage which may render the JES valueless.

Factors

8.61 Factors are clearly identifiable aspects of a job that can be defined and measured which provide the basis for assessing and comparing the relative overall worth of different jobs. Examples of factors are 'responsibility for people', 'knowledge', 'communication skills', 'physical demands', 'emotional demands', 'mental skills' and 'initiative'. Except in very broad terms, there is no standard set of factors that are applicable to all jobs. Clearly factor choice is crucial since the final rank order of jobs is most heavily affected by the selection of factors.

8.62 The exclusion of a factor that is important for a job will result in it being undervalued relative to other jobs. This is particularly important if factors are excluded which occur in predominantly female jobs as this will result in these jobs being placed unfairly at the bottom of a grading structure.

- 'Working conditions' and 'physical strength' are often included in schemes covering manual workers; both these factors will appear in jobs performed by men.

- On the other hand, factors associated with work done by women, for example, 'manual dexterity', 'caring skills' and 'working with people', may not be used as factors at all.

It is essential therefore that the factors chosen are representative of the whole range of work being evaluated. It is important to check the factor scores of the jobs performed predominantly by female employees and, if there are a lot of low scores or if the set of factors makes no provision for scoring aspects of the female jobs, which reflect their value to the organisation, then the set of factors is discriminatory and should be changed.

8.63 Where large numbers of jobs are involved, factors are often broadly defined, so it is essential that proper descriptions be provided for the meanings of each factor. The definitions should be closely scrutinised to ensure that unjust sex bias does not occur.

- For example, a definition of 'working conditions' which included shift work could discriminate against women, as could a definition of 'experience' which included length of service.

- For the purposes of job evaluation, it is not important if the jobholder has 20 years' service if the job could be learned in 2 months. Such matters should be dealt with outside the remit of the JES.

- If 'numeracy' is a factor a proper definition should be provided to avoid subjective judgments, for example, that women are less numerate than men.

8.64 Individual factors often have a number of levels within each factor. For example, a factor such as 'initiative' could have five levels ranging from the lowest defined as 'following detailed instructions under close supervision' to the highest defined as 'working within overall policy and having very wide discretion over a broad range of activities with minimal managerial direction'. This is a form of implicit weighting and therefore the considerations identified below in relation to weighting also apply to levels within factors. Care should be taken to avoid sex bias in the number of levels between factors. It is important to ensure that factors, which are characteristics of jobs largely held by one sex, do not unjustifiably have greater numbers of levels than those factors, which are contained in jobs mainly held by the other sex.

Scoring

8.65 Scoring is the method of attaching values to the various levels within each factor so that a total score for each factor and therefore the overall job can be calculated. It is important to ensure that the method of scoring for each factor is reasonably similar, so that the problem does not arise where factors with the same or similar numbers of levels can result in widely differing scores. For example, a factor of 'responsibility for financial resources' may have five levels with scores increasing by multiples of five. The maximum score for this factor would be 25. However, the factor of 'responsibility for caring' could also have five levels but with scores increasing in multiples of three. Therefore the maximum score for this factor is 15. Clearly the effect of this means that a form of implicit weighting has been applied to the 'responsibility for financial resources factor'. In the context of sex discrimination it is particularly important to ensure that factors, which are characteristics of male dominated jobs, do not have a wider dispersion of scores than factors which are characteristics of female dominated jobs.

Weighting

8.66 Once the important components of the jobs in an organisation have been identified and converted into job factors with scales for measuring those factors, it will be recognised that they are not all equally important to the work of the organisation. It is therefore normal practice to apply weights to the factor scores in an effort to reflect the relative importance of the various factors. A very important sub-factor may be weighted even as high as 10% (whilst an unimportant sub-factor may be only weighted 1%). Deciding what these weights shall be *is a highly subjective process* and it is extremely easy for sex discrimination to appear in a job evaluation procedure as a result of discriminatory weightings being applied to the factors.

8.67 To avoid discrimination resulting from the weighting of factors, extreme weights (either very high or very low) should *not* be given to factors that are exclusively found in jobs performed predominantly by one sex. An analysis showing the percentage of total points (after weighting) attributable to each factor should be compiled. This would assist in highlighting factors with heavy weightings and provide a relative comparison between factors. The factors with the heaviest and the lightest weightings should then be looked at again to ensure these can be justified and are not likely to penalise the jobs of one sex.

Ranking

8.68 The rank order resulting from the job evaluation exercise should be compared with that implied by the previous grading structure, with analyses of the two rank orders by gender. This should be a rank order of individual employees as job titles can disguise disparate impact. Also the order should be based on all employees not just the benchmark jobs.

8.69 Where the previous grading structure was also based on an analytical job evaluation exercise, this is a straightforward comparison of rank positions of jobs. Where the previous grading structure was not based on such an exercise then it will be necessary to compare the new rank order with the grouped rank order implied by the old grades, that is, by assuming that all jobs from each old grade shared an equal position in the old overall rank order. In either situation, relevant monitoring questions include:

- How many jobs have changed their relative position in the rank order? How many of these are predominantly male jobs? How many are predominantly female jobs? How many are of mixed gender?
  Where the number and proportion of jobs which have changed their relative position in the rank order is very small, implying a very similar rank order to the previous one, then every aspect of the design and implementation of the JES should be checked to ensure that the exercise does meet equal opportunities and equal value principles.

- How many jobs have moved up the relative rank order? How many of these are predominantly male jobs? How many are predominantly female jobs? How many are of mixed gender?

  Where predominantly male jobs have moved up the relative rank order, can this be demonstrably justified by an increase in overall demand since jobs were last reviewed, for instance, through an increase in responsibilities resulting from a re-organisation or re-distribution of work? If not, review the scheme design (including any hidden weighting) and application process.

- How many jobs have moved down the relative rank order? How many of these are predominantly male jobs? How many are predominantly female jobs? How many are of mixed gender?

  Where predominantly female jobs have moved down the relative rank order, can this be shown to have decreased in overall demand since jobs were last reviewed, for instance, through a decision in responsibilities resulting from a re-organisation or re-distribution of work? If not review the scheme design (including any hidden weighting) and application process.

Grading

8.70 Sometimes there are only a few points between jobs usually performed by men and similar jobs usually performed by women. When the grades are allocated, the cut-off mark in the points scale should not be placed so as to segregate scores and thereby create male and female grades. The result of this would be that grade differentials would occur leading to pay and status differentials which would be sex discriminatory. The selection of grade boundaries, therefore, should be objectively based on the evidence provided by the evaluation, irrespective of the sex of the jobholders.

8.71 Where analytical schemes are used which produce numerical scores for the jobs, grade boundaries should be placed only at points in the hierarchy where there is a gap in the scores. If, for example, a set of jobs produced the following scores; 56, 56, 57, 59, 60, 60, 61, 62, 64, 64, 72, 72, 73, 74, 75, 76, 76. These numbers show two clusters: 56–64 and 72–76. The grade boundary should fall roughly in the middle of the gap between the two clusters, at say 68 or 69, and not through the middle of either cluster. Where points are to be converted into a salary grade this will be integral to the scheme so that if there are different points but the same grade applies the work will be rated as equivalent (as in *Springboard Sunderland Trust v Robson* [1992] IRLR 261 where scores of 410 and 428 fell into the same grade).

8.72 The main determinant of the relationship between the rank order of jobs resulting from a job evaluation exercise and the new wage/salary structure is the positioning of the evaluation scheme grade boundaries. In order to ensure that the positioning of the grade boundaries has not contributed to discrimination against female employees, the following monitoring questions are relevant:

- Which jobs were used to determine grade boundaries – was it all jobs, benchmark jobs, or average result for clusters of similar jobs?

- Do the grade boundaries occur at natural breaks in the scores? If not, why not and can it be justified without reference to either the gender of the jobholders or to the previous grading/pay structures?

- If there are no natural breaks in the job scores, can the points chosen for the grade boundaries be demonstrably justified, for example, by the even size of grades or some other systematic and non-discriminatory principle?

- What if any, is the gender dominance of the jobs falling immediately below or immediately above each grade boundary? If jobs immediately above a grade boundary are carried out predominantly by men and/or those immediately below the grade boundary are carried out predominantly by women, can the positioning of the boundary be justified without reference to either the gender of the relevant jobholders or to the previous pay/grading structure?

- Are these grades that are comprised only of jobholders of one gender, either male or female? If so, can this be demonstrably justified by reference to the demands of the relevant jobs and how they were assessed under the JES?

8.73 Jobs may be re-evaluated if they are very near to the boundary of a higher grade. If the original evaluation is confirmed, however, discretionary points are sometimes added to bring the jobs into the higher grades. Care must be taken to avoid allocating points in a discriminatory way.

Benchmarks

8.74 Woolf LJ stated in *Bromley v H & J Quick Ltd* that there is no objection to benchmarking provided that there is no material difference between the benchmark jobs and other jobs in the group. Most schemes involve the selection of benchmark jobs which are used as a standard because they are considered to be typical of a grade or group of jobs. Discrimination can take place in the selection of benchmark jobs if they do not represent a fair spread of the work done in the organisation. Even this is not adequate where there are small numbers of female staff employed. In such cases it is important to ensure a representative sample of the female jobs is also included amongst the benchmarks. This is a means of ensuring that the scheme takes due account of job elements which are particularly contained in these predominantly female jobs, rather than continuing to rely on evaluating the jobs of female employees against a factor plan appropriate primarily to work of a different nature.

8.75 'Women's' jobs should not be excluded as benchmark jobs. It is commonplace that the factors and factor weights to be used in a job evaluation procedure are derived by reference to a detailed study of the benchmark jobs. If 'women's' jobs are not included in the selection of benchmark jobs then it is unlikely that elements in their work will be fairly represented in the factors and factor weights which are chosen. In order to avoid sex discrimination through job evaluation it is essential that a number of jobs performed predominantly by women and representing the range of such jobs be incorporated into the set of benchmark jobs which are used in the evaluation process.

Red circling

8.76 Anomalies can arise in the payments system as a result of the job evaluation exercise. Some of the existing rates of pay may be above rates newly set for the grades appropriate to those particular jobs. 'Red circling' occurs when the jobholders are allowed to maintain their current pay terms and conditions, but when they leave the particular job it reverts to its evaluated rate. Alternatively, jobholders' pay can be phased into line with the rest of the grade by withholding or restricting future wage increases. Red circling should not be used on such a scale that it amounts to sex discrimination. If red circling results in men receiving a higher rate than women doing the same or broadly similar work this may give rise to an equal pay claim. In any cases brought before them Tribunals will have to make a careful study of the circumstances of each case, taking into account the length of time the red circle has been in operation, whether the initial reason for the pay discrepancy remains justifiable, whether the employer acted in accordance with good industrial relations practices, and whether their actions were based upon any direct or indirect sex discrimination. The following issues may be considered under red circling:

• How many jobholders have had their wages/salaries red circled or personally protected?

• How many of these are men and how many are women?

• If the proportions are significantly different can this be demonstrably justified in terms of the features of the JES and job demands?

• In particular, if the numbers and proportions of men whose wages/salaries are red circled or personally protected in the new salary structure is significantly greater than the numbers and proportions of women, is it demonstrable that the red circling is not a means of evading paying the higher rates to women?

Revising scores: practical questions

8.77 It is sometimes necessary to revise evaluations of jobs after the initial evaluation phase, in order to rectify an inconsistency which crept into the evaluations, or, more probably, on account of new job information. Where this occurs, it should obviously not be used as an opportunity to re-evaluate jobs to a position in the relative rank order closer to their original position, unless this can be justified in terms of the demands of the job and the features of the JES.

8.78 Where revisions to evaluation take place after the initial phase, the following monitoring questions may apply:

- How many jobs have the original assessments been revised?

- How many of these are jobs carried out mainly by women?

- How many of these are jobs carried out mainly by men?

- How many are carried out by both men and women?

- Where there is a significant difference in the numbers and proportions, can this be demonstrably justified?

- How many jobs have the original assessments been revised upwards?

- How many of these are jobs carried out mainly by women?

- How many of these are jobs carried out mainly by men?

- How many are carried out by both men and women?

- If more men's than women's jobs are involved in these upward revisions can this be demonstrably justified without reference to either the gender of the jobholders or the previous grading/pay structures?

- How many jobs have the original assessments been revised downwards?

- How many of these are jobs carried out mainly by women?

- How many of these are jobs carried out mainly by men?

- How many are carried out by both men and women?

- If more women's than men's jobs are involved in these downward revisions can this be demonstrably justified without reference to either the gender of the jobholders or the previous grading/pay structures?

PROCEDURE

8.79 As set out above, the employee, trade unions and other representatives should be involved so far as is possible if the JES is to have validity and it is important to consider whether the JES will cover the whole workforce. Another consideration that employers will need to have in mind will be the application of the Information and Consultation of Employees Regulations 2004 since employment contracts are likely to be affected under the terms of the Regulations.

8.80 Provision is normally made for a formal appeals procedure to deal with those cases where the employees believe their job has been unfairly evaluated. A representative committee is usually set up, and it is important that this committee should be trained both in job evaluation and sex discrimination. The appeals committee members should not be prepared to condone sex discrimination, and in particular the chairs should be someone with an interest in ensuring both fair evaluations and the elimination of sex discrimination. All employees should be informed that care has been taken to ensure that the job evaluation procedure has not discriminated against employees of either sex. Employees should also be informed that the appeals procedure could be used if they feel that they have been wrongly graded because of their sex or if they feel that the scheme has resulted in sex discrimination in some way.

Chapter 9

WORK OF EQUAL VALUE

9.1   The third route by which a woman may claim equal pay is by showing that her work is of equal value. The Equal Pay Act 1970 (EqPA 1970), s 1(1)(c) states:

> 'where a woman is employed on work which, not being work in relation to which paragraph (a) or (b) above applies, is, in terms of the demands made on her (for instance under such headings as effort, skill and decision), of equal value to that of a man in the same employment—
>
> (i)   if (apart from the equality clause) any term of the woman's contract is or becomes less favourable to the woman than a term of a similar kind in the contract under which that man is employed, that term of the woman's contract shall be treated as so modified as not to be less favourable, and
>
> (ii) if (apart from the equality clause) at any time the woman's contract does not include a term corresponding to a term benefiting that man included in the contract under which he is employed, the woman's contract shall be treated as including such a term.'

9.2   The EqPA 1970, s 2A makes specific provision for the procedures to be adopted in relation to claims for work of equal value, which is further fleshed out by Sch 6 to the Employment Tribunals (Constitution and Rules of Procedure) Regulations 2004, SI 2004/1861 (as amended by the Employment Tribunals (Constitution and Rules of Procedure) (Amendment) Regulations 2004, SI 2004/2351) (see below at **9.8** onwards).

THE POINT IN TIME AT WHICH EQUAL VALUE IS CONSIDERED

9.3   The issue of the point in time at which an expert is to consider the facts in deciding whether there has been equal value was considered in *Potter and Others, Ms Casson and Others v North Cumbria Acute Hospitals NHS Trust* UKEAT/0004/08/CEA, [2009] IRLR 12. In one sense this is an issue which goes to the heart of equal value claims; if a claimant may claim back 6 years and the job has changed a number of times then there will be an issue as to how many comparisons the claimant may make as well as important limitation issues (see Chapter 18 at **18.6-18.9**). The expert tasked with providing a report where the equal pay claim extends over a period has the invidious task of identifying whether there is a point in time for the comparison or whether it must be made over the whole of the period. The claim in *Potter* involved grade

D, E and F nurses and some medical secretaries, a sub-multiple of the massive NHS litigation of some 800. Thirteen lead claimants had been selected, comparing themselves with twelve comparators. The periods of the claims varied but some went back to the full 6 years as permitted by *Levez* [2000] ICR 58. Some of the lead claimants had been in entirely different jobs but the claims considered only the most recent job. The parties sought to agree Job Analysis Reports (JARs) for each lead claimant and comparator. These were finalised following a Stage 2 decision. A difference arose as to the date when the JARs were to set out the facts and therefore the date at which the experts should prepare their reports. The respondent asserted that this should be only at the date of the claims being made whilst the claimants contended that it should cover the entire period. The Employment Tribunal held that the correct comparison period for the evaluation of equality was the date of the presentation of the claim.

9.4   The Employment Appeal Tribunal (EAT) refused to proffer any abstract observations as to when a change may occur, though changes brought about by technological developments were discussed as an example. The EAT stated that the claim is based upon the failure to pay a sum due on a distinct pay date over the period to which the claim relates. In many cases there would be no reason to suppose that the material facts were any different at any point in the period. Where the facts materially differed they would have to be stated on a distinct basis in respect of different parts of the period. If the claimed differences are very great the sensible course would be to have two distinct statements. In other cases it may be convenient to produce a statement at a given base and to identify the respects in which they differ for other periods. The base date would normally be the date of presentation of the claim but there is no reason why the beginning of the claim period could not be taken.

9.5   A Tribunal can, however, split the periods and decide first in relation to one part of the period, dealing later, if necessary with the other periods pre or post the alleged change. The Tribunal should be told at an early stage whether there have been changes and a claimant may be debarred from raising the point if it has not done so. In *Potter* the issue of possible changes was not identified at an early stage; the JARs stated only the fact at the date of presentation of the claim. The Employment Tribunal held that there must be a fixed point at which the claim could be evaluated by the expert and the Tribunal to consider the impact of any alleged changes in job content at a later stage in light of these reports. The EAT held that this was a case management decision with which it would not interfere. It was, however, noted by the EAT that if in due course an issue did arise about the effect of any changes in job content, it was possible that the Tribunal would have to appoint an expert to report on that issue. This would not necessarily be the case as the Tribunal may feel able to reach a safe conclusion without a further report. There would be no technical impediment to dispensing with a further report.

9.6   It was also noted that the Tribunal's ruling did not exclude tasks that were not being performed at the date of the evaluation but which remained part of the jobs in question. There were many employments where tasks were performed only occasionally or at long intervals but this did not mean that they were therefore not part of the package of tasks though their infrequency may be important in assessing their weight. The EAT also noted a different approach taken by another Employment Tribunal in another sub-multiple *Broadhurst* that all changes should be identified at an early stage rather than emerge at the final hearing. It stated that it may be that the *Broadhurst* approach is preferable but it did not follow that the Tribunal was wrong in this case as he had to decide the best course for the particular circumstances (see the EAT at para 29).

9.7 It is apparent from *Potter* that provided the Tribunal has good reasons it can order that the expert consider all changes at the outset or focus on one point in time and then later consider the impact of any changes. Neither approach is wrong though it is certainly preferable that changes be identified as soon as possible so that the parties know where they stand.

THE EQUAL VALUE PROCEDURE

9.8 The Tribunal procedures are regulated by the Employment Tribunals (Constitution and Rules of Procedure) Regulations 2004 and the procedures for equal value claims is set out in Sch 6, the Employment Tribunals (Equal Value) Rules of Procedure. There has for many years been judicial and extra-judicial complaint about the serious delays and expense of equal value claims; the EOC – (now the EHRC) complained as long ago as 1986 that the procedures served individuals badly. Indeed, there were only 23 successful claims in the ten years commencing 1 January 2004 when s 1(2)(c) was first introduced. The new procedures apply to equal value claims after 1 October 2004 and are intended to streamline the procedures. The Employment Tribunals (Equal Value) Rules of Procedure contains an indicative timetable of how long an equal value claim should take from commencement to finish. It has to be said that the timetable is somewhat optimistic but at least does focus minds on getting the case to a hearing. The timetable is as follows:

The indicative timetable

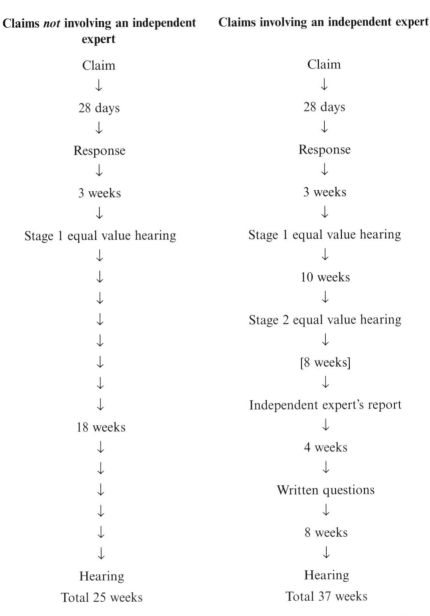

Claims *not* involving an independent expert	Claims involving an independent expert
Claim	Claim
↓	↓
28 days	28 days
↓	↓
Response	Response
↓	↓
3 weeks	3 weeks
↓	↓
Stage 1 equal value hearing	Stage 1 equal value hearing
↓	↓
↓	10 weeks
↓	↓
↓	Stage 2 equal value hearing
↓	↓
↓	[8 weeks]
↓	↓
↓	Independent expert's report
18 weeks	↓
↓	4 weeks
↓	↓
↓	Written questions
↓	↓
↓	8 weeks
↓	↓
Hearing	Hearing
Total 25 weeks	Total 37 weeks

9.9   A claim for equal pay for work of equal value is only necessary when a claim for like work or work rated as equivalent has not succeeded. This position was considered in *Pickstone v Freemans plc* [1987] 3 All ER 756, [1987] IRLR 218, [1987] ICR 867, CA, [1988] 2 All ER 803, [1988] IRLR 357, [1988] ICR 697. The claimants were warehouse operatives. They had sought to compare themselves with checker warehouse operatives who were paid more. Their claim for like work failed in the Employment Tribunal and EAT as they had men on like work and it was held that the words 'not being work in relation to which paragraph (a) or (b) above applies' excluded a claim for equal value. The House of Lords, however, held that after the word 'applies' there should be implied the words 'as between the woman and the man with whom she claims equality'. This purposive interpretation, in order to comply with Art 141 of the EC Treaty, meant that the claim for equal value could be made against the comparators chosen even though there were other men on 'like work'. The House of Lords did not expressly decide whether Art 141 was directly enforceable, though Lord Oliver doubted that this was the position, as this was not necessary for the decision.

9.10 The procedures in Schedule 6 involve a two-stage process where no expert is appointed and a three-stage process where there is an expert.

- The standard case will involve a *Stage 1* equal value hearing. If there is a valid job evaluation study (JES) which has rated the jobs as not being equal then the Tribunal may strike out the claim unless there are reasonable grounds for believing that the JES is tainted by sex discrimination or is unsuitable. If the claim is not struck out the Tribunal will decide whether to appoint an expert or decide the case without the assistance of an expert.

- If an expert has been appointed there will be a *Stage 2* hearing to resolve any disputed facts so that the expert can then proceed to make an evaluation of the claimant and comparator.

- The *Equal value hearing* at the second or third stage will determine if there is equal value. The expert's report may be admitted at this hearing and the question of equal value decided as well as any material factor defence. The party who disagrees with the expert's report may challenge its methodology at this hearing, though not the facts on which it is based (*Middlesbrough Borough Council v Surtees (No 2)* [2007] IRLR 981).

9.11   In an equal value claim, it is for the claimant to prove this element of the claim (*Nelson v Carillon* [2003] EWCA Civ 544, [2003] IRLR 428) and this remains so whether the assertion of indirect discrimination is put on the basis of statistics or otherwise. However, the principle of transparency (see **10.56**) does raise the issue whether the burden of proving equal value rests on the claimant where it is contended that the employer's pay system is not transparent (*Handels-OG Kontorfunktionaerernes Forbund i Danmark v Dansk Arbejdsgiverforening (acting for Danfoss)* (Case C-109/88), [1989] IRLR 532). This may be a particular issue where the employer awards a discretionary bonus and the basis of the exercise of discretion is far from clear. This position was considered in *Barton v Investec Henderson Crosthwaite Securities Ltd* [2003] IRLR 332 approved in *Igen v Wong* [2005] EWCA Civ 142, [2005] IRLR 258, as to which see **10.14-10.15**. It is apparent that lack of transparency will mean that the employer has to show objective justification when equal value has been demonstrated; it is going too far to say that it will have the burden of *disproving equal value* when there is lack of transparency, though clearly if the employer does not give some explanation at the equal value stage the Tribunal may decide to draw the inference that the work is of equal value. It should be remembered that the questionnaire procedure may have been used to interrogate the employer about the reasons for the pay system and an adverse inference can be drawn if the employer fails to give or gives an evasive reply.

9.12 As noted, the Equal Value Rules in Sch 6 modify and supplement the Employment Tribunals Rules of Procedure contained in Sch 1 to the Employment Tribunals (Constitution and Rules of Procedure) Regulations 2004 and need to be considered in conjunction with these Rules. These provisions are considered in more detail below.

Tribunal's general powers

9.13 A Tribunal is given specific powers to regulate its proceedings by Sch 6, rule 3, in addition to the general power of Tribunals contained in Sch 1, rule 10.

9.14 By rule 3 the Tribunal or Employment Judge is given power (subject to rules 4(3) and 7(4) as set out further below) to make the following orders:

(a) the standard orders set out in rules 5 or 8, with such addition to, omission or variation of those orders (including specifically variations as to the periods within which actions are to be taken by the parties) as the chairman or Tribunal considers is appropriate. Rules 4 and 7 deal with the Stage 1 and 2 hearings and are considered below;

(b) that no new facts shall be admitted in evidence by the Tribunal unless they have been disclosed to all other parties in writing before a date specified by the Tribunal (unless it was not reasonably practicable for a party to have done so). This general provision is intended to ensure that the equal value hearing will be on the basis of facts that have been admitted and considered before the hearing;

(c) that the parties may be required to send copies of documents or provide information to the other parties and to the independent expert. The Tribunal is able to ensure that the claimants and respondent give full disclosure and provision of information to the expert and the other side to ensure that the expert is fully appraised of all relevant facts;

(d) that the respondent is required to grant the independent expert access to his premises during a period specified by the Tribunal or chairman in order for the independent expert to conduct interviews with persons identified as relevant by the independent expert;

(e) when more than one expert is to give evidence in the proceedings, that those experts present to the Tribunal a joint statement of matters which are agreed between them and those matters on which they disagree. There may be more than one expert where the Tribunal has appointed an expert and the parties have an expert. The rules contain the sensible provisions which will allow the parties to agree facts so far as is possible;

(f)   where proceedings have been joined, that lead claimants be identified. This is an essential rule, particularly in recent cases where there have been many hundreds of claims.

Independent expert

9.15   One of the central facets of the procedure is the use by the Tribunal of a panel of independent experts recommended by the Advisory, Conciliation and Arbitration Service (ACAS). By the EqPA 1970, s 2A(1):

> 'Where on a complaint or reference made to an employment tribunal . . . a dispute arises as to whether any work is of equal value as mentioned in section 1(2)(c) . . . the tribunal may either—
>
> (a)   proceed to determine that question; or
> (b)   . . . require a member of the panel of independent experts to prepare a report with respect to that question . . .'

9.16   Where the claimant's job and that of the comparator had been assessed under a JES as having different values (the JES not being tainted by discrimination) a Tribunal had the power to decide that there were no reasonable grounds for determining that the work was of equal value. This 'reasonable grounds' defence has been removed so that a Tribunal cannot simply strike out the claim on this basis. Where there has already been a JES this may be presumed to be accurate so that a Tribunal may make a determination under s 2(2), 2A(2A) and 2A(3). By s 2A(2), s 2(2A) will apply in a case where a Tribunal is required to determine whether any work is of equal value as mentioned in s 1(2)(c) above, and the work of the woman and that of the man in question have been given different values under a JES. By s 2A(2):

> 'The tribunal shall determine that the work of the woman and that of the man are not of equal value unless the tribunal has reasonable grounds for suspecting that the evaluation contained in the study—
>
> (a)   was (within the meaning of subsection (3) below) made on a system which discriminates on grounds of sex, or
> (b)   is otherwise unsuitable to be relied upon.'

9.17   Section 2A(3) provides that an evaluation contained in a study such as is mentioned in s 1(5) is made on a system which discriminates on grounds of sex where a difference, or coincidence, between values set by that system on different demands under the same or different headings is not justifiable irrespective of the sex of the person on whom those demands are made. This makes clear the meaning of s 2A(2)(a).

Withdrawal of an independent expert

9.18 The section gives powers to the Tribunal to withdraw the requirement for an expert. By s 2A(1A), s 2A(1B) and (1C) apply in a case where the Tribunal has required a member of the panel of independent experts to prepare a report under s 2A(1)(b). The Tribunal may withdraw the requirement, and request the member of the panel of independent experts to provide it with any documentation specified by it or make any other request to him connected with the withdrawal of the requirement (s 2A(1B)). Thus the Tribunal may have the advantage of the expert's work up to the time when it decides to dispense with the expert's services. If the requirement has not been withdrawn the Tribunal shall not make any determination unless it has received the report from the expert (s 2A(1C)).

9.19 A reference to a member of the panel of independent experts is a reference to a person who is for the time being designated by ACAS for the purposes of that paragraph as such a member, being neither a member of the Council of that Service nor one of its officers or servants (s 2A(4)).

9.20 The circumstances in which the Tribunal should withdraw the requirement for an independent expert where a JES has been carried out was considered in *Mrs F A Hovell v Ashford and St Peter's Hospital NHS Trust* UKEAT/1063/08. The claimant was employed by the respondent as a social services administrator. Under the NHS Agenda for Change a valid JES produced nine pay bands, with band 9 subdivided into four. The claimant was placed into band 4, 271–325 points, along with her three named male comparators. She scored 274 points; her comparators respectively scored 296, 298 and 305 points. The jobs were rated as equivalent from 1 October 2004. The question was whether the claimant was employed on work of equal value under s 1(2)(c) prior to that date. It was common ground there was no material change in the job content over the previous 6 years. The claimant sought an order that the requirement for an expert be withdrawn on the basis that the JES was determinative. Employment Judge Malone concluded that the same banding was not determinative or sufficient evidence of equal value where the points score for the claimant was lower under the JES. (In an earlier case, *Jones v Wirral Hospital NHS Trust*, referred to in the EAT judgment, he had withdrawn the requirement for an expert where the point score was higher for the claimant). HHJ Clark did not accept that a same banding principle under s 1(2)(b), which is concerned with work rated as equivalent under a JES, necessarily applies to a claim under s 1(2)(c). The fact that jobs were rated as equivalent may be evidence that they were of equal value at an earlier stage but it does not follow that the employer is bound to accept that the jobs are of equal value for a period prior to implementation of the JES. HHJ Clark did not rule on whether *Jones* was wrong but it is submitted that it must be by parity of reasoning.

The stage 1 equal value hearing

9.21 Rule 4 sets out the conduct of what is called a 'stage 1' hearing which must be conducted when there is a dispute as to whether any work is of equal value as mentioned in the EqPA 1970, s 1(2)(c), in accordance with both rule 4 and the rules applicable to pre-hearing reviews in Sch 1.

9.22 By rule 4(6) when the Secretary of State gives notice to the parties of the stage 1 equal value hearing under rule 14(4) of Sch 1, he shall also give the parties notice of the matters which the Tribunal may and shall consider at that hearing, which are described in paras (3) and (5) of rule 4 and notice of the standard orders in rule 5 are also to be given.

9.23 Rule 4(2) provides that, notwithstanding rule 18(1) and (3) of Sch 1, a stage 1 equal value hearing shall be conducted by a Tribunal composed in accordance with the Employment Tribunals Act 1996, s 4(1). It is therefore necessary to have a full panel for a stage 1 hearing.

At the stage 1 equal value hearing, by rule 4(3), the Tribunal is to consider seven matters as follows.

Strike out

9.24 Rule 4(3)(a) provides that the Tribunal may:

> '(a)   where section 2A(2) of the Equal Pay Act applies, strike out the claim (or the relevant part of it) if, in accordance with section 2A(2A) of that Act, the tribunal must determine that the work of the claimant and the comparator are not of equal value.'

If consideration is going to be given to striking out the claim, by rule 4(4), before a claim or part of one is struck out under para 4(3)(a), the Secretary shall send notice to the claimant giving him the opportunity to make representations to the Tribunal as to whether the evaluation contained in the study in question falls within para (a) or (b) of EqPA 1970, s 2A(2A). A notice need not be sent if the claimant has been given an opportunity to make such representations orally to the Tribunal as to why such a judgment should not be issued.

9.25 The right of the Tribunal to dismiss a claim on the basis of no reasonable grounds was removed by the 2004 amendments. The Tribunal may, however, decide that a claim should be struck out where a valid JES has been produced which shows that the jobs are not of equal value. Claims which are misconceived may also be struck out; for example, where sample cases have been decided which are similar to the claimant's case so that the claimant is effectively seeking to relitigate an issue decided against him in the sample cases (cf *Ashmore v British Coal Corporation* [1990] IRLR 283, [1990] ICR 485).

9.26   By rule 7(7) it is noted that the Tribunal's power to strike out the claim or part of it under para (3)(a) is in addition to powers to strike out a claim under rule 18(7) of Sch 1, which sets out various grounds on which a Tribunal may strike out a claim, including striking out a claim on the basis that it is 'scandalous, or vexatious or has no reasonable prospect of success'. These Rules may be used in addition to the Equal Value rules.

Requirement for an expert?

9.27   The Tribunal will decide whether it can proceed to hear the case itself without the benefit of an expert or whether it will need the assistance of a member of the panel of experts to prepare a report. Rule 4(3)(b) provides that the Tribunal shall:

> '(b) decide, in accordance with section 2A(1) of the Equal Pay Act, either that (i) the tribunal shall determine the question; or (ii) it shall require a member of the panel of independent experts to prepare a report with respect to the question.'

9.28   The Tribunal may decide that the case is so hopeless that it would be a waste of time and money to appoint an expert. If the Tribunal decides that it does not wish to call an expert then the parties will be entitled to insist upon calling an expert and the Tribunal will have to decide the case on the basis of that evidence. In *Wood v William Ball Ltd* [1999] IRLR 773 a Tribunal dismissed claims based on equal value as it thought they were bound to fail and did not see the need to call expert evidence. The EAT held that there had been a requirement to allow the parties to adduce expert evidence themselves. The claimants were entitled to commission a report if they wished.

9.29   The Tribunal may decide not to appoint an expert if there has already been a JES and different values have been given to the work. The claim will then be struck out unless there is reason to suspect that the study discriminated on the basis of sex or there is some other reason that the JES is not suitable to be relied upon (s 2A(2) above). The existence of a JES in these circumstances will not be a bar to a reference to an expert (*Elbogen v Royal Institute of British Architects* EAT/480/90). Where the JES is not analytical, as set out in *Bromley v H & J Quick Ltd* [1988] IRLR 249, ICR 623 there shall be no bar to a reference. The Tribunal may decide the case themselves in such circumstances.

9.30   In cases where the claimant has brought a claim, the employer may then commence a JES. This will not prevent a claim being heard but it was held in *Avon County Council v Foxall and Webb* [1989] IRLR 435, [1989] ICR 470 that the Tribunal has a discretion to stay a claim. It was stated in *Webb* by Knox J that:

> 'The fact that the right which the proceedings aim at enforcing is an absolute right not fettered by judicial discretion, does not prevent the Court from having a discretion, where an appropriate power exists under the Rules of Procedure, as it does here, to grant or refuse a stay according to the weight of the arguments for

and against a stay ... prosecute their claims under the Act. For a stay to be ordered a case for doing so needs to be shown. The principal reason relied upon in order to establish this is identified as being the undesirable risk of the Hay Scheme's results being adversely affected by a result more favourable to the claimants of the report of an expert appointed by the Industrial Tribunal and that is not one which impresses me as having much force. The Hay Scheme will proceed and will not in itself be impeded by the existence of these proceedings although I accept some additional expense will be incurred. Once the Hay Scheme is properly and effectively completed, if it is, it will protect Avon completely against future claims from employees whose jobs are covered by the Hay Scheme. In these circumstances the possible loss to these claimants of rights which the successful prosecution of their claim under s.1(2)(c) would secure in my view significantly outweighs the disadvantages to Avon in the refusal of a stay.'

9.31 Where the employer carries out such a JES then the results will be admissible to decide whether the s 2A(2) defence can be relied upon (*Dibro Ltd v Hore* [1990] IRLR 129, [1990] ICR 370). The employer may produce a JES right up until the hearing of the claim and, if it does so, such a JES will be admissible in defending the claim. Wood J stated:

'Provided that a job evaluation scheme is analytical and a valid one within s.1(5) and is relevant to the issues which the Tribunal has to decide, it seems to us to matter not at all that it came into existence after the initiation of proceedings provided it relates to facts and circumstances existing at the time when those proceedings were initiated. The s.2A expert, if so ordered, will carry out just such a scheme or study, so will the experts advising each of the parties. Each will give an opinion based upon such an evaluation most of which work or assessment will come into being after proceedings commenced.'

9.32 The Tribunal may also decide that there is no point appointing an expert if it takes the view that the employer will have a good s 1(3) defence to the claim. In this case it may be that it will decide to hear the material factor defence before it hears the question of equal value (cf *McGregor v General Municipal Boilermakers and Allied Trades Union* [1987] ICR 505).

9.33 The respondent may wish the defence to be heard before the issue of equal value is dealt with. By rule 4(5) the Tribunal may, on the application of a party, hear evidence upon and permit the parties to address it upon the issue contained in s 1(3) (defence of a genuine material factor) before determining whether to require an independent expert to prepare a report under para (3)(b)(ii). If the s 1(3) defence does not succeed the employer will not be precluded from arguing equal value and the Tribunal may, at that stage, refer to an independent expert.

Standard orders

9.34 Rule 4(3)(c) provides:

'(c) subject to rule 5 and with regard to the indicative timetable, the Tribunal will make the standard orders for the stage 1 equal value hearing as set out in rule 5.'

The standard orders are considered under **9.39** below.

Provision of information to the expert

9.35 Rule 4(3)(d) provides:

'(d) if the tribunal has decided to require an independent expert to prepare a report on the question, the Tribunal will require the parties to copy to the independent expert all information which they are required by an order to disclose or agree between each other.'

Date of stage 2 hearing

9.36 Rule 4(3)(e) provides:

'(e) if the tribunal has decided to require an independent expert to prepare a report on the question, [the tribunal will] fix a date for the stage 2 equal value hearing, having regard to the indicative timetable.'

Date of hearing where no expert

9.37 Rule 4(3)(f) provides:

'(f) if the tribunal has not decided to require an independent expert to prepare a report on the question, the Tribunal will fix a date for the Hearing, having regard to the indicative timetable.'

Other Orders

9.38 Rule 4(3)(g) provides that the Tribunal may:

'(g) consider whether any further orders are appropriate.'

This is likely to take the form of preparation of schedules of comparators and consideration of what disclosure orders are appropriate. In the North East litigation involving National Health Trust, the Newcastle Tribunal has developed sophisticated standard orders which are now in their 14th edition.

Standard directions at the stage 1 hearing

9.39 Rule 5 provides that at a stage 1 equal value hearing a Tribunal shall, unless it considers it inappropriate to do so (and subject to para 5(2), which provides that any of the standard orders for the stage 1 equal value hearing may be added to, varied or omitted as the Tribunal considers appropriate order) make a variety of orders. The rules specify time periods, which can of course be varied as per rule 5(2). The Tribunal is to make the orders within the following time periods unless it is considered inappropriate.

Before the end of 14 days after the stage 1 hearing: identification of the comparator

9.40 Rule 5(1)(a) provides that the Tribunal can make an order that before the end of the period of 14 days after the date of the stage 1 equal value hearing the claimant shall:

'(i) disclose in writing to the respondent the name of any comparator, or, if the claimant is not able to name the comparator he shall instead disclose such information as enables the comparator to be identified by the respondent; and

(ii) identify to the respondent in writing the period in relation to which he considers that the claimant's work and that of the comparator are to be compared.'

Before the end of 28 days after the stage 1 hearing: identification of comparator, written job descriptions and relevant facts

9.41 Rule 5(1)(b) provides that the Tribunal can make an order that before the end of the period of 28 days after the date of the stage 1 equal value hearing:

'(i) where the claimant has not disclosed the name of the comparator to the respondent under sub-paragraph (a), if the respondent has been provided with sufficient detail to be able to identify the comparator, he shall disclose in writing the name of the comparator to the claimant;

(ii) the parties shall provide each other with written job descriptions for the claimant and any comparator.

(iii) the parties shall identify to each other in writing the facts which they consider to be relevant to the question.'

Access to the comparators

9.42 By rule 5(1)(c) the respondent is required to grant access to the claimant and his representative (if any) to his premises during a period specified by the Tribunal or chairman in order for him or them to interview any comparator.

Before the end of 56 days after the stage 1 hearing: agreed joint statement

9.43 By rule 5(1)(d) the parties shall before the end of the period of 56 days after the date of the stage 1 equal value hearing present to the Tribunal a joint agreed statement which is to include those matters listed in the rule; that is:

'(i) job descriptions for the claimant and any comparator;

(ii) facts which both parties consider are relevant to the question;

(iii) facts on which the parties disagree (as to the fact or as to the relevance to the question) and a summary of their reasons for disagreeing.'

At least 56 days prior to the hearing: disclosure of written statement of facts

9.44 By rule 5 (1)(e) the parties shall, at least 56 days prior to the hearing, disclose to each other, to any independent or other expert and to the Tribunal written statements of any facts on which they intend to rely in evidence at the hearing.

At least 28 days prior to the hearing: presentation of statement of facts and issues

9.45 By rule 5(1)(f) the parties shall, at least 28 days prior to the hearing, present to the Tribunal a statement of facts and issues on which the parties are in agreement, a statement of facts and issues on which the parties disagree and a summary of their reasons for disagreeing.

The role of the independent expert in fact finding

9.46 Rule 6 applies to proceedings in relation to which the Tribunal has decided to require an independent expert to prepare a report on the question. A Tribunal or chairman may if it or he considers it appropriate at any stage of the proceedings order an independent expert to assist the Tribunal in establishing the facts on which the independent expert may rely in preparing his report (rule 6(1) and 6(2)).

9.47 Rule 6(3) gives examples of the circumstances in which the Tribunal or Employment Judge may make an order, described as including:

'(a) a party not being legally represented;
(b) the parties are unable to reach agreement as required by an order of the tribunal or chairman;
(c) the tribunal or chairman considers that insufficient information may have been disclosed by a party and this may impair the ability of the independent expert to prepare a report on the question;
(d) the tribunal or chairman considers that the involvement of the independent expert may promote fuller compliance with orders made by the tribunal or a chairman.

(4) A party to proceedings may make an application under rule 11 of Schedule 1 for an order under paragraph 6(2).'

The stage 2 hearing: conduct at the hearing

9.48 Rule 7 applies to proceedings in relation to which the Tribunal has decided to require an independent expert to prepare a report on the question. In such proceedings the Tribunal is required to conduct a 'stage 2 equal value hearing' in accordance with both rule 7 and the rules applicable to pre-hearing reviews in Sch 1. A stage 2 equal value hearing shall be conducted by a Tribunal composed in accordance with the Employment Tribunals Act 1996, s 4(1) (rule 8(2)); that is a full Tribunal.

9.49 By rule 7(3) at the stage 2 equal value hearing the Tribunal shall make a determination of facts on which the parties cannot agree which relate to the question and shall require the independent expert to prepare his report on the basis of facts which have (at any stage of the proceedings) either been agreed between the parties or determined by the Tribunal (referred to as 'the facts relating to the question'). The reason for the Stage 2 hearing is to decide the facts which will form the basis for the expert to decide whether or not there is equal value and from which he will prepare his report.

9.50 Further, by rule 7(4) at the stage 2 equal value hearing the Tribunal shall:

'(a) subject to rule 8 and having regard to the indicative timetable, make the standard orders for the stage 2 equal value hearing as set out in rule 8.
(b) make any orders which it considers appropriate;
(c) fix a date for the Hearing, having regard to the indicative timetable.'

The facts relating to the question shall be the only facts on which the Tribunal shall rely at the equal value hearing (rule 7(5)). By rule 7(6) at any stage of the proceedings the independent expert may make an application to the Tribunal for some or all of the facts relating to the question to be amended, supplemented or omitted.

9.51 By rule 7(7), when the Secretary gives notice to the parties and to the independent expert of the stage 2 equal value hearing under rule 14(4) of Sch 1, he shall also give the parties notice of the standard orders in rule 8 and draw the attention of the parties to paras (4) and (5) of rule 7.

9.52 It has already been noted that the Tribunal will not prevent another expert from being called by the parties though the expert will not be able to challenge the facts on which the independent expert has based his report (see *Middlesbrough Council v Surtees (No 2)* [2007] IRLR 981 below at **9.64**).

Standard orders for stage 2 equal value hearing

9.53 Rule 8(1) provides that at a stage 2 equal value hearing a Tribunal shall, unless it considers it inappropriate to do so and subject to the proviso that any of the standard orders for the stage 2 equal value hearing may be added to, varied or omitted as the Tribunal considers appropriate, order that:

'(a) by a date specified by the tribunal (with regard to the indicative timetable) the independent expert shall prepare his report on the question and shall (subject to rule 14) have sent copies of it to the parties and to the tribunal; and

(b)   the independent expert shall prepare his report on the question on the basis of the facts relating to the question and no other facts which may or may not relate to the question.'

The hearing

9.54   By rule 9(1) in proceedings in relation to which an independent expert has prepared a report, unless the Tribunal determines that the report is not based on the facts relating to the question, the report of the independent expert shall be admitted in evidence. If the Tribunal does not admit the report of an independent expert in accordance with para 9(1), it may determine the question itself or require another independent expert to prepare a report on the question (rule 9(2)).

9.55   The expert's report is not conclusive but is evidence only and it is for the Tribunal to make a decision on equality based upon the whole of the evidence, of which the expert evidence is a part. The statements in *Tennants Textile Colours Ltd v Todd* [1989] IRLR 3 are apposite in this respect:

> ' . . . whoever conceived the ideas of a reference to an independent expert intended that expert's report to be conclusive but then drew back . . . Reports obtained in the circumstances created by the present Act and Rules must obviously carry considerable weight, as was clearly intended, but there is no provision or principle that the party challenging an independent expert's report has to "persuade the Tribunal that the independent expert's report should be rejected" or that the Tribunal "could only reject the independent expert's report if the evidence were such as to show that it was so plainly wrong that it could not be accepted". The burden of proving a claim under the Act of 1970 is on the applicant. The burden does not in point of law become heavier if the independent expert's report is against the applicant. Nor, if that report is in favour of the applicant is the burden of proof transferred to the employer.'

9.56   By rule 9(3) the Tribunal may refuse to admit evidence of facts or hear argument as to issues which have not been disclosed to the other party as required by the rules or any order made under them, unless it was not reasonably practicable for the party to have so complied.

THE INDEPENDENT EXPERT

9.57   Notwithstanding the above sentiments, the expert's report is likely to carry great weight with any Tribunal. The expert is independent and the Tribunal will be reliant upon the expert for assistance. Rules 10, 11 and 12 contain further provisions which set out the duties and powers of the expert, the use of expert evidence and the way in which experts may be questioned.

Duties and powers of the independent expert

9.58 By rule 10(1) when a Tribunal requires an independent expert to prepare a report with respect to the question of equal value or an order is made under rule 6(2), the Secretary shall inform that independent expert of the duties and powers he has under rule 10. By rule 10(2) the independent expert has a duty to the Tribunal to:

'(a) assist it in furthering the overriding objective in regulation 3;
(b) comply with the requirements of the rules and any orders made by the tribunal or a chairman in relation to the proceedings;
(c) keep the tribunal informed of any delay in complying with any order in the proceedings with the exception of minor or insignificant delays in compliance;
(d) comply with any timetable imposed by the tribunal or chairman in so far as this is reasonably practicable;
(e) inform the tribunal or a chairman on request by it or him of progress in the preparation of the independent expert's report;
(f) prepare a report on the question based on the facts relating to the question and (subject to rule 14 which relates to National Security proceedings) send it to the tribunal and the parties;
(g) make himself available to attend hearings in the proceedings.'

9.59 Rule 10(3) provides that the independent expert may make an application for any order or for a hearing to be held as if he were a party to the proceedings. This is an important provision since it is necessary for the expert to be able to get to the facts by compulsion from the Tribunal if necessary.

9.60 The Tribunal may at any stage, after giving the independent expert the opportunity to make representations, withdraw the requirement on the independent expert to prepare a report (rule 10(4)). If it does so, the Tribunal may itself determine the question, or it may determine that a different independent expert should be required to prepare the report. When rule 10(4) applies the independent expert who is no longer required to prepare the report shall provide the Tribunal with all documentation and work in progress relating to the proceedings by a date specified by the Tribunal. Such documentation and work in progress must be in a form which the Tribunal is able to use. Such documentation and work in progress may be used in relation to those proceedings by the Tribunal or by another independent expert (rule 10(5)). These provisions mean that the Tribunal can decide at any stage that an expert is no longer needed but the work that has been done to date may still be used.

9.61 Further, by rule 10(6) when an independent expert has been required to prepare a report in proceedings the Secretary shall give the independent expert notice of all hearings, orders or judgments in those proceedings as if the independent expert were a party to the proceedings and when the rules require a party to provide information to another party, such information shall also be provided to the independent expert. In other words, the expert is to be kept in the loop.

Use of expert evidence

9.62   The expert evidence is to be restricted to that which, in the opinion of the tribunal, is reasonably required to resolve the proceedings (rule 11(1)). By rule 11(2) an expert has a duty to assist the Tribunal on matters within his expertise. This duty overrides any obligation to the person from whom he has received instructions or by whom he is paid. We have already seen the specific duties contained in rule 10(2) on the part of the expert.

9.63   It is provided by rule 11(3) that no party may call an expert or put in evidence an expert's report without the permission of the Tribunal. No expert report shall be put in evidence unless it has been disclosed to all other parties and any independent expert at least 28 days prior to the hearing. By rule 11(4), in proceedings in which an independent expert has been required to prepare a report on the question, the Tribunal shall not admit evidence of another expert on the question unless such evidence is based on the facts relating to the question. Unless the Tribunal considers it inappropriate to do so, any such expert report shall be disclosed to all parties and to the Tribunal on the same date on which the independent expert is required to send his report to the parties and to the Tribunal. If an expert (other than an independent expert) does not comply with the rules or an order made by the Tribunal or an Employment Judge, the Tribunal may order that the evidence of that expert shall not be admitted (rule 11(5)).

9.64   In *Middlesbrough Borough Council v Surtees (No 2)* [2007] IRLR 981 the EAT considered when a party could produce an expert to adduce a report. The Employment Tribunal ordered an independent expert to notify steps he was taking and he therefore sent a list of 'possible job elements' and then in greater detail a 'review of job descriptions against a possible and tentative factor plan'. He began his approach by looking at certain factors. In his final report he isolated 21 factors and attributed seven levels to the jobs and scoring for them. Breaking down a factor according to levels and allocating scores was part of his methodology. The Council commissioned an expert who identified two aspects of methodology not included within the earlier provisional statements, in particular that the methodology did not include weightings to be given to particular factors and conventions which the independent expert would use to prevent double counting. This would make a difference to the scores. However, the Employment Judge refused to admit the report on the ground that he did not have the power to do so but that he would not have admitted the report, anyway, in the exercise of his discretion. The EAT held that the Employment Judge was wrong to refuse to admit the report and that rule 11(4) envisaged expert evidence but limited its reach. The party expert could not deal with the facts which are not challenged and which represent a sacrosanct position following findings or agreement at an earlier stage in the proceedings. However, the expert could be there to challenge methodology given the restricted scope of challenge to facts. It was noted that the system of job evaluation, for which there is uniquely by statute the designation of an expert, is one which is susceptible to different methodologies and this is what the appointed expert could be challenged upon.

9.65 By rule 11(6) where two or more parties wish to submit expert evidence on a particular issue, the Tribunal may order that the evidence on that issue is to be given by one joint expert only. When such an order has been made, if the parties wishing to instruct the joint expert cannot agree who should be the expert, the Tribunal may select the expert.

Written questions to experts

9.66 Further, by rule 12(1) when any expert (including an independent expert) has prepared a report, a party or any other expert (including an independent expert) involved in the proceedings may put written questions about the report to the expert who has prepared the report.

9.67 By rule 12(2), unless the Tribunal or Employment Judge agrees otherwise, written questions under para (1):

'(a)   may be put once only;
(b)   must be put within 28 days of the date on which the parties were sent the report;
(c)   must be for the purpose only of clarifying the factual basis of the report;
(d)   must be copied to all other parties and experts involved in the proceedings at the same time as they are sent to the expert who prepared the report.'

When written questions have been put to an expert in accordance with para (2) he shall answer those questions within 28 days of receiving them (rule 12(3)). By rule 12(4) an expert's answers to questions put in accordance with para (2) shall be treated as part of the expert's report.

9.68 By rule 12(5) where a party has put a written question in accordance with rule 12 to an expert instructed by another party and the expert does not answer that question, or does not do so within 28 days, the Tribunal may order that the party instructing the expert may not rely on the evidence of that expert.

Procedural matters

9.69 Three sets of procedural rules are made clear by rule 13:

'(1)   In proceedings in which an independent expert has been required to prepare a report, the Secretary shall send him notices and inform him of any hearing, application, order or judgment in those proceedings as if he were a party to those proceedings.
(2)   For the avoidance of doubt, any requirement in this Schedule to hold a stage 1 or a stage 2 equal value hearing does not preclude holding more than one of each of those types of hearing or other hearings from being held in accordance with Schedule 1.

(3)   Any power conferred on a chairman in Schedule 1 may (subject to the provisions of this Schedule) be carried out by a tribunal or a chairman in relation to proceedings to which this Schedule applies.'

National security proceedings

9.70   Rule 14 contains provision for national security in equal pay cases. By rule 14(1) in equal value cases which are also national security proceedings, if a Tribunal has required an independent expert to prepare a report on the question, the independent expert shall send a copy of the report to the Tribunal and shall not send it to the parties. In such proceedings if written questions have been put to the independent expert under rule 12, the independent expert shall send any answers to those questions to the Tribunal and not to the parties.

9.71   It is then provided that before the Secretary sends to the parties a copy of a report or answers which have been sent to him by the independent expert under para (1), he shall follow the procedure set out in rule 10 of Sch 2 as if that rule referred to the independent expert's report or answers (as the case may be) instead of written reasons, except that the independent expert's report or answers shall not be entered on the Register (rule 14(2)). Schedule 2, rule 10 contains procedures to be adopted in national security cases.

9.72   The report or answers will be sent to the relevant Minister under Sch 2. If the Minister does not give a direction under rule 10(3) of Schedule 2 within the period of 28 days from the date on which the Minister was sent the report or answers to written questions the Secretary shall send a copy of the independent expert's report or answers to written questions (as the case may be) to the parties (r 14(3)).

THE PRACTICAL APPROACH: THE STANDARD DIRECTIONS IN THE NORTH EAST CASES

9.73   Employment Tribunals in Newcastle are exercising phenomenal case management powers in light of the many thousands of claims that have been brought in the NHS and in relation to Local Authorities. The NHS cases have spawned a set of directions which have gone through many editions. The latest edition provides a very useful and practical insight as to the approach to take in an equal value claim in the Tribunal. These directions are commended as the ones to consider for anyone who has an equal value claim.

Chapter 10

DISCRIMINATION

10.1 Where a claimant has demonstrated that she is engaged on like work, work related as equivalent or work of equal value the issue then arises of how a breach of the EqPA 1970 will be proven. It has repeatedly been said that the legislation is not aimed at achieving 'fair wages' but at eradicating discrimination in pay and conditions based upon sex. The employer may seek to demonstrate that there is a reason for the pay differential, not based upon sex, which explains and justifies the disparity; the genuine material factor defence. It will be seen that there has been a live issue as to whether the employer is required to show objective justification in all cases when relying upon the material factor defence. The recent cases show that where the pay disparity is not in any way tainted by discrimination it may be sufficient for the employer to provide an explanation for the difference. If the pay disparity is 'tainted' by discrimination, the employer will have to go further and provide objective justification for the difference.

10.2 It will be seen that there has been considerable debate in the cases as to how disparate treatment is to be established under Community law. The aim of Art 141 of the EC Treaty is to eliminate pay practices that have the effect of depressing pay in occupations which are carried out by women. The three limbs required for an equal pay claim, (i) a comparator (ii) engaged in like work/work rated as equivalent/work of equal value (iii) in the same establishment, would, on the face of it, mean that there is a claim for equal pay if these three elements are made out, without the need to show discrimination, so that, subject to the material factor defence, the employee is entitled to equal pay. However, the European Community jurisprudence shows that there is a need, in addition, to show discrimination. In *Jämställdhetsombudsmannen v Örebro Läns Landsting* (Case C-236/98), [2000] IRLR 421, the position was put as follows:

> '. . . in order to establish whether it is contrary to Article 119 of the Treaty and to Directive 75/117 for the midwives to be paid less, the national court must verify whether the statistics available indicate that a considerably higher percentage of women than men work as midwives. If so, there is indirect sex discrimination, unless the measure in point is justified by objective factors unrelated to any discrimination based on.'

10.3 The issue of whether and when it is necessary to demonstrate discrimination is considered in some detail below. It is to be noted, however, that statistics alone may in some cases lead to an inference of discrimination.

10.4 Issues of direct and indirect discrimination, burden of proof and the material factor defence tend to blur and run into each other at this stage. Moreover, the European cases are not always easy to reconcile with the judgments in the UK courts.

10.5 It is necessary to consider:

(1) the approach to be followed once like work, work related as equivalent or work of equal value has been demonstrated and the material factor defences comes into play. The importance of the burden of proof cannot be underestimated here;

(2) the position where there is disparate treatment but no discrimination is alleged or demonstrated. In this case it will be necessary to consider what an employer will need to demonstrate in order to effectively invoke the material factor defence;

(3) the position where direct discrimination is demonstrated. In particular, it is necessary to consider whether the genuine material factor (GMF) defence can be put forward in a case of direct discrimination and, if so, what has to be demonstrated by the employer;

(4) the position where indirect discrimination is alleged:
   (a) the approach under EC law. It will be seen that the European Court of Justice has considered when statistical evidence or lack of transparency may lead to an assumption of indirect discrimination and the scope of the burden of proof on the employer;
   (b) the SDA 1975 and the EqPA 1970. The concept of indirect discrimination is expressly envisaged by the SDA 1975. It is necessary to consider the extent to which it applies under the EqPA 1970 and what needs to be demonstrated;

(5) objective justification and the EqPA 1970, s 1(3). This section will consider, as a matter of general principle, how the material factor defence applies.

THE APPROACH TO BE FOLLOWED ONCE LIKE WORK, WORK RELATED AS EQUIVALENT OR WORK OF EQUAL VALUE HAS BEEN DEMONSTRATED: THE MATERIAL FACTOR DEFENCE AND THE BURDEN OF PROOF

10.6 The components of the material factor defence will be considered in the next chapter. The present consideration is what the employer needs to show where the claimant has proven like work, work related as equivalent or work of equal value in order to defend the case. In these circumstances, the employer will wish to run the s 1(3) defence and argue that the variation between the man's contract and the woman's contract is genuinely due to a material factor that is not the difference of sex. There may be a number of reasons that justify the differential, which are considered in the next chapter, but the questions arise as to how the burden of proof will operate in these circumstances and what, as a matter of law, the employer will have to show to provide justification.

Burden of proof

10.7 It is important to know where the burden of proof lies in discrimination claims, especially given that discrimination is often covert and, in the case of equal pay, the discrimination may have arisen due to historical practices and be demonstrated by statistical evidence as opposed to deliberate acts. Lord Nicholls set out the process by which discrimination must be proven in *Glasgow City Council v Marshall* [2000] 1 WLR 333 as follows:

> 'The scheme of the Act is that a rebuttable presumption of sex discrimination arises once the gender-based comparison shows that a woman, doing like work or work rated as equivalent or work of equal value to that of a man, is being paid or treated less favourably than the man. The variation between her contract and the man's contract is presumed to be due to the difference of sex. The burden passes to the employer to show that the explanation for the variation is not tainted with sex. In order to discharge this burden, the employer must satisfy the tribunal on several matters. First, that the proffered explanation, or reason, is genuine and not a sham or pretence. Second, that the less favourable treatment is due to this reason. The factor relied on must be the cause of the disparity. In this regard, and in this sense, the factor must be a "material" factor, that is, a significant and relevant factor. Third, that the reason is not "the difference of sex". This phrase is apt to embrace any form of sex discrimination, whether direct or indirect. Fourth, that the factor relied upon is or, in a case within section 1(2)(c) may be a "material" difference, that is, a significant and relevant difference between the woman's case and the man's case.
>
> When section 1 is thus analysed, it is apparent that an employer who satisfies the third of these requirements is under no obligation to prove a "good" reason for the pay disparity. In order to fulfil the third requirement, he must prove the absence of sex discrimination direct or indirect. If there is any evidence of sex discrimination, such as evidence that the difference in pay has a disparately adverse impact on women, the employer will be called upon to satisfy the tribunal that the difference in pay is objectively justified. But if the employer proves the absence of sex discrimination he is not obliged to justify the pay disparity.'

10.8 In *Redcar & Cleveland Borough Council v Bainbridge, Surtees v Middlesbrough BC* [2008] EWCA Civ 885, [2008] IRLR 776 Mummery LJ referred to the above and stated:

> 'However, the incidence of the burden of proof is not important in any case where the evidence (from whatever source) enables the tribunal to be (properly) satisfied that the pay differential was or was not caused by indirect sex discrimination.

Burden of proof is only important where the evidence (from whatever source) fails to satisfy the tribunal. Then the result is determined against the party which bore the burden of proof on that issue.'

10.9 In *Nelson v Carillion Services Ltd* [2003] EWCA Civ 544, [2003] IRLR 428 the Court of Appeal stated that the burden of proving that there is disproportionate adverse impact falls upon the claimant. Once the claimant has established a prima facie case the burden shifts to the employer to prove that the difference in pay is not objectively justified. In *Nelson, the* claimant was employed as a steward with her pay being £5 per hour. A man who was taken on after the claimant was paid the same but a man who had been taken on some time before received a higher pay rate plus benefits. The employer argued that the man was paid more because he was employed as a result of a transfer to which the Transfer of Undertakings (Protection of Employment) Regulations 1981, (TUPE) applied and this particular comparator was protected because of the transfer. It was argued by the claimant that there was indirect discrimination since 80% of the men who had remained employed since the transfer had benefited from TUPE compared to 66.6% of women. The pool for comparison consisted of six employees who had originally transferred (four men and two women) plus herself and the man who had been taken on at the same rate. The Tribunal thought that the pool was too small to be meaningful and that the explanation was a GMF which was not in any way tainted with discrimination. The Court of Appeal stated that the Tribunal had been correct in holding that the claimant had to prove that the material factor was tainted by discrimination and rejected the argument that once she had raised a credible suggestion of indirect discrimination the burden then moved. The burden of proving sex discrimination lies initially on the employee (*Enderby v Frenchay Health Authority and Another* [1993] IRLR 591, [1994] ICR 112). A prima facie case must be established to shift that burden.

10.10 The Court of Appeal held in *National Vulcan Engineering Insurance Group Wade* [1978] IRLR 225, ICR 800 that the employer's burden of proving the difference between the man and the woman's case is on a balance of probabilities. The claimant claimed equal pay with a man who was younger and had less service but who was graded higher. Lord Denning stated that, under s 1(3), the burden of proof was on the employer on a balance of probabilities, the burden not being a heavy one.

10.11 The House of Lords in *Rainey v Greater Glasgow Health Board Eastern District* [1987] ICR 129, IRLR 26 did not see a great difference in principle between having to show objectively justified grounds under s 1(3) and justifying a discriminatory requirement or condition under the SDA 1975 (now a provision, criterion or practice – PCP). The claimant had sought to put forward an argument based on the test for showing justifiability in cases of indirect discrimination but Lord Keith stated that there would not appear to be any material distinction so that it was unnecessary to consider the matter further.

10.12   The impact of this statement was considered in *Calder and Another v Rowntree Mackintosh Confectionery Ltd* [1992] ICR 372, [1992] IRLR 165. The claimant was employed on work of equal value. They were paid at the same rate but the comparator received an additional premium of 20% of salary. The claimant brought a claim but did not argue that there was sex discrimination, it expressly being stated that any argument was not founded on indirect discrimination. The respondent argued that the comparator worked a rotating shift which caused inconvenience and justified the shift premium. The claimant argued that the respondent had not justified the whole of the premium and, based on Lord Keith's comments in *Rainey*, it was argued that the employer had to show that the pay differential was objectively justifiable. The Employment Appeal Tribunal held that this argument could not be accepted as the House of Lords in *Rainey* held that, if the material factor had an indirectly discriminatory effect, it would be necessary to show justification but Lord Keith had not stated a principle that the employer must always show objective justification for a variation, even in cases such as *Calder* where direct discrimination was alleged. The *Rainey* case involved indirect discrimination and there was no reason to extend his remarks beyond this. It was stated that the introduction of a requirement for objective justification in cases of direct discrimination would run counter both to existing well-established authority and to the basic scheme of the sex discrimination legislation.

10.13   The difficulties with the burden of proof led to Directive 97/80/EC on the Burden of Proof which seeks to resolve any problem of the shifting burden. The Consolidating Directive (2006/54/EC), in Article 19 sets out provisions with regard to burden of proof as follows:

> '1. Member States shall take such measures as are necessary, in accordance with their national judicial systems, to ensure that, when persons who consider themselves wronged because the principle of equal treatment has not been applied to them establish, before a court or other competent authority, facts from which it may be presumed that there has been direct or indirect discrimination, it shall be for the respondent to prove that there has been no breach of the principle of equal treatment.
>
> 2. Paragraph 1 shall not prevent Member States from introducing rules of evidence which are more favourable to plaintiffs.
>
> 3. Member States need not apply paragraph 1 to proceedings in which it is for the court or competent body to investigate the facts of the case.
>
> 4. Paragraphs 1, 2 and 3 shall also apply to:
>
> (a)   the situations covered by Article 141 of the Treaty and, insofar as discrimination based on sex is concerned, by Directives 92/85/EEC and 96/34/EC;
>
> (b)   any civil or administrative procedure concerning the public or private sector which provides for means of redress under national law pursuant to the measures referred to in (a) with the exception of out-of-court procedures of a voluntary nature or provided for in national law.

5. This Article shall not apply to criminal procedures, unless otherwise provided by the Member States.'

10.14 The Article reverses the burden of proof where facts have been established from which it may be presumed that there has been direct or indirect discrimination. The employer must prove that there has been no discrimination. The Article applies in respect of the equal pay provisions and Art 141. The SDA 1975, s 63A first came into effect on 12 October 2001 and applied the Burden of Proof Directive to cases commenced but not determined at that time. The court considered the reversed burden in *Barton v Investec Henderson Crosthwaite Securities Ltd* [2003] IRLR 332 where the claimant was employed as a media analyst, with her remuneration based upon basic salary, an annual bonus, share options and long-term incentive plans. The bonus was discretionary and not governed by the contract. The claimant brought a claim in 2001 on the ground that a male comparator on 'like work' received a higher salary and higher contractual benefits. She also claimed sex discrimination when the comparator and another colleague received substantially higher bonuses, She had not received a proper reply to her SDA questionnaire. The bank asserted that the comparator's salary had been increased to the highest level possible as he was being headhunted and the Tribunal found that there was a s 1(3) defence. It considered that the increases were 'conscientious, unscientific efforts to secure the employee's services for the future by putting his benefits in line with those of other key players' and were proportionate. The EAT held that the Tribunal had erred in law. The Tribunal had failed to take into account the lack of transparency in the pay system. The Tribunal had failed to take account of the failure to answer the questionnaire and to consider whether there were objective reasons for the difference in pay, whether there was proportionality or any real need for the difference to exist.

10.15 The EAT set out guidance, which was approved and slightly amended by the Court of Appeal in *Igen Ltd v Wong* [2005] EWCA Civ 142, [2005] IRLR 258 as follows:

'(1) Pursuant to section 63A of the SDA, it is for the claimant who complains of sex discrimination to prove on the balance of probabilities facts from which the tribunal could conclude, in the absence of an adequate explanation, that the respondent has committed an act of discrimination against the claimant which is unlawful by virtue of Part II or which by virtue of s 41 or s 42 of the SDA is to be treated as having been committed against the claimant. These are referred to below as "such facts".

(2) If the claimant does not prove such facts he or she will fail.

(3) It is important to bear in mind in deciding whether the claimant has proved such facts that it is unusual to find direct evidence of sex discrimination. Few employers would be prepared to admit such discrimination, even to themselves. In some cases the discrimination will not be an intention but merely based on the assumption that "he or she would not have fitted in".

(4) In deciding whether the claimant has proved such facts, it is important to remember that the outcome at this stage of the analysis by the tribunal will therefore usually depend on what inferences it is proper to draw from the primary facts found by the tribunal.

(5)   It is important to note the word "could" in s 63A(2). At this stage the tribunal does not have to reach a definitive determination that such facts would lead it to the conclusion that there was an act of unlawful discrimination. At this stage a tribunal is looking at the primary facts before it to see what inferences of secondary fact could be drawn from them.

(6)   In considering what inferences or conclusions can be drawn from the primary facts, the tribunal must assume that there is no adequate explanation for those facts.

(7)   These inferences can include, in appropriate cases, any inferences that it is just and equitable to draw in accordance with s 74(2)(b) of the SDA from an evasive or equivocal reply to a questionnaire or any other questions that fall within s 74(2) of the SDA.

(8)   Likewise, the tribunal must decide whether any provision of any relevant code of practice is relevant and if so, take it into account in determining, such facts pursuant to s 56A(10) of the SDA. This means that inferences may also be drawn from any failure to comply with any relevant code of practice.

(9)   Where the claimant has proved facts from which conclusions could be drawn that the respondent has treated the claimant less favourably on the ground of sex, then the burden of proof moves to the respondent.

(10) It is then for the respondent to prove that he did not commit, or as the case may be, is not to be treated as having committed, that act.

(11) To discharge that burden it is necessary for the respondent to prove, on the balance of probabilities, that the treatment was in no sense whatsoever on the grounds of sex, since "no discrimination whatsoever" is compatible with the Burden of Proof Directive.

(12) That requires a tribunal to assess not merely whether the respondent has proved an explanation for the facts from which such inferences can be drawn, but further that it is adequate to discharge the burden of proof on the balance of probabilities that sex was not a ground for the treatment in question.

(13) Since the facts necessary to prove an explanation would normally be in the possession of the respondent, a tribunal would normally expect cogent evidence to discharge that burden of proof. In particular, the tribunal will need to examine carefully explanations for failure to deal with the questionnaire procedure and/or code of practice.'

10.16   The above thought process is the one that should now be followed in considering how to apply the burden of proof. It is important to note that it is necessary for the facts from which discrimination can be inferred to be proven. In the sex discrimination case of *Ms Andrea Madarassy v Nomura International plc* [2007] EWCA Civ 33, [2007] ICR 867, [2007] IRLR 246 the requirement to prove facts from which an inference could be drawn were emphasised by Mummery LJ:

'56.   The court in *Igen v. Wong* expressly rejected the argument that it was sufficient for the complainant simply to prove facts from which the tribunal could conclude that the respondent "could have" committed an unlawful act of discrimination. The bare facts of a difference in status and a difference in treatment only indicate a possibility of discrimination. They are not, without more, sufficient material from which a tribunal "could conclude" that, on the balance of probabilities, the respondent had committed an unlawful act of discrimination.

57.   "Could conclude" in section 63A(2) must mean that "a reasonable tribunal could properly conclude" from all the evidence before it. This would include evidence adduced by the complainant in support of the allegations of sex discrimination, such as evidence of a difference in status, a difference in treatment and the reason for the differential treatment. It would also include evidence adduced by the respondent contesting the complaint. Subject only to the statutory "absence of an adequate explanation" at this stage (which I shall discuss later), the tribunal would need to consider all the evidence relevant to the discrimination complaint; for example, evidence as to whether the act complained of occurred at all; evidence as to the actual comparators relied on by the complainant to prove less favourable treatment; evidence as to whether the comparisons being made by the complainant were of like with like as required by section 5(3) of the 1975 Act; and available evidence of the reasons for the differential treatment.

58.   The absence of an adequate explanation for differential treatment of the complainant is not, however, relevant to whether there is a prima facie case of discrimination by the respondent. The absence of an adequate explanation only becomes relevant if a prima facie case is proved by the complainant. The consideration of the tribunal then moves to the second stage. The burden is on the respondent to prove that he has not committed an act of unlawful discrimination. He may prove this by an adequate non-discriminatory explanation of the treatment of the complainant. If he does not, the tribunal must uphold the discrimination claim.'

See also *Appiah and Another v Bishop Douglass Roman Catholic High School* [2007] IRLR 264, CA and *Brown v Croydon London Borough Council and Another* [2007] EWCA Civ 32, [2007] ICR 909, CA.

The questionnaire procedure

10.17   Tied in with the burden of proof considered in the last section is likely to be the issue of just *how* the claimant can prove her case when the information that is relevant is likely to be in the possession of the employer. It is obvious that it will normally be the employer that has the statistical information and other detail (employees' job descriptions etc) that go to prove disparate treatment. In the context of race and sex discrimination there has, for many years, been a questionnaire procedure which a potential claimant can utilise to ask for information which may go to demonstrate disparate treatment. From 6 April 2003 the employer can serve a questionnaire under the EqPA 1970 Act. A new s 7B was incorporated into the Act by the Equal Pay (Questions and Replies) Order 2003, SI 2003/722.

10.18   Section 7B provides that the Secretary of State may prescribe forms by which the complainant may ask questions with a view to helping a complainant to decide whether to institute proceedings and, if she does so, to formulate and present her case in the most effective manner. The respondent may, if it wishes, reply within 8 weeks of service of the questionnaire. The questions and replies will be admissible in evidence (s 7B(3)).

10.19 By s 7B(4) where the Tribunal considers that the respondent deliberately and without reasonable excuse, within the prescribed period, omitted to reply or the respondent's reply is evasive or equivocal, it may draw any inference which it considers it just and equitable to draw, including an inference that the respondent has contravened a term modified or included by virtue of the complainant's equality clause or corresponding term of service. The section is without prejudice to any other enactment or rule of law regulating interlocutory and preliminary matters in proceedings before an Employment Tribunal. The fact that the time-limits have not been complied with will not automatically mean that an inference will be drawn as in *Steel v Chief Constable of Thames Valley Police* EAT 0793/03 where the reply was 21 months late and some answers were evasive but the Tribunal found that the main issue of comparators was dealt with. For a case where the Tribunal failed to answer the claimant's questions so that an inference was drawn see *Dattani v Chief Constable of West Mercia Police* [2005] IRLR 327.

10.20 The essential point behind the procedure is that it will enable an employee to get details of other persons' pay where she thinks that there is discrimination (the Secretary of State may also serve a questionnaire). However, the procedure may be used to devastating effect by cross-examining the employer about such matters as skill sets, red circling, market forces or the bona fides of a job evaluation scheme. The EOC (now the EHRC) has a set of sample questions on its website (see Appendix 1 which sets out the questionnaire and sample questions and also the questions that are contained in Chapter 11).

10.21 The questionnaire must be served before proceedings are commenced or within 21 days of commencement. By Article 4 of the Equal Pay (Questions and Replies) Order 2003 the employer has 8 weeks to reply to the questionnaire. As noted, inferences may be drawn where the employer does not reply or the response is evasive.

10.22 The employer may take the view that the provision of information may breach the Data Protection Act 1998 (DPA 1998) so that there may be a reasonable excuse not to provide the information, such as where another employee (data subject) objects to the provision of the information. A Tribunal order will get around this difficulty as the employer will then be under a legal obligation to provide the information (DPA 1998, Sch 2, para 3). The Woman and Work Commission recommended in September 2006 that the law be changed to make it clear that the DPA 1998 does not prevent the provision of information under the questionnaire procedure. It may be that this is a matter that will be dealt with in due course in the Equality Bill since the Government has accepted this proposal.

NO DISCRIMINATION ALLEGED OR SHOWN

10.23   In cases where there is a statistical disparity in wages between men and women in the same group this may lead to an inference of indirect discrimination so that objective justification has to be shown. Where, however, no discrimination is alleged or proven it may be enough that the employer can provide a genuine and material reason without having to go on to show that there is objective justification for the reason in the sense enunciated in such decisions as *Bilka-Kaufhaus GmbH v Weber Von Hartz* (see below at **10.28**).

10.24   This is an issue which has been considered in some detail in the cases and, stemming from the House of Lords decision in *Rainey v Greater Glasgow Health Board* [1987] ICR 129, it was at one time thought that objective justification had to be proven whenever the material factor defence was asserted. In order to attract prosthetic fitters from private practice, the NHS in Scotland offered posts to employees from the private sector at their claimant, who had been directly recruited into the NHS and was paid a lower salary, brought an equal pay claim. It was accepted that there was nothing indirectly discriminatory in the decision to pay one group of works, from private practice, more than those directly recruited into the NHS and that men and women were not disproportionately affected. The respondent relied on market forces (see **11.99**) as a material factor defence. The House of Lords held that the material factor defence was made out, Lord Keith stating that the facts relied on by the Board were capable of constituting a relevant difference for the purpose of s 1(3) and 'they were objectively justified'. The impression given by the House of Lords in the case that there is a need for objective justification, even where no discrimination is alleged, whenever the material factor defence is relied on, has however, been shown by later cases to be unfounded.

10.25   That this is not so, has been shown by the House of Lords in *Strathcylde Regional Council v Wallace* [1998] ICR 205, IRLR 146. In this case, un-promoted women teachers were required to perform the duties of a principal teacher without being paid the salary for the post. The claimants sought equal pay with a male comparator who was employed as a principal teacher and paid at that rate. The statistics revealed that the majority of un-promoted teachers carrying out the duties were in fact men. The respondent relied upon budgetary constraints as the reason for the practice. The House of Lords held that the factor was not gender tainted so that it was not necessary for the employer to show that the material factor was 'objectively justified' and the Tribunal had been wrong to hold that it was. Lord Browne Wilkinson stated that:

> '... the only circumstances in which questions of "justification" can arise are those in which the employer is relying on a factor which is sexually discriminatory. There is no question of the employer having to "justify" (in the Bilka sense) all disparities of pay. Provided that there is no element of sexual discrimination, the employer establishes a subsection (3) defence by identifying the factors which he

alleges have caused the disparity, proving that those factors are genuine and proving further that they were causally relevant to the disparity in pay complained of.'

10.26 Where there is a reason for the disparity and no discrimination is alleged this will be sufficient to provide a defence otherwise the EqPA 1970 would be concerned with fair wages as opposed to the elimination of discrimination. The approach adopted in cases such as *National Coal Board v Sherwin* [1978] ICR 700 and *Barber v NCR (Manufacturing) Ltd* [1993] IRLR 95 was decisively rejected. It is only necessary to show that the material factor itself was not based on sex. Where the factor advanced to explain the variation is genuine and is not based on sex the employer will have a defence. Objective justification, as explained at **10.76** is not required. This point received further endorsement from the House of Lords in *Glasgow City Council v Marshall* [2000] ICR 196, [2000] IRLR 272. The claimants were employed as instructors at a special school for children with learning difficulties. The staff at the school included teachers who were professionally qualified and though some instructors were qualified the minimum level for teachers was higher than that for instructors. Teachers were paid considerably more. The reason for the disparity in pay was historical, with the instructors' salary being related to a local authority scale. The Tribunal found that the instructors and teachers were engaged on like work but that the s 1(3) defence did not succeed. The House of Lords noted that the Tribunal had accepted the employer's explanation that the reason for the variation in pay was a purely historical reason not tainted by sex discrimination. Lord Nicholls set out the scheme of the Act and the approach to be taken in such a case:

'I do not believe the EqPA 1970 was intended to have this effect. Nor does the statutory language compel this result. The scheme of the Act is that a rebuttable presumption of sex discrimination arises once the gender-based comparison shows that a woman, doing like work or work rated as equivalent or work of equal value to that of a man, is being paid or treated less favourably than the man. The variation between her contract and the man's contract is presumed to be due to the difference of sex. The burden passes to the employer to show that the explanation for the variation is not tainted with sex. In order to discharge this burden the employer must satisfy the tribunal on several matters. First, that the proffered explanation, or reason, is genuine, and not a sham or pretence. Second, that the less favourable treatment is due to this reason. The factor relied upon must be the cause of the disparity. In this regard, and in this sense, the factor must be a "material" factor, that is, a significant and relevant factor. Third, that the reason is not "the difference of sex". This phrase is apt to embrace any form of sex discrimination, whether direct or indirect. Fourth, that the factor relied upon is or, in a case within S.1(2)(c), may be a "material" difference, that is, a significant and relevant difference, between the woman's case and the man's case.

When S.1 is thus analysed, it is apparent that an employer who satisfies the third of these requirements is under no obligation to prove a "good" reason for the pay disparity. In order to fulfil the third requirement he must prove the absence of sex discrimination, direct or indirect. If there is any evidence of sex discrimination, such as evidence that the difference in pay has a disparately adverse impact on women, the employer will be called upon to satisfy the tribunal that the difference in pay is objectively justifiable. But if the employer proves the absence of sex discrimination he is not obliged to justify the pay disparity.'

10.27 If justification had been in point, ie there had been discrimination, a purely historical explanation would not, of itself have sufficed. The position was different where the absence of sex discrimination was not an issue. A similar approach is to be found in *Tyldesley v TML Plastics Ltd* [1996] ICR 356 at 361–362 (which Lord Nicholls in *Marshall* stated was a clear exposition) and, more recently *Armstrong v Newcastle upon Tyne NHS Hospital Trust* [2005] EWCA Civ 1608, [2006] IRLR 124 (where the Tribunal had erred in finding that a decision to contract out domestic work and not portering was tainted by discrimination and had therefore erred in finding objective justification was necessary).

Is objective justification necessary in all cases where disparate treatment has been shown?

10.28 The House of Lords cases set out the principle clearly. However, some ECJ decisions appeared to suggest that objective justification was necessary for all pay differences. In *Brunnhofer v Bank der österreichischen Postsparkasse AG* [2001] IRLR 571 the employer argued that the comparator received higher pay because he was a better worker than the claimant. The ECJ held that these factors could not have been determined objectively at the time of appointment when the salary was determined. The ECJ, however, suggested that objective justification is necessary in all cases of disparity regardless of whether there is discrimination, stating that European equality law precludes unequal pay as between men and women for the same work or work of equal value, whatever the mechanism which produces such inequality, unless the difference in pay is justified by objective factors unrelated to any discrimination linked to the difference in sex. The EAT, Judge Ansell presiding, in *Sharp v Caledonia Group Services Ltd* [2006] ICR 218, [2006] IRLR 4 held that *Brunnhofer* was authority that there was a need for objective justification in all equal pay cases and that it must be followed.

10.29 Other divisions of the EAT took a different view. In *Parliamentary Commissioner for Administration and Another v Fernandez* [2004] ICR 123, IRLR 22 a majority held that the ECJ was not laying down a principle that where the factor relied upon is not tainted by direct sex discrimination, and where no suggestion of prima facie indirect discrimination is raised, that it is nevertheless necessary for the employer to objectively justify the pay difference, since the ECJ itself stated that the differences in treatment which were prohibited are exclusively those based in the difference in sex of the employees concerned. The Court of Appeal adopted a similar approach in *Armstrong and Others v Newcastle upon Tyne NHS Hospital Trust* [2005] EWCA Civ 1608, [2006] IRLR 124, where Arden LJ stated that, based on *Marshall*, there is no need for an employer to provide justification for a disparity unless the disparity is due to sex discrimination, whilst Buxton LJ was of the view that 'the proper approach to cases of indirect discrimination not only starts but also finishes with the guiding passage of the speech of Lord Nicholls'. *Brunnhofer* and *Fernandez* were not cited.

10.30 In *Villalba v Merrill Lynch and Co Inc and Others* [2006] IRLR 437 the claimant was employed as a market executive. Her employment was terminated in July 2003 and she brought a number of claims, including a claim for equal pay. She compared herself to nine male comparators and argued that her bonus payments were significantly lower. The Tribunal dismissed the equal pay claim. It assessed the explanations given by the employer, including the performance of the claimant and stated that the methods of fixing the bonuses were opaque but the differences were not based on sex. There was no need for the Tribunal to show objective justification. On appeal by the claimant it was argued that the employer had to show objective justification and it was not enough that it had nothing to do with sex. The EAT held that the employer was under no duty to objectively justify the difference in pay as there was no evidence that the difference was directly or indirectly discriminatory. The mere fact that the woman was paid less was not enough to trigger the duty to objectively justify the difference in pay. If it were otherwise the legislation would be concerned with fairness rather than sex discrimination.

10.31 The issue was further considered in *Middlesbrough Borough Council v Surtees* [2007] IRLR 869 in which Elias P resiled from some of the comments that he had made in *Villalba*.

10.32 The case arose out of the single status agreement under which a collective agreement was reached nationally to unify terms and conditions of manual and of administrative, professional, technical and clerical (APTC) workers under one agreement, to be known as the 'Green Book'. Prior to 1997 manual workers were governed by the 'White Book', APTC workers were governed by the 'Purple Book' and craft workers by the 'Red Book'. The Green Book provided for a new job evaluation for all APTC and manual jobs, which were to be at a local level, pending which provisions of the White and Purple Books would remain in force until superseded. A JES in Middlesbrough came into effect on 1 April 2005. An important aspect of these negotiations was the issue of protected pay. Protections were agreed as follows: there was full protection for the first year, but it was reduced to 75% of the difference between old and new pay in the second year, falling to 50% in the third year. In the fourth year the protection only applied to a loss of pay exceeding £2,000 per annum, and thereafter there was no protection at all. That agreement was finally reached in February 2005, less than 2 months before the JES took effect.

10.33 There were a number of equal pay claims which were pending and more were commenced. An issue arose whether the pay protection scheme was discriminatory. An Employment Tribunal found that there was no disparate impact on women in operation of the pay protection itself. The groups eligible for pay protection were those who lost bonuses who were almost exclusively male and those who suffered a loss of pay on evaluation which group was predominately female. The Tribunal took the view that, though proportionately more men benefited, the statistics were not sufficiently detailed to justify the conclusion that there was disparate impact so that there was no need to show the treatment was justified. However, it found that the reason for the difference was so closely related to the sex of the claimants that the presumption of sex discrimination had not been discharged. At that stage, the difference which had to be justified was not extending the pay protection in the scheme to those who, albeit unbeknown to the employer at the time when the scheme was introduced, were in fact also subsequently found to be entitled to equal pay. That group was overwhelmingly female. The Employment Tribunal held that the policy should have been extended to such employees.

10.34 The EAT allowed an appeal, stating that the Employment Tribunal had erred in finding that the pay protection policy should be extended to those women who, after its introduction, were found to have been discriminated against in their pay in relation to the period before the policy was implemented so that the respondent was justified in not extending protection to that group. It stated that proof of a non-sex-based reason will be a complete answer to direct or indirect discrimination. The EAT noted that there had historically been much stereotyping of jobs with assumptions being made about what work was suitable for men and women and what pay was appropriate for these jobs, which had led to much de facto job segregation. It stated that this history continued to leave its mark on pay structures therefore a Tribunal has to be alive to the real possibility of adverse impact identified by sufficiently cogent statistics that may be the result of factors which are sex tainted. The Court of Appeal did not agree with the analysis of the EAT on pay protection. This is considered in more detail at **11.67** onwards. However, on the issue of *when* objective justification is necessary, the judgment of the EAT remains of some importance.

10.35 Elias P noted that the EAT was bound by *Armstrong* though *Enderby* had not been cited in that case. The statement in *Villalba* in that where the arrangements have a sufficiently strong disparate impact there is always an irrebuttable presumption of prima facie indirect sex discrimination, went too far, although in many cases the presumption would be extremely difficult to rebut in practice. The EAT concluded that:

> ' . . . logically it ought in principle to be open to an employer to show that even although there is disparate adverse impact, that it is not in any way related to any act of the employer which is sex tainted, and thereby avoid the need to establish justification.'

10.36 In *Enderby*, the employers demonstrated that the processes of collective bargaining were not sex tainted and yet prima facie discrimination, that is, unlawful discrimination in the absence of objective justification, was held to arise from the statistics alone. Elias P had stated in *Villalba* that *Armstrong* was inconsistent with *Enderby*. In *Surtees* he resiled from this view on the ground that in *Enderby* the independent processes of collective bargaining had led to different terms and conditions and neither process taken independently identified discrimination. However, that did not meet the possibility that with regard to each of the bargaining arrangements there were stereotypical assumptions as to the appropriate pay for what were historically perceived to be male and female jobs. In other words, discrimination had not been ruled out of each independent process of collective bargaining in each case.

10.37   The EAT concluded:

> 'The purpose of the equal pay legislation – both domestic and European – is to eliminate discrimination on grounds of sex. It is not to correct pay differentials for other reasons. If the employer adduces evidence which satisfies the tribunal that the variation in pay is not for sex reasons, that objective has been satisfied and there is no reason in policy or logic for requiring a non-sex based distinction to be objectively justified.'

10.38   It has been noted that the problem with this analysis is that it collapses the distinction between direct and indirect discrimination since indirect discrimination is not based on sex but adverse impact. Once adverse impact is shown then justification should be necessary. The analysis in *Surtees* means that one questions why there is an adverse impact before moving on to justification. The effect of this approach was set out by the EAT:

> ' . . . that proof of a non-sex based reason will be a complete answer to any discrimination claim, direct or indirect.'

In the Court of Appeal, the claimants criticised this approach as putting in an additional hurdle for claimants.

10.39   The EAT did state that Tribunals should be astute to recognise that there has been historical discrimination so that Tribunals must be alive to the very real possibility that where there is adverse impact, identified, where necessary, by sufficiently cogent statistics, this may be the result of factors which are sex tainted.

10.40   Elias P considered the practical significance of this approach:

* First, in all cases of classic examples of indirect discrimination the very criterion which the employer chooses to differentiate pay scales, such as part timers being paid more than full timers, will adversely affect women rather than men. The criterion itself is the factor that causes the disparate impact. The pay arrangements are tainted by sex and justification is necessary.

* Secondly, there will be cases where women claim that the pay arrangements adversely impact as a group but there is no obvious feature which causes the differentiation. It may not be possible to point to a single factor but where the disadvantage, gleaned from statistics is sufficiently striking, it may be justified to draw the inference that the difference in pay

reflects traditional attitudes about what is appropriate male and female work and pay, even though no obvious discriminatory factor is identified. This may include situations where there have been separate negotiating structures, as in *Enderby*. However, the EAT stated that, even then, it may be possible to envisage how the charge of sex discrimination has been discharged:

> 'For example, it may be shown that a particular group of workers (group A) has always been paid less than another group (group B) even although the jobs are of equal value. If both groups were originally predominantly male, but group B has over time become mainly female (such as might well be the case with lawyers or academics, at least in certain fields), a tribunal might readily be satisfied that despite the current adverse effect, there is no proper basis for inferring prima facie discrimination, whether based on historical stereotyping or otherwise. The factors leading to the difference in pay may be long established but the history suggests that they do not have their roots in sex discrimination but have operated independently of the sex of the job holders.'

- The third situation is where the employer identifies a particular and specific factor which causes the difference in pay and which is applied predominately to the male group. The factor does not create two pools but is applied to one of them. In this case it will be sex tainted unless the employer can show that notwithstanding that the factor has been applied so as to benefit only the male group, there are non-discriminatory reasons why that is so. The EAT stated that:

> ' . . . this may involve not merely focusing on why the men receive more but also why similar opportunities to earn the higher pay were not afforded to the women. For example, where the difference results from a bonus arrangement, the employer might show that the bonus scheme was offered to both groups and the predominantly female group chose not to adopt.'

The above three examples show where an employer may be able to defend an equal pay claim without having to show objective justification even though there prima facie appears to be indirect discrimination. The express issues considered in *Surtees* were that of pay protection and the issue of whether employees who had been discriminated against and would have been in the pool of protected employees but for the discrimination was entitled to claim such protection. The EAT also considered the issue of whether there was a valid GMF based upon separate collective bargaining. These matters are considered at **11.65-11.71**. The decision of the EAT that there had not been discrimination with regard to pay protection was reversed by the Court of Appeal.

10.41 The third situation was found to be the position in *Cumbria County Council v Dow (No 1)* [2008] IRLR 91 which, like *Surtees* concerned issues arising out of single status. The claimants comprised 23 different grades within three broad occupational groups which worked in the care sector, in cleaning and in catering. The claimants were almost exclusively female and graded under the White Book. The comparators worked in the direct services organisation, the principle comparators being road workers. The comparators worked in almost exclusively male occupations. Many had been evaluated under the White Book. There were various kinds of special pay, such as incentive bonuses and shift allowances. Where work had been evaluated the claimants asserted that they had been deprived of bonuses made payable to the comparators. In equal value claims it was alleged that there was discrimination with pay and bonuses. The Tribunal rejected the respondent's GMF defence. It accepted that objective justification did not arise if the authority was able to show that the difference in pay was genuinely not due to a difference in sex. It was satisfied that there was disparate impact and was not satisfied that the difference was wholly untainted by sex. It considered that objective justification was not established as the benefit of productivity arrangements was at best tenuous. It considered that similar schemes could have been provided for cleaners and caterers though not carers, when compared with road workers, so that the GMF was made good as regards carers. However, no link between productivity and bonus in relation to other comparators so that the authority could not rely on the GMF defence against the carers with respect to those comparators. The Tribunal also rejected a market force argument.

10.42 On appeal to the EAT it was stated that the case fell into the third category of sex tainting identified in *Surtees (No 1)* in which the employer chose to benefit a predominately male group or groups and did not give that opportunity to a predominately female group. The onus was on the employer to show that it did not reflect sex tainting. Elias P stated that:

> 'The real issue is whether the employer has satisfied the Tribunal that there is no element of traditional stereotyping, either consciously or unconsciously, in the fixing of wages. In our view, the Tribunal was fully entitled to find that the employers have failed to discharge that burden here. We accept that the Tribunal's decision could on one interpretation be taken to be saying that the degree of disparate impact was of itself sufficient to rebut the Council's contention that the productivity payments were paid and applied in a sex free way. That would be wrong; the Tribunal would need to engage with the specific reason put forward as to why that inference was not justified in the particular case, even in circumstances where there was job segregation along traditional sex lines. That fact does not inevitably mean that the particular differential must be sex tainted although in such cases the difficulty of establishing otherwise is a heavy one.'

The Tribunal was entitled, on the evidence to find that the authority had failed to discharge the burden. However, the Tribunal had been wrong in the manner it had reviewed a market forces argument and this issue was remitted to another Tribunal.

10.43 The Tribunal also considered an issue in relation to the removal of enhancements from particular groups of care workers with an improvement in basic pay, but which overall led to a reduction in pay. The deterioration in terms was reluctantly accepted by the Union in a collective agreement. The Employment Tribunal stated that it had concluded that a 'significant factor in this difference in treatment was a perception that female part-time workers would be prepared to agree to a pay reduction to retain a job which was particularly suited or more likely to be suited to their personal circumstances than to a man's, namely working around the requirements of child care. Those considerations did not apply to the male dominated full time jobs because they did not have child care responsibilities and were able to be more flexible in the labour market. There were in this respect close parallels with the facts and conclusions in *Ratcliffe v North Yorkshire County Council*. The EAT held that the Tribunal's decision rejecting the GMF was unsatisfactory. It stated that crucially there was no independent evidence at all that the pay was being reduced to a rate which could properly be described as a women's rate. There was no evidence, or at least none referred to by the Tribunal, as to the sex distribution in the private market at the material time so that it was difficult to avoid the conclusion that the Tribunal simply assumed that the reduction of pay in a predominantly female market necessarily involved adopting a discriminatory rate. This was impermissible.

DIRECT DISCRIMINATION

10.44   Where there is a disparity because of direct discrimination on the part of the employer the issue arises whether the material factor defence can be relied upon at all and, if so, whether objective justification is required. There is no concept of direct and indirect discrimination in the same way as they apply under the SDA 1975 (though the SDA 1975 itself does not use this terminology) and, indeed, in *North Yorkshire CC v Ratcliffe* [1995] ICR 833 and *Strathcylde Regional Council v Wallace* [1998] ICR 205, [1998] IRLR 146 the House of Lords considered that the distinction was largely irrelevant to equal pay, Lord Slynn in the former case stated that it was not helpful to import the distinction, whilst in the latter Lord Browne-Wilkinson thought that a strict demarcation was not necessary though this was not to be taken as meaning that the concept of justification for indirectly discriminatory pay practices could be ignored or eschewed. Lord Browne-Wilkinson stated that:

> '. . . even where the variation is genuinely due to a factor which involves the difference of sex, the employer can still establish a valid defence under subsection (3) if he can justify such differentiation on the grounds of sex, whether the differentiation is direct or indirect. I am not aware as yet of any case in which the European Court of Justice has held that a directly discriminatory practice can be justified in the Bilka sense. However, such a position cannot be ruled out since, in the United States, experience has shown that the hard-and-fast demarcation between direct and indirect discrimination is difficult to maintain.'

10.45   Thus, the House of Lords contemplated that there may be justification even though the employer adopts a policy or practice that deliberately discriminates against one sex. It is difficult to see how this can be squared with the wording of s 1(3) which refers to a material factor 'which is not a difference of sex'. The remarks in *Wallace* run counter to the statements of the House of Lords in *Ratcliffe and Others v North Yorkshire County Council* [1995] IRLR

439. The Council reduced the pay of its almost exclusively catering staff in order to compete during a competitive tendering exercise. A majority of the Tribunal stated that the wages were low in the catering industry where the employees were largely women because of 'the general perception in the United Kingdom, and certainly in North Yorkshire, that a woman should stay at home to look after the children and if she wants to work it must fit in with that domestic duty and a lack of facilities to enable her, easily, to do otherwise'. The House of Lords held that the reduction of the women's wages below men rated as equivalent was the very type of discrimination that the Act was aimed at. The women could not have found other suitable work and were obliged to take the wages offered if they were to continue with this work. Lord Slynn noted:

> 'The fact is that the employers re-engaged the women at rates of pay less than those received by their male comparators and no material difference other than the difference of sex has been found to exist between the case of the women and their male comparators.'

Although it is dubious whether the discrimination in this case was truly direct, since if a man had been employed in the same job as the women his salary would have been decreased, it is apparent from the case that it will be very difficult for any employer to run a material factor defence which is based on disparity due to sex.

10.46 The Consolidating Directive distinguishes between direct and indirect discrimination and defines the concepts (see **2.27;** and see *Redcar* at **11.71** where Mummery LJ took the view that direct discrimination could not be justified).

INDIRECT DISCRIMINATION

10.47 Since the equal pay legislation is aimed at pay systems that have an adverse effect on women the concept of indirect discrimination fits well into the scheme of equal pay. Practices, criteria or provisions which have the effect that women are paid less than men for like work, work rated as equivalent or work of equal value call out for a justification from the employer as to why the situation has arisen. The EqPA 1970 does not, unlike the SDA 1975, differentiate between direct and indirect discrimination, though the Consolidating Directive does so. One has to look to the jurisprudence to see the approach that has been taken by the courts.

10.48 Indeed, the courts have questioned the value of the distinction between direct and indirect discrimination in the equal pay context and have also disapproved adopting the same formulaic approach as the SDA 1975 (see *Armstrong* at **10.71**). Nevertheless, the concept of indirect discrimination is of importance in the equal pay field, as unintentional practices etc which lead to pay disparities are precisely the type of factual situation that the Act was intended to grapple with. Since the EqPA 1970 does not contain the same formula as the SDA 1975, the question arises as to what is the correct test for a finding that there has been indirect discrimination. It will be seen that the ECJ has adopted a rather different approach under Art 141 which is, on one view, less restrictive.

The approach under EC law

10.49 The Burden of Proof Directive contained a definition of indirect discrimination which is now in the Consolidating Directive and Article 2 provides:

> '"indirect discrimination": where an apparently neutral provision, criterion or practice would put persons of one sex at a particular disadvantage compared with persons of the other sex, unless that provision, criterion or practice is objectively justified by a legitimate aim, and the means of achieving that aim are appropriate and necessary.'

10.50 The EqPA 1970 is to be read in a way that gives effect to the European jurisprudence. It was made clear in *Bilka-Kaufhaus v Karin Weber von Hartz* [1986] IRLR 317, [1987] ICR 110 that Art 119 (now Art 141), applied to indirect pay discrimination. The employer's occupational pension scheme excluded part-time workers unless they had worked full time for at least 15 years out of a total of 20 years. The claimant had worked full time from 1961 to 1972 but from then until 1976 had worked part time. She was refused a pension and challenged the legality of this in the German Federal Labour Court which referred the following questions to the ECJ:

> '1. May there be an infringement of Article 119 of the EEC Treaty in the form of "indirect discrimination" where a department store which employs predominantly women excludes part-time employees from benefits under its occupational pension scheme although such exclusion affects disproportionately more women than men?
>
> 2. If so:
>
> (a) Can the undertaking justify that disadvantage on the ground that its objective is to employ as few part-time workers as possible even though in the department store sector there are no reasons of commercial expediency which necessitate such a staff policy?
> (b) Is the undertaking under a duty to structure its pension scheme in such a way that appropriate account is taken of the special difficulties experienced by employees with family commitments in fulfilling the requirements for an occupational pension?'

The ECJ ruled:

> '1. Article 119 of the EEC Treaty is infringed by a department store company which excludes part-time employees from its occupational pension scheme, where that exclusion affects a far greater number of women than men, unless the

undertaking shows that the exclusion is based on objectively justified factors unrelated to any discrimination on grounds of sex.

2. Under Article 119 a department store company may justify the adoption of a pay policy excluding part-time workers, irrespective of their sex, from its occupational pension scheme on the ground that it seeks to employ as few part-time workers as possible, where it is found that the means chosen for achieving that objective correspond to a real need on the part of the undertaking, are appropriate with a view to achieving the objective in question and are necessary to that end.

3. Article 119 does not have the effect of requiring an employer to organise its occupational pension scheme in such a manner as to take into account the particular difficulties faced by persons with family responsibilities in meeting the conditions for entitlement to such a pension.'

On the issue of 'pay' see **6.26-6.39** and for 'part time work' see Chapter 14. The case confirms that Art 141 applies to indirect pay discrimination and, though the phrase was not used in the judgment, it has been used in many subsequent cases (see the cases on part time workers at **14.12** onwards).

10.51   In *Paterson v London Borough of Islington* UKEAT/0347/03/DA, Rimer J held that objective justification was necessary only where there was a prima facie case of indirect discrimination. The EAT held that something in the nature of a provision, criterion or practice was necessary and the operation of a bonus scheme in that case did not amount to a practice. The explanation was not related to a sex difference so that objective justification was not necessary.

Assumption of indirect discrimination

10.52   The ECJ held that a prima facie case of discrimination will be established where valid statistics reveal a disparity in pay between two jobs of equal value in circumstances where the lower paid group is almost exclusively women and the higher paid group is predominately men in *Enderby v (1) Frenchay HA (2) Secretary of State for Health* [1993] IRLR 591, [1994] ICR 112. Senior speech therapists in the NHS claimed that they were employed on work of equal value with male senior pharmacist and clinical psychologists (see under 'Material factor, Market Forces' at **11.100** for the statement of facts which was referred to the ECJ). The ECJ stated that it is normally for the person alleging facts in support of a claim to adduce proof of the facts so that in this case the burden of proving sex discrimination lies with the worker, however:

' . . . it is clear from the case law of the Court that the onus may shift when that is necessary to avoid depriving workers who appear to be the victims of discrimination of any effective means of enforcing the principle of equal pay. Accordingly, when a measure distinguishing between employees on the basis of their hours of work has in practice an adverse impact on substantially more members of one or other sex, that measure must be regarded as contrary to the objective pursued by Article 119 of the Treaty, unless the employer shows that it is based on objectively justified factors unrelated to any discrimination on grounds of sex (judgments in Case 170/84 *Bilka-Kaufhaus* [1986] IRLR 317, at paragraph 31; Case C-33/89 *Kowalska* [1990] IRLR 447, at paragraph 16; and Case C184/89 *Nimz* [1991] IRLR 222, at paragraph 15). Similarly, where an undertaking applies a system of pay which is wholly lacking in transparency, it is for the employer to prove that his practice in the matter of wages is not discriminatory, if a female worker establishes, in relation to a relatively large number of employees, that the average pay for women is less than that for men (judgment in Case 109/88 *Danfoss* [1989] IRLR 532, at paragraph 16).'

10.53 There may be an *assumption* of discrimination where the figures warrant it; in this case the speech therapists were 'almost exclusively women' whilst the pharmacists were 'predominately men' so that there was a prima facie case of sex discrimination. The ECJ noted that it was for the national court to assess whether it may take into account the statistics, that is, whether they covered enough individuals, whether they illustrated purely fortuitous or short-term phenomena and whether they appeared to be significant. In other words, it is for the national court to interpret the raw data, including consideration of whether they illustrated purely fortuitous or short-tem phenomena and whether they appeared to be significant. Such prima facie evidence of discrimination will mean that the employer will have to show that there are objective reasons for the difference in pay. The ECJ therefore stated that:

' . . . where significant statistics disclose an appreciable difference in pay between two jobs of equal value, one of which is carried out almost exclusively by women and the other predominantly by men, Article 119 of the Treaty requires the employer to show that that difference is based on objectively justified factors unrelated to any discrimination on grounds of sex.'

10.54 The ECJ further considered the circumstances in which a disparity may raise a prima facie case of indirect discrimination in *Specialarbejderforbundet i Danmark v Dansk Industri, acting for Royal Copenhagen A/S* (Case C-400/93) [1995] IRLR 648; [1996] ICR 51 in which it was said that:

' . . . the national court must satisfy itself that the two groups each encompass all the workers who, taking account of a set of factors such as the nature of the work, the training requirements and the working conditions, can be considered to be in a comparable situation and that they cover a relatively large number of workers ensuring that the differences are not due to purely fortuitous or short-term factors or to differences in the individual output of the workers concerned.'

A comparison cannot be made by forming groups in an arbitrary manner to achieve the result that one comprises predominantly women and the other predominantly men with a view to carrying out successive comparisons and thereby bringing the pay of the group consisting predominantly of women to the level of that of another group also formed in an arbitrary manner but which consists predominately of men.

10.55 The circumstances in which indirect discrimination has been assumed by the ECJ involve cases where the work carried out by the female is done almost exclusively by women. The practical effect of the above two cases was considered in *British Road Services Ltd v Loughran and Others* [1997] IRLR 92 by the Northern Ireland Court of Appeal, in which there were separate pay structures, relating to the claimant clerical officers and the comparator, warehouse operatives, based on different collective bargaining agreements. The women comprised a significant proportion (75%) of the group claiming equal pay. The employer argued that the *Enderby* case meant that the claimant group had to be almost exclusively female. This was rejected by a majority of the Northern Ireland Court of Appeal who stated that, in using the phrase 'almost exclusively' the ECJ had been referring to the factual situation before them where 98% were female. It was not intended to lay down a principle that the presumption did not arise unless the group was almost exclusively female. If the female group is sufficiently representative to identify it as a female group that will be sufficient. The Court of Appeal reversed the Tribunal's decision that a history of separate pay structures without more provided justification. A group of 75% females and 25% males was sufficiently representative to provide a reliable indication of unequal treatment.

Transparency

10.56 Another line of ECJ cases consider whether there may be a presumption of discrimination where there is a lack of transparency in the employer's pay structures. In *Handels og Kontorfunktionaerernes Forbund i Danmark v Dansk Arbejdsgiverforening (acting for Danfoss)* [1989] IRLR 532, [1991] ICR 74 the Clerical Union brought a claim on behalf of two members. The claimants were subject to a collective agreement under which pay depended on grades and job classification; employers could increase employees' wages based on a number of factors including seniority, vocational training and flexibility. The statistical evidence over a 4-year period relating to 157 employees showed women were paid on average 6.85% less than men in the same grades. It was contended that this was sufficient to show discrimination. The employer argued that the burden of proof should not shift because of this statistical evidence and it was for the claimants to show that the disparity was due to discrimination. The ECJ was asked 'who has the burden of showing that the difference in pay is or is not due to considerations related to sex'.

10.57 The employees were only informed of the amount of their increased wages, without being able to establish the effect each of the criteria for the increases has had. Those who fell into a particular pay grade were, therefore, unable to compare the different components of their pay with those of the pay of their fellow workers who are part of the same grade. The ECJ stated that:

> ' . . . the Equal Pay Directive must be interpreted as meaning that, where an undertaking applies a pay system which is characterised by a total lack of transparency, the burden of proof is on the employer to show that his pay practice

is not discriminatory, if a female worker establishes that, by comparison with a relatively high number of employees, the average pay of female workers is lower than that of male workers.'

In such a case it will be necessary for the employer to show objective justification.

10.58 It is important to note that the mechanisms for deciding the individual increases were applied in such a way that a female worker was not able to identify the reasons for the difference in pay between her and a male worker carrying out the same work. The workers did not actually know the criteria for the increases which were applied to them and how they were applied. They were only informed of the amount of their increased wages, without being able to establish the effect each of the criteria for the increases has had. The workers who fell into a particular pay grade were, therefore, unable to compare the different components of their pay with those of the pay of their fellow workers who were part of the same grade. It was this total lack of transparency which meant that the employer had the burden of proof to show that the pay practice was not discriminatory if it was shown, by statistics with a relatively high number of employees that the average pay of female workers was lower than that of female workers.

10.59 The important implication of the case is its requirement for the reasons for direct or indirect differential treatment to be made overt. It also makes it clear that *statistical evidence* is sufficient to place the duty of explanation on the employer.

Statistics

10.60 It is apparent from *Enderby* that the employer can be required to show objective justification for a difference in pay where there is no evidence that any disparity has been brought about intentionally if the statistics show an appreciable difference in the two jobs of equal value, where one is carried out almost exclusively by women and the other predominately by men. In *Tyne and Wear PTE v Best* [2007] ICR 523, HHJ Serota in the EAT stated that statistical arguments based on small numbers should not be taken as indicative of indirect discrimination (and see similar sentiments in *Paterson v London Borough of Islington* UKEAT/034/03/DA). The issue, then, arises as to the statistical threshold for proving indirect discrimination based upon statistics.

10.61 This statistical approach to establishing a presumption of indirect discrimination was considered by the ECJ in *R v Employment Secretary ex p Seymour Smith* [1999] IRLR 253. The ECJ stated at para 60 of its judgment that:

'... it must be ascertained whether the statistics available indicate that a considerably smaller percentage of women than men is able to satisfy the condition of two years' employment required by the disputed rule. That situation would be evidence of apparent sex discrimination unless the disputed rule were justified by objective factors unrelated to any discrimination based on sex.'

Further:

> '... if the statistical evidence revealed a lesser but persistent and relatively constant disparity over a long period between men and women who satisfy the requirement of two years' employment. It would, however, be for the national court to determine the conclusions to be drawn from such statistics.'

10.62 The ECJ noted in both *Enderby* and *Seymour-Smith* that it is for the national court to decide whether the statistics are valid, taking into account whether they cover enough individuals, whether they illustrate purely fortuitous or short-term phenomena, and whether, in general, they appear to be significant. In *Seymour-Smith*, for example, the ECJ stated (at paras 62–63) that it was for the national court to decide whether the 1985 statistics concerning the respective percentages of men and women fulfilling the requirement of 2 years' employment under the disputed rule were relevant and sufficient for the purposes of resolving the case before it. The ECJ, however, noted that, in 1985, 77.4% of men and 68.9% of women fulfilled the condition of 2 years' employment and thought that such statistics did not, on the face of it, appear to show that a considerably smaller percentage of women than men were able to fulfil the disputed requirement.

10.63 The two ECJ cases left a number of issues either uncertain or unanswered.

(1) In *Enderby* the ECJ differentiated between a group of employees who were almost exclusively female compared with a group which was predominantly male, whilst in *Seymour-Smith* the focus was on statistical percentages. It is necessary to consider the degree of disparity that may give rise to an inference of indirect discrimination.

(2) In making the comparison there may be an issue as to whether the Tribunal should look at statistics concerning the advantaged or disadvantaged group.

(3) The pools for comparison will need to be drawn up and there is likely to be an issue as to how wide the pool should be drawn. In particular, the question may arise whether the pool should cover the workforce or be more widely drawn.

10.64 In *Home Office v Bailey* [2005] EWCA Civ 327, [2005] IRLR 369 it was held that there was a need for objective justification where the comparator groups were predominately male whilst the claimant group was equally male and female. Over 2,000 administrative, executive, secretarial and support staff in the prison service brought a claim comparing their pay to grades that were predominately occupied by men. Claimants who were Higher Executive Officers were paid less than the grades of governor 4 and 5 and principal officer even though it was accepted that a prison service job evaluation had rated the jobs as equivalent. It was argued by the employer that the differences were due to separate pay bargaining arrangements for the two groups that had operated for many years which amounted to a GMF. The Tribunal considered whether the employer had to objectively justify the difference in pay because there was evidence of indirect discrimination or whether it was only necessary to show that the difference in pay bargaining arrangements *was the cause of the difference.*

10.65 The Tribunal applied *R v Secretary of State for Employment ex p Seymour-Smith and Another.* It found that there was a condition or requirement that to obtain the advantages of the comparator group one had to belong to that group. The disadvantaged group consisted of men and women in approximately equal numbers and the comparator group was predominately male. The proportion of disadvantaged women was considerably greater than that of disadvantaged men. It concluded that there was prima facie evidence of indirect discrimination. The EAT held that the requirement or condition was wholly artificial and that there was a difference between a requirement or condition which presented a barrier to becoming a member of a group and considering whether a disparity of pay which has arisen for historical reasons evidences sex discrimination. In the former case it was sensible to compare the extent to which men and women across a pool could satisfy the requirement to become a member of the group and to measure disparate impact in this way. In the latter case the approach, as in *Enderby*, was to consider if the advantaged group was predominately male and the disadvantaged predominately female, so that there could be a prima facie case of discrimination. However, the EAT thought that if the advantaged group was predominately male but the disadvantaged group *not* predominately female it was not possible to say that there was prima facie discrimination.

10.66 On appeal to the Court of Appeal it was held that the Tribunal had not erred in finding a prima facie case of discrimination. The EAT had not erred in rejecting the requirement or condition argument that to obtain the advantages of the comparator group it was necessary to belong to the group as this was a circular argument. However, the Tribunal had been entitled to refer to the statistical evidence and conclude that there was a prima facie case of indirect discrimination *notwithstanding that the composition of the disadvantaged group was gender neutral.* The ECJ did not purport to exhaustively define the only circumstances in which a prima facie case of discrimination could be established in *Enderby*. According to *Enderby*, a prima facie case of discrimination is established if valid statistics show an appreciable difference in pay between two jobs of equal value, one of which is carried out almost exclusively by women and the other predominantly by men.

10.67 However, the statistical approach in *Seymour-Smith* can apply in cases where there is no requirement but there is a pay disparity between two groups. The national court has to verify whether the statistics indicate that a considerably smaller percentage of women than men are able to fulfil the requirement. If the Tribunal is satisfied as to the validity and appropriateness of the statistics it can use the statistical approach to determine whether there is a prima facie case of discrimination. Lord Justice Peter Gibson stated:

> 'Usually the disparity of pay between two work groups will reflect the fact that they do different work, and there may well be features of the work of the advantaged group which could be elevated to a requirement or condition. For example, where the disadvantaged group works in ordinary office or shop hours and the advantaged group does shifts or unsocial hours, it might be said that there was a requirement or condition for entry into the advantaged group of availability to work shifts or unsocial hours.'

The Court of Appeal stated that it could not be correct that a case could lead to a prima facie finding of discrimination, on the *Seymour-Smith* approach, where there was a requirement or condition whereas if the case involved disparity of pay it would be necessary that the disadvantaged group was predominantly of one gender and the advantaged group predominantly of the other.

10.68 The court in *Seymour-Smith* were of the view that it was for the national court to consider what statistics were appropriate, provided that the differences between the statistics were valid and significant. In *Rutherford v Secretary of State for Trade and Industry (No 2)* [2004] IRLR 892 the upper age limit for claiming unfair dismissal was in issue and the Court of Appeal considered the statistic issue. Mummery LJ stated that in assessing the disparate adverse impact of the upper age limit on male and female employees, the Tribunal should have defined the relevant pool by reference to the entire workforce to which the requirement of being under 65 applies, including those who were not adversely affected by the upper age limit because they are able to comply with the requirement at the relevant time (the advantaged group), rather than referring only to those who were disadvantaged by the upper age limit. It should then have compared the respective proportions of men and women who could satisfy that requirement rather than referring only to those who were disadvantaged by the upper age limit. The proportions of men and women who could qualify for statutory unfair dismissal and redundancy rights and who satisfied the test of being under the age of 65 (98.88% of men and 99.0% of women in 2001) clearly and unequivocally showed that there was no disparate impact.

10.69 The House of Lords upheld the Court of Appeal judgment though on different grounds. The pool for the purposes of comparison was all employed persons still in the workforce at 65. The House of Lords disagreed with the approach of the Court of Appeal which placed emphasis on the statistics for those who *could* comply with the preconditions for having rights to unfair dismissal compensation and redundancy pay. Since the statutory bar applied to everyone over age 65 and could apply to nobody under that age, the Burden of Proof Directive, 97/80/EC's requirement that it disadvantaged a higher proportion of the members of one sex than of the other was not satisfied. There were no proportions to compare as the rule applied to the same proportion of women over age 65 as it applied to men. Lord Walker, who gave the fullest speech, advocated an *advantage*-led approach though noting that there may be some cases where an approach which considered the disadvantaged pool may be more appropriate.

10.70 The issue of whether the advantaged or disadvantaged group should be focused upon was considered in *Grundy v British Airways plc* [2008] IRLR 74. Mrs Grundy had been employed full time as cabin crew (CC) but, in 1987, took employment as support cabin crew (SCC). A new collective agreement provided that SCC worked between 15 and 20 days in a 28-day period. This was the only way that SCC could work until 1994 when recruitment of SCC was halted and crew were offered the option of working percentage hours or full time. Mrs Grundy opted for a 75% contract. Full-time CC received increments and from 1994 so did part-time CC but Mrs Grundy had received no such increments so that she was earning nearly £4,000 less than a man doing like work who had benefited as CC from increments. The Employment Tribunal adjusted her pay to the top of the CC scale, holding that there had been a policy, criterion or practice which was to the detriment of a considerably larger proportion of women than men and was not justified. The statistics shows that the ratio of women to men in CC was constant at about 2:1 throughout these years, the female to male ratio in SCC averaged almost 18:1 and at its lowest was 14:1. In other words, anything which impacted adversely on SCC was going to hurt a far larger proportion of women than if it were to impact on CC. But because of the relative size of the two groups, it was going to hurt far fewer women in absolute numbers: in 1994, 471 as against 6,273; in 1998, 99 as against 8,501; in 2002, 42 as against 8,592. The disadvantaged female to male ratio within the total CC workforce moved accordingly in these years from above 9:1 to 7:1; but the advantaged ratio remained almost constant, at marginally (1:1.07) above and latterly at 1:1. Everything therefore depended on where the Employment Tribunal decided to focus its analysis.

10.71 It was held by the EAT that the Employment Tribunal had erred by focusing on the small disadvantaged SCC group rather than the advantaged CC group. If there had been focus on the latter there would have been no disparate impact. On appeal to the Court of Appeal it was held that the EAT erred in holding that the Tribunal had erred by focusing on the small disadvantaged group. The correct principle is that the pool must be one which suitably tests the particular discrimination complained of but there is not always a single suitable pool. As stated by Cox J in *Ministry of Defence v Armstrong* [2004] IRLR 672 the question is whether there is a causative link between the claimant's sex and the fact that she is paid less than the true value of her job as reflected in the pay of her named comparator. The pool chosen by the Employment Tribunal was permissible as it identified a cohort within which the defence could be objectively tested. Sedley LJ stated:

> 'The dilemma for fact-finding tribunals is that they can neither select a pool to give a desired result, nor be bound always to take the widest or narrowest available pool, yet have no principle which tells them what is a legally correct or defensible

pool . . . In discrimination claims the key determinant of both elements is the issue which the claimant has elected to pose and which the tribunal is therefore required to evaluate by finding a pool in which the specificity of the allegation can be realistically tested. Provided it tests the allegation in a suitable pool, the tribunal cannot be said to have erred in law even if a different pool, with a different outcome, could equally legitimately have been chosen. We do not accept that *Rutherford* is authority for the routine selection of the widest possible pool; nor therefore that any question arises of "looking at" a smaller pool for some unspecified purpose short of determining the case.'

The Court of Appeal held that the Tribunal had been right to look at all staff, both disadvantaged and advantaged, but to concentrate, in deciding disparate impact, on the disadvantaged group.

10.72 The Court of Appeal in *Armstrong v Newcastle Upon Tyne NHS Hospital Trust* [2005] EWCA Civ 1608, [2006] IRLR 124 endorsed the view of the Court of Appeal in *Rutherford* that there has to be evidence that the Tribunal has applied 'logic, relevance and common sense' in analysing the statistics. There was no evidence in the particular case that it deployed these considerations. Buxton LJ stated:

'The EAT did not directly confront this problem, but in its paragraph 38 it referred to the disparities between men and women identified in the speech of Lord Nicholls in *Seymour-Smith*, and concluded that the employment tribunal "was entitled to come to conclusions that it did based on the applicants' statistical evidence, showing greater and more persistent disparity than in the *Seymour-Smith* case". But the percentages in *Seymour-Smith* were based on the whole of the British workforce. It cannot be enough, in applying the approach required by *Rutherford*, to take the raw numbers extracted from the context of that case and apply them without more, as some sort of guideline or bench-mark, to reach conclusions that relate only to a limited number of workers in a particular employment. It may be that further exploration of the latter issue would lead to a conclusion that the employment tribunal's finding, however inadequately reasoned and expressed, could be supported; and that in that process the outcome in *Seymour-Smith* was of potential relevance even if it could not be determinative. But, as it stands, the EAT's analysis does not respect the need to assess disparate adverse impact separately from case to case, as this court required in *Rutherford*.'

10.73 It is clear that disparate impact needs to be assessed separately from case to case and the appropriateness of the pool for the particular case needs to be carefully considered. Buxton LJ stated that it is not enough to take the raw numbers extracted from the context of that case and apply them without more, as some sort of guideline or benchmark, to reach conclusions that relate only to a limited number of workers in a particular employment. Thus the pools may be drawn up to cover:

• the workforce as a whole (cf *Price v Civil Service Commission* [1978] ICR 27);

- those qualified for the particular position, ie those qualified for civil service employment (cf Sedley LJ's comments in *Grundy*);

- the particular workforce.

See further the decision of HHJ McMullen QC in *Pike v Somerset County Council* UKEAT/0046/08/ZT in which the test in *Rutherford (No 2)* was considered. An average of 42.45% of the disadvantaged pool in this case were men and an average proportion of 57.55% were women, a disparity of roughly 15%. The EAT, agreeing with the Employment Judge's tentative view, held the claimant had shown disparate impact.

10.74 It will be important to consider whether the groups selected have been drawn up in an artificial or arbitrary manner, such as in *Cheshire & Wirral Partnership NHS Trust v Abbott* [2006] EWCA Civ 523, [2006] IRLR 546 where the wrong groups were used, as ancillary workers, who received a bonus, had not been included. Otherwise the group had been domestics, mainly female, who were excluded and porters, male, who received a bonus. Keane LJ stated that:

> 'As a matter of statistics, a more reliable result is likely to be forthcoming if one takes as large a group as possible, so long as that group shares the relevant characteristics and can be seen as doing work of equal value. It does not appear to have been suggested in the present case that the caterers did not qualify on those grounds.'

SDA 1975 and EqPA 1970

10.75 As noted above, in *North Yorkshire CC v Ratcliffe* [1995] ICR 833 the House of Lords stated that it was neither right nor helpful when interpreting the EqPA 1970 to import concepts of direct and indirect discrimination, but in *Strathcylde Regional Council v Wallace* [1998] ICR 205, [1998] IRLR 146 it resiled from this position, though noting that there is no need to apply the hard and fast distinction between direct and indirect discrimination to be found under the SDA 1975. Whilst the approach may have a difference in emphasis under the two Acts it is clear that indirect discrimination is firmly within the ambit of the EqPA 1970. The test stated by Lord Nicholls in *Glasgow City Council v Marshall* [2000] IRLR 272 (see **10.7**) perhaps still remains the best starting point in this respect. Further, the consolidation of the Equal Pay Directive and the Equal Treatment Directive confirms that indirect discrimination is firmly within the ambit of equal pay.

OBJECTIVE JUSTIFICATION AND S 1(3)

10.76 This section considers the standard to be applied where the s 1(3) defence is engaged. The text has already considered the circumstances when the need for objective justification arises at **10.28** There may be no need to consider the s 1(3) defence where the claimant does not succeed in showing that there was direct or indirect discrimination. If the employee has not demonstrated that she has been treated in a manner which shows that discrimination has occurred this may be the end of the matter. In *Barry v Midland Bank plc* [1999] ICR 859, [1999] IRLR 581 it was held by the House of Lords that there was no discrimination where payment under a contractual redundancy scheme was based on the hours worked at the time of dismissal. The Tribunal found that the objectives of Midland Bank's scheme were to compensate for loss of the job and for loyalty to the bank. Length of service and loyalty to the bank, which the former denotes, was an element of the scheme and this increases in importance as length of service increases. The Tribunal also found that 'a scheme which fails to take into account, to a significant extent, the full service of an employee does not meet the objectives of the scheme' so that there was discrimination. Lord Slynn stated:

'. . . the bank's scheme is lawful. Its objects are of sufficient importance to override the weight to be given to the fact that under a different scheme with a different object a group of employees, mostly women, would be better off. To decide otherwise would be to compel Midland Bank to abandon its scheme and substitute a scheme where severance pay is treated and calculated, not as compensation for loss of a job, but as additional pay for past work.'

Barry v Midland Bank plc was applied in *Trustees of Uppingham School Retirement Benefit Scheme for Non-Teaching Staff v Shillcock* [2002] EWHC 641 (Ch), [2002] 2 CMLR 1029.

10.77 In *Bilka-Kaufhaus GmbH v Weber von Hartz* the employer's case was that the exclusion of part-time workers was intended to discourage part-time work, since part-time workers generally refused to work in the late afternoon or on Saturday. The ECJ held that it was for the national court to determine whether and to what extent the ground put forward by the employer might be regarded as an objectively justified economic ground. The court stated:

'If the national court finds that the measures chosen by Bilka correspond to a *real need* on the part of the undertaking, are appropriate with a view to achieving the objectives pursued and are *necessary* to that end, the fact that the measures affect a far greater number of women than men is not sufficient to show that they constitute an infringement of Article 119 [now Art 141].' (emphasis added)

Where the practice is indirectly discriminatory the employer will need to show that the discrimination is objectively justified, according to *Bilka-Kaufhaus*: that the means chosen for achieving that objective correspond to a real need on the part of the undertaking, are appropriate with a view to achieving the objective in question and are necessary to that end. The House of Lords applied the *Bilka-Kaufhaus* test in *Rainey v Greater Glasgow Health Board* [1987] ICR 129 to s 1(3).

10.78 We have seen above at **10.56–10.73** that the courts have considered when there is a need to show objective justification, based upon statistical evidence, lack of transparency or where it is not shown that the reason for discrimination is non-sex-based. Recently in *Voss v Land Berlin* (Case C-300/06) [2007] All ER (D) 87 (Dec) at paras 27 and 28 the test was succinctly stated:

> '27. ...it is necessary initially to determine, first, whether that legislation establishes a difference in treatment between part-time workers and full-time workers, and, secondly, whether that difference in treatment affects a considerably higher number of women than men.
> 28. If there is an affirmative answer to those two questions, it must be asked whether there are objective factors wholly unrelated to sex discrimination which can justify the difference in treatment found.'

10.79 It was stated in *Voss* that:

> 'If the statistics available indicate that, of the workforce, the percentage of part-time workers who are women is considerably higher than the percentage of part-time workers who are men, it will be necessary to hold that such a situation is evidence of apparent sex discrimination, unless the legislation at issue in the main proceedings is justified by objective factors *wholly unrelated to any discrimination based on sex.*' (emphasis added)

See also *Jämställdhetsombudsmannen v Örebro Läns Landsting* (Case C-236/98) [2000] IRLR 421.

10.80 The Court of Appeal considered the justification issue in *British Airways plc v Grundy* [2008] EWCA Civ 875, the second appeal in the case to go to the Court of Appeal. It held that justification was not made out even though the position had been achieved by collective bargaining. The Court of Appeal stated:

> ' . . . one of the important messages sent out by the Equal Pay Act has been that attention must be paid by negotiators to the possibility that such differentials will have a disparate impact on employees of one gender. If this is overlooked, with a consequent breach of one group's equality clauses, the oversight cannot logically be justified by reference to the agreement which resulted.'

The fact that the employer has not applied its mind at the time may make it more difficult to justify the position after the event.

10.81 It may be that in the case of indirectly discriminatory *legislation* the test for objective justification is not as stringent. In *Rinner-Kühn v FWW Spezial-Gebäudereinigung GmbH & Co KG* (Case C-171/88), [1989] IRLR 493 the ECJ applied the *Bilka-Kaufhaus* test to indirectly discriminatory employment legislation. The ECJ considered German social security law in which individuals who worked less than 15 hours per week and whose income did not exceed one-seventh of the monthly reference wage were termed 'minor' or 'marginal' workers and were not subject to old age, sickness and invalidity benefit schemes in the two cases of *Inge Nolte v Landesversicherungsanstalt Hannover (Social policy)* (Case C-317/93) (14 December 1995) and *Megner* (Case C-444/93). They did not have to pay contributions as the Government took the view that compulsory payments would lead to avoidance techniques and an increase in unlawful employment. The ECJ stated that:

> 'It should be noted that the social and employment policy aim relied on by the German Government is objectively unrelated to any discrimination on grounds of sex and that, in exercising its competence, the national legislature **was reasonably entitled** to consider that the legislation in question was necessary in order to achieve that aim.' (emphasis added)

10.82 The introduction of the reasonableness test would appear to dilute the *Bilka-Kaufhaus* necessity test (see also *C B Laperre v Bestuurscommissie beroepszaken in de provincie Zuid-Holland (Social policy)* (Case C-8/94) (8 February 1996) and *Posthuma-van Damme v Bestuur van de Bedrijfsvereniging voor Detailhandel (Social policy)* (Case C-343/92) (1 February 1996)). In *R v Secretary of State for Employment ex parte Seymour-Smith* (Case C-167/97) [1999] ECR I-623, [1999] IRLR 253, the dichotomy between the two lines was considered and the ECJ stated at para 77 that:

> '... if a considerably smaller percentage of women than men is capable of fulfilling the requirement of two years' employment imposed by the disputed rule, it is for the Member State, as the author of the allegedly discriminatory rule, to show that the said rule reflects a legitimate aim of its social policy, that that aim is unrelated to any discrimination based on sex, and that it could **reasonably consider** that the means chosen were suitable for attaining that aim.' (emphasis added)

Thus it would appear that there may be a 'sliding scale' of tests depending upon the nature of the alleged discriminatory treatment which is being justified.

Proportionality

10.83 Where objective justification has to be proved the court will apply principles of proportionality as set out in *Hampson v Department of Education and Science* [1990] 2 All ER 513, [1989] IRLR 69, [1989] ICR 179. In *Barry v Midland Bank plc* [1999] IRLR 581 Lord Nicholls explained proportionality as meaning that:

> '... the ground relied upon as justification must be of sufficient importance for the national court to regard this as overriding the disparate impact of the difference in treatment, either in whole or in part. The more serious the disparate impact on women, or men as the case may be, the more cogent must be the objective justification. There seem to be no particular criteria to which the national court should have regard when assessing the weight of the justification relied upon.'

10.84 It was noted in *Seymour-Smith* that mere generalisations will not be sufficient to show that the measures were proportionate; in that case 'generalisations concerning the capacity of a specific measure to encourage recruitment [were] not enough to show that the aim of the disputed rule is unrelated to any discrimination based on sex nor to provide evidence on the basis of which it could reasonably be considered that the means chosen were suitable for achieving that aim' (see also *Steinicke v Bundesanstalt fur Arbeit* (Case C-77/02) [2003] IRLR 892).

10.85 In considering specific defences that have been argued under s 1(3) as set out in the next chapter, the above general principles are to be borne in mind.

Chapter 11

THE MATERIAL FACTOR DEFENCE

11.1 Where the claimant has shown 'like work', 'work rated as equivalent' or 'work of equal value' there will be a presumption that the equality clause applies. The equality clause will then operate to place the claimant in the same position as the comparator unless the material factor defence applies. The EqPA 1970, s 1(3) provides:

> 'An equality clause falling within subsection 2(a), (b) or (c) above shall not operate in relation to a variation between the woman's contract and the man's contract if the employer proves that the variation is genuinely due to a material factor which is not the difference of sex and that factor—
>
> (a) in the case of an equality clause falling within subsection (2) (a) or (b) above, must be a material difference between the woman's case and the man's; and
>
> (b) in the case of an equality clause falling within subsection (2)(c) above, may be such a material difference.'

11.2 It is at the defence stage that the Tribunal will expressly consider whether the pay differentials are due to any reason of sex. The defence will be raised in 'like work' and 'work rated as equivalent' claims at the stage when the claimant has proven her case. With 'work of equal value' cases the issue may be raised at the initial hearing when the Tribunal is considering whether to refer to an independent expert (and this may be a matter of tactics; see Chapter 9) or after the expert has reported.

11.3 It was stated in *Capper Pass Ltd v Lawton* [1976] IRLR 366, [1977] ICR 83 that:

> 'Section 1(3) has nothing to do with the question whether a woman is employed on like work with a man, and confusion seems to have been caused in some of the cases cited to us by assuming that it has. Subsection (3) is concerned with the operation of an equality clause which, apart from the provisions of the subsection, would apply. For example, suppose a man and a woman to be engaged on like work but the man to be paid a higher rate than the woman. Despite the application of the equality clause in such a situation, it is not to operate if the variation in remuneration is genuinely due to a material difference (other than the difference of sex) between her and him.'

11.4 Where the employer can show that the claim has nothing to do with sex then the claim will fail regardless of the fairness of the position (*Chief Constable of W Midlands Police v Blackburn* UKEAT/007/07; and see the Court of Appeal judgment *Blackburn v Chief Constable of the West Midlands*

[2008] EWCA Civ 1208, which considered the issue of justification as deciding the case). The Act only seeks to eliminate discrimination and not to establish fairness in pay. Where the material factor relied upon is tainted we have seen in Chapter 10 that it is necessary to provide 'objective justification' for the difference. There are a large number of factors that an employer may seek to put forward as an explanation for the differential.

11.5 It is to be noted that s 1(3)(a) and (b) import different approaches as the factor *must* be a material difference with regard to 'like work' and 'work rated as equivalent' whilst it *may* be such a difference with regard to 'work of equal value'. It is questionable whether the different wording is necessary. Section 1(3)(b) was intended to reverse the ruling in *Clay Cross (Quarry Services) Ltd v Fletcher* [1978] IRLR 361, [1979] ICR 1. The Court of Appeal had stated that, when applying s 1(3) to like work or work rated as equivalent the Tribunal should have regard to personal circumstances and regard should not be had in this context to any extrinsic forces which have led to the man being paid more. When the right to equal pay for work of equal value was introduced in 1984 the altered wording of the statutory defence in s 1(3)(b) was intended to make clear that an employer could rely on extrinsic factors such as market forces. Subsequently, in *Rainey v Greater Glasgow Health Board* [1987] IRLR 26, ICR 129 the House of Lords held that the restriction in *Clay Cross* of the defence to personal circumstances was too restrictive. The House of Lords considered whether market forces could be used as a defence in a 'like work' case and held that it could. Thus, the wording remains in s 1(3)(a) and (b) but, for all practical purposes, make no difference.

11.6 In *Armstrong v Newcastle Upon Tyne NHS Hospital Trust* [2005] EWCA Civ 1608, [2006] IRLR 124, Arden LJ summarised the law as follows at para 32:

'I have set out in paragraph 17 above the well-known passage from the speech of Lord Nicholls in the *Marshall* case. (The remainder of the House agreed with his speech.) That passage sets out a step by step guide to proving a genuine material factor defence. For the purposes of this appeal, the steps can be summarised as follows:

(1)   the complainant must produce a gender-based comparison showing that women doing like work, or work rated as equivalent or work of equal value to that of men, are being paid or treated less favourably than men. If the complainant can produce a gender-based comparison of this kind, a rebuttable presumption of sex discrimination arises.

(2)   the employer must then show that the variation between the woman's contract and the man's contract is not tainted with sex, that is, that it is genuinely due to a material factor which is not the difference of sex. To do this, the employer must show each of the following matters:

(a)   that the explanation for the variation is genuine,

(b)   that the more favourable treatment of the man is due to that reason, and

(c)   that the reason is not the difference of sex.

(3)   if, but only if, the employer cannot show that the reason was not due to the difference of sex, he must show objective justification for the disparity between the woman's contract and the man's contract.'

TIME AT WHICH TO HEAR GENUINE MATERIAL FACTOR (GMF) DEFENCE

11.7   Under the equal value procedure the Tribunal will consider whether to hear the GMF defence before the issue of equal value is decided (see **9.33**).

11.8   In *Sunderland City Council v Mrs Brennan and Others, UNISON GMB* UKEAT/0219/08 the Employment Appeal Tribunal (EAT) considered whether a Tribunal should hear GMF defences in relation to two periods, pre- and post-October 2005, in respect of which there were different defences. A hearing was ordered with regard to both periods on the basis that the jobs were of equal value or had been rated as equivalent under a job evaluation scheme (JES). The lawyers for the claimants subsequently stated that they wished to amend to challenge the validity of the JES. The employer sought to have the application stayed until the amendment was determined but the Employment Tribunal decided to adjourn the issue of amendment until the hearing of the GMF defence. On appeal it was held that the Employment Tribunal was entitled to hold that the hearing would continue with the pre-October 2005 GMF as it would remain in issue whatever the outcome of the JES challenge. However, the Employment Tribunal erred in deciding that the post-October 2005 GMF should also be determined. The EAT noted that the claimants were not prepared to accept if the GMF defences failed they would not pursue the challenge to the JES so that the outcome of the GMF defences might be wholly irrelevant to the case being advanced. As Elias J noted:

> 'The real concern, in my judgment, is the potentially damaging effect on the proceedings if the GMF defence is heard first. The result may be that the GMF defence post-October fails. The claimants whose jobs are rated as equivalent in a valid JES will then have succeeded in their claims, albeit not to the same extent as if they had made a successful equal value claim with respect to a higher paid comparator. If the attack on the JES were then made and succeeded, it would defeat their claims. Moreover, given the nature of the challenge, it is possible that the challenge would succeed in part only, in which event some claimants would have their claims defeated and some would not . . . I do not think that it is justified to allow the claimants to keep this amendment in their back pocket and perhaps not to press it if their cases are successful. Logically, the challenge should be considered before the GMF defence and in my judgment it is unfair to the other parties not to deal with the issues in that order. There is nothing intrinsically unjust in the claimants running both horses; but if they do so then the Tribunal should determine the JES challenge before dealing with the GMF defence. If the JES challenge succeeds then it may remove the need for any further post-October GMF hearing at all.'

11.9   The following should be considered in relation to the s 1(3) defence:

(1)   the factors which may be considered under the defence;

(2)   justifying the defence;

(3)   the burden and standard of proof;

(4)   the meaning of 'genuine';

(5)   the meaning of 'material'; and

(6)   A to Z of specific factors that may amount to a defence.

The factors which may be considered under the defence

11.10 In considering the three heads of claim – like work, work rated as equivalent and work of equal value – factors may be put forward to assert that the claimant is not entitled to equal pay with the comparator. Where the Tribunal rejects these factors and holds that the claimant is entitled to claim equal pay, it is possible for the employer to rely upon any such factors for the purpose of the s 1(3) defence (*Davies v McCartneys* [1989] IRLR 439; *Christie v John E Haith Ltd* [2003] IRLR 670).

Justifying the defence

11.11 The issue is whether the employer is required to simply provide an explanation for the differential, which is not related to a difference of sex, or to go further and provide objective justification for the factor that is used to explain the differential. The case-law has been considered in some detail in Chapter 10 and the position may be summarised as follows:

(a)   Where there is no allegation of discrimination in relation to the differential, it should not be necessary to show objective justification provided that it is shown that the factor is genuine and is not tainted by discrimination.

(b)   We have seen in Chapter 10 where the material factor is based upon direct discrimination it is unlikely that it can be justified under s 1(3) (see the discussion at **10.44**) but, if there is any such possibility (because of the dicta of Lord Browne-Wilkinson in *Strathclyde*) then objective justification would need to be shown.

(c)   In cases where there is indirect discrimination it will be necessary to show objective justification as outlined at **10.47** et seq.

11.12 The issue, then, arises as to what factors may provide objective justification and these are considered under the A to Z categories below.

The burden and standard of proof

11.13   This is considered in detail at **10.7** et seq. Given that the claimant has proven like work, work rated as equivalent or work of equal value the burden will move on to the respondent to show the material factor defence whether in respect of direct or indirect discrimination. As stated by Lord Browne-Wilkinson in *Strathclyde Regional Council v Wallace* [1998] IRLR 146:

> 'The correct position under s 1(3) of the Equal Pay Act 1970 is that even where the variation is genuinely due to a factor which involves the difference of sex, the employer can establish a valid defence under subsection (3) if he can justify such differentiation on the grounds of sex, whether the differentiation is direct or indirect. I am not aware as yet of any case in which the European Court of Justice has held that a directly discriminatory practice can be justified in the Bilka case. However, such a position cannot be ruled out since, in the United States, experience has shown that the hard and fast demarcation between direct and indirect discrimination is difficult to maintain.'

The meaning of 'genuine'

11.14   It is necessary to show that the differential is 'genuinely' due to a factor that is material and not the difference of sex. The Tribunal will have to find that the reason or factor which is put forward is the genuine reason for the difference. The factor must not be a sham or pretence (see *Strathclyde Regional Council v Wallace* [1998] ICR 205). It is important that the reason is not simply a cloak or disguise for discrimination and, to some extent, the requirement that the factor be material ties in with genuineness. In *Shield v E Coomes (Holdings) Ltd* [1978] IRLR 263, in which it was argued that men were paid more for working as counter clerks in troublesome branches (see **7.10**), it was held that the differential was not due to a GMF as the employer had not considered any personal attributes. A male employee may have been more timid than a female employee so that it could not be said that the differential was 'genuinely' due to the personal attributes of the comparator.

11.15   The requirement for the factor to be genuine is illustrated by *Hawker Fusegear Ltd v Allen* EAT/794/94 in which it was argued that the comparator's qualifications, calibre and potential to be 'an asset for the Company' for the future constituted a good defence under s 1(3). The Tribunal had found as a fact that the comparator had not been employed to do anything different from what his female predecessor had done and she had been paid the same as the claimant. The employer had been impressed by the comparator's qualifications but this did not in any way relate to the job and so could not be a genuine factor.

The meaning of 'material'

11.16   A factor may be material even though it docs not have any bearing on the actual work that is carried out. Thus the parties may be carrying out like work but there may still be a material factor defence which has nothing to do with the work such as market forces. Care must, however, be taken that this does not simply disguise discrimination. In *Murray v Lothian Council* EAT/530/76 a male schoolteacher who worked as a counsellor complained he was paid £642 per annum less than a female comparator because she had an honours degree and he had an ordinary degree. The claim was rejected on the basis that the parties were employed on like terms but the Tribunal also stated that there was no material difference because an honours degree or an ordinary degree had no bearing on the actual work carried out. The EAT overruled the judgment on both grounds, but dismissed the appeal as the onus on the employer under s 1(3) had been satisfied. The EAT stated that:

> 'The question is whether the variation is due to a material difference other than sex. This can be due to length of service (Capper Pass Ltd v JB Lawton 1976 IRLR 366). It can be due to differences in custom between one place of employment and another (NAAFI v Varley EAT 20 October 1976). In our opinion it can very clearly be due to a difference in academic qualification. The tribunal have held that this can be a material difference but it must be relevant to the like work which is being performed. This is contrary to what was said by Phillips J in Capper Pass Ltd v Lawton where he points out in terms that section 1(3) has nothing to do with the question of like work. The reason for the variation must not, of course, be capricious. If so it is neither genuine nor material.'

11.17   The meaning of the word 'material' was considered in *Rainey v Greater Glasgow Health Board* [1987] ICR 129. The NHS in Glasgow offered employment at the same salary to 'private' prosthetic fitters though directly employed fitters (not coming in from private practice) were paid at Whitley Council rates. The latter claimed equal pay with a private, male, fitter. The House of Lords held that a difference will be material if it is 'significant and relevant'. These factors go beyond personal factors and will cover extrinsic factors such as market forces, economic considerations and administrative efficiency. Where arguments based upon factors such as 'market forces' are put forward the Tribunal should examine such arguments carefully in order to ensure that they are not being used to mask discrimination. The factor must explain the reason for the difference between the claimant and the comparator. Where there is no assertion that the factor is tainted by discrimination the employer will not have to objectively justify it in order for there to be a finding that the factor is material (see *Strathclyde Regional Council v Wallace and Others* [1998] ICR 205 and the cases in Chapter 10).

Number of factors

11.18   There may be a number of factors which the employer wishes to rely on as genuine material factors and there is no reason why there should be any limitation, as was made clear in *Davies v McCartneys* [1989] IRLR 439. Where there are several factors it will be necessary to identify which factor or factors justify any differential between the claimant and comparator. This was considered in *Calder v Rowntree Mackintosh Confectionery Ltd* [1993] ICR 811, a case in which it was conceded that the work carried out was of equal value.

The employees worked on a rotating shift basis. The claimant worked part time from Monday to Friday, 5.30 pm to 10.30 pm, the twilight shift. The comparator worked on a full-time rotating 2-week cycle of one week from 8 am to 4 pm and the next week from 4 pm to midnight. In addition to his basic salary he received a shift premium of one-fifth of his salary to reflect the inconvenience caused to him as a result of having to work rotating shifts. Women on the twilight shift did not receive the premium, although women who were employed on rotating shifts received the same rate of pay as the men. The Tribunal decided that the company had established a s 1(3) defence. In the Court of Appeal, Evans LJ stated:

'Had the tribunal found that the variation in pay was due to two factors, the inconvenience of the rotating shift and the unsocial hours, both of which were material, then the applicant's case might have succeeded. But what the tribunal in fact found was that, though the unsocial hours were an element in the premium, the inconvenience of the rotating shift was the sole direct or effective cause of the payment of the premium and thus of the variation of pay. This was a conclusion which the tribunal were entitled to reach on the facts of the case.'

11.19 Kennedy and Balcombe LJJ, however, thought that if there was a combination of factors that had been taken into account and only one of the factors was relevant this did not mean that a claimant would necessarily succeed. Balcombe LJ stated:

'Even if the industrial tribunal had found that the material factor was the combination of the rotating shift and unsocial hours, it does not necessarily follow that someone who could show that one only of these factors was relevant to her case was entitled to the operation of an equality clause. In the course of his submissions on behalf of the employer, Mr Elias suggested the case of employers who agreed to pay a bonus to all their employees who were aged and infirm. Could it seriously be suggested, he asked, that the bonus had to be divided into two parts: one for age and the other for infirmity, and that other (female) employees who were young but infirm, or old but healthy, could claim to have the operation of an equality clause which entitled them to the relevant part of the bonus, to be calculated presumably, although on what basis is not clear, by the industrial tribunal? This example is not too far removed from the facts of Methven v Cow Industrial Polymers Ltd, where a similar argument by female employees was rejected by this court.'

11.20 It may be that it would be necessary to apportion where there are several factors at play. However, a claimant is not entitled to claim equal pay on the basis that she should be paid a proportion of the comparator's salary based on respective values. If this is the position then the woman's work cannot fall within one of the heads of claim. Once 'like work', 'work rated as equivalent' or 'work of equal value' has been shown the employer is liable to the extent that it cannot defend the whole of the pay differential based upon a material factor other than sex. If the factor accounts for some but not all of the differential this will not be enough unless the precise differential can be calculated. This was made clear in *Enderby v (1) Frenchay HA (2) Sec of State for Health* [1993] IRLR 591, [1994] ICR 112 in which the ECJ stated that:

'If, as the question referred seems to suggest, the national court has been able to determine precisely what proportion of the increase in pay is attributable to market forces, it must necessarily accept that the pay differential is objectively justified to the extent of that proportion. When national authorities have to apply Community law, they must apply the principle of proportionality.

If that is not the case, it is for the national court to assess whether the role of market forces in determining the rate of pay was sufficiently significant to provide objective justification for part or all of the difference.'

11.21 It may be that the employer will need to set out the precise proportions of salary that are attributable to a specific factor if the defence is to succeed. The employee should therefore be entitled to details of such percentages (but cf *Byrne and Others v Financial Times Ltd* [1991] IRLR 417).

A to Z of genuine material factors: personal (employee factors)

11.22 This section considers the types of GMF defences that may be run and which have been considered in the very voluminous case-law on this topic. As noted at **10.17-10.22** the claimant may want to interrogate the employer as to the reasons why a particular pay structure etc has been adopted and to probe the validity of any alleged GMF via the questionnaire procedure. Equally, the employer should 'stand back' and ask whether the reasons put forward really do have validity. At the end of each GMF, where appropriate, I have therefore set out a series of questions that the claimant or employer may want to ask as a checklist to whether the GMF may be a good reason. These questions may be incorporated into the questionnaire procedure. It is suggested that the starting point would be the following questions which would then be asked in the context of the specific questions tailored to each GMF:

- Provide a breakdown of the workforce/department by reference to sex, stating the number of men and women and in relation to each employee – the salaries and other benefits, the job title/grade of each employee, the length of service.

- State whether it is accepted that the claimant is carrying out like work or work of equal value with certain grades.

- If there is a differential in pay, identify what is said to be the reason that the claimant was paid less than other employees.

- What criteria were applied which are said to be unrelated to sex?

11.23 A set of questions may be asked in relation to each GMF to tease out how the decision to use the specific factor in deciding the level of pay that was awarded (who, why, when, what):

- Who actually decided to use the criteria of (length of service, experience, etc) to fix salary or benefits?

- Why was this criteria adopted as opposed to some other criteria that would not have a disparate impact upon women?

- When was this decision reached and, in the case of a decision that was historical, has it been reviewed from time to time – if so by whom, etc?

- What was the benefit to the employer in adopting this criteria as opposed to some other criteria and, where there is disparate impact? Consider the *Bilka* questions at **11.24**.

11.24 It should be noted that, where it is alleged that there is prima facie discrimination and the employer is relying on the *Bilka*-type arguments, the following questions may be legitimate:

- What is the specific GMF relied upon as the objective reason for the difference in pay?

- In what way is it alleged that the reasons were objective differences unrelated to sex?

- How did the reason for the differential pay correspond to a real need on the part of the business?

- Did the employer consider whether there were any alternative approaches which would not have led to the disparity in pay?

The above set of questions may be considered for each of the GMFs that follow.

Age

11.25 Any pay and benefits based upon age alone are likely to amount to direct discrimination so that the Employment Equality (Age) Regulations 2006, SI 2006/1031 will apply. Experience may be used as a synonym for age, as to which see **2.54** It is to be noted that the courts have been fairly relaxed about accepting seniority as an acceptable factor, as to which see **11.80**.

Questions

- Is seniority and length of service used as a factor in deciding the level of pay and benefits?

- Why has this criteria been adopted?

- Does seniority and length of service tie in with experience thus justifying higher pay and benefits the longer the length of service?

- Is there a point in time when the employee has gained all the experience that he or she can so length of service thereafter makes no difference?

- Has the employer considered the impact of the Employment Equality (Age) Regulations 2006?

- Consider the *Bilka*-type questions above.

Demotion but salary preserved

11.26 See under 'Red circling' at **11.44** et seq.

Experience

11.27 Experience may either consist of familiarity with the specific position over a period of time, which may be equated with seniority or length of service, or know-how acquired during the course of one's working life. A grading system may be based upon experience in the job. It was stated in *ARW Transformers Ltd v Cupples* [1977] IRLR 228 that employers will rarely be able to rely on additional experience as constituting a material difference without leading evidence. The claimant and comparator were employed on like work but the man who was aged 53 was paid £60 per week compared with the claimant who was paid £40.75 and was aged 27. The comparator had greater experience of being a study work engineer though he had been employed later. The Tribunal held that the greater experience did not amount to a material difference as it was not a significant factor in the work. The EAT held that s 1(3) was not concerned with the nature of the work so that the Tribunal's reasoning was flawed but the Tribunal was correct in finding that the employers had provided no evidence to establish that the difference in pay was genuinely due to a material difference other than sex.

11.28 The case may be contrasted with *Baker and Others v Rochdale Health Authority* (unreported) 14 January 1994, CA, in which a male nurse's special expertise with regard to male catheterisation was a material factor other than sex, though this experience had only been gained as a result of a gender-based policy that only male workers could undertake male catheterisation. The comparator's expertise had become such that he trained other nurses. Farquharson LJ stated that:

> 'It is true that his ability to train became available because of his experience in fitting male catheters, but the industrial tribunal were entitled to find that this function was independent and that he should be additionally rewarded for it.'

Questions

- How did the employer decide to reward its employees based upon experience?

- Are the employees carrying out different job functions based upon experience?

- What criteria is actually adopted in deciding 'experience'; is it based on mere length of service or is there some other criteria which relates to the requirements of the job?

- Is there a point in time when an employee becomes 'fully experienced'? If so what is it and what happens to pay and other benefits at that point?

- Has the claimant had an opportunity to gain experience if this involves carrying out particular tasks/courses etc?

- What does the 'experience' bring to the job which merits a greater salary?

Hours of work

11.29 The House of Lords considered whether a difference in hours and holidays could amount to a GMF in *Leverton v Clwyd County Council* [1989] IRLR 28, [1989] ICR 33. The claimant, a qualified school nursery nurse, claimed her work was of equal value with one or more of 11 higher paid comparators. The employees were employed under the conditions of service of the NJC for Local Authorities' Administrative, Professional, Technical and Clerical Services (the 'Purple Book'), which set out various pay scales. The claimant worked 32.5 hours and had 70 days holiday a year whilst her comparators worked 37 or 39 hours and had 20 days holiday plus increments. It was argued that the differences defeated the claims. In the House of Lords it was held that where the regular working hours were translated into a notional hourly rate which yielded no significant differences it was a legitimate, if not necessary inference that the difference in salary was due to and justified by the hours worked in the course of the year and was nothing to do with sex. The House of Lords effectively endorsed a 'notional calculation' approach to determining whether or not pay differentials were genuinely due to differences in hours or holiday entitlement. Lord Bridge stated:

> 'I should conclude that this was a finding of fact which was amply justified by the evidence as a whole, but perhaps particularly by the comparison between the rates of pay and hours worked. Where a woman's and a man's regular annual working hours, unaffected by any significant additional hours of work, can be translated into a notional hourly rate which yields no significant difference, it is surely a legitimate, if not a necessary, inference that the difference in their annual salaries is both due to and justified by the difference in the hours they work in the course of a year and has nothing to do with the difference in sex.'

Incentive bonus

11.30 Productivity arrangements may provide a GMF where an incentive bonus is paid in order to increase productivity. However, where the bonus has become wholly unrelated to any genuine productivity benefits to the employer then the reason may have disappeared so that the employer cannot rely on this as a GMF (See *Redcar & Cleveland Borough Council v Bainbridge and Others* [2007] IRLR 91).

- Give precise details of how the productivity bonus is worked out setting out the genuine productivity benefits which it is alleged to relate to.

- Set out why the claimant did not receive the same productivity bonus as the comparators.

Location

11.31 Where the male comparator is paid a different rate because he is in a different geographical location this may be a material difference. In *Navy, Army and Air Forces Institutes v Varley* [1976] IRLR 408, [1977] ICR 11 the claimant, who was based in Nottingham, worked a 37-hour week compared to a male comparator in London who worked 36.5 hours. A Tribunal upheld her claim that the contract should be amended to bring it into line with the London terms. The EAT held that the difference was due to a geographical difference in conditions between those working inside and outside of London which existed for historical reasons which the EAT did not consider that it needed to go into. The s 1(3) defence was established.

Mistake

11.32 A mistake of fact may be put forward as a defence (*Yorkshire Blood Transfusion Service v Plaskitt* [1994] ICR 74 – employee mistakenly put on wrong salary grade). However, once the mistake is discovered it will not be possible to objectively justify the lower pay and it does not matter that there is no intention to discriminate (*McPherson v Rathgael Centre for Children and Young People and Northern Ireland Office (Training Schools Branch)* [1991] IRLR 206).

Motherhood

11.33 The Tribunal in *Coyne v Exports Credits Guarantee Department* [1981] IRLR 51 held that motherhood was not a material difference other than sex and less favourable treatment because of motherhood is sex discrimination. See also *Dekker v Stichting Vormingscentrum voor Jong Volwassenen (VJV-Centrum) Plus* (Case C-177/88) [1991] IRLR 27.

Overtime

11.34 See **11.37** for a consideration of this issue.

Part-time work

11.35 The position of part-time workers has received considerable attention in recent years culminating in the Part Time Workers (Prevention of Less Favourable Treatment) Regulations 2000, SI 2000/1551 (see Chapter 14). In the context of equal pay, a pay differential that treats part-time women (or has that indirectly discriminatory effect) less favourably will have to be justified under s 1(3). An intention to discourage part-time work by discriminating against part timers will not be justified as stated in *Jenkins v Kingsgate (Clothing Productions) Ltd (No 2)* [1981] IRLR 388, ICR 715. Further:

> 'Even if the employers had no such intention, for s 1(3) to apply the employer must show that the difference in pay between full-time and part-time workers is reasonably necessary in order to obtain some result (other than cheap female labour) which the employer desires for economic or other reasons.'

Cases such as *Kearns v Trust House Forte Catering Ltd* EAT/782/77 and *Durrant v North Yorkshire Health Authority* [1979] IRLR 401 in which part-time work was viewed as a different type of job cannot stand in light of *Jenkins*.

11.36 In *Handley v H Mono Limited* [1978] IRLR 534, [1979] ICR 147 part-time workers were paid less than full-time workers, the part-time workers becoming entitled to overtime pay earlier than full time. Two-thirds of the workforce were men and all worked full time. It was held that the claimant's contribution to production was different as her use of equipment was less and she was entitled to overtime pay earlier so that there was a material difference. Women who worked full time were treated the same as men who worked full time so that it was clear that the difference was not based on sex (though there was a slight differential). The problem with this case is that it is not clear how the 6 pence difference in pay was equated to a difference in productivity.

11.37 Although in *Handley* overtime was paid where work had been carried out in excess of the normal overtime hours, there is nothing to prevent the employer paying overtime only when the full-time hours have been reached. In *Stadt Lengerich v Helmig* [1996] ICR 35 the ECJ held that a collective agreement could exclude overtime supplements for part-time work where work had not been carried out in excess of full-time hours. There would be discrimination if the overall treatment of full-time workers was more beneficial than that of part-time employees. The assertion of indirect discrimination was made out:

> 'The principle of equal pay excludes not only the application of provisions leading to direct sex discrimination, but also the application of provisions which maintain different treatment between men and women at work as a result of criteria not based on sex where those differences of treatment are not attributable to objective factors unrelated to sex discrimination' (*Stadt Lengerich v Helmig* [1995] IRLR 216 at para 20)

11.38   Where the employer pays increments based upon length of service or seniority this may have an effect on part-time employees. In *Gerster v Freistaat Bayern* [1998] ICR 327 part-time employees' salary was calculated on a pro rata basis with full-time employees, based upon hours worked. Promotion was based upon pro rata length of service. Although the ECJ held that the claim did not fall within the equal pay provisions but the Equal Treatment Directive, it held that the provisions were indirectly discriminatory unless the employer could justify them on an objective basis.

Questions

•   Does the employer pay its part-time workers on a pro rata basis?

•   Does the employer exclude employees from any benefits/scheme because the employee works on a part-time basis?

•   If it is asserted that part timers are paid less because they are more expensive administratively or do not contribute, pro rata, as much financially, provide a complete breakdown of the figures.

Pay system

11.39   It is clear from *Handels-OG Kontorfunktionaerernes Forbund i Danmark v Dansk Arbejdsgiverforening* (Case C-109/88) [1989] IRLR 532 that, under Art 141, a pay scheme cannot be relied upon where the average pay of women is lower and the system is not transparent. The employer will need to demonstrate that there is an absence of sex discrimination where, for example criterion such as flexibility and adaptability are used.

Performance

11.40   In *Brunnhofer v Bank der österreichischen Postsparkasse AG* [2001] IRLR 571 the claimant received a monthly salary supplement at a lower rate than her male colleague. The respondent argued that this was because the male comparator was a better worker. The ECJ held that the difference in pay could not be objectively justified where the difference in pay was awarded at the time of appointment but was said to be based on personal ability or the quality of the work actually done. Circumstances linked to the individual employee which cannot be determined objectively at the time of the person's appointment but become clear only during performance, such as the quality of the work done, cannot be relied upon to justify a difference in pay which is awarded at the time of appointment as work performance can only be assessed after appointment. The ECJ stated:

> '76 In so far as the questions clearly concern work paid at time rates, as the national court has, moreover, stated in its order for reference, it follows from the foregoing that circumstances linked to the person of the employee which cannot be determined objectively at the time of that person's appointment but come to

light only during the actual performance of the employee's activities, such as personal capacity or the effectiveness or quality of the work actually done by the employee, cannot be relied upon by the employer to justify the fixing, right from the start of the employment relationship, of pay different from that paid to a colleague of the other sex performing identical or comparable work.

77 As the Commission has rightly pointed out in relation to work paid at time rates, an employer cannot therefore pay an unequal salary on the basis of the effectiveness or quality of the work done in the actual performance of the tasks initially conferred except by conferring different duties on the employees concerned, for example by moving the employee whose work has not met expectations to another post. In circumstances such as those described in the previous paragraph, there is nothing to stop individual work capacity from being taken into account and from having an effect on the employee's career development as compared with that of her colleague, and hence on the subsequent posting and pay of the persons concerned, even though they might, at the beginning of the employment relationship, have been regarded as performing the same work or work of equal value.'

Questions

- To what period in time does the assessment based upon performance relate?

- Who made the decision that the claimant was assessed on her performance as not being as good as/to be paid as much by way of bonus etc as her comparator?

- What were the precise criteria that were applied?

- Did the employer rely on appraisals or assessments?

- What additional benefit did the comparator bring to the business on an objective basis that justified an increase in salary/bonus, etc?

- This is an area where documents are likely to be important so that employers should keep careful records and claimants ask for all relevant documents.

Physical effort

11.41 In *Christie and Others v John E Haith Ltd* [2003] IRLR 670 a number of female packers claimed equal pay with male packers. The claim was dismissed on the ground that the greater physical effort and unpleasantness of work carried out by male packers was a GMF within s 1(3). The female packers dealt with packages weighing up to 12 kg whilst the men dealt with heavier packages up to 30 kg. The men also loaded and unloaded the delivery vehicles and wheeled and emptied rubbish trolleys. The Tribunal dismissed the claim and the EAT held that there was no basis for excluding factors that had already been considered in deciding whether the jobs were of equal value. The case has been criticised on the basis that the result may have been more correctly achieved by deciding that the demands placed on male employees meant that the work was not of equal value in the first place.

Question

- To what degree is the comparator paid more for the extra physical work that is alleged?

- Precisely what physical work is alleged to differentiate the comparator from the claimant?

- Was the claimant offered the opportunity to carry out this work?

- If not, did the employer carry out any assessment of the ability of the claimant to carry out this work?

Potential

11.42   Potential will be irrelevant to the issue of like work where the same work is being carried out. The potential of an employee may, however, constitute a material difference even though the same work is being carried out at that time. In *Guest v Ferro (Great Britain) Ltd* EAT 287/77 the claimant and comparator were working as laboratory assistants, though the comparator was paid more. It was contended that the comparator was only working as an assistant on a temporary basis to equip him for a more important position. The Tribunal held that the two were carrying out like work and rejected the s 1(3) defence. The EAT considered that the potential for promotion was relevant under s 1(3) and the case was remitted to a different tribunal.

> 'The alleged material difference would be that, as already stated, he was employed with a view to being trained for a more important job and was only resting, so to speak, temporarily in the laboratory while equipping himself for that purpose.'

It is to be noted, however, that the EAT did not wish to express any view on the outcome but noted that the employer had a 'substantial burden of displacing' the prima facie position that there was discrimination.

11.43   In *Edmonds v Computer Services (South West) Ltd* [1977] IRLR 359 it was argued that a male employee, who was older and more experienced, was paid more because he had greater potential despite having been taught the job by the claimant. The Tribunal thought that this amounted to a s 1(3) defence because the employer wanted the comparator to have more responsibility in due course, but the EAT stated that:

> 'No one directed his mind to the distinction between paying you more because of the present exercise of responsibility (which the tribunal thought was an insufficient difference here to warrant the full wages differential), and paying you

more because in view of your age and experience you have the potential to exercise responsibility, something which we think a tribunal would certainly be entitled, if it thought fit, to consider to be a material difference.'

It is submitted that this case is wrong; if the employees were doing like work then it is difficult to see how a belief in greater potential can be justification. There is a difference with actual achievement.

Productivity

11.44 The EAT held in *Hartlepool Borough Council (1) Housing Hartlepool Ltd (2) v M Dolphin and Others: M Dolphin and Others v Hartlepool Borough Council (1) Housing Hartlepool Ltd (2)* UKEAT/0007/08/CEA, UKEAT/0008/08/CEA that a Tribunal did not err when it found that bonus schemes created in the 1970s in order to improve productivity were a sham and could not be used in justification as a GMF to a claim of equal pay. Collective bargaining had been conducted on behalf of male-dominated groups who were densely organised in trade unions. The Employment Tribunal had found that there was no genuine basis for the bonuses which had been paid to the men and which in reality were not related to productivity but 'were not the genuine reasons for the difference in pay and served to disguise the true reason which itself was tainted by sex'.

Qualifications

11.45 It may be possible that different qualifications can provide a s 1(3) defence provided that they relate to the job and the differential is genuinely due to the qualifications (see *Hawker Fusegear Ltd v Allen* EAT/794/94 and *Glasgow City Council and Others v Marshall* (21 October 1997, Court of Session)).

Questions

- Set out the precise qualifications that are relied upon as justifying any pay etc differential.

- How do they relate to the benefits that are brought to the job which objectively justifies such a differential?

Red circling – pay protection

11.46 Red circling may have the effect that a man is paid at a higher level than a woman who is carrying out the same job. This has become an important issue of late where many employers seek to reorganise their pay structures to comply with the equal pay legislation but, at the same time to protect employees for a period of time where they would otherwise lose out. The typical 'red circle' will apply where the employee is graded at a lower level than his current salary would warrant, but that salary is protected or 'red circled' for a period of time or until the salary rate for the job catches up. Red circling may also occur where the employee is moved to a lower paid job, whether due to incapacity or to avoid redundancy and it is agreed that the salary will be protected for a period. Red circling may apply in respect of individual jobs or classes of positions. See, for example, *Methven & Musiolik v Cow Industrial Polymers Ltd* [1980] **IRLR** 289, [1980] **ICR** 463 where the comparator's position was red circled when he was transferred to light work due to ill-health but his pay remained fixed to correspond to his predecessors. A threefold test was set out:

> '(1) was there a variation between the woman's contract and the man's? The answer in this case was "Yes, there was a variation between their rates of wages." (2) Was there a material difference (other than the difference of sex) between her case and his? The answer again was "Yes, Mr Munn was old and infirm, the employees were not." (3) Have the employers proved on the balance of probabilities that the variation in wages was due to the material differences? . . . the words "due to" indicated that the question was one of causation, that like all questions of causation it was a question of fact and degree and that there was ample evidence to support the decision of the industrial tribunal.'

This type of red circling raises the immediate problem that women may be employed on work of equal value or even become employed in the same jobs but paid less and so have an equal pay claim. The reason that the man is paid more is that his pay has been red circled.

11.47 The employer will have to argue that the red circling is a material difference not related to sex so that the s 1(3) defence applies. It is likely that, even if a red circle provides a defence, it will only provide a s 1(3) defence for a limited period of time. The protection is also likely to be lost if protection is extended to someone who should not be within the circle.

11.48 The nature of red circling was considered in *Snoxell & Davies v Vauxhall Motors Ltd* [1977] **IRLR** 123, [1977] **ICR** 700. The claimants worked as inspectors alongside male inspectors who had been on separate grades until 1970 when the wage scale was revised by agreement with the unions. Male inspectors who had been graded X2 were placed at a lower grade, H3, but the former X2 inspectors were red circled and put into a special grade, 02, which was to remain until they ceased to be employed. There were no women in the 02 grade. In 1975 women were re-graded with the men as H3 and were paid the same rate as the H3 grade men, save for the red circled 02 grade. The claimants sought equal pay with the red circled inspectors. The Tribunal held that the s 1(3) defence applied. On appeal the EAT held that a defence cannot be established based on red circling where past discrimination on the grounds of sex contributed to the pay differential. Phillips J noted that for a case to fall in to s 1(3) it must be genuine, clear and convincing:

> ' . . . caution is required before accepting an employer's answer under S.1(3) that the variation is due to a "red circle" anomaly. In particular, we are anxious about whether it would be in conformity with the principle of equal pay to allow a claim to be permanently or semi-permanently defeated by an answer based on a "red

circle" anomaly. In other words, such an anomaly may provide an immediate answer, but can it be allowed to be valid indefinitely?'

11.49   The women were not in the red circle because they were unable to enter grade X2. It was stated that an employer can never establish a s 1(3) defence where it can be seen that past discrimination has contributed to the discrimination.

11.50   The EAT also noted that:

> ' . . . it seems to us desirable where possible for red circles to be phased out and eliminated, for they are bound to give rise to confusion and misunderstanding. One of the difficulties seems to be that although understood and accepted as fair when first introduced, with the passage of time memory dims, the reason for their institution is forgotten, and they are seen as examples of discrimination.'

11.51   The nature of the defence was considered by the Court of Appeal in *Benveniste v University of Southampton* [1989] IRLR 122, [1989] ICR 617. The claimant was recruited as a university lecturer at a time when the university was subject to severe financial constraints so that the salary she was paid was less than someone of her age and qualifications would normally be paid. By the end of the year of her appointment these pressures had eased and she was given increments over the next 4 years. She was unhappy with the salary that she was paid and refused to perform certain duties, as a result of which she was dismissed.

11.52   In relation to her equal pay claim, the Tribunal found that there were four comparators doing like work and that her salary should have been adjusted to catch up with these salaries. The university argued that there was no term in the contract that was less favourable than a similar term applying to the male comparators as s 1(2)(a)(i) required. Further, even if there was a less favourable term, s 1(3) applied. The Tribunal held that the relative qualifications and experience of lecturers and the point they were placed on the scale was a matter for the university and that the point on the scale was not related to sex. There was no term in the contract that was less favourable. It was also held that there was a material difference as the claimant had been taken on when there were financial pressures and the university had not been able to pay a higher rate.

11.53   On appeal to the Court of Appeal, it being accepted that the claimant was doing like work, it was held that the Tribunal and EAT had erred in holding that there was no relevant term in the contract which was less favourable and that the material factor defence applied. The special factors which justified the salary had disappeared so that she should not have continued to be paid at the lower rate. On the first point, Neill LJ noted that no one had drawn any relevant distinction between the claimant and comparators on the basis of skill or experience. There was a term relating to her salary which was less favourable to her than the terms of a similar kind in the contracts of the comparators who were paid more.

11.54 On the material factor defence, Neill LJ, after referring to the above cases stated:

> 'I do not find any assistance in the red circle cases where certain individual employees have been treated as falling into a special or different category because on humane grounds their salaries have been protected at a higher rate over a period. They remain protected employees. In the present case, however, once it is accepted that the financial constraints came to an end in 1981, or at any rate by October 1982, the special factors which justify the lower salary disappear. I am not persuaded that it can be right that the appellant should continue to be paid on a lower scale once the reason for payment at the lower scale had been removed. There was no justification for the lower rate of pay other than the circumstances existing at the date of her appointment.'

There was no continuing financial constraints that could be pointed to which justified the lower salary.

11.55 It is necessary for the employer to show that any pay differential can be justified in relation to each person who has been brought into the 'red circle' and that the reason has not disappeared at a time when an employee is brought into the circle. In *United Biscuits Ltd v Young* [1978] IRLR 15 a female day shift packing supervisor claimed equal pay with five night shift packing supervisors. It was accepted that they were on like work. The night shift supervisors had in 1974 been paid an uplift for responsibility but this was removed in 1976 as anomalous so that new recruits were paid at the same rate as the day shift. The employer argued that there was a red circle so that s 1(3) applied. However, the Tribunal found that two of the night shift supervisors had been employed in 1975 and that there was no evidence that responsibility was a factor at that time. The EAT stated that:

> ' . . . where an employer seeks to discharge the onus which rests upon him under s.1(3) by what may be described as a "red circle defence", he must do so under reference to each employee whom it is claimed is within the circle. He must prove that at the time when that employee was admitted to the circle his higher remuneration was related to a consideration other than sex. It may be that in some cases he can rely upon a presumption that considerations which apply to existing members of the circle apply to subsequent entrants. But where, as here, these considerations are accepted as having eventually disappeared we consider that it is for the employer to establish by satisfactory evidence that this occurred after the latest entrant was accepted.'

11.56 The EAT took the same approach in *Honeywell Ltd v Farquhar* EAT/554/77 where the claimant and male employee were employed as clerks at grade 2 but the male employee had previously been a security guard and was given a higher salary to preserve his remuneration. When another man was placed in the same grade, at the same salary as the claimant, he complained that he was not paid the same as his male colleague, who was on the higher salary, and was a given a salary rise when he was promoted to senior clerk. The claimant was not given a similar rise when promoted and claimed equal pay. The Tribunal thought that the promotion of the man had been a device and all three employees had been engaged on like work. Though the treatment of the male employee who had previously been a security officer had been justified, the subsequent male employee was not in the red circle and the award of equal pay should be backdated from the time that this employee was paid more. The promotion of that employee had not been genuine so that the defence failed.

11.57 Time is likely to be an important factor in considering whether the red circle is justified as open-ended protection may perpetuate discrimination and the reasons for protection may not continue. The undesirability of red circling continuing indefinitely was stated in *Snoxell & Davies v Vauxhall Motors Ltd* [1977] IRLR 123, ICR 700, above. The possibility of phasing out after a period of time should be considered. The EAT in *Outlook Supplies Ltd v Parry* [1978] IRLR 12 did not agree with the Tribunal that a period of two and a half years was too long for a red circle. The claimant, an accounts supervisor, claimed equal pay with a comparator who had been an accounts supervisor and assistant accountant until some of his duties were taken away when he became ill but his higher salary was preserved. The Tribunal held that a red circle continuing for two and a half years was too long. The EAT were of the view that the time which had elapsed was relatively short. It also made the following observations:

> 'We wish to draw attention to the following matters: (i) We stress the point that cases arising under section 1(3) can never be solved by rule of thumb, or by attaching a label, such as saying "This is a red circle case". It is necessary to look at all the circumstances; (ii) the "protection" of wages, even when done for good reason, gives rise to much misunderstanding and upset, which increases as time goes on, and it is accordingly desirable that where possible such arrangements should be phased out; (iii) for the same reason joint consultation is desirable where it is intended to introduce such a practice or, if it has been introduced, to continue it; (iv) in such cases, when determining whether the employer has discharged the onus upon him under section 1(3), it is relevant for the industrial tribunal to take into account the length of time elapsed since the "protection" was introduced, and whether the employers have acted in accordance with current notions of good industrial practice in their attitude to the continuation of the practice.'

See also *Charles Early and Marriott (Witney) Ltd v Smith & Ball* [1977] IRLR 123.

11.58 A distinction may be drawn between the factors which gave rise to the red circle ceasing to exist and whether the material difference has ceased to exist. In *Avon and Somerset Police Authority v Emery* [1981] ICR 229 the pay differential was based upon additional responsibilities of training. When this function ceased the employees were kept on grade 6 though new recruits were on grade 5. There were eight employees on grade 6 and 42 on grade 5. The EAT held that the employer was entitled to maintain the difference. The extra pay had been given because of the extra responsibilities which they undertook by reason of their experience. It was impossible to say that, because of the passage of time, the material difference ceased. A different result was reached in *Post Office v Page* EAT/554/87. The claimant was appointed, with 24 others, to a new grade. A number of employees were paid a higher grade based on direct production experience. However, the Tribunal held that, whilst experience may have been a factor at the time of appointment, by the time of the hearing it had ceased to be, so that the defence did not succeed.

Questions

- The employer will need to be asked to provide all of the details of those who are red circled and those who are outside the red circle.

- When was it decided that the comparators should be red circled?

- What was the reason for the red circling?

- Is it accepted that, at the time of the red circling, the claimant was being discriminated against in relation to her salary, etc?

- Provide a breakdown of the salary and remuneration for those in the red circle and those outside throughout the relevant period.

- How long was the red circle to continue?

- What steps have been taken by the employer to monitor the effect of the red circle?

- Why do the red circled employees continue to receive rises etc that perpetuate the effect of the red circle?

- Has the employer taken any steps to redress the impact of the red circle on those employees who are not within it but who would have been in it at the time of the red circling but for the discrimination that was taking place?

Red circling – pay protection – duty to establish a scheme

11.59 In *Redcar & Cleveland Borough Council v Bainbridge and Others* [2007] IRLR 91, EAT, [2008] IRLR 776, CA, women whose jobs had been rated as equivalent with comparator men (and in some cases had been rated higher) were paid less because of the effect of bonuses and other extra payments known as attendance allowances and wet weather payments. Disparate impact was conceded and indeed, in the case of a number of claimants who submitted their claims before a particular date, it was conceded that they were entitled to the bonuses. However, for claims submitted after that date the employers claimed that the difference in pay was objectively justified because it resulted from productivity schemes which conferred real efficiency savings on the Council and were largely self-financing.

11.60 The Tribunal held in some cases the bonuses no longer reflected any genuine incentive bonus scheme, and even with respect to the group of workers where they did, namely refuse collectors, the extra bonus was not justified because it would have been possible to *construct a different kind of bonus scheme for the claimants*, albeit not one which made any relevant cost savings. It was conceded by the employer that where the claimants could have been subject to a similar productivity scheme, then the bonus payments could not be justified. The Tribunal therefore had to consider whether this would have been possible. They found that although in some cases analogous productivity schemes could not have been constructed, in a number of other cases there was no evidence before them to suggest that they could not, and since the burden was on the employer, these cases succeeded. The Tribunal also held that the attendance allowances were not justified but that the wet weather payments were justifiably paid only to those who worked in inclement weather. They also held that claimants could legitimately compare themselves with a comparator rated lower in the JES.

11.61   The claims related to a period pre-April 2004. Since that date a new JES has been entered into. This provided pay protection (red circling) for those whose pay was adversely affected as a consequence. The claimants contended that if their claims succeeded (and some had been conceded) then they should also be given the benefit of pay protection on the basis that although they were not in fact in receipt of the higher pay, they ought to have been had they been given equal pay. Accordingly they contended that the employers could not rely upon a GMF defence under s 1(3) because the factor relied upon was not a material factor 'other than sex' within the meaning of that section. It was sex tainted. The employers contended that the historic sex discrimination was irrelevant. The purpose of pay protection was to cushion employees from the practical consequences of having to move towards lower pay; if they had not in fact been in receipt of that pay, and adjusted their financial arrangements accordingly, it was wholly reasonable that they did not qualify for the payment. The Employment Tribunal found against the Council.

11.62   There were various appeals and cross appeals. The Council appealed the finding that there was no objective justification with respect to the refuse workers; that comparison could be made with those rated lower; that there was no evidence that bonus incentive schemes could not have been introduced for certain of the claimant groups; and the conclusion that the claimants should receive the protected pay which would have been available to them had they been paid their legal entitlement at the relevant time. The claimants cross-appealed certain detailed findings relevant to particular claimants, principally on perversity grounds.

11.63   The EAT upheld two of the grounds of appeal. They held that the Tribunal had erred in finding that the fact that some other non-incentive based bonus scheme could have been introduced for some claimants defeated the Council's GMF defence with respect to those claimants; and that the Tribunal was wrong to say that there was no evidence relating to the issue whether some of the claimant groups could or could not be subject to a productivity scheme. The other grounds of appeal, and the grounds raised in the cross-appeal, were all dismissed.

11.64   On the issue whether the employer would fail in any GMF defence if it did not seek to implement some form of scheme. The EAT stated:

> '57. We accept that in assessing the issue of proportionality it may be necessary to focus on the disadvantaged as well as the advantaged group and to ask why the disadvantaged group were not given the same benefits, or opportunities to benefit, as the advantaged group. The council has implicitly accepted as much by conceding that their GMF defence will not succeed if a similar productivity scheme could have been implemented for these claimants. Here, however, there was an obvious and vital difference between the situation of the claimants and their chosen comparators. The refuse collectors were employed in work which enabled a productivity scheme to be adopted and which, as a consequence, brought savings and greater efficiency to the work being carried out for the council. That opportunity did not exist in relation to these particular claimants. The comparators were fortuitously in posts where they could largely pay for their own bonuses by productivity improvements. These particular claimants could not. Mr Allen submitted that a merit based scheme might have resulted in greater efficiencies. However, the Tribunal recognised in terms that they could not be formulated in a way which would save money or be self financing for these particular groups.

> 58. It cannot in our judgment be the case that in order to seek to bring the pay back into equilibrium that the employer should be under some obligation to adopt some other technique, be it a bonus scheme or some other way, of seeking to pay the claimants more. That is simply adding costs to the employer without any corresponding benefits. That argument would always be available where a GMF had been established; if correct it would fundamentally undermine the scope of the GMF defence . . .

> 64. It follows that in our judgment the Tribunal made an error which goes to the heart of its finding on this matter. Once the Tribunal had concluded that the higher bonus paid to the refuse workers was justified because of the arrangement they made they ought not, in our judgment, to have found that the material factor defence was not made out because of the failure to apply a wholly different kind of scheme for the benefit of these comparator groups. As the Tribunal accepted, no such scheme could finance itself or indeed involve any savings to the council. We conclude that the council has objectively justified the difference in pay, and we quash that part of the Tribunal's decision and substitute a finding that there was a GMF defence explaining the differential between these particular claimants and the refuse workers.'

Red circling – pay protection – excluding the discriminated employee from the scheme

11.65   In *Redcar* the EAT also held at paras 158–166 that an employee may be able to claim that she was entitled to pay protection in circumstances where 'had they been in receipt of their lawful pay by the date of implementation then there would be no answer to their claim to pay protection'. The EAT stated, at para 160:

> 'The council can surely not pray in aid … its own failure to implement equality as a justification for defeating it. It would frustrate the fundamental principle of equality to deny them benefits which, as everyone accepted, they were legally entitled to receive. Had the employers corrected the inequality when they ought to have done, then there can be no doubt that these women would have been in exactly the same situation as the comparators. They would have had the benefit of the pay protection. (We recognise that had the true cost been appreciated then the council may have structured a different scheme with lesser pay protection. To that extent the claimants may receive more than they would have done had their pay been equalised earlier. But this is no more than speculation.)'

The EAT were concerned about the difficulties that local authorities may face when seeking to manage their way out of historical discrimination. It noted that if the employer could show a carefully crafted and costed scheme negotiated for the purpose of cushioning the effects of a drop in pay without any reason to suppose when it was implemented that it would have a discriminatory effect, then it may be that objective discrimination could be demonstrated.

11.66 The EAT decision was appealed to the Court of Appeal; see below at **11.69** et seq.

11.67 The facts of *Middlesbrough Borough Council v Surtees* [2007] IRLR 869 are set out at **10.32**. It will be recalled that the issue in the case was whether the employer had to justify not extending the pay benefit of the pay protection scheme to those who, *albeit unbeknown to the employer at the time when the scheme was introduced*, were in fact also subsequently found to be entitled to equal pay when the scheme was introduced. That group was overwhelmingly female. Having considered whether objective justification has to be shown in all cases where there was an inference of indirect discrimination, the EAT first considered the natures of the claims made. The Employment Tribunal had held that GMF defences failed in respect of claims where the comparators were paid bonuses that no longer represented genuine productivity arrangements. In addition these successful claimants sought the benefit of the protected pay arrangements. They argued that if they had been receiving equal pay when they ought then they would have been in receipt of higher pay and would therefore have had the benefit of the pay protection arrangements. The Tribunal found that the pay arrangements did not adversely impact on the women. The statistics were not sufficiently detailed to justify the conclusion that there was disparate impact. The Tribunal held that the reason for the difference could properly be described as being a GMF other than sex within the meaning of s 1(3) and there was no need to show objective justification.

11.68 The EAT noted that the Tribunal decision on protected pay was heavily influenced by the EAT's decision in *Bainbridge* above. The EAT thought that the arguments which had been put forward missed the point. It stated that the difference which had to be justified was not extending the pay benefit of the scheme to those who, albeit unbeknown to the employer at the time when the scheme was introduced, were in fact also subsequently found to be entitled to equal pay when the scheme was introduced. The group was overwhelmingly female and since there was sex tainting, the need for objective justification arose. However, the justification which had to be shown was in not extending the arrangement to women who subsequently established their right; the relevant question being whether it infringed the principle of equal pay to fail to apply the scheme retrospectively to those persons The EAT held that the case was different from *Bainbridge* since the scheme when implemented was not, to *the actual knowledge of the council*, exacerbating existing discrimination. It held that the Council was justified in not applying the scheme to the claimants who might succeed after its introduction in establishing an equal pay right. It stated that:

> ' . . . given that the purpose of the scheme was to cushion employees from the potentially disastrous effects of a sudden drop in pay, the council was entitled to take the view that it should limit the benefit to those actually in that group and to exclude all others even if some of them ought to have been in the group. Unless the pay was actually being received, there was nothing to protect. We think that is itself sufficient justification, but it is reinforced by the fact that the need to reach a protected pay arrangement, with the agreement of the unions, was crucial to the making of the job evaluation scheme. Any assessment of future costing would inevitably be highly speculative and would undermine the ability to obtain agreement for the scheme.'

11.69   The case was appealed to the Court of Appeal and consolidated with the *Redcar* case as *Redcar & Cleveland Borough Council v Bainbridge and Others (Bainbridge 1 and 2), Surtees and Others v Middlesbrough Borough Council, Equal and Human Rights Commission intervening* [2008] EWCA Civ 885, [2008] IRLR 776. The Court of Appeal agreed with the approach in *Redcar* but thought that the approach taken by the EAT in *Surtees* had been wrong. In relation to *Redcar*, Mummery LJ stated, at para 105, that the reason for the post changeover pay differential must be considered on its own merits. He noted that:

> ' . . . if one then looks at the underlying reasons why the men suffered a wage drop on changeover and the women did not, the questions and answers go as follows: Why did the men suffer a drop in pay? Because they lost their old bonuses. Why did the women not suffer a drop in pay on that day? Because they had been underpaid in the period preceding changeover. Why had they been underpaid in the preceding period? Because they were being unlawfully discriminated against in that period. They too had been entitled to the same pay as the men who had been on bonuses. Thus the reason for the new pay differential was causally related to the historic unlawful sex discrimination.'

11.70   The following matters had been considered:

• the protection was temporary;

- it was closed and limited to existing employees;

- it had been negotiated;

- on the other hand there was no evidence that the women's views had been taken into account;

- there was no evidence that the women could not have been included in the scheme;

- no evidence was given of the likely cost of including the claimants. On costs, Mummery LJ stated:

  'The ET considered that the circumstances were not at all like those in *Cross v British Airways plc* [2005] IRLR 726 CA where cogent reasons, including economic costings, had been provided. The ET would have been willing to take the cost of including the women into account as relevant but they had been given no evidence.'

- the Council was aware that there were a number of claims to which it had no defence.

11.71 The Court of Appeal thought that one could not avoid the conclusion that the new arrangements were sex tainted. The employer therefore had to justify its reason for excluding women from pay protection on *Barry/Cadman* grounds. The Court of Appeal considered the issue of justification and noted that it was important to distinguish between direct and indirect discrimination as the former can never be justified. The approach of the Employment Tribunal and EAT was upheld. Mummery LJ noted:

' . . . The ET's task was then to consider whether the means Redcar had adopted of achieving its legitimate objective (which means had entailed excluding the women) were appropriate and necessary to achieve that objective. Or, in the language of Lord Nicholls in *Barry*, whether the ground relied on for justification (the legitimate objective) was sufficiently important for the court to regard it as overriding the effect of the discriminatory treatment of the women. The ET considered various factors. It mentioned that in *Snoxell* the red-circling had been permanent but here the pay protection advantage was only temporary. That was a point in favour of the employer; the discrimination would only last for three years and was reducing. It observed that the class of those receiving pay protection was closed; no one was to be admitted after 1 April 2004. That was also a point in favour of the employer; the advantaged group was limited to existing employees. On the other hand, it noted that the pay protection scheme had been the subject of negotiation with the representatives of the comparators but there was no evidence that the views of the women had been taken into account. The ET was of the view that Redcar has simply not applied its mind to the discriminatory effect of the exclusion of the women claimants from pay protection. Even after the event, no evidence had been given as to why the women could not have been included in the scheme. No evidence had been given as to the likely cost of including the women claimants. The ET considered that the circumstances were not at all like those in

Cross v British Airways plc [2005] IRLR 423 CA where cogent reasons, including economic costings, had been provided. The ET would have been willing to take the cost of including the women into account as relevant but they had been given no evidence. It should be noted that the ET did not specifically mention that the employer was aware at the time when it implemented the pay protection scheme that a number of claimants were alleging that they were entitled to the same pay as the men who were going to receive pay protection and that, in respect of at least some of those women, the employer had no defence to the claims. However, the ET was clearly aware of that factor and must be taken to have had it in mind when it commented, adversely, that the employer had not applied its mind to the discriminatory effect of excluding the women from the scheme.'

11.72 The only difference between *Bainbridge* and *Surtees* was that in the latter equal pay claims had not been conceded before the changeover date. However, the test was objective. The underlying reason in both cases why the women did not receive a drop in pay was because they had been discriminated against and not received the wages to which they were entitled. The Court of Appeal held that the EAT had been wrong to overturn the findings of the Tribunal in *Surtees*. Mummery LJ expressed reservations over the passage in the EAT's judgment cited above (at **11.66**). The reasoning was inconsistent with that in *Redcar*. Moreover:

'The argument accepted by the EAT in the Middlesbrough case is that in such circumstances, the employer will always be entitled to say that it must continue to discriminate against the women for another three or four years (albeit to a reducing extent) because it cannot afford to bring them into line with the men at the time of reorganisation. We find that a very surprising and undesirable general conclusion. We accept that a large public employer might be able to demonstrate that the constraints on its finances were so pressing that it could not do other than it did and that it was justified in putting the need to cushion the men's pay reduction ahead of the need to bring the women up to parity with the men. But we do not accept that that result should be a foregone conclusion. The employer must be put to proof that what he had done was objectively justified in the individual case.'

11.73 Mummery LJ was of the view that the Tribunal had been entitled to reach the decision it did in *Surtees* and that the EAT should not have reversed the judgment:

'... the scheme when implemented was not, to the actual knowledge of the Council, exacerbating existing discrimination. The Council was not structuring an arrangement in a way which it knew would perpetuate such discrimination. Payments were made to those in receipt of the higher pay – and these included all those who to the Council's knowledge were entitled to the higher pay – when the scheme was introduced. That was not direct discrimination nor anything analogous to it.

However, we have no doubt that the Tribunal was entitled to find that the Council must have realised that some of the outstanding claims at least were likely to succeed ... Since the claimants were overwhelmingly female, the decision to limit the benefits to those who to the knowledge of the Council were in receipt of the higher pay when the scheme was introduced required objective justification.'

11.74 The importance of the Court of Appeal decision is that it will be very difficult for an employer to justify red circling in cases where the persons in the red circle are mainly male and the red circle has arisen in this way as a result of historical discrimination.

Red circling – other issues

11.75 Where an outsider is let into the red circle the defence under s 1(3) will be destroyed (*United Biscuits v Young* [1978] IRLR 15). The length of time the jobs are red circled will also be taken into account (*Outlook Supplies v Parry* [1978] IRLR 12) though in *Charles Early and Marriott (Witney) Ltd v Smith and Ball* [1977] IRLR 123, ICR 700 it was held that indefinite red circling was permitted on the facts of that case.

11.76 It is, however, a matter of good industrial relations to phase out the red circle as soon as possible as appears from *Outlook Supplies Ltd v Parry* [1978] IRLR 12, [1978] ICR 388 and *Avon and Somerset Police Authority v Emery* [1981] ICR 229. In *Home Office v Bailey* [2005] IRLR 757 a practice of doubling pensionable years for prison officers for each year of service after 20 years was phased out in 1987 but retained for officers employed at that time. Administrative staff who had commenced work prior to 1987 brought a claim based on the comparators being those prison officers employed prior to 1987. The Tribunal rejected the s 1(3) defence, holding that the red circling could not be shown to be justified in 1999. The EAT held that the employer had failed to lead evidence to show that there was still justification in 1999.

Responsibility

11.77 It was held in *Edmonds v Computer Services (South West) Ltd* [1977] IRLR 359 that greater responsibility may constitute a material difference other than sex. The claimant, aged 23, had been employed as a control clerk for 6 months when the respondent engaged a man, aged 40, who had considerably more clerical experience though the claimant taught him the job of control clerk and there was no significant difference in their work but the man was paid more. The Tribunal found that the employer wanted the comparator to exercise responsibility as senior control clerk and this was a material difference. The EAT held that the Tribunal had failed to distinguish between present exercise of responsibility and future potential for exercising responsibility in the future. The former related to the work done whilst the latter could be considered to be a material difference.

Rotating shifts

11.78 Where employees work on rotating shifts which causes part of their work to be done at inconvenient or unsocial hours this may result in benefits being conferred which are not given to those who are not on such hours. In *Montgomery v Lowfield Distribution* EAT/932/95 full-time workers had variable shifts whereas part timers always worked fixed hours. This was a GMF which justified differential pay.

Shift premium

11.79 It was held in *Calder v Rowntree Mackintosh Confectionery Ltd* [1993] IRLR 212 that the payment of a shift premium could be grounds for a material factor defence though it was not possible to demonstrate that the extra money was wholly attributable to the difference. The comparator was paid because he worked rotating shifts whereas the claimant worked late hours. She argued that she worked unsocial hours for which she received no premium. The Court of Appeal held that the s 1(3) defence could be relied upon as the reason for the differential had been made clear. This decision has been criticised as making it more difficult to challenge discrimination where there are a number of reasons for the differential and the employer cannot point to the reason for the differential being wholly due to the reason put forward.

Seniority/length of service

11.80 Seniority in the form of length of service has frequently been used as a means by which to fix remuneration. Employees may be paid increments on an annual basis etc so that length of service becomes a determinative factor in fixing pay. Such a criterion may have a discriminatory effect on women who have entered the labour market at a later stage or have been out of the labour market for some time. In *Handels og Kontorfunktionaerernes Forbund i Danmark v Dansk Arbejdsgiverforening (acting for Danfoss)* [1989] IRLR 532, [1991] ICR 74 one of the criteria by which the employer could increase salary was seniority. The ECJ stated that:

> ' . . . as regards the criterion of seniority, it cannot be ruled out either that, like that of vocational training, it may result in less favourable treatment of female workers than for male workers, insofar as women have entered the labour market more recently than men or are subject to more frequent interruptions of their careers. However, since seniority goes hand in hand with experience which generally places a worker in a better position to carry out his duties, it is permissible for the employer to reward it without the need to establish the importance which it takes on for the performance of the specific duties to be entrusted to the worker.'

11.81 The position was considered in *Nimz v Freie und Hansestadt Hamburg* [1991] IRLR 222 in which length of service was rewarded by increase in pay depending also on whether the employee was full time or part time. The ECJ stated that where employers reward their employees based upon length of service and the pay structure indirectly discriminates the employer must prove that 'that such a provision is justified by factors which depend for their objectivity in particular on the relationship between the nature of the duties performed and the experience afforded by the performance of those duties after a certain number of working hours have been worked'.

11.82 The position was considered in *Cadman v Health and Safety Executive* [2006] ICR 1623, [2006] IRLR 969. The claimant transferred to the HSE after working for five and a half years in the DSS. She was in due course promoted up to principal inspector in band 2 but was paid less than four male comparators who were also employed at band 2. There was a differential between £4,000 and £9,000, principally because the comparators had longer service. It was submitted that the length of service was a GMF which was justified on grounds unrelated to sex. The employer relied on *Danfoss* but the Tribunal was of the view that the case has been watered down by subsequent cases such as *Nimz* where objective justification had been found to be necessary. The Tribunal decided that the HSE had not shown objective justification but was overruled by the EAT. The Court of Appeal referred the case to the ECJ. In the ECJ the principle in *Danfoss* was stated to establish that it was not necessary to provide special justification for recourse to the criterion of length of service. The decision did not preclude the possibility that there may be situations where the criterion of length of service must be justified in detail. This was so when the worker had provided evidence which gave rise to serious doubts whether recourse to the criterion was appropriate to attain the employer's objectives.

11.83 The Employment Equality (Age) Regulations 2006, SI 2006/1031 will also be of relevance. The Regulations exempt any service-related benefits based on length of service up to 5 years, but an employer using length of service above 5 years must show that the criterion 'fulfils a business need', such as experience. In the light of the general approval given by the ECJ to length of service as a legitimate criterion, it may well be that employers will not have too much difficulty justifying age discrimination that results from the use of such a criterion.

Union pressure

11.84 In *Farthing v Ministry of Defence* [1980] IRLR 402 there were negotiations between the union and employer when pay banding took place which disadvantaged women with the result that the employer was placed under pressure to achieve a settlement whereby the women received special treatment which resulted in them being paid more. The Court of Appeal held that the union pressure and the personal equation of the women meant that there was a defence to the claim. Lord Denning MR stated:

> 'It seems to me that these 51 ladies were in a very special category. They attained the higher rate of wages because of their special position (because of the pressures which had been brought to bear on the Ministry) and not because of any difference of sex. Therefore I would take a different view from the Tribunals below. I would say that the employers have sufficiently proved "that the variation is genuinely due to a material difference (other than the difference of sex) . . ."'

The decision is a dubious one in that it appears to permit market forces in the guise of union pressure to negate the effect of EqPA 1970 (men were doing like work and cf *Allen v GMB* at **2.61**). It was stated by the Court of Appeal in *Redcar* that the actual facts of *Farthing* were not sustainable and should be consigned to history.

A to Z of genuine material factors: external factors

Administrative error

11.85 It was held in *Young v The University of Edinburgh* EAT/244/94 that an administrative error may provide a s 1(3) defence provided that it is a genuine one and there are reasons why it cannot be remedied. The comparator had been placed on the wrong clinical scale as a result of a clerical error as it had not been noted that she was not medically qualified. The Tribunal accepted that the university could not rectify the error because the comparator was in tenured employment and the employer was bound to pay at the agreed rate. If the claimant had been paid the same this would have created a second anomaly. The EAT held that an administrative error may, in appropriate circumstances amount to a s 1(3) defence. However:

> ' . . . it is manifestly of the greatest importance that administrative reasons, or administrative circumstances, should not be permitted to become a cloak for disguised inequality or discrimination. In any case, therefore, in which it is said that the explanation for a difference in pay between persons of different sex, doing like work, is an administrative error, the circumstances must be scrutinised in order to ensure that the error was a genuine one, and that it was properly approached with a view to bringing it to an end.'

Collective bargaining structures

11.86 Given that, in many workforces, pay and other benefits are agreed through collective bargaining it may be argued that such collective bargaining is an external factor that may provide a s 1(3) defence. However, it has been clear since *Enderby v (1) Frenchay Health Authority (2) Secretary of State for Health* [1993] IRLR 591, [1994] ICR 112 that the mere fact there are separate collective bargaining structures will not be sufficient where one relates almost exclusively to women and the other predominately to men, which though taken separately have no discriminatory effect, if women are paid less than comparable men. The existence of separate collective bargaining is not sufficient objective justification in itself in such a case. The ECJ stated:

> 'The fact that the rates of pay at issue are decided by collective bargaining processes conducted separately for each of the two professional groups concerned, without any discriminatory effect within each group, does not preclude a finding of prima facie discrimination where the results of those processes show that two groups with the same employer and the same trade union are treated differently. If the employer could rely on the absence of discrimination within each of the collective bargaining processes taken separately as sufficient justification for the

difference in pay, he could, as the German Government pointed out, easily circumvent the principle of equal pay by using separate bargaining processes.'

It will be necessary for the separate bargaining structures and the results of such bargaining to be objectively justified. There is a danger otherwise that separate collective bargaining in itself imports discriminatory assumptions.

11.87 This is not to say that collective bargaining should not be taken into account as is apparent from *Specialarbejderforbundet i Danmark v Dansk Industri, acting for Royal Copenhagen A/S* [1995] IRLR 648, [1996] ICR 51. In this case 60% of the workforce were women, the employees being divided into three groups of turners, painters and unskilled workers. The turners and the painters consisted of a number of sub-groups, including blue pattern painters and ornamental plate painters. Workers were covered by a collective agreement under which pay was partially dependent on individual output and in practice 70% of the turners and painters were paid by the piece, with a basic hourly rate and a variable rate dependent on output. The ornamental plate painters had the highest average hourly pay followed by automatic machine operators with the blue pattern painters receiving the lowest pay. All but one in the latter group were women whereas all but one of the automatic machine operators were men. The union sought a declaration that the blue pattern painters carried out work of equal value to the automatic machine operators. The ECJ held that:

> '... the principle of equal pay for men and women also applies where the elements of the pay are determined by collective bargaining or by negotiation at local level but that the national court may take that fact into account in its assessment of whether differences between the average pay of two groups of workers are due to objective factors unrelated to any discrimination on grounds of sex.'

11.88 In *British Road Services Ltd v Loughran and Others* [1997] IRLR 92 the Northern Ireland Court of Appeal considered whether a Tribunal had been correct to find that discrimination was objectively justified due to there being separate pay structures based on different collective bargaining agreements. The respondent argued that the effect of *Enderby* was that it was necessary for the claimant's group to be almost exclusively female in order to refute the s 1(3) defence. A majority of the Court of Appeal rejected this argument. Where a significant number of the claimant's group are women the employer cannot rely on separate bargaining processes per se as a defence under s 1(3). The claimant's group did not have to be almost exclusively women; in *Enderby* the ECJ was merely stating the facts of that case. The issue of whether the proportion of the women in the group raises a presumption of discrimination is a question of fact for the Tribunal.

11.89 The EAT further considered the effect of collective bargaining in *Barber and Others v NCR (Manufacturing) Ltd* [1993] IRLR 95. The clerical workers at the respondent's factory consisted of direct clerical workers, whose jobs related to shop floor production, whose contracts were for 39 hours a week, and indirect clerical workers not related to shop floor production whose contracts were for 35 hours a week. Male and female employees were employed on the same terms in each group. Rates of pay had been equalised by collective bargaining but when direct employees were conceded a 38 hour week and there was no increase in hourly rates for indirect employees the latter claimed the same rates of pay. The Tribunal found that the collective bargaining agreements were untainted by sex and the employers had justified the agreement on objective grounds by establishing the pay agreement was due to the need to harmonise the pay structure of the employees. The EAT held that the employers had only demonstrated the historical process by which the hourly rates of pay were arrived at and had not shown any objective factors which justified or supported the results. The EAT stated that:

> ' . . . there is a small, but critical, difference between saying that the variation is genuinely due to a material factor other than sex, on the one hand, and saying that the cause of the variation was free from sex discrimination, on the other. It seems to us that these expressions do not have the same meaning, and that there may well be a "cause" for a variation which is not a "material factor" other than the difference of sex. To substitute one expression for the other, as the employers' argument requires, therefore involves placing a gloss upon the provisions of S.1 of the 1970 Act for which there is no warrant in the statutory words.'

Therefore:

> ' . . .the proper approach, in applying the 1970 Act to the present case, is to consider whether the employers have shown that the difference between the appellants and their comparators is genuinely due to a material factor other than sex. If that is correct, it follows, in our view, that . . . evidence led in the case established the historical process by which the difference in hourly rates of pay had been arrived at, but did not show any objective factor which justified, or even supported, the result which had been produced . . . It is, however, the result which has to be looked at, and the result was a pay difference which was not due to any material factor other than difference of sex.'

The employees therefore succeeded in their claims.

11.90 In *Middlesbrough Borough Council v Surtees* [2007] IRLR 869 one of the arguments was that there had been separate bargaining structures which justified the differences. However, the EAT stated there had been unlawful sex discrimination in the operation of the bargaining processes applicable to them. The EAT stated that:

> 'In short, in our view once the tribunal had found that the bonus differential could not be demonstrated to be free of sex discrimination, the separate collective bargaining argument was doomed to fail. It would explain the fact that bonuses were paid to one group and not in the other, but the fixing of the comparator's pay could not then be free of sex discrimination, and the fact that the claimants pay was separately negotiated could not alter that fact.'

On appeal to the Court of Appeal it was held that the Tribunal was entitled to infer that there was sex taint between the two groups.

11.91 It will not avail an employer to argue that it is 'locked into' a potentially discriminatory pay structure due to a longstanding collective agreement where the agreement itself is tainted by discrimination in that it maintained higher pay for positions traditionally reserved for men (*William Ball Ltd v Wood* EAT/89/01).

11.92 The right to equal pay extends to setting aside discriminatory provisions that may be contained in a collective agreement (*Kowalska v Freie und Hansestadt Hamburg* [1992] ICR 29; *Nimz v Freie und Hansestadt Hamburg* [1991] IRLR 222). It is apparent from *Nimz* that the mere fact of the criteria being in a collective agreement will not make them self-evidently objective. Further, an agreement cannot be relied on if it is, itself, tainted with sex discrimination (*William Ball Ltd v Wood* EAT/89/01).

Questions

• When did the negotiations take place for the purpose of collective bargaining, who was involved and how were the decisions reached?

• Explain how the collective bargaining process objectively justifies the difference in salaries between the claimant and comparators.

• What were the factors that led to this disparity during the collective bargaining process?

Comparator

11.93 Where the claimant chooses an anomalous comparator the employer may rely upon this as a material factor defence (*British Coal Corporation v Smith* [1996] 3 All ER 97, [1994] IRLR 342).

Competitive tendering

11.94 Engaging or employing women on a lower salary in order to make the business more attractive for the purpose of tendering should not be a defence as it defeats the very object of the legislation (*Ratcliffe v North Yorkshire County Council* [1995] 3 All ER 597, [1995] IRLR 439).

Costs

11.95 The mere factor that getting rid of discrimination or discriminatory practices will cost more will not provide a defence (see *Steinicke v Bundesanstalt fur Arbeit* (Case C-77/02) [2003] IRLR 892 and *Schönheit v Stadt Frankfurt am Main* (Cases C-4/02 and C-5/02) [2004] IRLR 983 and see the decision of Burton J in *Cross v British Airways plc* [2005] IRLR 423). *Cross* was referred to by the Court of Appeal in *Bainbridge*. The difficulties with using cost as an argument that there is a GMF is clear from these cases.

Economic considerations

11.96 Increased costs to the employer cannot solely provide justification where there is indirect discrimination otherwise the fact of increased expense would always provide a justification and defeat the very purpose of the legislation (*Hill and Stapleton v Revenue Commission and Department of Finance* (Case C-243/95) [1998] IRLR 466).

Grading scheme

11.97 Grading schemes at which employees are placed in different grades or at a particular scale on the grade upon commencement of employment and in which employees thereafter progress through the scales or grades are quite common, particularly in local authorities. The grading scheme may have come about due to a JES or to negotiated wage scales. The evaluation itself must be free from the taint of discrimination (*Snoxell & Davies v Vauxhall Motors Ltd* [1977] IRLR 123, ICR 700). Provided that the grading is fairly and genuinely applied it is likely to provide a s 1(3) defence. In *National Vulcan Engineering Insurance Group v Wade* [1978] IRLR 225, [1978] ICR 800, 3 All ER 121, [1979] QB 132 clerks were graded on the basis of experience, capacity, skill and application and were paid according to their grade. The claimant claimed parity with male clerks who had been placed at a higher grade. In the Court of Appeal it was held that there was ample evidence that the grading had nothing to do with sex. The claimant had been assessed as 'easily distracted' compared with her comparator who was assessed as a 'young man going places'. Lord Denning MR stated:

> 'If it were to go forth that these grading systems are imperative and operate against the Equal Pay Act, it would, I think, be disastrous for the ordinary running of efficient business. It seems to me that a grading system according to ability, skill and experience is an integral part of good business management; and, as long as it is fairly and genuinely applied irrespective of sex, there is nothing wrong with it at all.'

This case should be seen in light of the Court of Appeal's ruling in *Bromley and Others v H & J Quick Ltd* [1988] ICR 623 (see **8.18** et seq).

11.98 The opposite result was reached in *Graviner Ltd v Hughes and Others* EAT/46/78. The claimants were employed as 'viewers' and the male comparators as 'inspectors'. The employer had three grades, grade 2 inspectors, grade 8, male viewers and grade 11, female viewers. Grade 11 was abolished and the women were moved to grade 8 but the only man in grade 8 was upgraded to grade 2. All the men in grade 2 were called inspectors though some were doing the task of viewers. The like work claim was upheld. The EAT held that the work was semi-skilled and it was lack of opportunity that prevented the women from being graded as inspectors. The grading was not related to skill. There was no system in force for the periodic testing of skill or aptitudes.

'In short, and in the view of the expert members of the Appeal Tribunal, a rational wages structure would have put all these inspectors and all the viewers in one grade, but with sub-gradings or bandings.'

If not in intent, in practice and effect the wages structure was still discriminatory.

Market forces

11.99   An employer may argue that market forces dictate the salary that is payable to a comparator; that is, it is necessary to pay the going (higher) rate to a comparator than to the claimant even though the work is like work, etc. This may be because of market shortages, a perceived need to pay the comparator the going rate in order to attract him to the position or because of the need to reduce turnover of staff by retaining an employee on attractive terms and conditions. It may be that the claimant is a member of a group of workers with weak bargaining power so that the employer only needs to pay a low rate. Market forces can be a GMF as was confirmed by the House of Lords in *Rainey v Greater Glasgow Health Board* [1987] ICR 129.

11.100   The defence was further considered in *Enderby v (1) Frenchay HA (2) Secretary of State for Health* [1993] IRLR 591, [1994] ICR 112. Senior NHS speech therapists claimed equal pay with male senior pharmacists and clinical psychologists in the NHS. It was asserted that it was necessary to pay members of the pharmaceutical profession more in order to avoid shortages of personnel. The Tribunal held that this factor did not justify the whole of the differential. The case was referred by the Court of Appeal to the ECJ, with the following question:

'If the employer is able to establish that at times there are serious shortages of suitable candidates for job B, and that he pays the higher remuneration to holders of job B so as to attract them to job B, but it can also be established that only part of the difference in pay between job B and job A is due to the need to attract suitable candidates to job B (a) is the whole of the difference of pay objectively justified? or (b) is that part, but only that part, of the difference which is due to the need to attract suitable candidates to job B objectively justified? or (c) must the employer equalise the pay of jobs A and B on the ground that he has failed to show that the whole of the difference is objectively justified?'

11.101   It was held that the state of the employment market which dictates that an employer has to pay higher rates if it wants to attract certain employees may be a GMF. The ECJ stated that:

'The state of the employment market, which may lead an employer to increase the pay of a particular job in order to attract candidates, may constitute an objectively justified economic ground within the meaning of the case law cited above. How it is to be applied in the circumstances of each case depends on the facts and so falls within the jurisdiction of the national court.

If, as the question referred seems to suggest, the national court has been able to determine precisely what proportion of the increase in pay is attributable to market forces, it must necessarily accept that the pay differential is objectively justified to the extent of that proportion. When national authorities have to apply Community law, they must apply the principle of proportionality.

If that is not the case, it is for the national court to assess whether the role of market forces in determining the rate of pay was sufficiently significant to provide objective justification for part or all of the difference.'

11.102   It is of importance that this factor is not used to justify differential payments for what may be perceived as 'womens' work' as such a factor could be used to perpetuate discrimination if taken too far. This may particularly be the case if an employer seeks to argue that it pays the 'market rate' for the job when the market rate undervalues the work carried out by women. Moreover, the fact that the woman may be prepared to work for that rate is not a sufficient answer as an employer cannot avoid its obligation by stating 'I paid her less because she was willing to come for less' (*Clay Cross (Quarry Services) Ltd v Fletcher* [1979] ICR 1, per Lord Denning). Such an approach may undermine the market forces argument if it is tainted by underlying discrimination, as was the case in *North Yorkshire County Council v Ratcliffe* [1995] ICR 833. The claimants were catering staff, 'dinner ladies', whose work was rated as equivalent with road sweepers, refuse collectors and gardeners. The womens' pay had been increased to match the comparators but when the work was put out to competitive tender, via the DSO, it took the view that it had to reduce the pay in order to compete. The catering assistants were dismissed and appointed a month later on less favourable terms. The claimants brought equal value claims. The Tribunal held that there was a material factor but that it was not a difference other than the difference in sex. The lower rates of pay resulted from 'the general perception in the United Kingdom, and certainly in North Yorkshire, that a woman should stay at home to look after the children and if she wants to work it must fit in with that domestic duty and a lack of facilities to enable her, easily, to do otherwise'. The House of Lords upheld the Tribunal's judgment. Although the employer had taken the decision because of its perceived need to compete in the marketplace, the women were paid less for work rated as equivalent and the s 1(3) defence was not made out.

11.103   Lord Slynn stated that:

'The fact that they paid women less than their male comparators because they were women constitutes direct discrimination and ex hypothesi cannot be shown to be justified on grounds "irrespective of the sex of the person" concerned . . . The fact is that the employers re-engaged the women at rates of pay less than those received by their male comparators and no material difference other than the difference of sex has been found to exist between the case of the women and their male comparators . . . I am satisfied that to reduce the women's wages below that of their male comparators was the very kind of discrimination in relation to pay which the Act sought to remove.'

It is difficult to understand why Lord Slynn arrived at the conclusion that the claimants were paid less *because they were women.* The employer's argument was that the women were paid less not on account of any gender factor but due to the need to compete with rival tenders. This was not dealt with head on by the House of Lords. In effect the House decided that in a case where the reason for reducing the wages of an exclusively female workforce is to compete in the labour market with rivals who also employ predominantly women this will not constitute a GMF defence because the women are being paid less because of the fact that they are women. In such a case, at the very least, the employer will need to provide objective justification for the pay rates which are unrelated to sex.

Checklist for market factors

11.104 The checklist, which is taken from the EOC (now the EHRC) documentation, which follows will assist in identifying potential equal pay issues. If the employer answers 'no' (or the employer does not know the answer) to any of the questions in the checklist the employer will need to further investigate the pay data and pay practice to ensure that it is free from sex discrimination.

Market factors checklist

Can the employer clearly identify an appropriate external market(s) for the jobs within the pay systems?	Yes	☐
	No	☐
Does the employer apply the same principles and guidance for using market rates in pay determination to all internal jobs?	Yes	☐
	No	☐
Is there an even distribution of male and female jobs in the external labour market database?	Yes	☐
	No	☐
Has the employer asked the provider of market comparisons/databases for confirmation that the process has been 'equality proofed'?	Yes	☐
	No	☐
If you uses a job evaluation scheme for internal and external matching for market purposes has it been audited for sex bias (see separate Guidance Note)?	Yes	☐
	No	☐
Have those involved in preparing market rate data, advising on its use and applying this to pay determination been trained/given guidance in avoiding gender bias?	Yes	☐
	No	☐

Is there clear and objective justification for pay rates which are determined by market comparisons?	Yes	☐
	No	☐
Are market rate additions checked regularly to ensure that they are still justified?	Yes	☐
	No	☐

Mistakes

11.105   A genuine but mistaken belief may amount to a GMF under s 1(3) (see *King's College London v Clark* EAT/1049/02). The reason for the difference in this case was the genuine and gender-neutral reason that the comparator's pay was protected by the operation of TUPE. HHJ Clark noted that a sham or non-genuine explanation is a false one, designed to disguise the true reason for the difference in pay, and would itself be tainted by sex

Negotiations

11.106   It has been seen that separate collective bargaining may still not prevent a successful claim for equal pay as it may not be sufficient to provide a GMF defence. By the same token, negotiations which are based upon discriminatory assumptions may unravel any defence and, indeed, there may be a claim against the union if it does not fully represent the interests of the women (see *GMB v Allen* [2008] IRLR 690 and see the next section).

Separate pay structures

11.107   Where there are separate pay structures this may constitute a material factor defence. In *Reed Packaging Ltd v Boozer & Everhurst* [1988] ICR 391, [1988] IRLR 333 women dispatch clerks claimed equal pay with a male dispatch clerk who carried out work of a different nature. The claimants were members of ACTSS and were graded on the staff pay structure, with a basic weekly rate of £124.56. The comparator was a member of the GMBATU and was graded for hourly paid workers which resulted in him receiving an extra £17 per week. The separate pay structures were due to negotiations with two different unions and not to access to the schemes or their operation. The respondent raised the defence that the difference in pay was justified by the separate pay structures. The Tribunal decided that s 1(3) could not apply as equal pay principles could not take kindly to artificial differences between staff and hourly paid employees which were due to historical reasons. However, the EAT held that, so long as the separate pay structures were genuinely operated and were not tainted by sex-based grounds they could be the basis for a material factor defence under s 1(3). The present case showed an objectively justified administrative reason and therefore a material factor that was genuine or sound.

11.108 Whilst the above case sets out the principle, it has been criticised on the basis that the EAT only considered whether each pay structure was not based on sex grounds but did not consider whether there was discrimination between the two pay structures. The approach adopted by the EAT in *Barber and Others v NCR (Manufacturing) Ltd* [1993] IRLR 95 (above at **11.89**) reveals a more critical approach which is likely to be adopted.

Social objectives

11.109 It was held in *R v Secretary of State for Employment, ex p Equal Opportunities Commission* [1991] IRLR 493 that the state may put forward considerations of social policy in justifying legislation that has a discriminatory effect. See further *R v Secretary of State for Employment, ex p Seymour-Smith and Perez (No 2)* [2000] IRLR 263 in which the Government was able to justify the 2-year service requirement for claims of unfair dismissal by reference to policy, though the ECJ has stated that policy cannot be used to frustrate the principle of equal treatment in *Kutz-Bauer v Freie und Hansestadt Hamburg* (Case C-187/00) [2003] IRLR 368.

Statutory provisions

11.110 In *R v Secretary of State for Social Services, ex p Clarke* [1988] IRLR 22 speech therapists claimed equal value with male pharmacists and psychologists. The Tribunal held that the health authorities were bound to comply with regulations and directions from the Secretary of State as to the fixing of salaries. The claimants applied for judicial review on the basis that the Regulations were contrary to EC law. However, the Divisional Court held that the Tribunal should first decide whether the work was of equal value and whether the material factor defence was available. It did hold that the fact that there were Regulations did not per se provide a defence. Taylor J stated:

> 'The submission on behalf of the applicants that a "material factor" under s.1(3) must be a reason based on the merits and that a mere executive act is not a "material factor" was correct. S.1(3) requires the employer to prove that his decision to effect a variation is genuinely due to a "material factor" (ie reason) which is not the difference of sex. It might be that the wording of s.1(3) is infelicitous where the wage-fixer stands above and behind the employer, but there is no reason why what the employer has to prove should be any different in that type of case from what he has to prove in the usual case.

> In the present case, since the Industrial Tribunal were invited to deal with the employers' preliminary submission on the assumption that the applicants brought themselves within s.1(2)(c), that assumption imported that there was *prima facie* evidence of the applicants' contracts being less favourable than the contracts of men doing work of equal value in the same employment. Therefore, the presumption that the Secretary of State had acted lawfully in approving the rates was assumed to be displaced and the burden was on the employers to satisfy the requirements of s.1(8).

If the rate of remuneration approved by the Secretary of State turned out on evidence presented to the Tribunal to be less favourable to a woman applicant than the rate applied to a man doing work of equal value, the Tribunal could treat the rate as being modified under s.1(2)(c) to iron out the inequality. It was neither necessary nor appropriate to take the sledge hammer via judicial review of seeking a declaration that the Secretary of State's original approval was *ultra vires*.'

TUPE

11.111 It was held in *King's College London v Clark* EAT/1049/02 that the fact that terms and conditions of the claimant's comparator were protected as a result of a transfer under the Transfer of Undertakings (Protection of Employment) Regulations 1981 (now 2006) could amount to a GMF under s 1(3). The Tribunal had concluded that it was the employer's genuine but erroneous belief which was the reason for the difference in pay so that there was no defence. However, this failed to take into account the historical reason for the difference in pay which was that the employee was protected under TUPE. It was also stated that if the employer had genuinely but mistakenly believed that the claimant was at a lower grade this was of itself capable of amounting to a material factor under s 1(3).

Chapter 12

MATERNITY AND EQUAL PAY

12.1 It is beyond the scope of this book to set out the detailed provisions relating to maternity leave and pay, paternity and parental leave, etc. Women are protected during pregnancy and maternity leave from discrimination in relation to their working conditions and remuneration. However, pay during maternity leave is governed by statutory provision and a failure to pay equal pay to that of a man during the maternity period will not of itself be unlawful discrimination (see *Gillespie* below).

12.2 In some circumstances a woman may be more favourably treated as the EqPA 1970, s 6(1)(b) expressly provides that the equality clause does not operate in relation to terms 'affording special treatment to women in connection with pregnancy or childbirth'. An additional payment to a woman during maternity leave will be governed by this provision.

12.3 The SDA 1975 contains provisions which outlaw discrimination on the basis of pregnancy or maternity (s 3A). The Sex Discrimination Act 1975 (Amendment) Regulations 2008, SI 2008/656, reg 2 amends SDA 1975, s 3A to provide that there is no need for a comparator where the discrimination is on the ground of pregnancy or maternity. This was necessary as a result of the decision of Burton J in *Equal Opportunities Commission v DTI* [2007] IRLR 327 that inter alia the requirement of a comparator meant that the law was not compliant with Community law. Regulation 5 imports a proviso to SDA 1975, s 6 (which relates to discrimination in employment):

> '6A.—(1) Subject to subsection (2), section 6(1)(b) and (2) does not make it unlawful to deprive a woman who is on maternity leave of any benefit from the terms and conditions of her employment relating to remuneration.
>
> (2) The reference in subsection (1) to benefit from the terms and conditions of a woman's employment relating to remuneration does not include a reference to—
>
> (a) maternity-related remuneration (including maternity-related remuneration that is increase-related),
> (b) remuneration (including increase-related remuneration) in respect of times when the woman is not on maternity leave, or
> (c) remuneration by way of bonus in respect of times when a woman is on compulsory maternity leave.

(3) For the purposes of subsection (2), remuneration is increase-related so far as it falls to be calculated by reference to increases in remuneration that the woman would have received had she not been on maternity leave.

(4) In this section—

"maternity-related remuneration", in relation to a woman, means remuneration to which she is entitled as a result of being pregnant or being on maternity leave;

"on compulsory maternity leave" means absent from work in consequence of the prohibition in section 72(1) of the Employment Rights Act 1996;

"on maternity leave" means—

(a)   on compulsory maternity leave,
(b)   absent from work in exercise of the right conferred by section 71(1) of the Employment Rights Act 1996 (ordinary maternity leave), or
(c)   absent from work in exercise of the right conferred by section 73(1) of that Act (additional maternity leave); and

"remuneration" means benefits—

(a)   that consist of the payment of money to an employee by way of wages or salary, and
(b)   that are not benefits whose provision is regulated by the employee's contract of employment.'

This section makes it clear that remuneration is generally excluded from the SDA 1975 but narrows the exception in that it facilitates claims for discrimination in relation to eligibility for remuneration by way of bonus while on compulsory maternity leave. In addition, it enables claims for discrimination in relation to terms and conditions of employment in relation to periods of additional maternity leave to the same extent to which they are available in relation to periods of ordinary maternity leave. There are also amendments to the Maternity Regulations, set out below at **12.9**.

12.4 It is important to note that this is an area where the dichotomy between equal treatment and equal pay is crucial. Where the claim is in relation to pay it must be brought under the EqPA 1970 or the Equal Pay Directive (or the corresponding provisions of the Consolidating Directive). Where it is in relation to benefits the claim must be under the SDA 1975 or the Equal Treatment Directive (or corresponding provisions). The importance of this distinction is that the ECJ has accepted differential treatment in relation to maternity pay so that it is possible for workers on maternity leave to be treated differently to a man at work.

12.5 There are a number of areas of equal pay that need to be specifically considered in relation to pregnancy and maternity:

(1)   the interaction between contractual rights and statutory maternity legislation;

(2)   the level of maternity pay during leave;

(3)   the impact of pay rises that are given whilst the pregnant worker is on maternity leave;

(4)   the position with regard to bonuses;

(5)   bursaries and maternity leave;

(6)   the effect of sick leave provisions in the contract of employment.

CONTRACTUAL AND STATUTORY MATERNITY PAY

The Maternity and Parental Leave etc Regulations 1999 (MAPLE Regs 1999), SI 1999/3312

12.6   The MAPLE Regs 1999 distinguish between ordinary maternity leave (OML) during the first 6 months of maternity and additional maternity leave (AML) during the second 6 months. It is now necessary to distinguish between cases where the expected week of childbirth (EWC) begins on or after 5 October 2008.

Where EWC is before 5 October 2008

12.7   The MAPLE Regs 1999, reg 9 provides that an employee who takes OML is entitled, during the period of leave, to the benefit of all of the terms and conditions of employment which would have applied if she had not been absent, and is bound, during that period, by any obligations arising under those terms and conditions, save that the ERA 1996, s 71(5) applies so that remuneration is not included. Regulation 9(3) provides that only sums payable to an employee by way of wages or salary are to be treated as remuneration.

12.8   With AML, reg 17 provides that the employee is entitled, during the period of leave, to the benefit of her employer's implied obligation to her of trust and confidence and any terms and conditions of her employment relating to: (i) notice of the termination of the employment contract by her employer; (ii) compensation in the event of redundancy; or (iii) disciplinary or grievance procedures. The employee is bound, during that period, by her implied obligation to her employer of good faith and any terms and conditions of her employment relating to: (i) notice of the termination of the employment contract by her; (ii) the disclosure of confidential information; (iii) the acceptance of gifts or other benefits; or (iv) the employee's participation in any other business.

Where EWC is after 5 October 2008

12.9 The Maternity and Parental Leave etc. and the Paternity and Adoption Leave (Amendment) Regulations 2008, SI 2008/1966, regs 4–7 apply to remove distinctions between the rights of employees on OML and those of employees on AML.

12.10 Regulation 4 amends regs 9 and 17 of the MAPLE Regs 1999, so that an employee taking AML is, like an employee taking OML, entitled to the benefit of (and bound by any obligations arising from) all the terms and conditions of employment which would have applied if she had not been absent.

12.11 This does not include terms and conditions about remuneration, as defined in the MAPLE Regs 1999, reg 9.

12.12 Regulation 5 amends reg 18A of the MAPLE Regs 1999, so that the seniority, pension and similar rights of an employee returning from AML are, like those of an employee returning from OML, unaffected by her absence. There are similar provisions with regard to adoption.

12.13 Statutory Maternity Pay (SMP) is currently payable for 39 weeks and this has not been altered by the above, though the Government has stated that it intends SMP to be increased to 52 weeks by 2010.

Contract and statute: benefits and pay

12.14 It was held in *Boyle v Equal Opportunities Commission* [1998] IRLR 717 by the European Court of Justice (ECJ) that a public sector contractual maternity leave scheme that preserved accrual rights during OML, but not during AML, did not contravene the Equal Treatment Directive.

12.15 Against this background, the ECJ in *Land Brandenburg v Sass* (Case C-284/02) [2005] IRLR 147 considered the way in which differences between the statutory maternity leave schemes of the former German Democratic Republic (DDR) and the Federal Republic of Germany were to be reconciled post-reunification so as to be consistent with EU law. Mrs Sass, who was employed in the former DDR, complained that it was sex discrimination for the collective agreement for civil servants, to which she became subject following reunification, not to count as service the part of her maternity leave which was longer than the 8 weeks provided for by the Federal Republic's legislation to which the agreement referred. In the DDR this would have amounted to 20 weeks so that Miss Sass claimed that she should have attained a higher grade salary 12 weeks earlier than she otherwise did. It was argued that the Pregnant Workers Directive 92/85/EC provided for 14 weeks so that the period longer than the minimum period was simply a 'benefit available to her'. This was rejected by the ECJ since 'the fact that a piece of legislation grants women maternity leave of more than 14 weeks does not preclude that leave from being considered to be maternity leave as referred to in Article 8 of Directive 92/85 and, therefore, a period during which the rights connected with the employment contract must, under Article 11, be ensured'.

12.16 The ECJ linked maternity leave firmly with the contract of employment. It stated:

> 'A woman who is treated unfavourably because of absence on maternity leave suffers discrimination on the ground of her pregnancy and of that leave. Such conduct constitutes discrimination on the grounds of sex within the meaning of Directive 76/207 (Case C-342/93 *Gillespie and others* [1996] IRLR 214, paragraph 22; Case C-136/95 *Thibault*, paragraphs 29 and 32; and Case C-147/02 *Alabaster*, [2004] IRLR 486, paragraph 47).
>
> Against that background, it must be held that Mrs Sass is in a worse position than a male colleague who started work in the former GDR on the same day as she did because, having taken maternity leave, she will not attain the higher salary grade until 12 weeks after he does.
>
> However, the referring court takes as the premise for its reasoning that the disadvantage suffered by Mrs Sass is not based on sex but on the fact that her employment relationship was in abeyance for the 12 weeks in question.
>
> In that regard, it must be pointed out that a woman is still linked to her employer by a contract of employment during maternity leave (see *Gillespie and others*, paragraph 22; *Thibault*, paragraph 29, and *Alabaster*, paragraph 47). The way in which a female worker is paid during such leave does not affect that conclusion.'

12.17 Since the 20 weeks' leave was 'intended to ensure the physical recovery of the mother following the birth and to allow her to care for her child herself' (para 51) it must be considered to be statutory leave intended for the protection of the women who have given birth and must also count towards a qualifying period for access to a higher salary grade, otherwise Miss Sass would suffer discrimination on the grounds of sex within the meaning of Directive 76/207 in that she would not attain the higher salary grade until 12 weeks after a male colleague who started work in the former GDR on the same day as she did. The ECJ distinguished *Boyle* on the basis that it concerned additional leave granted by the employer rather than statutory leave.

12.18 The ECJ makes it clear that pregnant workers, who take up their statutory rights are entitled to the same rights and benefits under their contract of employment, whilst on leave, as if they were at work (subject to express provisions as to remuneration). This raised the specific issue of whether the AML provisions breached European law, since the benefits under the contract of employment, with the limited exceptions of reg 17, remained in abeyance. This has now been addressed with regard to employees who have post 5 October 2008 as the EWC. The more generalised point may be made that the case makes it clear that the statutory rights granted must be seen within the context of the contract of employment so that, unless there are exceptions (such as relating to remuneration), the pregnant worker is entitled, so far as possible, to the same rights under the contract of employment as other workers or there will be discrimination. It is important to note that the ECJ case makes it clear that discriminatory treatment as regards *benefits* (in this case seniority) will be a breach of the Equal Treatment Directive/SDA 1975. This is a point which should be borne in mind in drafting maternity policies and in considering the case-law below, which reveal a continuing trend to seek to obtain the same benefits on maternity leave as when an employee is at work. The position differs with regard to remuneration so that it is more difficult for the employee to claim equal pay.

12.19   The importance of the above decision is that the claimant may have a claim for discrimination under the Equal Treatment Directive or the SDA 1975 for less favourable treatment in relation to provision of benefits. Now that the MAPLE Regs 1999 provide for the same rights during OML and AML regarding accrual of pension, seniority, etc this will have to be taken into account in relation to pay and other contractual benefits. However, there is a dichotomy between pay and benefits as the next section makes clear.

THE LEVEL OF MATERNITY PAY DURING LEAVE

12.20   The fact that the level of pay may be reduced during maternity leave is exemplified by *Gillespie v Northern Health and Social Services Board* [1996] IRLR 214. The ECJ dealt with the argument that women who are on maternity leave should be entitled, under the Equal Pay Directive to the same pay as when they worked, on the basis that that if the only reason why a woman's pay is reduced is that she is off work due to pregnancy and maternity, since that can only affect women, it must be treated as direct discrimination based on sex. This argument was rejected by the ECJ on the ground that women taking maternity leave are in a special position 'which is not comparable either with that of a man or with that of a woman actually at work'. The ECJ decided:

> 'The principle of equal pay laid down in Article 119 [now Art 141] of the EEC Treaty and set out in detail in Council Directive 75/117/EEC of 10 February 1975 on the approximation of the laws of the Member States relating to the application of the principle of equal pay for men and women *neither requires that women should continue to receive full pay during maternity leave, nor lays down specific criteria for determining the amount of benefit payable to them during that period, provided that the amount is not set so low as to jeopardise the purpose of maternity leave.* However, to the extent that it is calculated on the basis of pay received by a woman before the commencement of maternity leave, the amount of benefit must include pay rises awarded between the beginning of the period covered by reference pay and the end of maternity leave, as from the date on which they take effect.' (emphasis added)

However, since the person on maternity leave remains governed by the relationship of the contract of employment, a woman on maternity leave must receive a pay rise awarded before or during maternity leave:

'As to the question whether a woman on maternity leave should receive a pay rise awarded before or during that period, the answer must be "yes".

The benefit paid during maternity leave is equivalent to a weekly payment calculated on the basis of the average pay received by the worker at the time when she was actually working and which was paid to her week by week, just like any other worker. The principle of non-discrimination therefore requires that a woman who is still linked to her employer by a contract of employment or by an employment relationship during maternity leave must, like any other worker, benefit from any pay rise, even if backdated, which is awarded between the beginning of the period covered by reference pay and the end of maternity leave. To deny such an increase to a woman on maternity leave would discriminate against her purely in her capacity as a worker since, had she not been pregnant, she would have received the pay rise.' (paras 21-22)

Monies paid during maternity leave are covered by Art 141 of the EC Treaty and the Equal Pay Directive so that such pay cannot be covered by the Equal Treatment Directive as well.

THE IMPACT OF PAY RISES THAT ARE GIVEN WHILST THE PREGNANT WORKER IS ON MATERNITY LEAVE

12.21   However, whilst the Equal Pay Directive may permit different treatment in respect of levels of maternity pay, it is not permissible to treat employees on maternity leave differently when it comes to pay rises. In *Alabaster v Woolwich plc and Secretary of State for Social Security* [2004] IRLR 486 the ECJ ruled that any pay rise awarded after the beginning of the period used to calculate SMP but before the end of maternity leave must be included in calculating the amount of SMP payable. This requirement is not limited to cases where the employer agrees to backdate a pay award to a date within the calculation period. The amount of SMP is calculated by the earnings during the 8-week period ending with the 15th week before the EWC. This calculation can be affected by a pay rise that is backdated to the calculation period. The Statutory Maternity Pay (General) Regulations 1986, SI 1986/1960, reg 21(7) (enacted to deal with the pay rise argument in *Gillespie*) provided that:

'In any case where a woman receives a back-dated pay increase which includes a sum in respect of a relevant period, normal weekly earnings shall be calculated as if such sum was paid in that relevant period even though received after that period.'

12.22   The ECJ decided that normal weekly earnings must include all pay increases and not just those which are backdated to the calculation period. It was then for the national authorities to determine *how a pay rise should be taken into account when calculating SMP*. The ECJ declined to give guidance on the position where there is a *pay decrease* after the calculation period but before the end of the maternity leave period. Regulation 21(7) has accordingly been amended to provide:

'In any case where—

(a)   a woman is awarded a pay increase (or would have been awarded such an increase had she not then been absent on statutory maternity leave); and

(b)   that pay increase applies to the whole or any part of the period between the beginning of the relevant period and the end of her period of statutory maternity leave,

her normal weekly earning shall be calculated as if such an increase applied in each week of the relevant period.'

12.23   The case was remitted to the Court of Appeal, [2005] IRLR 576, to determine whether Mrs Alabaster was entitled to an effective remedy in accordance with the ECJ's ruling or whether her claim for increased maternity pay was barred because she did not issue her claim until after the expiration of the time-limit under ERA 1996. The Government argued that the claim must be brought under ERA 1996 (it would then have been out of time) even though the case was clearly a sex discrimination case.

12.24   The chronology of the case was that:

•   Mrs Alabaster became pregnant in May 1995 and her EWC was the week commencing 11 February 1996;

•   the normal weekly earnings during the 8-week period beginning with the EWC covered the 8 weeks up to 31 October 1995, at which time her annual salary was £11,619;

•   a pay rise was awarded with effect from 1 December 1995 which increased her salary to £12,801. Mrs Alabaster remained at work during December 1995;

•   Mrs Alabaster started her maternity leave on 8 January 1996;

•   her SMP was calculated by reference to the reference period – based upon the lower salary. If it had been calculated by reference to the pay rise she would have received an additional £204.53;

•   Mrs Alabaster brought a complaint under Art 141 and EqPA 1970 on 21 January 1997. She later, on 9 June 1997, amended her claim to claim an unlawful deduction under ERA 1996, s 13 (after the 3-month time-limit).

12.25   The Court of Appeal noted that, in accordance with the ECJ decision, Mrs Alabaster was entitled to have the pay increase which she received before the start of her maternity leave taken into account even though it was not backdated to the relevant reference period. The Employment Tribunal had held that the unlawful deduction claim was time barred and dismissed the Art 141 and the EqPA 1970 claim as it considered that the correct route was under the ERA 1996. This had been upheld by the EAT and the Court of Appeal had remitted the claim to the ECJ, as set out above, so that on remission back to the Court of Appeal, Mrs Alabaster's contention that she should have an effective remedy had become a live issue.

12.26 It was argued for Mrs Alabaster that the EqPA 1970 was the domestic implementation of the equal pay regime created by Art 141 and that, because the ERA 1996 was not a discrimination statute, it was not appropriate to enforce equal pay rights. The Court of Appeal set out the different statutes and then (at para 30) stated that it was against this statutory background:

> ' . . . and because it became increasingly clear during the hearing that we needed to obtain a clearer understanding of the differences between, on the one hand, the regime for enforcing a woman's right to recover her full lawful entitlement to maternity pay if she has to have recourse to the ERA, and on the other hand the regime that is available under English legislation for all the other complaints someone may have against his/her employer in respect of unfair treatment in the field of pay, that we made a request to the parties for more assistance in this respect.'

12.27 Counsel for Mrs Alabaster provided a list of differences, which are tabulated below:

ERA 1996	EqPA 1970
Time-limits 3 months, subject to a power to extend time where it is not reasonably practicable to present a claim within time	*Time-limit* 6 months from the date of termination of employment, except in cases of 'concealment' and 'disability'
Composition of the tribunal Chairman sitting alone, subject to a discretion contained in the Employment Tribunals Act 1996, s 4(5)	*Composition of the tribunal* Full tribunal
Interest to date of judgment No interest payable from the date of the unauthorised deduction until judgment	*Interest to date of judgment* Interest payable from half way between the date of contravention and the date of judgment at a current rate of 6%
Interest from date of judgment Interest payable at judgment rate from 42 days after the relevant decision	*Interest from date of judgment* Interest payable at judgment rate from the relevant decision (unless full award is paid within 14 days after that date)

Free legal advice and legal services	*Free legal advice and legal services*
Legal Services Commission funding not available. No assistance from the EOC (now the EHRC)	Advice and assistance available from the EOC (now the EHRC)
Provision for service of a statutory questionnaire	*Provision for service of a statutory questionnaire*
No provision	Provision under the EqPA 1970, s 78 and the Equal Pay (Questions and Replies) Order 2003, which prescribes that an adverse inference may be drawn from any failure to respond, or an evasive response
Victimisation during continuing employment	*Victimisation during continuing employment*
No protection	Protection against discrimination (including victimisation) under SDA 1975, s 4
Victimisation as a reason for dismissal	*Victimisation as a reason for dismissal*
Dismissal of an 'employee' for alleging that his/her statutory rights have been infringed, including a breach of ERA 1996, s 13, constitutes unfair dismissal	Dismissal of both an 'employee' and a 'worker' by reason of victimisation constitutes unlawful discrimination
Victimisation post-dismissal	*Victimisation post-dismissal*
No protection	Post-employment victimisation of both 'employees' and 'workers' constitutes unlawful discrimination
Burden of proof	*Burden of proof*
The burden is on the claimant to establish an unlawful deduction	The burden of showing there has been no sex discrimination passes to the respondent once a prima facie case is established

Back pay is limited to 6 years under both an ERA 1996 claim and an EqPA 1970 claim, so that there are no differences between the two regimes in that respect.

12.28 The Court of Appeal held that differences on the above scale, which left Mrs Alabaster significantly disadvantaged in comparison to any others with an equal pay claim could not be justified. It was argued by the respondent that it would be sufficient to disapply the time-limit for ERA 1996 claims but the Court of Appeal did not think that this answered the other deficiencies in the ERA 1996 scheme. Binding authority meant that a claim could not be made directly under Art 141 and there was 'no value' *in carving out remedy under SDA 1975 by disapplying s 6(6)*. The Court of Appeal concluded:

> 'In our judgment the appropriate way to proceed is to follow the example shown by the House of Lords in *Webb* (see paragraph 24 above) and disapply those parts of s.1 of the EqPA which impose the requirement for a male comparator. In this way Mrs Alabaster can succeed in her claim for sex discrimination without the need for such a comparator, just as she would have done automatically if her claim had not related to the payment of an amount of money that was regulated by her contract of employment and had fallen within the SDA regime instead.'

12.29 The editors of the Industrial Relations Law Reports describe the reasoning of the Court of Appeal in disapplying the requirement of a comparator as skimpy, but the moral is clear: the courts will find ways to ensure that the domestic legislation is in line with European law even if it involves rewriting statute. From the practical point of view, employers should ensure that their maternity policies make provision for any pay rises that may be made from the relevant period to the end of the maternity leave period to be taken into account as appropriate, where it will mean an uplift in the statutory entitlement of 90% of salary during the first 6 weeks of leave. It is to be noted that the position where there is a pay *decrease* has not yet been clarified.

12.30 It was necessary to make amendments to the EqPA 1970 and these are to be found in s 1(2)(d)-(f) and (5A) and (5B). Section 1(2)(d)-(f) provides:

'(d) where—
    (i)   any term of the woman's contract regulating maternity-related pay provides for any of her maternity-related pay to be calculated by reference to her pay at a particular time,
    (ii) after that time (but before the end of the statutory maternity leave period) her pay is increased, or would have increased had she not been on statutory maternity leave, and
    (iii) the maternity-related pay is neither what her pay would have been had she not been on statutory maternity leave nor the difference between what her pay would have been had she not been on statutory maternity leave and any statutory maternity pay to which she is entitled,
    if (apart from the equality clause) the terms of the woman's contract do not provide for the increase to be taken into account for the purpose of calculating the maternity-related pay, the term mentioned in sub-paragraph (i) above shall be treated as so modified as to provide for the increase to be taken into account for that purpose;
(e) if (apart from the equality clause) the terms of the woman's contract as to—
    (i)   pay (including pay by way of bonus) in respect of times before she begins to be on statutory maternity leave,
    (ii) pay by way of bonus in respect of times when she is absent from work in consequence of the prohibition in section 72(1) of the Employment Rights Act 1996 (compulsory maternity leave), or

(iii) pay by way of bonus in respect of times after she returns to work following her having been on statutory maternity leave,

do not provide for such pay to be paid when it would be paid but for her having time off on statutory maternity leave, the woman's contract shall be treated as including a term providing for such pay to be paid when ordinarily it would be paid;

(f) if (apart from the equality clause) the terms of the woman's contract regulating her pay after returning to work following her having been on statutory maternity leave provide for any of that pay to be calculated without taking into account any amount by which her pay would have increased had she not been on statutory maternity leave, the woman's contract shall be treated as including a term providing for the increase to be taken into account in calculating that pay.'

Section 1(5A) and (5B) further provides:

'(5A) For the purposes of subsection (2)(d) to (f) above—

(a) "maternity-related pay", in relation to a woman, means pay (including pay by way of bonus) to which she is entitled as a result of being pregnant or in respect of times when she is on statutory maternity leave, except that it does not include any statutory maternity pay to which she is entitled;

(b) "statutory maternity leave period", in relation to a woman, means the period during which she is on statutory maternity leave;

(c) an increase in an amount is taken into account in a calculation if in the calculation the amount as increased is substituted for the unincreased amount.

(5B) For the purposes of subsections (2)(d) to (f) and (5A) above, "on statutory maternity leave" means absent from work—

(a) in exercise of the right conferred by section 71(1) or 73(1) of the Employment Rights Act 1996 (ordinary or additional maternity leave), or

(b) in consequence of the prohibition in section 72(1) of that Act (compulsory maternity leave).'

THE POSITION WITH REGARD TO BONUSES

12.31 Two issues may arise with respect to whether the female employee is entitled to the same bonus as a man where she has been on maternity leave or in respect of periods whilst the employee may have been absent due to pregnancy-related illness.

• What is the position where a bonus is awarded during a period whilst the employee is on maternity leave?

• How are absences due to maternity leave to be taken into account in future years in awarding a bonus?

Bonuses awarded during pregnancy or maternity absence

12.32 The first issue was considered in *GUS Home Shopping Ltd v Green & McClaughlin* [2001] IRLR 75 where the claim succeeded under the SDA 1975 and the Equal Treatment Directive. The respondent moved an office from Worcester to Manchester with effect from 1 April 1998, the employees at Worcester to be made redundant from that date. A discretionary loyalty bonus was introduced which was contingent on an orderly and effective transfer during the 6 months preceding the transfer and the employees being in post on 31 March 1998 or an earlier agreed date. Mrs McClaughlin did not receive a bonus as she was on maternity leave throughout the period. Mrs Green was absent for part of the period on pregnancy-related sickness and maternity leave and her bonus was reduced on a pro rata basis. An Employment Tribunal held that the claimants had been unlawfully discriminated against. On appeal it was argued that the scheme was one which provided for a definite payment for a definite purpose for a definite period. As such, it was analogous to the exceptional situation described by Lord Keith in *Webb v EMO Air Cargo (UK) Ltd (No 2)* [1995] IRLR 645 where a woman's absence due to pregnancy would have the consequence of her being unavailable for the whole of the work for which she had been engaged. This argument was rejected.

12.33 The EAT held that the bonus scheme was intimately linked with the contract of employment and that the employee had to do no more than comply with the contract to be awarded the bonus. It was:

> ' . . . not the case of a contract, whether separate and specific or a block within a continuing contract, for the performance of a specific task which explicitly required the employee to be at work performing the task in order to qualify for the payment. Rather this was a special scheme within a contract of indefinite duration offering a special loyalty payment for those who continued with the contract until a specific date. As such it was subject to all the regular incidences of an indefinite contract of employment such as absence by reason of illness or leave for whatever purpose.'

12.34 The EAT did envisage the possibility of devising a scheme which would be dependent upon attendance:

> 'It may be that, in a similar situation, a scheme could be devised by an employer which would operate separately from the contract of employment and require the employee to attend work to perform a specific task in order to qualify either for payment, or for employment under the special scheme.'

The EAT thus envisaged that terms may be drafted so that absences due to maternity leave disentitled the employee from a bonus, depending upon the nature and purpose of the bonus.

Taking into account maternity absences in calculating bonus

12.35 The position was considered in *Hoyland v Asda Stores Ltd* [2005] IRLR 438. During 2002, Ms Hoyland was absent from work for 183 days, of which 18 weeks were OML and 8 weeks were AML. In 2002 ASDA introduced an annual bonus based upon profits. Employees who were employed on 21 February 2003 with at least 6 months' service on 31 December 2002 were entitled to a bonus This was pro-rated to reflect part-time employment and absences of 8 consecutive weeks or more during the year. Maternity leave was treated as absence. Ms Hoyland expected to receive £189.47 but she was paid £94.48 to reflect the 183 days of absence.

12.36 An Employment Tribunal found that she had been subjected to a detriment under ERA 1996, s 47C but only for the compulsory maternity period of 2 weeks and she was awarded £5.20. The Employment Tribunal found that the bonus was 'wages or salary' within reg 9 of the MAPLE Regs 1999 and was thus regulated by her contract of employment so that SDA 1975, s 6(6) applied. The bonus was therefore paid under the EqPA 1970 and the differential treatment was permitted.

12.37 On appeal it was argued that Ms Hoyland had suffered a detriment and/or that there was a breach of Art 141. The EAT held that the Tribunal had been correct in deciding that the pro rata reduction could be made. There was no sex discrimination and the bonus scheme fell within the exclusion of s 6(6) in any event. A worker who took maternity leave during the bonus year must be paid in respect of the periods when she is at work and for the 2 weeks' compulsory maternity leave. A proportionate reduction may be made to reflect OML. European case-law meant that when a woman returns from maternity leave she must be treated for the purpose of future pay and conditions as though she had never been away but that was not the same as saying that she must be paid as though she had never been on leave. It was further held that it could not be said that there had been a detriment under ERA 1996, s 47C because reg 9 provides that a woman on OML is not entitled to the 'benefit of terms and conditions about remuneration' which covered 'sums payable to an employee by way of wages or salary' and the bonus was paid on this basis. It was therefore not required to be paid. The case could not be distinguished from *Gillespie*:

> 'Mr Napier argued that the present case can be distinguished from *Gillespie* because it was not concerned with payments made during the period of maternity leave. Like the tribunal we are unable to accept the distinction between the period when entitlement accrued and the date when the bonus was paid. Mrs Hoyland's entitlement to be paid bonus accrued during the period of maternity leave. It was a payment in recognition of work undertaken by the workforce during the period of that leave, and the tribunal found that the bonus payment was part of the wages of Mrs Hoyland and her colleagues. It would in our view lead to anomalous results if the case were to turn on whether the payment date for the annual bonus was shortly before or shortly after the end of the applicant's maternity leave. What is surely significant is the period during which the entitlement accrues.'

12.38 In the Court of Session, an attempt was made to bring the bonus within the provisions of the Equal Treatment Directive:

'Counsel submitted that the issue of bonus entitlement was entirely separate from any contractual provision in the employee's contract and as such did not therefore fall within the exclusion created by section 6(6) of the Act. He referred us to *GUS Home Shopping Limited* v *Green and McLaughlin* [2001] IRLR 75 and *Farrell Matthews and Weir* v *Hansen* [2005] IRLR 160. Both cases, he submitted, were illustrative of a situation where a bonus could be payable outwith the confines of the contract in a particular contract of employment. Counsel went further in as much that he submitted that discrimination based on pregnancy was in itself discrimination against a woman and in this respect he drew our attention to *Webb* v *Emo Air Cargo UK Limited*, a decision of the European Court in [1994] ICR 770. Given, he submitted, that the entitlement to bonus was entirely discretionary in terms of a proper construction of the contract, section 6(6) could not apply in any event.'

This was rejected, as it had been in the EAT. However, the wording of the judgment of Lord Johnston may lead to some difficulties. He stated:

'[14] In seeking to resolve this matter we consider that the important word in section 6(6) is "regulated". While we recognise that the word "discretionary" is used by the employer in referring to the bonus scheme, that can be construed as relating only to the amount being paid in any one year and we recognise that the Tribunal found, as a matter of fact, that every employee received a bonus. *We have no doubt that that entitlement, if it be such in law, arose out of the contract of employment and is regulated by it in the sense that but for the existence of the contract of employment the bonus would not be paid and it is therefore being paid as a consequence of its very existence. It does not seem to us to be necessary for section 6(6) to have any application in a given situation that the entitlement in question should be part of the formal contract of employment.* This conclusion reflects the dichotomy between equal pay and equal treatment, and avoids an employer being exposed to double jeopardy.

[15] We are therefore in no doubt that the Employment Tribunal and the Employment Appeal Tribunal reached the correct decision in construing the arrangements for bonus payments in respect of the appellant as falling within the terms of section 6(6) and thus excluding any claim for sex discrimination under the 1975 Act.

[16] We confess to be surprised that the issue of whether there was any discrimination at all was not taken before the lower Tribunals having regard to the fact that it appears that a man claiming paternity leave is in precisely the same position as a woman claiming maternity leave. It may be that some distinction is sought to be drawn because in the female's case pregnancy requires her to leave her employment temporarily, while a father, or potential father, has an option.

[17] Be that as it may, we recognise that we cannot determine this matter and if we had been in favour of the appellant's position we would have remitted the matter back for a further hearing before an Employment Tribunal on the issue of discrimination in principle.

[18] However, in the circumstances, for the reasons we have given the appeal will be dismissed and the order of the Employment Appeal Tribunal, itself supporting the order of the Employment Tribunal, will be endorsed.' (emphasis added)

12.39   The words in italics in the above quote would appear to encompass most bonuses as they are underpinned by the existence of a contract of employment. However, entitlement may depend on whether the bonus is contractual or discretionary, stated to be remuneration or outside the contract of employment and its stated purpose. The bonus in the present case was stated to be to reward attendance during the year and in recognition of the effort of the workforce, but it did expressly state that it would be reduced where the employee was absent on maternity leave. It is likely that a bonus based upon individual performance would be similarly treated if it was *contractual* as the remuneration exclusion would apply. The paradoxical position is that a bonus which is stated to be discretionary may have protection since it may be a benefit under the SDA 1975 as opposed to remuneration where the EqPA 1970 applies. The current position is that:

- where the bonus is retrospective pay for work done, then the employer cannot refuse to award the bonus to an employee merely on the ground that she is on maternity leave at the time payment is made;

- a contractual bonus can be pro rated to reflect periods of maternity leave although a payment must be made in respect of the 2-week compulsory maternity leave period, and any periods when the woman was at work; and

- where the bonus is discretionary it may be possible for a woman to bring a successful sex discrimination claim so that employers may not be able to pro rata it without there being a claim under the SDA 1975. It is to be noted that the bonus in *Hoyland* was treated as contractual though it was expressed to be discretionary. However, it is not clear whether the Court of Session's analysis is so wide that a discretionary bonus is caught by s 6(6) as it emanates, ultimately, from a contract of employment. It is thought unlikely that courts will adopt this position.

BURSARIES AND MATERNITY LEAVE

12.40   Although the result has been reversed by the Government, who have changed the bursary rules, the case of *Ms C Fletcher and Others v NHS Pensions Agency/Student Grants Unit & The Secretary of State for Health* [2005] IRLR 689 remains of importance in considering issues relating to vocational training grants. The effect on other types of trainees is of particular concern to the Government. The case raised for the first time the question whether vocational trainees, who are absent from their training for a specified period due to pregnancy and maternity, and for whom the facility of a bursary providing financial support during their training is terminated for the duration of that period, can claim the protection of the SDA 1975 interpreted so as to be consistent with the Equal Treatment Directive, and succeed in their complaints of unlawful discrimination.

12.41   The status of the claimants was to be distinguished from that of academic students. Whilst the claimants were not 'workers', for the purposes of domestic and European legislation, they were vocational trainees who combined academic study at higher education institutes with practical training in the working environment through clinical placements in the community and in NHS hospitals. The evidence was that academic study and practical training amounted to approximately 50% each of the course. Completion of the course and the attainment of the qualification permitted them then to be registered as qualified midwives and to obtain employment in the NHS. The bursary scheme was provided by the Pensions Agency as successors to Blackpool, Fylde and Wyre Hospitals. The complaints were that claimants ceased to be paid bursary instalments during absence for pregnancy and childbirth and in one case that the claimant was unable to take an appropriate period of absence from training because the bursary payments would have terminated and that part of a bursary has to be repaid after attendance was interrupted because of pregnancy and childbirth.

12.42   The EAT found that the facility of the bursary to the claimants was a working condition within Art 5, the domestic implementation of which was SDA 1975, s 14. The EAT concluded at para 76 that:

> 'In our judgment, therefore, the law is clear; and the Tribunal erred in concluding that the Applicants were treated in exactly the same way as other vocational trainees, male or female, who were absent from the course and that there was no discrimination contrary to sections 1 and 14 of the SDA. Treating the Applicants, who were absent because of pregnancy or maternity, in the same way as other trainee midwives who were absent for other reasons (save for short-term sickness) does not constitute a defence to less favourable treatment. The relevant circumstances in section 5(3) of the SDA were different, because the Applicants were pregnant and other trainees were not. The same rule was being applied to different situations; and the policy imperative of reducing or eliminating disadvantaged pregnant women because of their protected status means therefore that it was discriminatory to withdraw from them the facility of the bursary payment. There is no necessity, on this analysis, for the Applicants to compare their treatment with the more favourable treatment of trainees absent for reasons of sickness in order to succeed in their complaints of sex discrimination . . . in deciding whether less favourable treatment is on grounds of pregnancy, it is not permissible to say that the treatment is on grounds of absence from the course, rather than on grounds of pregnancy, and that other absent employees are treated equally so that there is no sex discrimination.'

Cox J further stated:

> 'Whilst it is not necessary for the pregnant woman to compare her treatment with that of a sick man in order to succeed in her claim of discrimination, and whilst an employer dismissing a woman on grounds of pregnancy cannot defend her

complaint of sex discrimination by stating that he would have treated a sick man in the same way, the purpose of the *Webb* principle is to protect pregnant women. It is not to prevent them from comparing their treatment with more favourable treatment afforded to sick men, where appropriate, in order to demonstrate that a different rule is being applied in comparable circumstances and that discrimination has occurred.'

Thus, how an employer deals with a sick man can never be a shield for an employer's treatment of a pregnant woman, but it can be a sword for a pregnant woman seeking to establish sex discrimination. The EAT also rejected the argument that the claimants were seeking to impose a regime that went beyond the maternity pay provisions required of employers as that did not apply because they were not employees. The case was heard by the Court of Appeal on 28 March 2006 but the view was taken that the arguments were academic as the rules had been changed.

THE EFFECT OF SICK LEAVE PROVISIONS IN THE CONTRACT OF EMPLOYMENT

12.43   The ECJ held in *North Western Health Board v McKenna* [2005] IRLR 895 that a sick pay scheme which provided for reductions after a certain period of time and which, subject to certain safeguards, treated absences due to pregnancy-related illness in the same way as other absences, was not in breach of European equal pay rules. Ms McKenna found that she was pregnant in January 2000 and she had to take the whole period of her pregnancy off as sickness. The sick leave scheme provided that employees were entitled to 365 days of paid sick leave in a 4-year period; the first 183 days in 12 months being at full pay and the additional days at half pay. Absence for pregnancy-related illness was treated the same as other illness, the policy stating that 'sickness as a result of maternity-related illness prior to the granting of 14 weeks' maternity leave falls to be considered under the Board's sick leave policy'. Ms McKenna exhausted her entitlement to full pay on 6 July 2000 and her pay was reduced to half. She was on maternity leave from 3 September to 11 December and was unfit to return so again received half pay. She brought a claim for sex discrimination before the equality officer who found that there was discrimination under the Equal Treatment Directive and that the reduction in pay was also contrary to Art 141 and the Equal Pay Directive. The following questions were referred to the ECJ by the Labour Court:

'1 Does the operation of a sick leave scheme which treats employees suffering from pregnancy-related illnesses and pathological illness in an identical fashion come within the scope of Directive 76/207?

2. If the answer to Question 1 is in the affirmative, is it contrary to Directive 76/207 for an employer to offset, against an employee's total entitlement to benefit under an occupational sick leave scheme, a period of absence from work due to incapacity caused by a pregnancy-related illness arising during pregnancy?

3. If the answer to Question 1 is in the affirmative, does Directive 76/207 require an employer to have in place special arrangements to cover absence from work due to incapacity caused by pregnancy-related illness arising during pregnancy?

4. Does the operation of a sick leave scheme which treats employees suffering from pregnancy-related illness and pathological illness (in the same way) come within the scope of Article 141 (EC) and Directive 75/117?

5. If the answer to Question 4 is in the affirmative, is it contrary to Article 141 (EC) and Directive 75/117 for an employer to reduce a woman's pay after she has been absent from work for a designated period where the absence is caused by incapacity due to a pregnancy-related illness arising during pregnancy in circumstances in which a non-pregnant woman or a man absent from work for the same period as a result of incapacity due to purely pathological illness would suffer the same reduction?'

12.44 The ECJ held that the sick leave scheme which treated female workers suffering from a pregnancy-related illness in the same way as other workers suffering from illness that was unrelated to pregnancy was 'pay' within Art 141 and the Equal Pay Directive. The payment of wages to a worker in the event of illness fell within the meaning of Art 141; the scheme defined the conditions governing maintenance of the worker's pay in the event of absence on grounds of illness, on the basis of an arithmetical formula. It stated that pay within the terms of Art 141 and the Equal Pay Directive cannot also come within the scope of the Equal Treatment Directive.

12.45 The scheme did not constitute discrimination contrary to Art 141 and the Equal Pay Directive so long as the amount of payment made was not so low as to undermine the objective of protecting pregnant workers since there was no principle that women should continue to receive full pay during maternity leave. It was not discrimination to treat all illnesses in an identical manner for the purpose of determining the total number of days of paid sick leave to which the worker was entitled during a given period and not to take account of the special nature of pregnancy-related illness. The ECJ further stated:

'If a rule providing, within certain limits, for a reduction in pay to a female worker during her maternity leave does not constitute discrimination based on sex, a rule providing, within the same limits, for a reduction in pay to that female worker who is absent during her pregnancy by reason of an illness related to that pregnancy also cannot be regarded as constituting discrimination of that kind.

In those circumstances, it must be concluded that, as it stands at present, Community law does not require the maintenance of full pay for a female worker who is absent during her pregnancy by reason of an illness related to that pregnancy . . .

However, the offsetting of absences during pregnancy on grounds of a pregnancy-related illness against a maximum total number of days of paid sick-leave to which a worker is entitled over a specified period cannot have the effect that, during the absence affected by that offsetting after the maternity leave, the female worker receives pay that is below the minimum amount to which she was entitled over the course of the illness which arose during her pregnancy (see paragraph 62 of the present judgment).

Special provisions must therefore be implemented in order to prevent such an effect.'

The ECJ ruled:

'1. A sick-leave scheme which treats identically female workers suffering from a pregnancy-related illness and other workers suffering from an illness that is unrelated to pregnancy comes within the scope of Article 141 EC and Council Directive 75/117/EEC of 10 February 1975 on the approximation of the laws of the Member States relating to the application of the principle of equal pay for men and women.

2. Article 141 EC and Directive 75/117 must be construed as meaning that the following do not constitute discrimination on grounds of sex:

–   a rule of a sick-leave scheme which provides, in regard to female workers absent prior to maternity leave by reason of an illness related to their pregnancy, as also in regard to male workers absent by reason of any other illness, for a reduction in pay in the case where the absence exceeds a certain duration, provided that the female worker is treated in the same way as a male worker who is absent on grounds of illness and provided that the amount of payment made is not so low as to undermine the objective of protecting pregnant workers;
–   a rule of a sick-leave scheme which provides for absences on grounds of illness to be offset against a maximum total number of days of paid sick-leave to which a worker is entitled over a specified period, whether or not the illness is pregnancy-related, provided that the offsetting of the absences on grounds of a pregnancy-related illness does not have the effect that, during the absence affected by that offsetting after the maternity leave, the female worker receives pay that is lower than the minimum amount to which she was entitled during the illness which arose while she was pregnant.'

12.46   The case vividly illustrates the inconsistencies which have arisen from the way the ECJ has dealt with pregnancy and maternity. On the face of it, if it is inherently sex discriminatory to dismiss a woman because of a pregnancy-related illness regardless of how a man with the same amount of illness is treated, the same principle of EU law should be applied to sick pay resulting from a pregnancy-related illness, so that the pregnant woman should be entitled to full pay. However, the regime governing pregnancy would then be entirely different from that governing maternity and post-maternity illness. The ECJ rationalised the resulting inconsistency between the treatment of pregnancy-related illness for dismissal purposes and its treatment for pay purposes by saying that:

' . . . so far as dismissals are concerned, the special nature of a pregnancy-related illness may only be accommodated by denying an employer the right to dismiss a female worker for that reason. By contrast, so far as pay is concerned, the full maintenance thereof is not the only way in which the special nature of a pregnancy-related illness may be accommodated. That special nature may, indeed, be accommodated within the context of a scheme which, in the event of the absence of a female worker.'

The important point for employers is that their sickness absence schemes may take account of absence for pregnancy-related illness provided it is treated the same as other absences.

12.47   Where the term is less favourable than that which would be applied to a man there may be discrimination under the EqPA 1970. In *Coyne v Expert Credits Guarantee Department* [1981] IRLR 51 the claimant was on paid maternity leave until 15 April 1978 but was not certified fit to return until 2 May 1978. She applied for sick leave under the Civil Service Regulations which provided that qualifying women were entitled to 3 months' maternity leave on full pay but that this would count against normal sick leave allowance. It was provided that further paid sick leave following maternity leave may be allowed within her normal allowance when a woman produces a doctor's statement which clearly indicates that the absence arises from some illness or condition unconnected with confinement. The claimant's request for sick pay was refused because the absence arose from a condition that was connected with confinement. The Tribunal held that the term in the contract relating to sick leave was less favourable than that applying to a man on like work. It was argued that the provision was excluded by s 6(1)(b) because the term related to maternity and that there was a material difference other than of sex. Section 6(1)(b) provides that the equality clause would not apply to a provision affording special treatment to women in connection with pregnancy or childbirth. The Tribunal held that the contract did not afford special treatment but deprived the employee of rights she would otherwise have. A man had unrestricted rights to 6 months' salary so that there was less favourable treatment and s 1(3) did not assist the employer.

12.48   Moreover, a woman may claim in respect of pre-maternity leave absences where a man is treated more favourably (*Handels-og Kontorfunktionærernes Forbund i Danmark v Fællesforeningen for Danmarks Brugsforeninger* (Case C-66/96) [1999] IRLR 5) or for any less favourable treatment that occurs whilst she is absent for a pregnancy related reason (*Caledonia Bureau Investment and Property v Caffrey* [1998] IRLR 110).

Chapter 13

PENSIONS AND EQUAL PAY

13.1 This chapter will consider and draw together the various strands relating to pensions and equal pay. The considerable jurisprudence of the European Court of Justice, which recognised that occupational pensions can be 'pay' so that Art 141 of the EC Treaty may apply has resulted in legislation, notably the Pensions Act 1995 and the Occupational Pension Schemes (Equal Treatment) Regulations 1995, SI 1995/3183. It is important to differentiate between occupational pensions and UK state pension provisions as the equality legislation will apply to the former.

THE DIFFERENT PENSION SCHEMES

13.2 The different types of pension schemes are as follows:

- *Occupational pension schemes.* These pension schemes come within Art 141. They are paid as a result of the employment relationship. Their terms may be covered by the contract of employment or a Trust Deed and legislative provision as set out below at **13.29** et seq. The schemes may be final salary/defined benefit schemes or money purchase/defined contribution schemes. A final salary scheme is based on the salary of the employee at the time of retirement or average salary over the final years of employment. The employer's contribution is calculated to cover the cost of the scheme. These have proved expensive and many schemes have been closed over recent years. A money purchase scheme is based on the investment of contributions by employer and employee. The pension will be calculated based on the annuity that can be purchased with the money that has been accumulated over the years of contribution. The sums must be within HM Revenue and Customs limits. Further points to be noted are that:
  - it is normally possible to receive a tax-free lump sum on retirement and a reduced pension;
  - under a money purchase scheme, actuarial factors are likely to play a part in calculating the pension since women, on average, live longer than men. Where the employer makes the same contributions for both, men are likely to receive a larger pension;
  - it may be possible for the employee to make additional voluntary contributions (AVCs) in order to secure additional benefits;
  - bridging pensions may bridge the gap between the occupational pension and the state pension since men get the state pension at 65

whilst women are entitled at 60. The pension scheme may therefore provide payments to men between 60 and 65 to cover the fact that they are not entitled to a state pension.

- *Personal pension schemes.* These schemes do not form part of the employment relationship, though employers may contribute so that the contributions will be employer-provided benefits. The 'stakeholder pension' was introduced by the Welfare Reform and Pensions Act 1999. Employers are under a duty to designate a scheme though not to contribute.

- *Public sector pension schemes.* It was held in *Bestuur van het Algemeen Burgerlijk Pensioenfonds v Beune* [1995] IRLR 103 that pensions paid under a statutory civil service scheme was 'pay' under Art 141. The decisive criterion is the employment relationship so that if the scheme 'is directly related to the period of service and if its amount is calculated by reference to the civil servant's last salary. The pension paid by the public employer is therefore entirely comparable to that paid by a private employer to his former employees'.

- *The basic state pension.* Entitlement is based upon national insurance contributions and having reached pensionable age. The basic state pension is not 'pay' under Art 141 and is covered by the Social Security Directive (79/7/EEC).

- *The additional pension,* being the old state earnings related pensions scheme (SERPS). This pension was replaced by the state second pension from 6 April 2002.

- *The state second pension.* It is possible to contract out of this pension where an occupational pension scheme or approved personal pension plan provide equivalent benefits, so that the employer and employee pay a lower contribution.

TRUSTEES

13.3 The pension scheme will normally be administered by trustees in accordance with the Rules of the Trust Deed. In *Coloroll Pension Trustees v Russell and Others* [1994] IRLR 586, [1995] ICR 179 the ECJ held that the direct effect of Art 141 may be relied upon by employees against trustees of an occupational pension scheme who are bound to observe the principles of equal treatment. Employers and trustees cannot be allowed to rely upon the rules of the pension scheme or those contained in a trust deed to evade their obligation to ensure equal treatment. If necessary, trustees should have recourse to the national courts in order to amend the pension scheme or trust deed. Employers and trustees are not required to ensure equal treatment in respect of level of pensions benefits before 17 May 1990 but equal access to pension benefits must have been given since the *Defrenne* judgment (see **1.3**). The ECJ noted that:

> ' . . . neither that Article (now 141) nor any other provision of Community law regulates the way in which that obligation is to be implemented by employers or by the trustees of an occupational pension scheme acting within the limits of their powers. It follows that the national court, whose duty it is to ensure ultimate performance of the obligation of result, may, in order to do so, make use of all means available to it under domestic law. Thus, it may order the employer to pay additional sums into the scheme, order that any sum payable by virtue of Article 119 must first be paid out of any surplus funds of the scheme or order that the sums to which members are entitled must be paid by the trustees out of the scheme's assets, even if no claim has been made against the employer or the employer has not reacted to such a claim.'

13.4 It was also held in *Coloroll* that where pension rights are transferred from one scheme to another owing to an employee's change of job, the second scheme will be obliged on the employee reaching retirement age to increase the benefits so as to make up any shortfall which arose due to the discriminatory treatment of the first scheme.

THE APPLICATION OF EC LAW TO PENSIONS

13.5 It is apparent that Art 141 will apply to contracts of employment and collective agreements which regulate the employment relationship in the public or private sector and may include pensions under a statutory civil service scheme, as found in *Bestuur van het Algemeen Burgerlijk Pensioenfonds v Beune* [1995] IRLR 103. On the other hand, social security benefits are not covered. In *Beune* the ECJ stated that the fact that the pension scheme is covered by statute points to it being a social security benefit rather than pay. It noted that:

> 'On the basis of the situations before it, the Court has developed inter alia the following criteria: the statutory nature of a pension scheme; negotiation between employers and employees' representatives; the fact that the employees' benefits supplement social security benefits; the manner in which the pension scheme is financed; its applicability to general categories of employees; and, finally, the relationship between the benefit and the employees' employment.'

13.6 State schemes may not be 'pay' within Art 141 since:

> ' . . . although consideration in the nature of social security benefits is not in principle alien to the concept of pay, that concept, as defined in Article 119, cannot embrace social security schemes or benefits such as, for example, retirement pensions, directly governed by statute to the exclusion of any element of negotiation within the undertaking or occupational sector concerned, which are obligatorily applicable to general categories of employees. Such schemes give employees the benefit of a statutory scheme, to whose financing the contributions

of workers, employers and possibly the public authorities are determined not so much by the employment relationship between the employer and the worker as by considerations of social policy.'

13.7   Thus, the case of *Griffin v London Pensions Fund Authority* [1993] ICR 564 in which the EAT decided that the local government superannuation scheme, the statutory pension scheme for council workers, did not come within Art 141 was probably wrongly decided. The scheme was described as a 'statutory scheme governed by exhaustive rules leaving the employer no discretion at all and applying to a general category of workers, ie local government workers throughout the country'. The EAT had been inclined to find that the scheme came within Art 141, based upon the Opinion of Advocate-General Slynn in *Liefting v Academisch Ziekenhuis bij de Universiteit van Amsterdam* [1984] ECR 3225 that the relevant question when dealing with civil service pensions is 'whether what is done is done by the State essentially as an employer' but considered itself bound to hold otherwise. In *Beune*, the ECJ effectively adopted the approach of Advocate-General Slynn as it stated that 'the only possible decisive criterion is whether the pension is paid to the worker by reason of the employment relationship between him and his former employer'. On this basis, the local government scheme would be 'pay'.

13.8   The seminal case of *Barber v Guardian Royal Exchange* [1990] ICR 616, IRLR 240 incorporated a temporal limit on claims relating to levels of benefits payable out of a pension scheme, as opposed to access, to 17 May 1990, the date of the ECJ's judgment. The claimant was employed by the Guardian Royal Exchange Assurance Group (GRE). He was a member of their non-contributory occupational pension scheme. As the scheme was contracted out, employees paid only the statutory minimum contributions to the state pension scheme and received benefits from the private scheme in substitution for the earnings-related element of the state scheme. The pensionable ages were 62 and 57 for men and women. Employees were entitled to immediate pensions if they retired within 10 years of normal pensionable age and GRE's severance terms provided that, if women over 50 and men over 55 were made compulsorily redundant, they would be deemed to have been retired and would receive an immediate pension. When the claimant was made redundant at 52 he did not qualify for an immediate pension but received a redundancy payment and a deferred pension. He claimed discrimination and the ECJ held that a pension paid under a contracted-out occupational pension scheme constituted 'pay' for the purposes of Art 141. The effect of the judgment was that any differential treatment which amounts to discrimination in relation to occupational pensions from 17 May 1990 would be a breach of Art 141.

13.9   The ECJ noted that the effect of *Defrenne v Belgium* [1971] ECR 445 was only to limit the effect of Art 141 in relation to benefits in the nature of social security 'which are directly settled by law without reference to any element of consultation within the undertaking or industry concerned, and which compulsorily cover without exception all workers in general'. The temporal limitation was applied because of the impact that the judgment would otherwise have in circumstances where the member states had been led to believe that such pension benefits were in the nature of social security so that the Article did not apply.

13.10 The temporal limitation distinguishes between access to a pension scheme and the amount of benefits payable under the scheme. In *Quirk v Burton Hospitals NHS Trust* [2002] ICR 602, [2002] IRLR 353 the National Health Service Pension Scheme Regulations 1995, SI 1995/300 provided that pension benefits payable to a male member of the scheme who took early retirement were to be calculated only by reference to his pensionable service from 17 May 1990, whereas the benefits payable to a female member on early retirement were calculated by reference to all of her pensionable service. These Regulations replaced earlier provisions as a result of the *Barber* decision. The claimant would be financially worse off than a female who retired at the same age of 55. He therefore sought a declaration that he was entitled to the same pension and lump sum as a female who retired at that age. The Court of Appeal held that there had not been discrimination as such disparity of treatment was permissible under the temporal limitation in *Barber*. There was a distinction between the calculation of benefits and right to join or be fully admitted. The disparity did not arise from the denial of access of the claimant to the scheme so that the temporal limitation applied. The European cases showed that men and women must be admitted to the scheme without discrimination but 'say nothing' of discrimination within the terms of the scheme.

13.11 The position would be different if the employee had already issued proceedings or made a claim at the date of *Barber* in which case the temporal limitation would not apply, though it was stated in *Howard v Ministry of Defence* [1995] IRLR 570 that merely asserting a claim was insufficient.

13.12 It was held in *Ten Oever v Stichting Bedrijfspensioenfonds voor het Glazenwassers- en Schoonmaakbedrijf* [1993] IRLR 60 that pensions paid after 17 May 1990 must not discriminate in relation to pension contributions made after that date. The limitation is now contained in Protocol No 2 annexed to the Treaty on European Union, which provides that:

> 'For the purposes of Article 119 of this Treaty, benefits under occupational social security schemes shall not be considered as remuneration if and in so far as they are attributable to periods of employment prior to 17 May 1990, except in the case of workers or those claiming under them who have before that date initiated legal proceedings or introduced an equivalent claim under the applicable national law.'

13.13 It is also clear from *Ten Oever* that the temporal limitation will apply where the benefits under a pension scheme are not linked to length of service, such as a lump sum payment on death, so that Art 141 applies if the death occurred after 17 May 1990. The temporal limit applies in relation to survivors pensions (*Coloroll*).

13.14   The temporal limit does not apply to the right to join a scheme. In *Vroege v NCIV Instituut voor Volkshuisvesting BV and Stichting Pensioenfonds NCIV* [1994] IRLR 651, [1995] ICR 635 it was held that a scheme which excludes part-time employees will be in contravention of Art 141 if the exclusion affects a much greater number of men than women. The limitation in *Barber* applies only to those kinds of discrimination which employees and the trustees of pension schemes could reasonably have considered to be permissible under European Law. Since *Bilka-Kaufhaus GmbH v Weber von Hartz* [1986] IRLR 317, [1987] ICR 110 it had been clear that the right to join a scheme came within the Article so that there was no reason to suppose that a person administering a scheme could have been mistaken as to the legal position. Direct effect could be relied upon from 8 April 1976 when the court held that Art 141 had direct effect (and see *Fisscher v Voorhuis Hengelo BV and Another* [1995] ICR 635, [1994] IRLR 662).

13.15   In *Dietz v Stichting Thuiszorg Rotterdam* [1996] IRLR 692 it was stated at para 23 that membership of a scheme would be of no interest to employees if it did not confer entitlement to the benefits provided by the scheme in question. Entitlement to a retirement pension under an occupational scheme was indissolubly linked to the right to join such a scheme.

13.16   Nor can the position be got around by retrospective 'levelling down' of the inequality the disadvantaged party must be given the same rights (*Smith and Others v Avdel Systems Ltd* [1994] IRLR 602; *Van den Akker and Others v Stichting Shell Pensioenfonds* [1994] IRLR 616). Once the discrimination is eradicated, the employer may then alter the scheme provided men and women are treated equally, though only if this is permitted by the trust deed; the general principle is that there must first be levelling up to eradicate discrimination (*Harland and Wolff Pensions Trustees Ltd v AON Consulting Financial Services Ltd* [2006] EWHC 1778 (Ch)). In *Van den Akker* men had a pensionable age of 60 and women of 55. The age was equalised in 1985 at 60 but women members had the option of keeping the age of 55. The ECJ held that it was possible to equalise but women could not then be treated more favourably after 17 May 1990. This meant that any more favourable treatment between that date and 1 June 1991 when equalisation was implemented had the effect that the pension rights for both had to be calculated on the basis of the lower retirement age of 55.

CONTRIBUTIONS

13.17   An employee will be under an obligation to pay the contributions relating to the period of membership in order to claim the right to retroactively join the pension scheme. In *Fisscher v Voorhuis Hengelo BV and Stichting Bedrijfspensioenfonds voor de Detailhandel* [1994] IRLR 662 the ECJ held that contributions must be paid. The employee argued that she should be able to join without facing obstacles such as paying contributions. However, the ECJ noted that this would entail more favourable treatment of the woman and stated 'that the fact that a worker can claim retroactively to join an occupational pension scheme does not allow the worker to avoid paying contributions relating to the period of membership concerned'. It is not clear from the judgment whether the employee must pay the full sum or can claim a pension based upon the contributions that can be made. In *National Pensions Office v Jonkmann/Vercheval/Permesaen* (Cases C-231/232/233), 21 June 2007, the ECJ held that where the pension rules are changed to allow female ex-employees to have the same benefits and women have to pay retrospective contributions it will be unlawful to require interest to be paid. The Social Security Directive also precludes a requirement that that payment be made as a single sum, where that condition makes the adjustment concerned impossible or excessively difficult in practice. That is the case in particular where the sum to be paid exceeds the annual pension of the interested party.

PAY

13.18   See the section on pay at **6.26** et seq.

13.19   Pay in this context will include:

• *Payments by employers to occupational pension schemes* (*Worringham & Humphreys v Lloyds Bank Ltd* [1981] ICR 558, [1981] IRLR 178). In that case, the ECJ stated:

> 'Sums such as those in question which are included in the calculation of the gross salary payable to the employee and which directly determine the calculation of other advantages linked to the salary, such as redundancy payments, unemployment benefits, family allowances and credit facilities, form part of the worker's pay within the meaning of the second paragraph of Article 119 of the Treaty even if they are immediately deducted by the employer and paid to a pension fund on behalf of the employee. This applies a fortiori where those sums are refunded in certain circumstances and subject to certain deductions to the employee as being repayable to him if he ceases to belong to the contractual retirement benefits scheme under which they were deducted.'

• *Compulsory schemes.* These will be included provided that they arise out of the employment relationship, though pension schemes in the UK cannot be compulsory (*Dietz*).

• *Pension benefits for dependants.* Pension benefits for dependants are likely to be regarded as pay; the fact that payments are made after the termination of the employment relationship should not matter.

• *Benefits paid to surviving spouses and civil partners.* A survivor's pension is paid by virtue of the membership of the spouse of the scheme and arises because of the pension relationship (*Coloroll Pension Trustees Ltd v Russell and Others* [1994] IRLR 586). It was held in *Maruko v*

Versorgungsanstalt der deutschen Bühnen (Case C-267/06), 1 April 2008, that these benefits amount to pay where it can be said that they arise as a result of the employment relationship. The claim would, however, not be under Art 141 as the survivor may not be a worker in the same employment, but under the Employment Equality Directive (2000/78/EC). The ECJ held as follows:

> '1. A survivor's benefit granted under an occupational pension scheme such as that managed by the Versorgungsanstalt der deutschen Bühnen falls within the scope of Council Directive 2000/78/EC of 27 November 2000 establishing a general framework for equal treatment in employment and occupation.
>
> 2. The combined provisions of Articles 1 and 2 of Directive 2000/78 preclude legislation such as that at issue in the main proceedings under which, after the death of his life partner, the surviving partner does not receive a survivor's benefit equivalent to that granted to a surviving spouse, even though, under national law, life partnership places persons of the same sex in a situation comparable to that of spouses so far as concerns that survivor's benefit. It is for the referring court to determine whether a surviving life partner is in a situation comparable to that of a spouse who is entitled to the survivor's benefit provided for under the occupational pension scheme managed by the Versorgungsanstalt der deutschen Bühnen.'

13.20   The following are not pay:

- *Compulsory deductions from salary.* In *Newstead v (1) Dept of Transport (2) HM Treasury* [1988] IRLR 66, [1988] ICR 332 the claimant contended that the civil service pension scheme discriminated against him. The Scheme provided that all male members had to contribute to a widows' pension fund by deductions from their gross salary. Women had an option to contribute to an equivalent widowers' fund. The claimant asserted that he had suffered discrimination:

  > ' . . . the factor which gives rise to the disparity at issue is neither a benefit paid to workers nor a contribution paid by the employer to a pension scheme on behalf of the employee, which might be regarded as consideration . . . which the worker receives, directly or indirectly. Men and women were paid the same gross salary and the deduction was like a contribution to a statutory social security scheme.'

- *Lump sums and transfer payments.* In *Neath v Hugh Steeper Ltd* [1995] ICR 158, [1994] IRLR 91 there was a defined benefit/final salary scheme which was funded by contributions from the employer and employees. The sums paid by the employer were higher for female employees due to the actuarial factors used to determine how much money was required to fund the scheme that women live on average longer than men and that the cost of providing a retirement pension for women was therefore greater. When the claimant was made redundant he had the option of transferring his pension to another scheme or taking a lump sum. The transfer value was lower as it equated to an amount which was actuarially equivalent to the benefits which the member had accrued as a result and the lump sum was less. The ECJ held that the transfer benefits and lump sum were not pay. The ECJ stated:

> 'The assumption underlying this approach is that the employer commits himself, albeit unilaterally, to pay his employees defined benefits or to grant them specific advantages and that the employees in turn expect the employer to pay them those benefits or provide them with those advantages. Anything that is not a consequence of that commitment and does not therefore come within the corresponding expectations of the employees falls outside the concept of pay ... The answer to be given to the national court must therefore be that the use of actuarial factors differing according to sex in funded defined-benefit occupational pension schemes does not fall within the scope of Article [141] of the EEC Treaty.'

The use of actuarial factors in final salary schemes will not be regarded as pay (*Coloroll Pension Trustees Ltd v Russell and Others* [1994] IRLR 586).

- *Additional Voluntary Contributions.* These additional benefits will not be regarded as pay (*Coloroll Pension Trustees Ltd v Russell and Others* [1994] IRLR 586).

- *Bridging Pensions.* In *Birds Eye Walls Ltd v Roberts* [1994] ICR 338, [1994] IRLR 29 it was held that there was no breach of Art 141 where an employer paid a full bridging pension to male employees between the ages of 60 and 65 but not to women of the same age on the basis that women were paid the state pension.

COMPARATORS FOR THE PURPOSE OF PENSIONS AND ART 141

13.21 Under the Equal Pay Act 1970 it will normally be essential for a comparator to be identified before a claim can be brought. In *Coloroll Pension Trustees Ltd v Russell and Others* [1994] IRLR 586, [1995] ICR 179 the ECJ were of the view that a worker cannot claim equal pay in relation to an occupational pension scheme in the absence of a comparator. However, in *Allonby v Accrington and Rossendale College and Others* [2004] IRLR 224 the ECJ considered whether a comparator was necessary in respect of an occupational pension scheme deriving from state legislation. The claimant claimed access to the teachers superannuation scheme which was a statutory scheme applying to all teachers. She was denied entry as she was a self-employed agency worker and all agency workers could not join the scheme. The issue for the ECJ was whether it was sufficient to rely upon statistics to show that the exclusionary rule amounted to indirect discrimination.

13.22 The ECJ held that Art 141 could not be applied where the pay and conditions of workers could not be attributed to a single source (see **5.48** on this point). The criterion on which the Article is based is the comparability of the work done by the workers of each sex. However, the ECJ in *Allonby* stated at paras 74–76:

> 'Thus, in the case of company pension schemes which are limited to the undertaking in question, the Court has held that a worker cannot rely on Article 119 of the EC Treaty (Articles 117 to 120 of the EC Treaty have been replaced by Articles 136 EC to 143 EC) in order to claim pay to which he could be entitled if he belonged to the other sex in the absence, now or in the past, in the undertaking concerned of workers of the other sex who perform or performed comparable work (case C-200/91 *Coloroll Pension Trustees* [1994] IRLR 586, paragraph 103). On the other hand, in the case of national legislation, in case 171/88 *Rinner-Kühn* [1989] IRLR 493 (paragraph 11), the Court based its reasoning on statistics for the numbers of male and female workers at national level.
>
> In order to show that the requirement of being employed under a contract of employment as a precondition for membership of the TSS – a condition deriving from State rules – constitutes a breach of the principle of equal pay for men and women in the form of indirect discrimination against women, a female worker may rely on statistics showing that, among the teachers who are workers within the meaning of Article 141(1) EC and fulfil all the conditions for membership of the pension scheme except that of being employed under a contract of employment as defined by national law, there is a much higher percentage of women than of men.
>
> If that is the case, the difference of treatment concerning membership of the pension scheme at issue must be objectively justified. In that regard, no justification can be inferred from the formal classification of a self-employed person under national law.'

The conclusion of the ECJ was that:

> ' . . . it must be held that a woman may rely on statistics to show that a clause in State legislation is contrary to Article 141(1) EC because it discriminates against female workers. Where that provision is not applicable, the consequences are binding not only on the public authorities or social agencies but also on the employer concerned.'

THE EFFECT OF ART 141

13.23 The legal effect of Art 141 and relevant Directives are as follows:

- *Direct or indirect discrimination in relation to access to an occupational pension scheme will be unlawful.* This will include less favourable treatment of part-time workers where it is shown that this is indirectly discriminatory and the discrimination cannot be objectively justified. It was held in *Bilka-Kaufhaus v Karin Weber von Hartz* [1986] IRLR 317, [1987] ICR 110 that exclusion of part-time workers from a pension scheme which adversely affected a greater number of women than men was a breach of Art 141 unless it could be objectively justified on grounds unrelated to sex discrimination (see further *Vroege v NCIV Instituut voor Volkshuisvesting BV and Stichting Pensioenfonds NCIV* [1994] IRLR 651, [1995] ICR 635).

- *Restriction of payments of survivors' pensions will be discriminatory.* It was held in *Razzouk v European Commission* [1984] ECR 1509 that restricting a payment to widows would be discriminatory.

- *The pension benefits under occupational pension schemes must be paid to men and women at the same age and equally.* This is clear from *Barber* (above at **13.8**). In *Moroni v Firma Collo GmbH* [1994] IRLR 130 it was confirmed that this applies to contracted in occupational pension schemes.

- *Pension contributions are pay and should be equal.* This principle was stated in *Worringham* above at **13.19**.

- *Actuarial factors may be applied as an exception to the equal treatment rule.* This was stated by the ECJ in *Neath v Hugh Steeper Ltd* (see **13.20**). *Neath* concerned a final salary pension scheme. The variations in pension pay will be lawful where it is due to actuarial calculations relating to the calculation of the employer's contributions or the payment or other benefits to a member. Different actuarial factors may also be applied to take account of different life expectancies in order to achieve equal pension benefits to men and women. This is provided for by the Pensions Act 1995 and the Occupational Pension Schemes (Equal Treatment) Regulations 1995, see below at **13.32**.
  There is no breach of the equality provisions where the pension scheme is compulsory for full-time employees but optional for part-time employees nor where the employer failed to tell staff that the barrier to access has been removed (*Preston v Wolverhampton Healthcare NHS Trust (No 3)* [2004] IRLR 96, ICR 993).

- *Transfers from one scheme to the other.* If the first scheme was discriminatory it will be necessary for the second scheme to eliminate the effect of the previous discrimination. The members of the scheme can claim to receive a payment in accordance with the *Barber* rule, limited to service after 17 May 1990 (*Coloroll*).

- *Absence on statutory maternity leave.* It was held in *Mayer v Versorgungsanstalt des Bundes und der Länder* (Case C-356/03) 13 January 2005, that the Equal Treatment in Occupational Social Security Schemes Directive (86/378/EC) precludes national rules under which a worker acquires no rights to an insurance annuity which is part of a supplementary occupational pension scheme during statutory maternity leave paid in part by her employer because the acquisition of those rights is conditional upon the worker receiving taxable pay during the maternity leave.

- *Part-time work – pro rata reduction.* It was held in *Schönheit v Stadt Frankfurt am Main* (Cases C-4/02 and C-5/02) [2004] IRLR 983 that it is permissible for a pension to be reduced pro rata to take account of the fact that the pensioner worked only part time, but any other reduction is potentially unlawful. Restricting public expenditure is not an element that can be relied upon.

THE CONSOLIDATING DIRECTIVE

13.24 Directive 2006/54/EC incorporated the Equal Treatment in Occupational Social Security Schemes Directive (86/378/EC), as part of the consolidation. It helpfully sets out the position regarding equal treatment for occupational schemes.

13.25 Article 6 provides that Chapter 2 covers:

'. . . members of the working population, including self-employed persons, persons whose activity is interrupted by illness, maternity, accident or involuntary unemployment and persons seeking employment and to retired and disabled workers, and to those claiming under them, in accordance with national law and/or practice'.

13.26 Article 7 provides that Chapter 2 applies to:

'(a) occupational social security schemes which provide protection against the following risks:
  (i)   sickness,
  (ii)   invalidity,
  (iii) old age, including early retirement,
  (iv)   industrial accidents and occupational diseases,
  (v)   unemployment;
(b) occupational social security schemes which provide for other social benefits, in cash or in kind, and in particular survivors' benefits and family allowances, if such benefits constitute a consideration paid by the employer to the worker by reason of the latter's employment.'

13.27 There shall be no direct or indirect discrimination on the grounds of sex in occupational social security schemes, in particular in relation to:

'(a) the scope of such schemes and the conditions of access to them;
(b) the obligation to contribute and the calculation of contributions;
(c) the calculation of benefits, including supplementary benefits due in respect of a spouse or dependants, and the conditions governing the duration and retention of entitlement to benefits.' (Article 5)

13.28 Article 9 provides examples of discrimination, which it can be seen, are culled from the case-law set out above:

'1. Provisions contrary to the principle of equal treatment shall include those based on sex, either directly or indirectly, for:

(a) determining the persons who may participate in an occupational social security scheme;

(b) fixing the compulsory or optional nature of participation in an occupational social security scheme;

(c) laying down different rules as regards the age of entry into the scheme or the minimum period of employment or membership of the scheme required to obtain the benefits thereof;

(d) laying down different rules, except as provided for in points (h) and (j), for the reimbursement of contributions when a worker leaves a scheme without having fulfilled the conditions guaranteeing a deferred right to long-term benefits;

(e) setting different conditions for the granting of benefits or restricting such benefits to workers of one or other of the sexes;

(f) fixing different retirement ages;

(g) suspending the retention or acquisition of rights during periods of maternity leave or leave for family reasons which are granted by law or agreement and are paid by the employer;

(h) setting different levels of benefit, except in so far as may be necessary to take account of actuarial calculation factors which differ according to sex in the case of defined-contribution schemes; in the case of funded defined-benefit schemes, certain elements may be unequal where the inequality of the amounts results from the effects of the use of actuarial factors differing according to sex at the time when the scheme's funding is implemented;

(i) setting different levels for workers' contributions;

(j) setting different levels for employers' contributions, except:
  (i) in the case of defined-contribution schemes if the aim is to equalise the amount of the final benefits or to make them more nearly equal for both sexes,
  (ii) in the case of funded defined-benefit schemes where the employer's contributions are intended to ensure the adequacy of the funds necessary to cover the cost of the benefits defined;

(k) laying down different standards or standards applicable only to workers of a specified sex, except as provided for in points (h) and (j), as regards the guarantee or retention of entitlement to deferred benefits when a worker leaves a scheme.

2. Where the granting of benefits within the scope of this Chapter is left to the discretion of the scheme's management bodies, the latter shall comply with the principle of equal treatment.'

STATUTORY PROVISION

13.29 The Directives and jurisprudence of the ECJ have had a fundamental impact upon equality of pension rights. The principles have been implemented in statutory form by the Pensions Act 1995 and the Occupational Pension Schemes (Equal Treatment) Regulations 1995.

13.30 The Pension Act 1995, s 62(1) provides that an occupational pension scheme which does not contain an equal treatment rule shall be treated as including one. The operation of s 62 is in similar terms to EqPA 1970, providing for equality in relation to like work, work rated as equivalent and of equal value and for a material factor defence. Section 63(1) provides that the dependants of members are covered. The equal treatment rule is to be construed as one with the EqPA 1970, s 63(4).

13.31 Section 62, so far as it relates to the terms on which members of a scheme are treated, is to be treated as having had effect in relation to any pensionable service on or after 17 May 1990 (s 62(6)). There are also exceptions relating to the application of actuarial factors (s 64(3)) and in relation to bridging pensions (s 64(2)).

13.32 The Occupational Pension Schemes (Equal Treatment) Regulations 1995 contain detailed provisions for the Tribunal or court to declare the rights of members and for the employer to provide extra resources. In particular, where there has been a breach of the equal treatment rule the court or Tribunal may declare that the employer shall provide resources to the scheme. The resources are defined as:

> '. . . such additional resources, if any, as may be necessary for the scheme to secure to the member, without contribution or further contribution by the member or by other members of the scheme, the same accrued rights in respect of the period falling before the date of the declaration as if that member had been treated equally in respect of that period.'

TUPE

13.33 Occupational pension schemes are excluded from the effect of the Transfer of Undertakings (Protection of Employment) Regulations 2006 (TUPE) but the Regulations specifically take into account pension transfers.

Chapter 14

PART-TIME WORKERS AND EQUAL PAY

14.1 As is already apparent from the cases considered so far, a vast amount of case-law relating to equal pay concerns disparate treatment of part-time workers. Access to pension benefits as well as terms and conditions of employment has much exercised the ECJ in the context of part-time work. In the UK the Part-time Workers (Prevention of Less Favourable Treatment) Regulations 2000, SI 2000/1551 (PTW Regs 2000) have sought to implement Community law.

14.2 It is a fact that the majority of part-time workers in the UK are women. It is also a fact that about eight million or about a quarter of the workforce are part-time workers. The use of part-time workers may satisfy the requirements of employers who want a flexible work force and also enable one partner in a family to work part-time whilst catering for domestic needs or even for both partners to work part-time so that they can spend time with the family. The status of a part-time worker is not, however, governed by the phrase 'part-time', but the status of the contractual relationship: the part-time worker may be self-employed, a worker, employee, home worker, freelance, an agency worker or a seasonal or casual worker and there are no doubt hybrid contractual relationships not encompassed in the foregoing. For many years statutory protection was really for the benefit of full-time workers, with thresholds in hours before there was sufficient continuity to make a claim. The decision of the House of Lords in *R v Secretary of State for Employment ex p Equal Opportunities Commission* [1994] IRLR 176 in which qualifying thresholds in terms of hours were held to be discriminatory led to the abolition of such thresholds for part-timers in 1995 and part-time employees now have the advantage of much of the legislation.

14.3 The Work and Parents Taskforce stated that prejudices against part-time staff are not uncommon and that part-time workers are more likely to be overlooked for promotion and perceived as not being committed to their jobs. It pointed out that the Work-Life Balance Baseline Survey of 2000 showed that most organisations have staff working in excess of their statutory hours and that over 20% of the work force with children under 5 wished to reduce their hours. The need for protection is therefore self-evident and there have been considerable developments in this area over the last decade.

14.4 At the time when domestic reforms were proceeding apace, the Government took steps to implement the Part-time Work Directive (97/81/EC) by implementing the Regulations which prohibit less favourable treatment of part-time workers unless such treatment can be objectively justified. The Regulations are not gender based and provide an easier route for the part-time worker than claims in sex discrimination, particularly indirect discrimination, and equal pay where the principles are complex and, in the equal pay context, cases have historically taken some time to be decided in comparison with cases under the PTW Regs 2000 (though the indicative timetable for equal value cases seeks to speed up proceedings). Nevertheless, the discrimination legislation contains similar concepts, particularly in relation to the defence of justification and the case-law already considered will be of assistance in approaching the PTW Regs 2000, though the courts have urged caution when applying cases which deal with one area of discrimination law to other areas.

THE SEX DISCRIMINATION ACT 1975: DIRECT AND INDIRECT DISCRIMINATION

14.5 Prior to the implementation of the PTW Regs 2000, claimants would have to rely on the provisions of the SDA 1975 in claiming inequality of treatment. The SDA 1975 can still be relied on and the dichotomy between the SDA 1975 and the EqPA 1970 applies (see **2.43**). There are many examples of cases involving direct or indirect discrimination in relation to part-timers as noted in this chapter and throughout the book. Some examples follow.

Direct discrimination

14.6 The fact that a woman is not allowed to job share or work part time is unlikely to amount to direct discrimination where a man would equally have been refused (*British Telecommunications plc v Roberts* [1996] ICR 625).

Indirect discrimination

14.7 In order to show indirect discrimination it is necessary that the employer operated a provision, criterion or practice equally to all employees which was to the disadvantage of women when compared with men and which could not be shown to be a proportionate means of achieving a legitimate aim, and which put the claimant at a disadvantage.

Provision, criterion or practice

14.8 Examples of cases in which a requirement or condition was applied and which would now be regarded as a provision, criterion or practice are:

- *Home Office v Holmes* [1984] IRLR 299 where there was a requirement to work full-time; and

- *Greater Glasgow Health Board v Carey* [1987] IRLR 484 where employees were permitted to work part time but the part-time hours had to be spread over 5 days which ruled out the possibility of job sharing.

Disadvantage for women when compared with men

14.9 It will be necessary for the Employment Tribunal to identify the pool for comparison. In *Keep v Lloyds Retail Chemists Ltd* EAT/319/97 the employee was refused sick and holiday pay on the basis that she worked insufficient hours. The employee claimed that this contravened EqPA 1970 but, taking the pools of comparison as the total of retail staff they found that 94% of those working part time were women and 94% of those full time were women. The employee argued that pharmacists should have been included but it was held that their work was entirely different. On the basis of the comparison made there was no discrimination. In *London Underground Ltd v Edwards (No 2)* [1998] IRLR 364 the rosters for drivers were changed so that a single parent could not work because of her child care responsibilities. There were over 2,000 drivers and 20 of the 21 female drivers could comply. However, it was held that there was indirect discrimination on the basis that where the pool was so small the Tribunal could rely upon the well-known fact that females were more likely to be single parents and unable to comply with any such requirement.

Proportionate means of achieving a legitimate aim: justifiability

14.10 The employer may justify why it is not possible for the work to be carried out on a part-time basis. It is necessary for the employer to objectively justify the reason for the discriminatory provision, criterion or practice. The Tribunal will balance the discriminatory effect against the reasonable needs of the party that applies the provision, criterion or practice; the means adopted must be proportionate to the legitimate aim that is sought to be achieved. There are many examples of employers refusing part-time work and the employee seeking to justify the discriminatory impact of a requirement to work full-time:

- *Abbey Textiles Ltd v Burgess* EAT/1265/97. The employee asked to return to her position as a sewing machinist after maternity leave on a part-time basis because of child-minding problems. She was told that she could not although a quarter of the work force was part time. It was argued by the employer that it was necessary for the job to be full time in order to foster team working. The Tribunal rejected this argument as the evidence was that the employee could use any machine in the team and that team meetings did not take place at any particular time so that there was no reason why she could not attend or, in any event, in her absence be told what had been said at the meetings.

- *Bullen v HM Prison Service* EAT/777/96. Refusal to permit a prison officer to work part time after maternity leave was justified as the prison would lose part of its staff budget if the job was not full time and the remoteness of the prison meant that two part-time jobs were not feasible.

- *Cast v Croydon College* [1998] ICR 500. The employer operated a discriminatory policy by requiring a job to be carried out full time and not by way of job share.

- *Eley v Huntleigh Diagnostics Ltd* EAT/1441/96. The employee worked as a telephonist/receptionist and resigned shortly after returning from maternity leave when it became clear she would not be allowed to start or finish early or work half days on Friday. It was held that the requirement to work full time was justified as the employee was more than just a receptionist since she played a role in clerical support and her absence would cause problems for the sales department. The cost of an alternative during this time was prohibitive due to the technical nature of the business and she was needed for customer continuity.

- *Greater London Glasgow Health Board v Carey* [1987] IRLR 484. It was not possible for a health visitor to work part time unless the hours were spread over 5 days as the need for the visitor to be available to people over the 5 days justified such requirement.

- *Nelson v Chesterfield Law Centre* EAT/1359/95. A requirement for a full-time post was justified where it was necessary for there to be ongoing collaboration between two workers at the same centre.

Detriment to complainant

14.11   Even if a considerably smaller proportion of women than men can meet the provision, criterion or practice the claimant must not be able to meet the provision, criterion or practice if she is to succeed. For example, in *Clymo v Wandsworth London Borough Council* [1989] ICR 250 the Employment Appeal Tribunal (EAT) were of the view that the claimant could comply with a requirement to work full time as some part of the combined income with her husband could be used for child care. In *Stevens v Katherine Lady Berkeley's School* EAT/380/97 a teacher resigned when the employer refused to permit her to work part time but, even though the employer could not justify the discriminatory requirement to work full time, the claim failed as the employee may have preferred to work part time but could work full time. In *Ogilvie v Chris Ross & Mike Hall t/a Braid Veterinary Hospital* EAT/1115/99 the employee could not work full time as a matter of practicality but the disturbance to the business justified the requirement.

EQUAL PAY CLAIMS AND PART-TIME WORKERS

14.12   The EqPA 1970 has long been used to assist part-time workers if they are treated in a way that disadvantages them and it can be shown that this has a disparate impact upon one sex. The reader is referred to the many cases in earlier chapters on this issue and to Chapter 13 on pensions from which it can be seen that many of the claims in relation to pensions are by part-time workers.

14.13   Any differential treatment relating to terms and conditions of employment which are on the basis that the employer is or has been part time is likely to be in breach of the EqPA 1970. It was held in *Hill and Stapleton v Revenue Commissioners and Department of Finance* [1998] IRLR 466 that an arrangement where employees who had been job sharers and became full time were paid less than those who had always been full time was indirectly discriminatory. See also *Rinner-Kühn v FWW Spezial-Gebäudereinigung GmbH & Co KG* (Case C-171/88) [1989] IRLR 493; *Arbeiterwohlfahrt der Stadt Berlin Ev v Bötel* (Case C-360/90) [1992] IRLR 423; *Magorrian and Cunningham v Eastern Health and Social Services Board and Department of Health and Social Services* (Case C-246/96) [1998] IRLR 86 referred to elsewhere in this book.

14.14 The genuine material factor (GMF) defence will depend upon the facts of the particular case and there may be justification based upon efficiency, costs and resources, business needs, market forces and the position of the employee which may all be factors that affect the payment of part-time workers. However, a variation in pay which sought to be justified merely on the basis that the man is full time whilst the woman is part time is bound to fail (*Jenkins v Kingsgate (Clothing Productions) Ltd (No 2)* [1981] IRLR 388; *R v Secretary of State for Employment, ex p Equal Opportunities Commission* [1994] 1 All ER 910, [1994] IRLR 176). Productivity may justify the differential rate, where it is more productive that a man uses a machine full time whilst the machine for the part-timer stands idle for part of the time (*Handley v H Mono Ltd* [1978] IRLR 534, [1979] ICR 147). The discrimination was not on the basis of sex but productivity and the fact that all the part-timers were women was coincidental.

14.15 A provision that part-time workers would not be paid an end of year bonus contained in a collective agreement could not be justified on the basis of broad social policy considerations (*Kruger v Kreiskranenhaus Ebersberg* [1999] IRLR 808, ECJ). It was held in *Kachelmann v Bankhaus Hermann Lampe KG* [2001] IRLR 49 that a provision in German law whereby part-time workers were not to be compared with full-time workers in deciding redundancy selection was not precluded by the Equal Treatment Directive but was potentially discriminatory as most women were part time. However, the difference in treatment could be objectively justified as the Government was entitled to balance the competing interests of different categories of workers. In *Montgomery v Lowfield Distribution Ltd* EAT/932/95 the employer was justified in giving double time and a day off in lieu for full-time workers where the same benefits were not given to part-time workers who were exclusively female, since the full-time employees worked on a rota shift which encompassed unsocial hours so that there was objective justification for the difference. See also *Lenderich v Helmig* [1996] ICR 35 where a collective agreement could lawfully exclude overtime supplements for part-time workers who did not work in excess of the number of hours of full-time workers even where the part-timers worked overtime

14.16 In *Elsner-Lakeberg v Land Nordrhein-Westfalen* (Case C-285/02) 27 May 2004, it was held that national legislation providing that full-time and part-time teachers were obliged to work the same number of additional hours before being entitled to remuneration could amount to indirect sex discrimination if the different treatment affected considerably more women than men. Part-time teachers had to work 5 hours before they received an enhanced payment whilst full-timers only worked 3 hours.

14.17   It was held in *Wippel v Peek und Cloppenburg GmbH und Co KG* (Case C-313/02), 12 October 2004, that an 'on demand' worker could not compare herself with a full-time worker for the purposes of claiming sex discrimination or less favourable treatment on the ground of part-time status. The right of part-timers to be able to refuse work was a GMF which justified the difference.

14.18   The fact that there is no intention to discriminate against part-time workers will not be a defence (*Barber v NCR (Manufacturing) Ltd* [1993] IRLR 95).

THE PART-TIME WORKERS (PREVENTION OF LESS FAVOURABLE TREATMENT) REGULATIONS 2000, SI 2000/1551 (PTW REGS 2000)

14.19   The PTW Regs 2000 came into force on 1 July 2000. The power to make the Regulations was given by Employment Relations Act 1999 (ERA 1999), s 19. The Regulations were enacted as a result of the Part-time Worker Directive (97/81/EC). Clauses 1–4 of the framework agreement adopted by the Directive were enacted by the Regulations but the vague aspirational obligations on member states and the social partners to review obstacles to opportunities for part-time work, and on employers to seek in various specified ways set out in clause 5, is not addressed in the PTW Regs 2000.

14.20   The ERA 1999, ss 20 and 21 give the Secretary of State power to issue a Code of Practice on part-time work which could cover the wider concerns that are addressed in clause 5 but to date this has not been done and all that has been produced is a guide, 'Part-time workers. The law and best practice', which is referred to in this chapter. However, it must be questioned whether the Directive has been properly transposed.

14.21   The schemes of the PTW Regs 2000 are that there are 17 clauses divided into four parts:

- Part I contains definition and interpretation regulations which are central to the way in which the Regulations operate;

- Part II contains the principle whereby part-time employees may not be less favourably treated than their full-time co-employees without objective justification;

- Part III contains amendments to principal legislation and provides for liability of employers and principals; and

• Part IV covers liability of special classes of persons.

Part I: definitions

Definitions of part-time and full-time workers

14.22 It was originally intended to apply the PTW Regs 2000 only to employees. However, the major change was to apply them to workers as with a number of other recent enactments. The definitions contained in the PTW Regs 2000 are largely from clause 3 of the framework agreement in Directive 97/81/EC.

14.23 The PTW Regs 2000 apply to workers unless otherwise stated. An 'employee' is defined as an individual who has entered into or works under or where the employment has ceased, worked under a contract of employment, being a contract of service or of apprenticeship, whether express or implied, and (if it is express) whether oral or in writing. The latter definition is the same as in the ERA 1996, s 230. An employer, except where the PTW Regs 2000 otherwise provide, means the person by whom the employee or worker is or where the employment has ceased, was employed. A worker, unless otherwise required by the Regulations, is an individual who has entered into or works under or where the employment has ceased, worked under:

'(a) a contract of employment; or
(b) any other contract, whether express or implied and (if it is express) whether oral or in writing, whereby the individual undertakes to do or perform personally any work or services for another party to the contract whose status is not by virtue of the contract that of a client or customer of any profession or business undertaking carried on by the individual.' (PTW Regs 2000, reg 1(2))

See the definition under EqPA 1970 at **3.2**.

Pro rata principle

14.24 The 'pro rata principle' is a central concept to the PTW Regs 2000 and means that, where a comparable full-time worker receives or is entitled to receive pay or any other benefit, a part-time worker is to receive or be entitled to receive not less than the proportion of that pay or other benefit that the number of his weekly hours bears to the number of weekly hours of the comparable full-time worker.

Hours of work

14.25 In the definition of the pro rata principle and in regs 3 and 4 'weekly hours' means the number of hours a worker is required to work under his contract of employment in a week in which he has no absences from work and does not work any overtime or, where the number of such hours varies according to a cycle, the average number of such hours.

Full-time worker, part-time worker and comparator

14.26 A worker is a full-time worker if he is paid wholly or in part by reference to the time he works and, having regard to the custom and practice of the employer in relation to workers employed by the worker's employer under the same type of contract, is identifiable as a full-time worker (reg 2(1)).

14.27 A worker is a part-time worker if he is paid wholly or in part by reference to the time he works and, having regard to the custom and practice of the employer in relation to workers employed by the worker's employer under the same type of contract, is not identifiable as a full-time worker (reg 2(2)). By reg 2(4), a full-time worker is a *comparable* full-time worker in relation to a part-time worker if, at the time when the treatment that is alleged to be less favourable to the part-time worker takes place:

  (a) both workers are–
    (i) employed by the same employer under the same type of contract, and
    (ii) engaged in the same or broadly similar work having regard, where relevant, to whether they have a similar level of qualification, skills and experience; and
  (b) the full-time worker works or is based at the same establishment as the part-time worker or, where there is no full-time worker working or based at that establishment who satisfies the requirements of sub-paragraph (a), works or is based at a different establishment and satisfies those requirements.'

14.28 It is possible for there to be a cross-establishment comparison where there is no comparable full-time worker in the same establishment but the establishments must apparently still be operated by the *same* employer, because the concept of associated employers is not adopted by these Regulations. This omission must be taken to be deliberate and cannot be filled by implication (see *Hardie v CD Northern Ltd* [2000] IRLR 87, EAT; *Colt Group Ltd v Couchman* [2000] ICR 327, EAT for reasoning on similar provisions). The framework agreement clause 2(2) permits a member state to exclude, for objective reasons, part-time workers who work on a casual basis but this has not been adopted in the Regulations. Regulation 2(3) states that, for the purposes of paragraphs 2(1), (2) and (4) the following shall be treated as employed on different contracts:

  '(a) employees employed under a contract that is neither for a fixed term nor a contract of apprenticeship;
  (b) employees employed under a contract for a fixed term that is not a contract of apprenticeship;
  (c) employees employed under a contract of apprenticeship;
  (d) workers who are neither employees nor employed under a contract for a fixed term;
  (e) workers who are not employees but are employed under a contract for a fixed term;

(f) any other description of worker that it is reasonable for the employer to treat differently from other workers on the ground that workers of that description have a different type of contract.'

Workers who become part-time workers

14.29 Under reg 3(1) and (2), notwithstanding reg 2(4), reg 5 shall apply as if there were a part-time worker, and as if there were a comparable full-time worker employed under the terms that applied immediately before a variation or termination, where the worker:

'(a) was identifiable as a full-time worker in accordance with regulation 2(1); and
(b) following a termination or variation of his contract, continues to work under a new or varied contract, whether of the same type or not, that requires him to work for a number of weekly hours that is lower than the number he was required to work immediately before the termination or variation.'

The regulation thus makes a comparison between the worker's part-time employment and full-time employment. However, by reg 3(3) any rights by virtue of reg 2(4) are not affected.

Workers returning to part-time work

14.30 By reg 4(1) the provisions of reg 5 shall apply to a worker who:

'(a) is identifiable as a full-time worker in accordance with regulation 2(1) immediately before a period of absence (whether the absence followed a termination of the worker's contract or not); and
(b) returns to work for the same employer within a period of less than twelve months beginning with the day on which the period of absence started;
(c) returns to the same job or to a job at the same level under a contract, whether it is a different contract or a varied contract and regardless of whether it is of the same type, under which he is required to work for a number of weekly hours that is lower than the number he was required to work immediately before the period of absence.'

14.31 The provisions apply as if the individual was a part-time worker and as if there were a comparable full-time worker employed under the contract under which the returning worker was employed immediately before his absence or alternatively where it is shown that, had the returning worker continued to work under the original contract and a variation would have been made to its term during the period of absence, the contract as varied. However, by reg 4(3) any rights by virtue of reg 2(4) are not affected.

Part II: rights and remedies

14.32 The central provision of the PTW Regs 2000 is contained in reg 5 which enacts the principle of non-discrimination required by clause 4 of the framework agreement in Directive 97/81/EC. Clause 4(4) allows a member state, for objective reasons, to make access to particular conditions of service dependent on a period of service, time worked or earnings qualification, but that has not been adopted in these Regulations.

Less favourable treatment

14.33 By reg 5(1) a part-time worker has the right not to be treated by his employer less favourably than the employer treats a comparable full-time worker:

> '(a) as regards the terms of his contract; or
> (b) by being subjected to any other detriment by any act, or deliberate failure to act, of his employer.'

14.34 The DTI Guidance Notes set out the areas in which an employer must secure equality of treatment of part-timers, on a pro rata basis if necessary, namely rate of pay, contractual sick and maternity pay, occupational pensions, access to training, leave/holidays/breaks, annual leave, maternity and parental leave, career breaks, and selection for redundancy. There must be equal treatment for overtime but this is subject to the part-time worker working past normal full-time hours (see reg 5(4)). It is important to note that the PTW Regs 2000 cover claims in relation to contractual benefits that would be made under EqPA 1970 and non-contractual benefits under SDA 1975.

14.35 In *Pipe v Hendrickson Europe Ltd* (15 April 2003, EAT, HHJ Prophet) the Appellant was placed under pressure to work full time when the employer took the view that it only required three full-time accounting assistants. She was unable to do so, but volunteered to work extra hours, but the employer did not accept that offer or look to see whether it could accommodate her, and it dismissed her. The Employment Tribunal held that the applicant had been unfairly dismissed. It also held that she had been subject to discrimination by reason of her status as a part-time worker. On appeal, it was acknowledged that by reg 5(1)(b), the protection to the part-time worker extended to 'any other detriment', such as the pressure to switch to full-time employment in the present case. The Employment Tribunal's decision regarding discrimination was based on a breach of reg 5. The EAT stated that there were four stages to be considered:

(i) What was the treatment complained of?

(ii) Was that treatment less favourable than that of a comparable full-time worker?

(iii) Was the less favourable treatment on the ground that the worker was a part-time worker?

(iv) If so, was it justified?

In the present case, although the Employment Tribunal had not worked through those stages with precision, it was apparent from its reasons that the applicant had been less favourably treated than the full-time accounting assistants and the Employment Tribunal had considered all the questions posted by reg 5 so that its analysis of reg 5 was correct. The appeal was dismissed.

14.36 The DTI document 'Part-time workers. The law and best practice' (which is currently on the website at: www.berr.gov.uk/whatwedo/employment/ employment-legislation/employment-guidance/page19479.html) sets out examples where the employer must take steps to comply with the law and is essential reading. There are a number of cases which illustrate less favourable treatment in relation to part-time workers under the PTW Regs 2000.

A to Z of less favourable treatment in part time work

Bank holidays

14.37 It was held in *McMenemy v Capita Business Services Ltd* [2007] IRLR 400 by the Court of Session that a part-time worker who does not work on Mondays does not suffer a detriment because his employers do not allow time off in lieu for bank holidays. It was held that there was no less favourable treatment; the reason that time off in lieu was not given was simply that the employee did not work on Mondays. The same would have applied to a full-time employee who did not work Mondays.

Bonuses

14.38 Part-time workers are entitled to a pro rata bonus. The failure to pay a non-contractual incentive bonus was held to be a detriment under equivalent provisions in the Fixed Term Employees (Prevention of Less Favourable Treatment) Regulations 2002, SI 2002/2034 in *Coutts v Cure* EAT/0395/04.

Grading and length of service

14.39 It was held in *Kording v Senator fur Finanzen* [1997] IRLR 710 that there would be indirect discrimination where total length of experience required for exemption from a professional exam was extended pro rata for part-timers, though this could be justified on an objective basis if the extra hours worked made a difference to competence (cf *Nimz* and *Cadman* at **11.80–11.83** and see *Rinke v Arttekammer Hamburg* (Case C-25/02) [2003] ECR I-8349 where the requirement of full-time work for training doctors was justified).

Holidays

14.40 Part-time workers are entitled to pro rata contractual holiday entitlement including parental and maternity leave, subject to the issue of objective justification.

Overtime

14.41 By reg 5(4), a part-time worker paid at a lower rate for overtime worked by him in a period than a comparable full-time worker is or would be paid for overtime worked by him in the same period shall not, for that reason, be regarded as treated less favourably than the comparable full-time worker where, or to the extent that, the total number of hours worked by the part-time worker in the period, including overtime, does not exceed the number of hours the comparable full-time worker is required to work in the period, disregarding absences from work and overtime (see *James v Great North Eastern Railways* EAT/0496/04).

Pay

14.42 Part-timers should not receive a lower basic hourly rate than full-time workers (see *James v Great Northeastern Railways* EAT/0496/04).

Sickness and maternity pay

14.43 The PTW Regs 2000 apply to contractual sickness and maternity pay so that the part-time worker should receive pro rata benefits (cf *Rinner-Kühn v FWW Spezial-Gebäudereinigung GmbH & Co KG* (Case C-171/88) [1989] IRLR 493 in which it was held that there was a breach of Art 141 where employees working less than 10 hours were excluded from sick pay).

Application of the pro rata principle

14.44 By reg 5(3), in determining whether a part-time worker has been treated less favourably than a comparable full-time worker the pro rata principal shall be applied unless it is inappropriate.

Objective justification

14.45 By reg 5(2) the right conferred by para (1) applies only if:

'(a)   the treatment is on the ground that the worker is a part-time worker; and
(b)   the treatment is not justified on objective grounds.'

14.46 The justification defence is permitted by clause 4(1) of the framework agreement though there is no definition of its meaning. The DTI Guidance Notes state:

'Less favourable treatment will only be justified on objective grounds if it can be shown that the less favourable treatment: (1) is to achieve a legitimate objective, for example a genuine business objective; (2) is necessary to achieve that objective; and (3) is an appropriate way to achieve the objective.'

14.47   In *Colman Coyle v Georgiou* EAT/535/00 a firm of solicitors was able to justify its refusal to allow an employed solicitor who had child care problems to work part time.

Less favourable treatment and written reasons

14.48   Where a worker considers that his employer may have treated him in a manner which infringes a right conferred on him by reg 5 he may request in writing from his employer a written statement giving particulars of the reasons for the treatment and the worker is entitled to be provided with such a statement within 21 days of the request (reg 6(1)). Such statement is admissible as evidence in any proceedings under the PTW Regs 2000 (reg 6(2)).

14.49   By reg 6(3), if it appears to the Tribunal in any proceedings under the PTW Regs 2000 that the employer deliberately, and without reasonable excuse, omitted to provide a written statement, or that the written statement is evasive or equivocal, it may draw any inference which it considers it just and equitable to draw, including an inference that the employer has infringed the right in question.

14.50   Regulation 6 does not apply where the treatment in question consists of the dismissal of an employee, and the employee is entitled to a written statement of reasons for his dismissal under ERA 1996, s 92 (reg 6(4)).

Unfair dismissal and detriment

14.51   The employee has the right not to be subjected to a detriment and any dismissal will be automatically unfair where a claim is made under the PTW Regs 2000. Complaint may be made to the Employment Tribunal (regs 7 and 8). The ERA 1996, s 203 applies so that it is *not* possible to exclude or limit the effect of the PTW Regs 2000 (reg 9).

Part III: miscellaneous

14.52   Regulation 10 applies amendments to primary legislation contained in the Schedule.

14.53   By reg 11(1), anything done by a person in the course of his employment shall be treated as also done by his employer, whether or not it was done with the employer's knowledge or approval.

14.54 By reg 11(2), anything done by a person as agent for the employer with the authority of the employer shall be treated for the purposes of the PTW Regs 2000 as also done by the employer.

14.55 By reg 11(3), in proceedings under the PTW Regs 2000 against any person in respect of an act alleged to have been done by a worker of his, it shall be a defence for that person to prove that he took such steps as were reasonably practicable to prevent the worker from doing that act or doing, in the course of his employment, acts of that description.

Part IV: special classes of person

14.56 By reg 12, the PTW Regs 2000 apply to Crown employment and persons in Crown employment as they have effect in relation to other employment and other employees and workers subject to reg 13. 'Crown employment' means employment under or for the purposes of a government department or any officer or body exercising on behalf of the Crown functions conferred by a statutory provision (reg 12(2)). References to employees and a worker are construed as references to a person in Crown employment and references to a contract in relation to an employee and references to a contract in relation to a worker shall be construed as references to the terms of employment of a person in Crown employment to whom the definition of employee or, as the case may be, worker is appropriate for the purpose of application of reg 12 (reg 12(3)). There is provision in reg 13 for the PTW Regs 2000 to apply to the Armed Forces with specific exceptions and qualifications. The PTW Regs 2000 apply to any 'relevant member of the House of Lords staff' which is any person employed under a contract with the Corporate Officer of the House of Lords by virtue of which he is a worker (reg 14). The PTW Regs 2000 also apply to any 'relevant member of the House of Commons staff' meaning any person who was appointed by the House of Commons Commission; or who is a member of the Speaker's personnel (reg 15).

14.57 By reg 16, the PTW Regs 2000 apply to the holding, otherwise than under a contract of employment, of the office of constable or an appointment as a police cadet which shall be treated as employment, under a contract of employment, by the relevant officer. The relevant officer is:

'(a) in relation to a member of a police force or a special constable or police cadet appointed for a police area, the chief officer of police (or, in Scotland, the chief constable);

(b) in relation to a person holding office under s 9(1)(b) or 55(1)(b) of the Police Act 1997 (police members of the National Criminal Intelligence Service and the National Crime Squad), the Director General of the National Criminal Intelligence Service or, as the case may be, the Director General of the National Crime Squad; and

(c) in relation to any other person holding the office of constable or an appointment as a police cadet, the person who has the direction and control of the body of constables or cadets in question.'

The PTW Regs 2000 do not apply to any individual in his capacity as the holder of a judicial office if he is remunerated on a daily fee-paid basis (reg 17).

The decision in *Matthews v Kent and Medway Towns Fire Authority*

14.58   The House of Lords considered the position of part-time firefighters in *Matthews v Kent and Medway Towns Fire Authority* [2006] ICR 365. In this case 12,000 retained firefighters brought claims that they were less favourably treated than whole time firefighters in that different terms and conditions were operated between the two groups. An Employment Tribunal found that the claimants were not employed under the same type of contract as the whole time firefighters within the meaning of reg 2. The full-time firefighters were employed under reg 2(3)(a) whereas the part-timers were employed under reg 2(3)(f) so that they were on different contracts. In the alternative the work was not the same or broadly similar under reg 2(4)(a)(ii). The Tribunal stated that, if it was wrong about the above it would have found that there was less favourable treatment so far as pensions, sick pay and pay for additional duties was concerned and that this was on the ground that the claimant was a part-time worker. There would have been no objective justification for the less favourable treatment. The EAT upheld the Tribunal's findings and the Court of Appeal upheld the findings in some respects and not others.

14.59   The case went to the House of Lords. Agreeing with the Court of Appeal, the House of Lords held that both the claimant retained firefighters and full-time firefighters were employed under 'a contract that is neither for a fixed term nor a contract of apprenticeship' for the purposes of reg 2(3)(a) and that therefore they were employed under the 'same type of contract' within the meaning of reg 2 so as to allow the retained firefighters to claim that they had been less favourably treated than full-time firefighters. The Employment Tribunal and the EAT erred in concluding that whereas the full-time firefighters were employed under a contract falling within reg 2(3)(a), the retained firefighters fell under reg 2(3)(f), which covers 'any other description of worker that it is reasonable for the employer to treat differently from other workers on the ground that workers of that description have a different type of contract'.

14.60   The House of Lords noted that reg 2(3)(f) is a long stop or residual category. It is there to fill any gaps that may have been left and is not designed to allow employers to single out particular kinds of part-time working arrangements and treat them differently from the rest. The purpose of reg 2(3) is only to provide a threshold to require the comparison between full- and part-time workers to take place. Part-time employment is inevitably different from full-time employment in a number of ways, yet the purpose of the PTW Regs is to secure that it is treated equitably. Their Lordships thought that if the threshold of comparability is set too high, this could only apply in the most straightforward of situations, for example where the full-timer and part-timer work in exactly the same way.

14.61 The argument on behalf of the employers that reg 2(3)(f) can take a relationship which would otherwise fall within one of the earlier paragraphs into a different category was rejected. The categories in reg 2(3) are designed to be mutually exclusive and para (f) refers to 'any other description of worker', which in the ordinary use of language means 'any description of worker other than those described in the preceding paragraphs'.

14.62 Further, the Employment Tribunal, the EAT and the Court of Appeal erred in finding that retained and full-time firefighters were not 'engaged in the same or broadly similar work having regard, where relevant, to whether they have a similar level of qualification, skills and experience' within the meaning of reg 2(4)(a)(ii).

14.63 The Tribunal erred in concentrating on the differences between the work rather the weight to be given to the similarities. The House of Lords stated that whether the work on which the full-time and part-time workers are engaged is 'the same or broadly similar' has to be approached in the context of regulations which are inviting a comparison between two types of worker whose work will almost inevitably be different to some extent. In making that assessment, particular weight should be given to the extent to which their work is exactly the same and to the importance of that work to the enterprise as a whole. If a large component of their work is exactly the same, the question is whether any differences are of such importance as to prevent their work being regarded overall as 'the same or broadly similar'. Where both full- and part-timers do the same work, but the full-timers have extra activities with which to fill their time, this should not prevent their work being regarded as the same or broadly similar overall.

14.64 The importance of the same work which they do to the work of the enterprise as a whole is also of great importance in this assessment. The fact that full-timers and part-timers both do some of the same work would not mean that their work was the same or broadly similar where the full-timers do the more important work and the part-timers are brought in to do the more peripheral tasks. The House of Lords stated that it is equally easy to imagine workplaces where the full-timers and part-timers spend much of their time on the core activity of the enterprise, so that the fact that the full-timers do some extra tasks would not prevent their work being the same or broadly similar.

14.65 Regard must also be had to whether the full-time workers and part-time workers have a similar level of qualification, skills and experience. This question is relevant only in so far as it bears on the exercise of assessing whether the work on which the workers are actually engaged at the time was the same or broadly similar.

14.66 The Tribunal treated the fact that there were differences in the levels of skills and experience as an additional factor leading to the conclusion that comparability could not be established, without assessing the extent to which these differences affected the work that the two different kinds of worker were actually engaged in. The Tribunal's conclusion that the job of the full-time firefighter was a fuller wider job than that of the retained firefighter was not the end of the exercise. They still had to address whether, notwithstanding this, the work on which both groups were engaged could nevertheless be described as broadly similar. The case was to be remitted to the Employment Tribunal for reconsideration.

14.67 The case demonstrates that a practical approach needs to be taken to the PTW Regs 2000. The Tribunal's judgment would have emasculated the effect of the Regulations. It is clear from the House of Lords' decision that focus must be carried on the tasks carried out by the part-time worker and consideration given to the importance of those tasks and whether they are broadly similar to the tasks carried out by the full-timer. It is obvious that the full-timer will be carrying out additional tasks to fill up the extra hours but this, in itself, cannot mean that the jobs are not the same or broadly similar otherwise the PTW Regs 2000 could never in reality apply. It is necessary to carry out a careful appraisal of the functions that are being carried out by the part-time workers and the comparators in order to consider whether the work is broadly similar.

Chapter 15

EQUAL PAY HEALTH CHECK

Extracts from Note 6 of the Equal Pay Review Kit and the Working Time Chart are reproduced by kind permission of the Commission for Equality and Human Rights, known as the Equality and Human Rights Commission 'the EHRC'.

15.1   This chapter considers the approach that an employer may adopt in deciding whether its employees are being paid equal pay for work of equal value. The benefits of having carried out a job evaluation in defending any equal pay claim have been referred to in earlier chapters. It is therefore important that the employer carries out an evaluation exercise.

15.2   The former EOC (now the Commission for Equality and Human Rights, known as the Equality and Human Rights Commission ('the EHRC'), produced an Equal Pay Review Kit and the Code of Practice on Equal Pay which contains a wealth of information to assist an employer seeking to devise an equal opportunities plan. ACAS has also recently produced a booklet on 'Job Evaluation, Considerations and Risks' which is available at www.acas.org. uk/CHttpHandler.ashx?id=922&p=0. The content of this chapter is very much based upon these documents.

15.3   This chapter also sets out the checklists that one should consider in relation to the contract of employment and work carried out by the employees in evaluating the work. It is helpful to run through these checklists in evaluating employment.

GENERAL CHECKLIST TO ENSURE THAT THERE IS NO DISCRIMINATION IN PAY

15.4   It will help the employer to undertake a general equality proofing process of the pay structure. If the employer cannot answer 'Yes' to any of the questions in the checklist the employer will need to check the pay structure to ensure it is free from gender-based discrimination. The former EOC (now EHRC) has the following checklist in the Equal Pay Review Kit: Guidance Note 6.

The employer should answer the following questions by *checking pay practice*, rather than relying on the pay policy.		
Design	*Yes*	*No*

	Yes	No
Is everybody in the organisation covered by the same, single job-evaluated pay structure?		
Is the job evaluation scheme analytical and free of sex bias? (see Guidance Note 4)		
Were those involved in the design of the structure trained in equal pay principles?		
Was the likely impact on men and women checked prior to implementation?		
Do the grade boundaries reflect distinct differences in the relative value of jobs?		
Is there an objective justification for the structure?		
Implementation	*Yes*	*No*
Were those involved in the implementation of the pay structure representative of the workforce and trained in equal pay principles?		
Is the structure transparent?		
Has the structure been clearly communicated to staff?		
Are men and women performing equal work receiving equal average basic pay and equal average total earnings?		
Does the statistical analysis confirm that neither men nor women predominate at the tops and bottoms of grades?		

Terms and conditions: pay on entry

15.5 The considerations in respect of possible sex inequality regarding pay on entry, pay protection and pay progression are similar, so one checklist is provided to cover pay policies and practices in these areas. The employer should apply the checks to pay on entry, pay protection and pay progression policies and practices. Where employees are first recruited and are carrying out the same work but there is a differential in pay the question may arise as to what extent qualifications or experience are relevant.

15.6 It is possible that the employer will need to ask other questions that are particular to the employer's organisation. Some of the considerations set out in Guidance note 6 are as follows:

* *Joining a pay band*
  Typically, employees will join a pay grade or job as a new recruit, a transferee, on promotion, on re-entry after a career break, or following a

restructuring of a pay and grading system. The 'entry' rate of pay on joining a job/grade may be determined using a set formula/rules or simply be an amount agreed by the parties. Where a formula is used, the impact should be tested to ensure that its operation is not favouring one gender over another. Where there is discretion over the entry rate of pay, the impact of decisions should also be checked by gender.

- *Pay protection arrangements*
  Red circling. is a widely used pay protection technique for protecting the pay of an individual whose job is downgraded following, for example, an internal reorganisation, grading review or implementation of a new job evaluation scheme (JES), or following a relocation. The use of red circling, which maintains a difference in pay between men and women over more than a reasonable phase-in period of time will be difficult to justify. The employer should check that pay protection arrangements operate over a reasonable period of time. There is no hard-and-fast guidance from employment tribunals on what constitutes a reasonable timescale (see Chapter 11). The danger of perpetuating discrimination where females would be in the red circle but for historical discrimination must be taken into account (see the cases on Red Circling in Chapter 11).

- *Pay progression*
  Differences in pay between men and women resulting from pay progression within a grade or job, whether by traditional increments or an alternative progression mechanism, may be objectively justified by the benefits to the organisation of increased experience ensuring greater expertise.

15.7 Guidance Note 6 states that problems, however, may arise from the legacy of past incremental progression systems, which have particularly benefited a male group of employees and which appear to lie at the root of some gender-based pay differences. It is essential that any new pay progression arrangements are rigorously scrutinised both for their impact on men and women, and for the strength of the increased expertise and value justification. The argument is likely to be stronger if progression is linked to the achievement of pre-determined criteria. The checklist which follows is taken from Guidance Note 6 and is intended to assist in identifying potential equal pay issues. If the Employer answers 'No' (or the employer does not know the answer) to any of the questions in the checklist then the employer will need to further investigate the pay data and pay practice to ensure that it is free from sex discrimination.

Equal Pay – Law and Practice

Pay on entry (recruitment), pay protection, pay progression (Guidance Note 6, p 5)

The employer should answer the following questions by checking pay practice, rather than relying on the pay policy.		
Design	*Yes*	*No*
Are there clear rules governing pay on entry, pay progression and pay protection?		
Were those involved in the design of the rules trained in equal pay principles?		
Were the rules checked for potential bias at the design stage?		
Was the likely impact on men and women of the rules checked prior to implementation?		
Was there an objective justification for the rules?		
Implementation	*Yes*	*No*
Do the rules apply in principle to all employees?		
Have those involved in the implementation of the rules been trained in equal pay principles?		
Are the rules transparent and have they been communicated clearly?		
Are the rules applied consistently and even-handedly in practice?		
Where managerial discretion applies, are there clear guidelines on the exercise of discretion over starting salaries?		
Is there a right of appeal against decisions?		
Impact	*Yes*	*No*
Does the statistical analysis show that men and women performing equal work are treated equally regarding entry salaries, pay protection and pay progression?		
If differences have been revealed, has the employer checked whether current pay practices are causing the pay gaps?		
If differences have been revealed, has the employer checked whether historical pay practices are causing the pay gaps?		
Monitoring and review	*Yes*	*No*

Does the employer regularly monitor and review entry salaries, pay protection and pay progression?		
Does the employer regularly review the objective justification for the rules and practice on entry salaries, pay protection and pay progression to ensure they remain valid?		
Do the rules and practice still meet standards of best equal pay practice?		

Performance-related pay

15.8 Performance-related pay (PRP) systems, include those pay schemes which have a competence-based element, and stand-alone competence-related pay schemes. There is no reason why the performance of women should not be equal to that of men. The Guidance Notes state that the performance/ competence measurement and pay system should, all other things being equal, generally deliver the same performance payments to women as to men. It refers to issues of concerns as being:

- groups of workers being excluded from the system or bonus arrangement;

- applying different performance/competence pay systems to different groups of employees; and

- performance/competence criteria which are potentially indirectly discriminatory by, for example, being more characteristic of male than female behaviour.

15.9 The Guidance Notes contain the checklist below on performance related competence based pay schemes. The first part of the checklist identifies those aspects of any performance/competence pay system where problems could arise. The remaining parts of the checklist deal with specific aspects of particular types of performance pay systems. The Notes state that to work through this checklist the employer will need:

- copies of the performance/competence appraisal/measurement guidance and instructions;

- analyses of performance/competence assessments, or equivalent, overall and by grade/band and gender; and

- analyses of performance/competence payments, overall and by grade/ band and gender.

This Guidance checklist is intended to assist in identifying potential equal pay issues. If the employer answers 'No' (or the employer does not know the answer) to any of the questions in the checklist the employer will need to further investigate the pay data and pay practice to ensure that it is free from sex discrimination.

A performance/competence based pay systems chart (Guidance Note 6, pp 7–9)

The employer should answer the following questions by checking pay practice, rather than relying on the pay policy.		
Access	*Yes*	*No*
Are all groups of workers included in the performance/competence pay system or systems?		
In particular, are part-time workers, temporary or casual staff, those on maternity leave or taking career breaks, or any other group which is likely to be predominantly female, included in the performance/competence pay system?		
Does the same performance/competence pay scheme apply to different groups of workers with jobs of equal value?		
Do men and women have equal access to opportunities to develop/acquire competencies and do they benefit equally from them?		
Design issues – the measurement of performance/competence	*Yes*	*No*
Have all those involved in the design and development of performance/competence appraisal schemes been trained in gender awareness and the avoidance of bias?		
Are the criteria/objectives that are rewarded by the performance/competence appraisal system objectively justified and have they been checked for potential gender bias?		
Are performance/competence criteria which may favour attributes and roles perceived to be 'male' (eg assertion, leadership, decision-making skills) and those perceived to be female (eg co-operation, consultation, and other people-related features) included in a balanced way?		
Do the performance/competence criteria/objectives avoid any which could be indirectly discriminatory, for example, those related to attendance, flexibility in hours of work?		
Are performance/competence targets or objectives equally achievable in jobs typically done by women and men?		

Implementation	Yes	No
Have all those involved in the implementation been trained in gender awareness and the avoidance of bias, as well as in the operation of the scheme?		
Where managerial discretion applies, are there clear guidelines on the exercise of discretion over performance/competence appraisal and payments?		
Is the performance/competence pay system transparent to all employees covered by it, eg does each employee receive information about her or his individual performance ratings and how they convert into pay?		
Impact – performance pay outcomes	**Yes**	**No**
Does the distribution of performance/competence assessments show that there may be gender bias between women and men employees within each grade?		
Is the distribution of performance/competence payments broadly similar as between women and men within each grade?		
Is the distribution of performance/competence payments broadly similar as between women and men across the organisation (within and between schemes)?		
In a scheme where performance/competence payments are consolidated, do men and women undertaking equal work achieve equal earnings over time?		
If differences have been revealed, has the employer checked whether historical practices are causing the pay gaps?		
In a scheme where performance/competence payments are not consolidated, are the average and distributions of such payments similar as between men and women undertaking equal work?		
If differences have been revealed, has the employer checked whether current practices are causing the pay gaps?		
If differences have been revealed, has the employer checked whether historical practices are causing the pay gaps?		
Can any differences in pay between men and women which are attributed to performance/competence be objectively justified?		

Is the treatment of non-consolidated performance/competence payments for pension purposes the same or similar as between men and women undertaking equal work?		
Monitoring and review	*Yes*	*No*
Are performance/competence objectives/targets/assessments/ratings regularly monitored by gender and by full/part time, etc?		
Are performance/competence payments regularly monitored by gender and by full/part time, etc?		
Have schemes been checked for their impact on women who have taken maternity leave?		
Is the exercise of managerial discretion within the performance/competence assessment and pay system monitored by gender?		
Incentive based productivity/bonus schemes	*Yes*	*No*
Is the base point for the measurement of productivity/bonus demonstrably at an equivalent level for work generally undertaken by women as for work generally undertaken by men?		
If the base point is not demonstrably equivalent, have adjustments been made to the measurement system to take account of this?		
Do the measurement steps above the base point represent equivalent levels of additional effort (mental and/or physical) for work generally undertaken by women and work generally undertaken by men?		
Does the system for converting productivity into bonus or other payment result in equivalent pro-rata payments for full-time and part-time staff where appropriate?		
Does the system for converting productivity into bonus or other payment result in broadly similar payments for women and men?		
Are the average payments to women over a suitable period equal to the average payments for men?		
If differences have been revealed, has the employer checked whether current practices are causing the pay gaps?		
If differences have been revealed, has the employer checked whether historical practices are causing the pay gaps?		

Can any differences in pay between men and women, which are attributed to performance/competence, be objectively justified?		

Hours of work

15.10 Checklist 6 to Guidance Notes 6, deals with what it describes as 'Working Time payments'. It notes that in some pay systems, pay includes a number of elements which are paid as work-related premia in addition to basic pay. These might include:

- working time premia, such as overtime, shift pay, on-call payments;

- working conditions allowances, such as 'dirty money';

- miscellaneous payments, such as travel-time payments.

15.11 This is an area, in particular, where women or part-time workers may be paid less as men may be paid more for shift work or unsociable hours. Equal pay problems with work-related premia arise from unequal access, for example, where:

- predominantly female jobs are excluded from the premium payments, or have restricted access to them;

- overtime is restricted to certain grades or jobs, or allocated on a discretionary basis; and

- working conditions allowances are paid to those in male dominated jobs as a result of past collective agreements or 'industrial muscle'.

15.12 If jobs of equal value do not receive equal payments/allowances there will be a claim if the employer cannot objectively justify the difference. If the exclusion or restricted access to work-related premia is itself discriminatory on grounds of gender, it is not necessary for the jobs to be of equal value for a case of gender discrimination in pay to be made. The Guidance Notes state that:

- objectively justifying differential access or payments can present a considerable challenge to employers; and

- the general format of the work-related premia checklist which follows may be adapted to analyse whatever work-related premia operate in the employer's own pay system.

15.13 The checklist below from Guidance Note 6 is designed to assist in identifying potential equal pay issues. If the employer answers 'No' (or does not know the answer) to any of the questions in the checklist the employer will need to further investigate the pay data and pay practice to ensure that it is free from sex discrimination.

Working time payments chart (Guidance Note 6, pp 14–15)

Where men and women are doing like work do they have equal access to payments?			Can the benefit still be objectively justified?		Where men and women are doing jobs of equal work, is their average payment equal?	
Personal Security	Yes	No	Yes	No	Yes	No
Overtime (Monday to Friday)						
Shift pay						
Unsociable hours payments						
Night duty payments						
On-call payments						
Time in lieu of overtime						
Travelling time payments						

Bonuses and other benefits

15.14 The Guidance Notes state that under the Sex Discrimination Act 1975 (SDA 1975) it may be discriminatory not to apply some benefits equally across the whole workforce if this results in a lower proportion of one gender not receiving the benefit (eg only offering child care assistance to women). In terms of equal pay law, each element of the pay package must be treated separately. As part of the Equal Pay Review process, each benefit must therefore be examined separately for equal pay problems. Issues of particular concern regarding gender equality in benefits include:

- unequal access – eg the exclusion of part-time workers from a benefit where the majority of part-time workers are women;

- providing different levels of benefit to different categories of employee; and

- providing different levels of benefit according to length of service.

15.15 Checklist 5, from Guidance Note 6, which follows provides a format which can be adapted to analyse the benefits provided by the employer's own organisation. The checklist will assist in identifying potential equal pay issues. If the employer answers 'No' (or the employer does not know) the answer to any of the questions in the checklist the employer will need to further investigate the pay data and pay practice to ensure that it is free from sex discrimination.

Benefits chart (Guidance note 6, pp 12–13)

Reason for Payment/ Benefit	Where men and women are doing equal work are the proportions of men and women receiving the benefit equal?		Where men and women are doing equal work, is their average payment/ benefit equal?		Can the benefit still be objec- tively justified?		Does the benefit meet current standards of best equality practice?	
Personal Security	Yes	No	Yes	No	Yes	No	Yes	No
Occupational pension								
Sick Pay								
Private health insurance								
Financial Assistance	Yes	No	Yes	No	Yes	No	Yes	No
Interest-free loans								
Mortgage assistance								

Season-ticket loans								
Fees to professional bodies								
Childcare allowances								
Leave	Yes	No	Yes	No	Yes	No	Yes	No
Holidays								
Special paid leave								
Career breaks								
Cars	Yes	No	Yes	No	Yes	No	Yes	No
Company cars								
Private petrol								
Car allowances								
Car parking								
Other benefits	Yes	No	Yes	No	Yes	No	Yes	No
Clothing allowances/ uniforms								
Mobile phones								
Subsidised meals								
Flexible working								

15.16 The Guidance Notes state that for certain benefits, the employer should also check whether all categories of staff regardless of equal work have access. Unequal access might indicate sex discrimination. An example would be childcare allowances.

15.17 The following issues also need to be borne in mind:

- *Maternity.* Special treatment afforded with regard to maternity is treated differently (see Chapter 12). A woman on maternity leave is not entitled to claim equal pay (*Gillespie* [1996] IRLR 214, ECJ). Pay awards after the beginning of the period used to calculate statutory maternity pay (SMP) but before the end of maternity leave must be included in calculating the amount of SMP payable. This requirement is not limited to cases where the employer agrees to backdate a pay award to a date within the calculation period (*Alabaster v Woolwich plc and Another* [2004] IRLR 486).

- *Part time work.* It is to be noted that the position of part-time workers is now likely to be covered by the Part-time Workers (Prevention of Less Favourable Treatment) Regulations 2000, SI 2000/1551; see Chapter 14.

Different termination payments

15.18 It was held in *Barry v Midland Bank plc* [1999] IRLR 581 that it was not unlawful to calculate a severance payment at the rate of pay that was being paid at the date of termination, even though the scheme made no allowance for the fact that the employee had worked part time over the years (though may have accrued as many hours as a full-time worker) and so the salary at termination was less (see further at **10.76**). In *Österreichischer Gewerkschaftsbund, Gewerkschaft der Privatangestellten v Wirtschaftskammer Österreich* (Case C-220/02), 8 June 2004, it was held that female workers in Austria were not discriminated against by national rules governing the calculation of termination payments which did not take account of periods of parental leave. Such employees could not be compared with employees who undertook national service. Nevertheless, employees will need to be extremely careful to ensure that employees are not treated differently in relation to termination payments.

Market factors

15.19 The Guidance Notes also contain a cautionary checklist where the employer pays differently based upon market factors. The notes refer to market factors that lead to inequality such as:

- over-reliance on data from sex segregated jobs;

- internal and external jobs are not accurately matched for 'size';

- failure to ensure that a representative sample of male and female jobs from organisations of a comparable size is included in the database;

- existing market premia cannot be justified and/or outdated market premia continue to be paid.

Market factors are considered in this book at **11.99**.

Market factors checklist

Can you clearly identify an appropriate external market(s) for the jobs within the pay systems?	Yes	☐
	No	☐
Do you apply the same principles and guidance for using market rates in pay determination to all internal jobs?	Yes	☐
	No	☐
Is there an even distribution of male and female jobs in your external labour market database?	Yes	☐
	No	☐
Have you asked your provider of market comparisons/databases for confirmation that the process has been equality proofed?	Yes	☐
	No	☐
If you use a job evaluation scheme for internal and external matching for market purposes has it been audited for sex bias (see separate Guidance Note)?	Yes	☐
	No	☐
Have those involved in preparing market rate data, advising on its use and applying this to pay determination been trained/given guidance in avoiding gender bias?	Yes	☐
	No	☐
Is there clear and objective justification for pay rates which are determined by market comparisons?	Yes	☐
	No	☐
Are market rate additions checked regularly to ensure that they are still justified?	Yes	☐
	No	☐

15.20 Completion of the above tables will give a good idea of whether there is likely to have been disparate treatment. Appendices 2–8 contain the process by which the employer should carry out a full equal pay review based on the information set out above. These documents set out the data that should be collated in carrying out job evaluations of employees and the methods that should be followed in carrying out the JES.

15.21 The employer should bear in mind the provisions of the EOC (now the EHRC) Code of Practice on Equal Pay. The Code is reproduced by kind permission of the Equality and Human Rights Commission (EHRC) in Appendix 9 and can also be found at www.equalityhumanrights.com/Documents/Gender/Employment/equal_pay_code_of_practice.pdf.

Chapter 16

EQUAL PAY AND TUPE

16.1 The Transfer of Undertakings (Protection of Employment) Regulations 2006 (TUPE), SI 2006/246 came into effect from 6 April 2006 and superseded the 1981 Regulations. The Regulations will apply where there has been a relevant transfer or a service provision change as defined in reg 3. There is much case-law on what amounts to a TUPE transfer and there are many issues thrown up by the Regulations which are beyond the scope of this book (the reader is referred to R Upex and M Ryley *TUPE: Law and Practice* (Jordan Publishing, 2006).

16.2 This chapter will consider specific TUPE issues which are likely to be thrown up when one is considering equal pay claims. There are a number of issues under TUPE as follows:

- Upon a transfer, any claims which the employee may have under the equal pay legislation will transfer to the transferee.

- There will be complications where the contracts of employment of women are transferred under TUPE but the contracts of comparators are not transferred. This will be especially so where there are no comparators employed by the transferee. The issue will arise whether the employee has a claim against the transferor or transferee, limitation periods and whether comparators still employed by the transferor can be used.

- However, as will be seen, pension rights do not transfer under TUPE and there are separate provisions in relation to pensions.

- There may be an issue whether the transferee may pray in aid, as a genuine material factor (GMF), the fact that comparators are on higher salaries because their contracts have been transferred from the transferor at that higher salary so that their salary is protected for TUPE reasons.

TRANSFER OF EQUAL PAY CLAIMS TO TRANSFEREE

16.3 By reg 4, upon a TUPE transfer, the terms and conditions of the contracts of the employee will be transferred as reg 4(2) provides that 'all the transferor's rights, powers, duties and liabilities under or in connection with any such contract shall be transferred by virtue of this regulation to the transferee'.

It is apparent that equal pay claims will transfer (cf *DJM International Ltd v Nicholas* [1996] ICR 214 in which a discrimination claim transferred).

COMPARATORS NOT TRANSFERRED

16.4 Where the comparators are not transferred to the transferee but the claimant had a claim against the transferor and has a continuing claim against the transferee issues will arise as to who the employee may claim against and time-limits. These were considered in detail in *Sodexo Ltd v Ms Gutridge and Others, North Tees and Hartlepool NHS Foundation Trust* UKEAT/0024/08, [2008] IRLR 752 in which the EAT considered the operation of the Equal Pay Act 1970 (EqPA 1970), s 2ZA when TUPE applied. The claimant, domestics or cleaners, were all employed by Hartlepool prior to 1 July 2001 at Hartlepool General Hospital. The comparators were maintenance assistants who were employed by Hartlepool prior to and after 1 July 2001. The claimants were transferred to Sodexo on that date but none of the comparators were transferred. The proceedings by the claimants were commenced on 28 December 2006. Since the right to recover back pay can go back 6 years full recovery in the case would have involved a period when the claimants were employed by the transferor. By s 2ZA the claim had to be brought within 6 months from the date of employment.

16.5 The EAT considered reg 5(2) of TUPE 1981. It noted that the issue was whether the claimants could pursue their claims for equal pay in circumstances where their comparators remained with the transferor and they did not initiate their claims until more than 5 years after the transfer. The claimants' case was that the effect of the equality clause was to confer upon them enhanced contractual rights which initially the transferor was obliged to honour, and which then transferred to the transferee as contractual rights on transfer. They took with them such rights as existed at the time of transfer. It was conceded that they could not continue to take the benefits of any improvements for the comparators who were not transferred. The EAT held that the effect of *Powerhouse Retail Ltd v Burroughs and Others* [2006] IRLR 381 was that the 6-month time-limit runs from the date of transfer itself for all equal pay claims which derive from the equality clause with the transferor, at least with respect to alleged breaches by the transferor. This is so whether liability for breach transfers pursuant to TUPE or not. On the alternative argument that the equality clause itself transfers from the transferor to the transferee, Elias J stated as follows:

> 'In my judgment, the true position after the transfer is that the claimant is enforcing a contractual right which is derived from the equality clause operating with respect to the transferor. She could enforce against the transferee such terms as were enforceable against the transferor. The issue is, therefore, what is the time limit for enforcing this particular contractual right, and is it relevant that it is derived from a contractual term arising out of employment with another employer which it would now be too late to enforce against that employer . . .

In short, in my judgment, regulation 5(2) transfers two kinds of relevant liabilities with respect to the equality clause. First, there is the liability for what was done (or not done) by the transferor prior to the transfer. Liability for such acts is transferred under TUPE regulation 5(2). However, the time limit for enforcing that claim is, following *Powerhouse*, six months from the date of transfer. The transferee stands in the shoes of the transferor, but this does not alter the time limits applicable to those claims. Accordingly the claimants are too late to enforce that aspect of their claims.

Second, there is a continuing liability to honour the contractual terms in place at the point of transfer and this placed an obligation on the transferee personally to fulfil those contractual obligations. This liability transfers under TUPE regulation 5(1). In so far as reliance has to be placed on the equality clause as it operated with respect to the transferor in order to establish the contractual right that has been transferred under TUPE, that clause must be deemed to have transferred also. The relevant employment under section 2ZA is therefore the employment with the transferee.'

16.6 It was held that a woman cannot continue to compare herself with the man once he ceases to be a comparator, but she does not lose such enhanced rights as have already been incorporated into her contract. Those rights are by then crystallised and she remains entitled to enforce them as a term of the contract. The claimants could therefore enforce their rights against the transferee for failure to honour their contracts but not against the transferor.

PENSIONS

16.7 Regulation 10 provides that the provisions for transfer relating to employment contracts (reg 4) or collective agreements (reg 5) do not apply:

'(a) to so much of a contract of employment or collective agreement as relates to an occupational pension scheme within the meaning of the Pension Schemes Act 1993; or

(b) to any rights, powers, duties or liabilities under or in connection with any such contract or subsisting by virtue of any such agreement and relating to such a scheme or otherwise arising in connection with that person's employment and relating to such a scheme.'

Provisions of an occupational pension scheme which do not relate to benefits for old age, invalidity or survivors shall not be treated as being part of the scheme (reg 10(2)). Thus pension provision is excluded but this will not cover terms allowing for early retirement on redundancy as it is the latter which is the reason for any payment (*Beckman v Dynamco Whicheloe Macfarlane Ltd* (Case C-164/00) [2002] IRLR 578; *Martin v South Bank University* (Case C-4/01) [2004] IRLR 74).

16.8 The Pensions Act 2004, ss 257 and 258 and the Transfer of Employment (Pension Protection) Regulations 2005, SI 2005/649, which came into force from 6 April 2005, make limited provision for the transferee to provide certain benefits to transferring employees. Where the transferor provided access to an occupational pension scheme the obligation will be triggered on the part of the transferee to provide access to either a defined benefits scheme or a money purchase scheme; in the case of the latter the employer will have to provide a contribution of up to 6% of the employer's basic pay.

16.9 Because pension rights do not transfer under TUPE the 6-month time-limit for bringing a claim will commence against the transferor from the date of transfer and not the date when employment with the transferee ceases (*Powerhouse Retail Ltd v Burroughs and Others* [2006] IRLR 381). In the context of equal pay the issue will be against whom a claim may be brought when a transfer takes place and the effect of the limitation periods.

16.10 However, where employees are transferred and the existing work force, who carry out the same work or work of equal value to the transferred employees, are given access to an occupational pension scheme, it is difficult to see why the transferred employee cannot use the existing employees as comparators to argue that they should receive the same benefits.

TUPE PROVIDING A GMF

16.11 Where the transferred employees are on a higher salary than the employees of the transferee before the transfer, it may be that the employer can argue that the higher pay which is paid to transferred employees must be retained or red circled because of the application of TUPE. This may provide a GMF if existing employees seek to compare themselves with transferred employees. On the other hand, there is nothing to prevent transferred employees on lower salaries comparing themselves with the existing employees where they receive higher salaries and are carrying out the same work or work of equal value.

Chapter 17

THE IMPACT OF THE STATUTORY GRIEVANCE PROCEDURES

17.1   Given that the Employment Act 2002 (EA 2002), Sch 4 provides that the statutory grievance procedures apply to the EqPA 1970, the claimant must get through the hurdle of having lodged a grievance before a claim can be made to the Employment Tribunal. Further, if the procedures have not been complied with and the employer is at fault there may be a statutory uplift of between 10% and 50% (EA 2002, s 31(3)). If the employee is at fault the compensation may be reduced (s 31(2)). The statutory disciplinary and grievance procedures have led to much case-law, particularly as regards the latter, and have been much criticised by employer and employee organisations as well as the judiciary. This chapter summarises the statutory procedures and case-law under EA 2002 and the Employment Act 2002 (Dispute Resolution) Regulations 2004, SI 2004/752 (EA Regs 2004). The provisions will be repealed in April 2009 but will continue to throw up problems in the meantime.

GRIEVANCE PROCEDURES (GPS)

17.2   By EA 2002, s 32, in relation to the jurisdictions listed in Sch 4 (which cover most claims that can be made to an Employment Tribunal and includes equal pay) a complaint may not be presented to a Tribunal if the requirements of Sch 2, paras 6 or 9 have not been complied with or the claimant has presented a complaint less than 28 days after they have been complied with (s 32(1) and (2)). If the 28-day period has not elapsed the Tribunal will not have jurisdiction to hear the case (*Basingstoke Press Ltd (in administration) v Clarke* [2007] IRLR 588).

17.3   By EA 2002, Sch 2, para 6 (standard procedure):

'The employee must set out the grievance in writing and send the statement or a copy of it to the employer.'

17.4   By EA 2002, Sch 2, para 9 (modified procedure):

'The employee must—

(a)   set out in writing—
        (i)   the grievance, and
        (ii)   the basis for it, and

(b)   send the statement or a copy of it to the employer.'

The standard procedure

17.5   After the employee has set out the grievance and sent a statement or copy to the employer:

- the employer must invite the employee to attend a meeting which must not take place until the employee has informed the employer of the basis for the grievance and the employer has had a reasonable opportunity to consider its response. The employee must take all reasonable steps to attend the meeting and the employer must inform the employee of his decision as to his response to the grievance and notify him of the right to appeal against the decision if he is not satisfied with it (EA 2002, Sch 2, para 7); and

- the employee must inform the employer if he wishes to appeal, the employer must invite him to attend a further meeting, the employee must take all reasonable steps to attend the meeting and, after the appeal meeting, the employer must inform the employee of his final decision (EA 2002, Sch 2, para 8).

Modified procedure

17.6   After the employee has sent the grievance and the basis for it, then the employer must set out his response in writing and send the statement or a copy of it to the employee (EA 2002, Sch 2, para 10).

GENERAL REQUIREMENTS

17.7   The general requirements that apply to both dismissal and disciplinary procedures *(DDPs) and GPs* are that:

- each step and action under the procedure must be taken without unreasonable delay (EA 2002, Sch 2, para 12); and

- timing and location of meetings must be reasonable; meetings must be conducted in a manner that enables both employer and employee to explain their cases and, in the case of appeal meetings which are not the first meeting, the employer should, as far as is reasonably practicable, be represented by a more senior manager than attended the first meeting (unless the most senior manager attended that meeting) (EA 2002, Sch 2, para 13).

MEANING OF A GRIEVANCE

17.8 Of crucial importance is the definition of when a grievance has been made since the draconian requirements of s 32 apply to prevent a claim to the Employment Tribunal if the employee has not made a grievance. By the EA Regs 2004, reg 2:

> '"grievance" means a complaint by an employee about action which his employer has taken or is contemplating taking in relation to him.'

17.9 The legislation does not provide for any particular form in which the grievance be made and the case-law has had to consider what may amount to a grievance. The cases to date decide the following (amidst much criticism on the part of the judiciary about the wording and undesirable effects of the legislation).

(1) What matters is that the grievance is set out in writing – it is not necessary for the employee to state that it is a grievance or the invocation of a grievance (*Shergold* at para 33 and see *Canary Wharf* at para 22) so that even a resignation letter will be sufficient.

In *Shergold v Fieldway Medical Centre* [2006] IRLR 76 the employee sent a letter of resignation setting out at length complaints about the way she had been treated by her manager. She had a meeting with the partners but her complaints went unresolved and her resignation was accepted. She claimed unfair constructive dismissal and referred to two specific incidents which led her to resign. The Employment Tribunal decided that she had never raised her grievances as the letter of resignation was not an invocation of a grievance and she had not given details of the two incidents. The Employment Appeal Tribunal (EAT) held that the requirements of para 6 had been satisfied and 'in terms of what is required. It is simply that the grievance must be set out in writing' (Burton J at para 30). In relation to the letter being one of resignation:

> ' . . . the fact that the written grievance in this case was contained in a letter of resignation makes, in our judgment, no difference at all, provided that it is the setting out of a grievance in writing. That can be done in a letter which also serves as the notice of resignation.'

In *Galaxy Showers v Wilson* [2006] IRLR 83 the employee sent a letter dated 9 December 2004 setting out a number of complaints, stating if matters were not resolved he would resign at the end of the month. The EAT upheld the Employment Tribunal's finding that the letter was a grievance. Langstaff J said at para 10:

> 'The definition of grievance does not upon the face of it contain any requirement that the complaint should go any further than being a complaint about what the employer has or has not done. There is no particular formality required by the statutory wording. There is no link at this stage which needs to be drawn between the making of the complaint and

any intention to follow the complaint through to a grievance process or a further hearing or a meeting. What is required at this stage is simply to identify whether there has been a complaint.'

(2) The question is whether on a fair reading of the document the employer could reasonably have been expected to appreciate that a grievance was being raised. In *Canary Wharf Management Ltd v Edebi* UKEAT/0708/05/DA, Elias P stated that:

> 'It seems to me that the objective of the statute can be fairly met if the employers, on a fair reading of the statement and having regard to the particular context in which it is made, can be expected to appreciate that the relevant complaint is being raised.'

(3) The grievance must still be extant. In *Canary Wharf* Elias P stated:

> 'There is no maximum time limit prior to the lodging of the claim to the Tribunal in which the grievance must have been raised. There is the minimum period of 28 days which must be allowed for the employer to deal with it and go through the relevant procedures, but no maximum period. That is not to say, however, that the act of raising a complaint months or years prior to lodging the Tribunal claim will necessarily constitute the appropriate raising of the grievance. The grievance must be extant.'

(4) With the step 1, standard procedure, the grievance letter need only set out the grievance and does not need to set out the basis. In *Thorpe & Soleil Investments Ltd v Poat & Lake* [2006] All ER (D) 30 (Jan), EAT a seven-page letter chronicling a litany of complaints was a grievance, though HHJ Clark did not in the event permit the point to be taken as to whether the statutory GPs applied since it was not taken below.

(5) The statutory procedure is separate from any contractual procedure so that it can be complied with, though a contractual procedure has not been followed, where the employee has written a letter that amounts to a grievance even though he was not specifically intending to commence the statutory grievance procedure (*Shergold* at para 34:

> ' . . . there is equally no requirement that an employee must comply with any company or contractual grievance procedure. It is simply a question of setting out the grievance in writing.'

(See also *Thorpe*.)

(6) A letter from a third party, such as a solicitor acting for the employee can be a step 1 grievance. In *Mark Warner Ltd v Aspland* [2006] IRLR 87 a solicitor's letter was written which stated that unless the employer took action against a manager who had allegedly bullied the claimant, she would treat the employer as being in fundamental breach of contract, resign and claim constructive dismissal. When no undertaking to discipline was given the employee resigned. The Employment Tribunal

held that the solicitor's correspondence amounted to a grievance and this was upheld by the EAT. HHJ Clark stated:

> '... it matters not whether the grievance is raised, for example, in a letter before action ... I see no warrant for reading the words "employee" and "employer" in para. 6 of Schedule 2(2) EA 2002 as excluding action taken by their agents, here the parties' solicitors.'

(7)   A letter from a solicitor which is expressed to be 'without prejudice' may even be a grievance. See, for example, *Arnold Clark Automobiles v Stewart and Others* UKEATS/0052/05/RN; per Lady Smith:

> 'How could it be said that a claimant was intimating a statement of grievance if, at the same time, he was reserving his right to say something different at a later date? However, the message did not change. The claim put before the tribunal was in respect of the matter complained of in his solicitor's letter. Given that the statement of grievance requires to relate to the subject matter of any subsequent claim, he would have been in difficulty if the claim presented to the tribunal was different in substance but it was not. On reflection, it seems to us that the use of the "Without prejudice" formula did not prevent the letter being viewed as a statement of grievance for the purposes of s.32 of the 2002 Act.'

(8)   A request for flexible working may be a grievance even where it does not expressly state that this is the position. In *Commotion Ltd v Rutty* [2006] IRLR 171 the employee made a formal request to work a 3-day week and appealed against the refusal after an informal request was refused. She resigned when the request was rejected. The Employment Tribunal found, amongst other matters, that the refusal was a breach of trust and confidence which entitled her to terminate her employment. It held that the presentation of the application for flexible working amounted to a presentation of a grievance. HHJ Burke QC stated that 'it cannot be the case in law that there must be a separate document instituting each of the two sets of procedures' (para 3).

(9)   A discrimination questionnaire cannot be a grievance as this is specifically excluded by reg 14 and this will include the statements in the questionnaire as well as the questions. In *Holc-Gale v Makers UK Ltd* [2006] IRLR 178 HHJ Clark stated:

> '... the policy behind reg 14 is to exclude the statutory anti-discrimination questionnaire procedure altogether from the statutory definition of grievance.'

It is therefore important to note that, in an equal pay claim, the fact that a questionnaire has been served will not be sufficient to be a grievance. It will be important for the employee to provide a document as well as the questionnaire which she makes clear amounts to a grievance.

(10) The grievance need not be identical to the subsequent proceedings provided that there is a material similarity. See, for example, *Shergold* per Burton J at para 35–36:

> ' . . . the grievance in question must relate to the subsequent claim, and the claim must relate to the earlier grievance, if the relevant statutory provision is to be complied with. It is clearly no compliance with the requirement that there must be a grievance in writing before proceedings if the grievance in writing relates, for example, to unpaid holiday pay and the proceedings, which are then sought to be issued, are based upon race discrimination or sex discrimination with no relevance to any question of holiday pay. In those circumstances, it is likely that it will be found that the proceedings were issued in breach of the statutory procedure because no grievance in writing had been set out beforehand . . . But that does not begin to mean that the wording of the simple grievance in writing required under paragraph 6, and the likely much fuller exposition of the case set out in proceedings, must be anywhere near identical; not least, as we have described, because, at any rate where the standard procedure is concerned, the basis of the grievance does not have to be set out in the first instance.'

(11) It does not matter that the employer is not given an opportunity to respond (*Shergold* at para 38).

(12) As stated, the step 1 stage only requires that the fact of a grievance is set out. The employee must set out the actual acts complained of before a meeting takes place of where the modified procedure is being followed. Where the modified procedure is followed and there is no specification of the grievances the Tribunal will have no power to entertain the claim. It was stated in *Clyde Valley Housing Association v MacAulay* [2008] IRLR 616 that the basics – who and why – are needed so that where the evidential basis for a generalised complaint is missing the procedures have not been complied with. It is apparent from this case that it will not be enough for a claimant to merely state that she has an equal pay claim as this hardly provides the basis for the grievance.

17.10 The statutory GP does not apply where the employer has dismissed or is contemplating dismissal of the employee but the employee will be obliged to commence the GP where constructive dismissal is claimed (the effect of the EA Regs 2004, regs 2 and 6).

EXTENSION OF TIME IN DDP AND GP CASES

17.11 The EA Regs 2004, reg 15 provides:

- where a complaint is presented, the DDPs apply and the employee:

> ' . . . presents a complaint to the tribunal after the expiry of the normal time limit for presenting the complaint but had reasonable grounds for believing,

when that time limit expired, that a dismissal or disciplinary procedure, whether statutory or otherwise (including an appropriate procedure for the purposes of regulation 5(2)), was being followed in respect of matters that consisted of or included the substance of the tribunal complaint.'

- where a complaint is presented, the GPs apply and the employee presents a complaint within the normal time-limit, but in circumstances where EA 2002, s 32 prevents the complaint from being presented; or the employee presents a complaint after the expiry of the normal time-limit for presenting the complaint having complied with para 6 or 9 of Sch 2 in relation to his grievance within that normal time-limit.

The normal time-limit for presenting the complaint is extended for a period of 3 months beginning with the day after the day on which it would otherwise have expired.

17.12 The automatic extension does not apply in cases of unfair dismissal where constructive dismissal is not alleged as the GPs do not apply to a grievance that the employer is contemplating dismissal (*Lothian Buses plc v Nelson* UKEATS/0059/05).

17.13 In *Piscitelli v Zilli Fish Ltd* UKEAT/0638/05/DZM the claimant was summarily dismissed on 2 February 2005. By letter dated 23 February the claimant's solicitors alleged the dismissal to be unfair. There were negotiations to compromise and the final contact took place on 9 May; on 11 May proceedings were lodged, the 3-month period having expired on 1 May. The Employment Tribunal held that the claimant did not have reasonable grounds for believing that a DDP was being followed when the primary limitation period expired. The letter of 23 February did not amount to an appeal. HHJ Clark accepted the contention that the letter on a proper reading did not raise an appeal so that there were no grounds for believing that a DDP was being followed when the primary limitation period expired. It was stated that where an employer had no appeal procedure what was required in the first place was to lodge an appeal. If the employer refused to entertain it there would be no ground for believing the disciplinary process was being followed so that a claim must be presented within the 3-month time period and the employer could be penalised in compensation if the claim succeeded.

17.14 The claimant presented a complaint one day late in *Mr R T Van Dieren v Mr and Mrs Edwards and Others* UKEAT/0166/06/LA where it was reasonably practicable to have presented the claim in time. The DDP applied and not the GPs as the Employment Tribunal had found. The case had to be remitted as the Employment Tribunal had not considered whether the employee had a reasonable ground for believing that when the time-limit expired the DDP was still being followed. In the important case of *Spillett v Tesco; v BUPA Care Homes Ltd v Cann* UKEAT/0475/05/DZM, HHJ Clark sitting alone, held that s 34 does not prevent the 'just and equitable' extension under the Disability Discrimination Act 1995 (DDA 1995), Sch 3, Part III being exercised. His Honour stated:

> 'The question raised directly in the Cann case is whether the expression "original time limit" contained in section 32(4) EA, itself not defined in the Act, refers to the primary 3 month limitation period or to the primary period as extended by the Tribunal where either it was not reasonably practicable to present a complaint of Unfair Dismissal in time (ERA section 111(2)(b)) or it is just and equitable to extend time in a DDA claim, applying Schedule 3 paragraph 3 to the Act.'

He concluded

> 'In my judgment the "original time limit for making the complaint" is the time limit provided for in the relevant legislation, here the DDA. That includes giving a tribunal the power to consider a complaint made outside the primary limitation period where it is just and equitable to do so.'

This case appears to put at rest the concern that employees may not be able to rely upon the provisions as to extensions of time in the various employment legislation.

EXCEPTIONS AND DEEMED COMPLIANCE

17.15 The Tribunal can still entertain a complaint where the statutory GP has not been complied with if the employer is violent, abusive or behaves in an unacceptable way (EA Regs 2004, reg 11(3)(a) and (b)) or where factors beyond the control of either party make if effectively impossible to go through the procedures (reg 11(3)(c)). Compliance will be deemed to have taken place where:

(1) the employee sent a step 1 statement before the appeal stage of the DDP (reg 7);

(2) the employee ceased to be employed and sent a step 1 statement but it was not reasonably practicable for the procedure to be completed (reg 8);

(3) a written grievance has been raised by a representative of more than one employee (reg 9); and

(4) the employee has raised a grievance via a collectively agreed dispute resolution procedure (reg 10).

ADJUSTMENT OF TRIBUNAL AWARDS

17.16 If the statutory procedures are not completed through the fault of either, the Tribunal may increase or reduce the award by not less than 10% or more than 50% (s 31) where the complaint falls within the list in Sch 3 (which does not include part-time workers or fixed-term employees) and the 10% lower limit may be disapplied in exceptional circumstances (EA 2002, s 31(4)).

17.17 It is, at least until the statutory procedures are repealed, necessary to take into account the way in which equal pay claims interact with the obligation to make a grievance under the statutory procedures.

17.18 In *City of Bradford Metropolitan District Council v Pratt* [2007] IRLR 192 the claimant was employed as a cleaner at the Alhambra Theatre and St George's Hall. The claimant wrote a letter after her employment had terminated stating:

> 'I have been subjected to unlawful sex discrimination in relation to my pay and conditions. This is a written statement of grievance in compliance with statutory dispute resolution requirements. My grievance is that I believe I have been paid less than male employees of this authority for which work is broadly similar or of equal value. I believe I have been denied equal access to additional payments enjoyed by male colleagues.'

Mrs Pratt opted to follow the modified procedure. Under the modified procedure it was necessary to set out the grievance and the basis for it. The employer wrote asking for details for the claim. The claimant stated that the comparators were at the Alhambra Palace and comprised the post of cleaner in which male colleagues work alongside doing the same task, the 'daymen' who worked alongside the female cleaners. In her claim the claimant compared herself to two 'litter pickers' who were grade 1 manual workers receiving a bonus. The EAT held that the letter did not set out the basis of the claim as required by the modified procedure. The letter did not contain any indication of the type of male colleague in respect of whom the grievance was said to apply or the type of additional payment in respect of which the claim was made, or the type of work in comparison to which equal value was claimed. The claimant's reply to the request for further information did set out the basis for the grievance but the claim form issued did not relate to the basis of the grievance put forward as it referred to employees of the same grade who received a bonus, rather than employees who did the same work but were paid more.

17.19 In *Bainbridge v Redcar and Cleveland BC (No 2)* [2007] IRLR 494 the EAT held that the Employment Tribunal was wrong to increase compensation by 5% because of the failure to 'go through the charade of individual interviews'. In the Court of Appeal it was stated at par 310:

> 'If, as in our view is the case, there was no relevant "blatancy", then the ET's rejection of there being no uplift and their choice, instead, of an uplift of 5% is left

unsupported by any acceptable reason. Hence it was an error of law. Moreover, having accepted in terms that there was "considerable force in [Redcar's] pointlessness argument", they failed, as far as one can tell, to have that in mind save in their rejecting an increase of "more than 10%". To judge from the reasons expressed, the ET had failed to take that into account as a factor which could lead to it being just and equitable to award no increase at all. A consideration of what is "just and equitable", which is what section 31(4) invites, requires a consideration of all relevant surrounding circumstances. Although, in an overall assessment, one factor may, of course, tip the balance one way or another, the ET's concentration on "blatancy" as the reason for rejecting a zero uplift, quite apart from being in any event misplaced, seems to have been part not of a consideration of all relevant circumstances, but of a focus upon one to the exclusion of the many others. We thus agree with the EAT's analysis that the ET had, in effect, wrongly directed itself on the meaning of "just and equitable". We hold that the ET's decision on uplift was in error of law.'

A GRIEVANCE RELATING TO A CLAIM UNDER EQPA 1970

17.20   In equal pay claims the claimant may choose to specify a range of comparators or may discover that there are different, more appropriate comparators, as a result of further investigations that have been carried out. In some cases the claimants have merely specified the job range with which they seek to compare themselves. Some of these issues were considered in *The Highlands Council v TGWU/Unison* [2008] IRLR 272 in which the EAT considered whether the claimants were prevented by EA 2002, s 32(2) from presenting complaints specifying certain comparators that were different from those that had been stated in the grievances. There was variation as between the comparators specified in the relevant grievance letters and those specified in the forms ET1. The forms ET1 included comparators which had not featured in the grievance letters. The Tribunal held that there had been compliance although the job types of the comparators identified in their subsequent claims to an Employment Tribunal, which were also rated in the Green Book, differed from those identified in their grievance. On appeal the EAT noted that the relevant issue referred to by the Tribunal was:

'. . . whether, in a claim of equal pay, a claimant is entitled to amend her chosen comparator during the course of the proceedings without having to submit a fresh grievance and a fresh claim, in order to comply with the statutory grievance procedure?'

17.21   The EAT was of the view that this was an erroneous way to proceed as the question was not one of amendment during the course of proceedings but whether s 32(2) prevents the proceedings at all. The Union argued that if it was necessary to identify a comparator in the grievance then it would mean that a claimant would have to issue proceedings whenever a new comparator was identified. It was argued that the employee was only required to set out at the first stage that he or she had an equal pay complaint. The employer argued that it would not be in a position to understand the nature of the grievance prior to the start of proceedings. Lady Smith noted that it is for the employee to identify the comparator and the onus only passes to displace the presumption if he can. It is 'only incumbent on an employer to volunteer information about comparators if he requires to do so when seeking to rebut the presumption of discrimination or if he has been ordered to do so either under the Freedom of Information Act provisions or by an Employment Tribunal in the course of proceedings'. In *Bainbridge* the EAT had held that claims against different comparators were separate causes of action so that *res judicata* did not apply. Lady Smith stated that:

> ' . . . it seems to me that the exercise of comparison is so fundamental to a complaint that an employer has failed in his equal pay obligations, that there must be some specification of comparator, at least by reference to job or job type in the grievance document. Without that, the employer cannot be expected to appreciate that a relevant complaint is being made. It cannot be enough to state that an equal pay claim is being made without saying more. That would not amount to a relevant complaint of breach of the 1970 Act requirements. I recognise that a distinction has to be drawn between the separate stages of the procedure. The employee does not have to set out the "basis" for the grievance at the first stage. It is, however, wrong, in my view, to regard the specification of a comparator as being a matter of setting out the basis for the grievance. Setting out the "basis" is not a matter of inserting the essentials required to render the complaint relevant but rather a matter of fleshing out those essentials.'

17.22   An employee is not being provided with enough simply to be told that there is an equal pay complaint. Where the employee discovers materially different comparators:

- if Tribunal proceedings have not commenced then, to comply with the statutory requirements, a further grievance document will require to be communicated if the claimant wishes, in the event that the grievance procedure does not resolve the issue, to rely on that comparator in a subsequent Employment Tribunal claim;

- if Tribunal proceedings have commenced then it is not a question of considering whether a claim can be presented or not. It has already been presented. The claimant could seek to amend the existing claim and if there was a good reason for the reference to the new comparator(s) not having been made at that stage then that would, no doubt, weigh in the claimants' favour. Alternatively, where Tribunal proceedings have already commenced, it would be open to the claimant, if so advised, to start afresh in respect of the new comparator, with a fresh grievance and, if the issue is not resolved through the grievance procedures (which should not be assumed to be without prospect of success) with a fresh Tribunal complaint.

17.23   The claim was remitted to consider the issue of whether EA 2002, s 32(2) applied so as to prevent the complaints being presented having regard to the fact that to determine that issue, it was necessary to consider whether in relation to each claimant they had previously communicated a grievance document to the respondents specifying comparators that were not materially different from those specified in their forms ET1.

17.24 On appeal in the Court of Session, the appeal was allowed in part: *Cannop and Others v Highland Council, Highland Council v TGWU* [2008] IRLR 634. The Court of Session held that the Employment Tribunal and EAT had erred in determining the matter on a hypothetical question, whether it was necessary under the standard procedure to specify comparators in the step 1 grievance document. The EAT had been right to allow the appeal but the terms on which it was remitted were varied. The Lord President stated that s 32 should not be construed any more widely than was necessary to give effect to the intentions of the statute. The court considered that it had been, neither necessary nor desirable for the Employment Tribunal or EAT to express an opinion on the question of whether comparators need to be specified in the grievance document in an equal pay dispute. The Tribunal had allowed itself to be drawn into discussion of what was in the circumstances a hypothetical question, namely, whether an employee who had simply stated that she had an equal pay grievance (and nothing more) had, for the purposes of any later equal pay claim, satisfied the requirement of EA 2002, Sch 2, para 6. In so far as the Employment Tribunal and the EAT had expressed opinions on those wider issues, those comments were obiter and the Court of Session did not approve of their pronouncements.

17.25 The EAT had been entitled to construe the Employment Tribunal's reasoning as meaning that it would not have mattered if the comparators referred to in the grievance documents were quite different from those relied on in the subsequent claims. To that extent, the EAT had been entitled to allow the appeal and remit the matter back to the Tribunal. However, the terms of the EAT's order remitting the matter to the Tribunal could be read as deciding that in every case the statement of grievance had to specify the comparator or comparators relied on. That issue did not arise for decision. Accordingly, the terms of the remittal would be varied, so that it would fall to be decided by the Employment Tribunal whether, in respect of each claim, the grievance underlying the Tribunal claim was essentially the same as the grievance earlier communicated.

17.26 See further *City of Edinburgh Council v Marr* [2008] IRLR 279 in which the EAT held that it was for the claimant to identify the comparator and it was not appropriate to require particulars of the employer which forces the employer to carry out this exercise. This has obvious implications in the way that the grievance must be framed.

17.27 The approach that was taken by the EAT in *Highland Council* was not followed by the EAT, Elias P presiding, in *Suffolk Mental Health Partnership NHS Trust v Hurst and Others* UK/EAT/0366/08/RN which was heard at the same time as a number of other cases on the same issue. Elias P launched a scathing criticism on the way that the procedures had worked in practice. He provided a useful summary of current principles, as follows:

'(i) The underlying purpose of the statutory grievance procedures is to seek to encourage conciliation and to avoid disputes having to be resolved by a tribunal (*Shergold* para 26; *Highland Council* (EAT) para 29). The provisions are to be construed having that purpose in mind.

(ii) In determining whether a statement amounts to a grievance or not, the appropriate test is the following (*Highland Council* para 10):

"the grievance document requires to be in such terms that, on a fair reading of it, the employer can be expected to appreciate that a relevant complaint is being raised (*Canary Wharf* at paragraphs 24 and 25); he needs to be able to understand from the grievance document what is the general nature of the complaint that is being made (*Shergold* at paragraph 37)."

(iii) When construing the grievance – and this must apply both to the issue of whether a statement raises a grievance at all, as well as what complaint is identified by the grievance – the context is important. The point was put by the Lord President, Lord Hamilton, in the *Cannop* case as follows (para 29):

"Moreover, the grievance document need not necessarily be read in isolation. There may have been earlier communications with the employer which provide a context in which the grievance document falls to be interpreted (*Canary Wharf*, paragraph 36). Thus, as seems to have been the case for some of the union-backed claimants in the present proceedings, prior communications between the unions on behalf of their members and the respondents, even if they do not give rise to deemed compliance by virtue of reg. 9 or 10 of the 2004 Regulations, may constitute a relevant context in which the grievance documents are to be understood. Events subsequent to the communication of the grievance document (for example, the giving of the "basis" prior to the step 2 meeting and exchanges between the parties at that meeting) may illuminate the nature and scope of the grievance."

(I confess to having some difficulty with the notion that the construction of the grievance can be made in the light of subsequent communications, but nothing turns on that issue in this case.)

(iv) It is inappropriate to carry out an unduly technical or over sophisticated approach to construing a grievance (*Shergold* para 27; *Edebi* para.41, approved in *Highland Council* (CS) para 29).

(v) It is enough in relation to step 1 of the standard grievance procedure to identify "the complaint" (Edebi para 21). That is to be distinguished from the obligation (arising at step 2 of the standard grievance procedure but in step 1 of the modified procedure) to set out the "basis" of the complaint.

(vi) The statement of grievance must be a statement of essentially the same complaint as the employee is seeking to have determined in the Tribunal (*Edebi* paras 16, 21); *Cannop* (Court of Session, at para 29). In this context, however, it must be borne in mind that the grievance document and the claim form are designed to achieve different objectives and are addressed to a difference audience. In *Cannop* (CS para 29) the Lord President explained it thus:

> "... We add only that in carrying out this exercise it should be recognised that the grievance document and the tribunal claim are designed to perform different functions and that their language can accordingly be expected commonly to be different. The correlation to be looked for is whether underlying the claim presented to the tribunal is essentially the same grievance as was earlier communicated"

(vii) In accordance with European law principles, the procedural requirements, looked at in context, should not be applied so as to render access to the Employment Tribunal impossible in practice or excessively difficult: Cannop (para 25). This question needs to be looked at broadly: *Unison and another v Brennan* [2008] IRLR 492 para.51.'

17.28   The EAT then stated that the issue before them was:

> ' . . . what detail is necessary to identify "the complaint" and what can properly be considered as "the basis" of the complaint. A related issue is how to determine whether the correlation principle is satisfied, i.e. whether underlying the claim made to the tribunal is the same grievance as that raised with the employer.'

17.29   Having considered the arguments and the above authorities, Elias P concluded:

> ' . . . only the minimum requirement is necessary when raising a statement of grievance. In my judgment, it is enough for the claimant to indicate that he or she is pursuing an equal pay claim. That is compatible with the definition of a "grievance". The employee has made it plain that she objects to action taken by the employer, namely the failure to pay the sum due to her, and by identifying the claim as an equal pay claim she is also revealing the reason why she is saying that. She is not, for example, contending that there has been a failure to pay as a result of some mistake or because overtime hours have not been counted, or because her rate is below the minimum wage, or anything of that nature. The employer knows that the allegation is that a comparable man doing equal work (whether that is work rated as equivalent, equal value, or like work) is receiving more than she is and he ought not to be. That much is inherent in the action being identified as an Equal Pay Act claim.
>
> I also consider that this construction best meets the injunction of the Lord President in *Cannop* that the appropriate construction should be one which goes no further than is strictly necessary to give effect to the intention of the legislature.
>
> This construction is supported, in my view, by considerations of policy. The effect of construing the concept of "the grievance" too widely is that claimants – who will often in this jurisprudence be litigants in person – are denied the opportunity to bring their claims altogether if they have not raised a relevant grievance in time. That is a draconian step to take for what might be a purely technical failure to comply with the regulations.'

17.30 Elias P therefore thought that the correlation principle could be satisfied as follows:

> 'If my construction of what constitutes a grievance is correct, it follows that the correlation principle will in practice be very easy to satisfy. If the grievance states that the complaint is an equal pay complaint, a claim form which reflects that fact will suffice whether the details of the claim are provided or not. Again, this does not make the exercise a pointless one. If the claim raises claims of a quite different jurisdiction, for example a dismissal claim or redundancy, there will obviously be no correlation.'

17.31 Bearing in mind that there were two conflicting decisions of the EAT, leave to appeal to the Court of Appeal was given.

Chapter 18

PROCEEDINGS AND REMEDIES

18.1 This chapter will consider specific issues that are likely to arise during any proceedings in which an equal pay claim is brought. It is not intended to be a comprehensive coverage of Tribunal procedure and the reader is referred to *Employment Law Practice 2008* (John Bowers QC et al) for the most comprehensive coverage in this area. A number of areas have already been covered in other chapters, in particular:

(a) grievance procedures in Chapter 17;

(b) questionnaire procedures at **10.17**; and

(c) equal value claims and the procedures to be followed in ascertaining equal value in Chapter 9.

18.2 The procedure in equal pay Tribunal cases is governed by the general provisions of Sch 1 of the Employment Tribunals (Constitution and Rules of Procedure) Regulations 2004, SI 2004/1861 and Sch 6 so far as equal value is concerned.

JURISDICTION

18.3 The right to equal pay takes effect by an equality clause being incorporated into the contract of employment. This means that the claimant will have a contractual right to equal pay so that it is possible to bring claims in the county court or High Court for damages, a declaration or an injunction. It may be possible to claim unlawful deduction from wages under Part II of the Employment Rights Act 1996 (ERA 1996). However, the most common action will be to seek a declaration and compensation in the Employment Tribunal.

18.4 The ordinary courts will have jurisdiction but the EqPA 1970, s 2(3) provides that the court can refer the issue to a Tribunal if it believes that it can be more conveniently disposed of by the Tribunal and the court may strike out the claim or counterclaim. The court may, alternatively adjourn the matter pending reference to a Tribunal, which it can make or require a party to make and, in the meantime, stay proceedings. The county court or sheriff court will treat any finding by a Tribunal as conclusive (SDA 1975, s 73(2)).

18.5 A complaint may be referred to a Tribunal:

- by the employee presenting a complaint (EqPA 1970, s 2(1));

- by the employer asking for a declaration if a dispute arises about the effect of the equality clause (EqPA 1970, s 2(1A));

- by the DTI on behalf of a group of women (EqPA 1970, s 2(2));

- by the High Court or county court (EqPA 1970, s 2(3));

- by the EHRC on certain issues.

TIME-LIMITS FOR MAKING A CLAIM

18.6 In some cases breaches of the EqPA 1970 may go back many years and there may be issues as to whether a claim has been brought in time and how far back the Tribunal may go in granting any remedy.

18.7 The EqPA 1970, s 2(4) provides that no determination may be made by a Tribunal unless the proceedings are instituted on or before the qualifying date, determined in accordance with s 2ZA. The latter section contains detailed provision as to when time starts to run. Section 2ZA differentiates between:

- a concealment case: where the employer deliberately concealed from the woman any fact (the qualifying fact) which is relevant to the contravention to which the proceedings relate, and
  - without knowledge of which the woman could not reasonably have been expected to institute the proceedings; and
  - the woman did not discover the qualifying fact (or could not with reasonable diligence have discovered it) until after the last day on which she was employed in the employment, or the day on which the stable employment relationship between her and the employer ended. In a case which is a concealment case (but not also a disability case), the qualifying date is the date falling 6 months after the day on which the woman discovered the qualifying fact in question (or could with reasonable diligence have discovered it) (s 2ZA(5)). In a case which is both a concealment and a disability case, the qualifying date is the later of the dates under the concealment or disability provisions (s 2ZA(7));

- a disability case: where the woman was under a disability at any time during the 6 months after the last day on which she was employed in the employment, the day on which the stable employment relationship between her and the employer ended, or the day on which she discovered (or could with reasonable diligence have discovered) the qualifying fact deliberately concealed from her by the employer.

In a case which is a disability case (but not also a concealment case), the qualifying date is the date falling 6 months after the day on which the woman ceased to be under a disability (s 2ZA(6));

- a stable employment case: where the proceedings relate to a period during which a stable employment relationship subsists between the woman and the employer, notwithstanding that the period includes any time after the ending of a contract of employment when no further contract of employment is in force.

  In a case which is a stable employment case (but not also a concealment or a disability case or both), the qualifying date is the date falling 6 months after the day on which the stable employment relationship ended (s 2ZA(3));

- a standard case: where a case is not a stable employment case, a concealment case, a disability case, or both a concealment and a disability case.

  In a standard case, the qualifying date is the date falling 6 months after the last day on which the woman was employed in the employment (s 2ZA(3)).

18.8 The 6-month limitation period for making a clam was held to be lawful in *Preston v Wolverhampton Healthcare NHS Trust* [2001] IRLR 237 following the European Court of Justice (ECJ) decision ([2000] IRLR 506) that there was no incompatibility with Community law. The best view is that there is continuing discrimination where, for example, a part-timer is excluded from a pension scheme or there is other such continuing inequality (cf *Barclays Bank plc v Kaptur* [1991] IRLR 136). The 6-month limitation period runs from the date of leaving employment or the termination of the contract (*National Power plc v Young* [2001] IRLR 32). In *Preston v Wolverhampton Healthcare NHS Trust (No 3)* [2004] IRLR 96, ICR 993 the Employment Appeal Tribunal (EAT) gave further assistance as to how to approach the limitation period.

- The EAT defines the characteristics of a 'stable employment relationship' as follows:

  'It is therefore necessary to consider the "features that characterise a stable employment relationship" (ECJ judgment paragraph 70) and these can be broken down as follows:
  (1) A succession of short-term contracts.
  (2) Concluded at regular intervals.
  (3) Relating to the same employment.
  (4) To which the same pension scheme applies.'

  As to (1), this devolves into two parts. The subject matter must be short-term contracts. The House of Lords in its Order for Reference and in its consideration of the ECJ judgment when referred back to it has in mind as "short-term" contracts which are termly, or for the academic or sessional year. It follows that those contracts and anything for a shorter period are

> "short-term". There must be a "succession" or a "sequence" (ECJ judgment, para 70). I interpret this to mean three or more, for the existence of two such contracts is not usually described as a sequence or a succession of such contracts. It would ordinarily be described as the repetition of a contract.
>
> As to (2), the intervals which must be regular, this is described as "periodicity" which of course implies regularity. The periods are regular because they are clearly predictable and can be calculated precisely; and they are also regular where the intervals between work, and the length of the spells of work, are not to be predicted with accuracy; but nevertheless it is possible to say that the teacher, for example, is frequently, or even customarily, called upon whenever a need arises. This arises, by definition in the field of supply teaching, several times a term and thus may be described as regularly; but the precise dates cannot be calculated or predicted and so the work may accurately be described as intermittent.
>
> As to (3) "same employment", no guidance is given. As to (4), the same pension scheme, it seems that the adoption of the expression "over-arching" is encompassed within the same scheme.'

- A move from a short-term contract to a permanent contract could not be characterised as a succession of contracts.

- There is no breach of the equality principle where the membership of a pension scheme is compulsory for full-time staff and optional for part-time staff nor where the employer failed to inform the staff of the removal of a barrier to full-time employment.

18.9 Where a series of short-term contracts is superseded by a permanent contract the critical period will be the date of the last contract forming part of the stable employment relationship, as stated by Elias P in *Jeffery v Secretary of State for Education* [2006] ICR 1062:

> 'In my judgment, it cannot be said that there is a continuation of the stable employment relationship into a new permanent contract. To put it in my own words, the concept of a stable employment relationship has the effect of requiring a series of intermittent contracts or temporary contracts to be treated as if they were a single contract terminating at the conclusion of the last of those sequential contracts. But this only modifies the basic principle that time runs from the end of each contract in the very precise circumstances identified by the European Court of Justice. It does not permit an employee to treat a succession of contracts not falling within those criteria as amounting to a single stable employment relationship. If that were right, it would mean that, in practice, in almost all cases employees would be able to bring claims within six months of the termination of the employment relationship with a particular employer, however many separate contracts there may have been during the course of those relationships, and whether they were short term, long term or, indeed, whatever form they took. That would involve a fundamental change in the law which is plainly not the effect of the decision of the European Court.'

18.10   In *Cumbria County Council v Dow (No 2)* [2008] IRLR 109 the respondent identified some 1,500 cases where it was alleged that the claims were out of time, many of the claimants having continuous service but there being a change to terms of employment in relation to status, hours or duties. A number of cases were before the Employment Tribunal which raised the question, in a variety of factual circumstances, whether the contract with respect to which the equal pay claim had been made had terminated more than 6 months before the claim was lodged. In some cases new documents had been issued, described as contracts of employment which stated that the contract superseded any previous contract of employment and had been signed. The issue for the EAT was to determine the principles for analysing when changes in a contract amounted to a variation and when they involved a termination of the contract and the creation of a new contract.

18.11   The EAT held that where the parties have agreed to effect changes by a fresh contract this will be decisive as the court must give effect to the parties' chosen mechanism. The mere fact that the document purports to be a new contract will not suffice otherwise the employer could unilaterally dictate the mechanism to be adopted. Where there is clear evidence that both parties have signed what is stated in terms to be a new contract that will be conclusive evidence that the termination route has been chosen. The approach had to be taken in accordance with traditional contractual principles so that if a new contract was signed this would have the effect of terminating the earlier contract even though it was extremely unlikely that any of the parties gave any thought to whether it was a new contract or a variation or termination. (On stable employment relationship, see further *McMaster and Others v Perth and Kinross Council* UKEAT/0026/08/MT).

18.12   In *Secretary of State for Health v Rance* [2007] IRLR 665 the EAT considered the power to reopen claims for backdated pension entitlement where it had been conceded that the claimants were entitled to claim equal access to occupational pension schemes in the NHS. Following *Preston (No 3)* calculations had been carried out to enable claimants to know their entitlements and what contributions they had to make. Periods of service were not disputed and Tribunals gave judgments in respect of those periods whilst dismissing or striking out claims in respect of disputed periods. Within weeks of the judgments the respondents carried out routine audits and found that periods should have been disputed. They sought reviews which were, in some cases refused and in other cases carried out so that the earlier declarations were maintained or varied. Appeals were presented to the EAT. The practical effect of reversing the judgments of the Tribunals was that the claims would be out of time under EqPA 1970, s 2(4). However, the EAT held that this, in itself is not a reason for refusing a review or permitting the point on appeal. The EAT set out, in some detail, the principles relating to opening new points on appeal at para 50 and, at para 51, stated:

> 'When applying those principles to the four test cases, some new problems emerge which require new rules. In deciding whether to exercise discretion in favour of the

respondents it is relevant to ask what the period of time has been since the date of the judgment or possibly from the date of the "concession". A short period of time, or a short period of time in the context of very protracted litigation, would point in favour of the respondents. It is also relevant to ask what the reason was for the change of position. An administrative mistake, or an oversight by a lawyer doing a routine audit of a very substantial number of files, is more venial than a tactical decision made by a representative in the proceedings. A mistake which arises in the course of handling 11,000 cases according to protocols directed by the employment tribunal from the centre should not readily be held against the respondents, even if the number is upwards of 120 out of the 11,000. That genuine attempts were made to raise the matter on review before the tribunals which were unsuccessful is also a relevant factor, as is the reason for the tribunal's refusal. It would generally be unjust to allow the reopening of a concession if the claimant had made an agreement to forego any part of her claim in exchange for the conceded point, unless the matter could be put right entirely on a financial settlement. Attention should also be paid to the nature of the judgment-making in the employment tribunal: a judgment on the papers without an investigation of the evidence would not command the same protection as one after a contested hearing. There is less repugnance about a respondent having a second bite of the cherry when the claimant has not been put to proof and the respondent has not suffered a contested defeat.'

TUPE

18.13 Where there is a transfer of an undertaking then any equal pay claim in relation to pension rights will be 6 months from the date of transfer (*Powerhouse Retail Ltd v Burroughs* [2006] UKHL 13, [2006] IRLR 381). The position differs where the case does not involve occupational pension rights; this is considered in detail in Chapter 16.

THE QUESTIONNAIRE PROCEDURE

18.14 Before any proceedings are commenced, the employer should make use of the questionnaire procedure in order to obtain evidence of likely comparators and to cross-examine the respondent about the reasons for any disparity in pay as well as to obtain statistical evidence of the composition of the workforce where the claim is likely to be based upon statistics. The employer will have to consider data protection issues under the Data Protection Act 1998 and may consider it more appropriate to await a Tribunal Order before disclosing personal details relating to other employees. It should be borne in mind that the primary purpose of the questionnaire procedure is for the employee to decide whether or not to bring a claim rather than seek early disclosure so that the employer may decide to refuse to give disclosure of documents which appear to amount to a fishing expedition.

18.15 The law relating to questionnaires is set out at **10.17**. The precedent questionnaire and suggested answers are set out at Appendix 1.

THE PLEADED CLAIM AND THE GROUNDS OF RESISTANCE

18.16 As noted in the last chapter, it is necessary for a proper grievance to have been made in order to comply with the statutory provisions before any complaint may be made to a Tribunal. However, the claimant should not approach the grievance as going through the motions to comply with the statutory procedures. It may be possible to seek documents and to probe the issue of comparators at the grievance stage by assertion that the claimant is entitled to equal pay in comparison with particular comparators. The employer will have to respond to such contentions. The provisions of the Data Protection Act 1998 and the Code on Data Protection need to be born in mind when seeking documents. On the other hand, the employer should use the grievance process in order to set out the strengths of its case since what happens during the process is likely to be looked at very carefully by the Employment Tribunal.

18.17 An equal pay claim will be commenced in the normal way by submitting a claim form to the Employment Tribunal. The claimant will need to consider whether there is also a claim under the SDA 1975 and whether Art 141 of the EC Treaty should be pleaded if there is a risk that the EqPA 1970 does not provide an appropriate route; ie where there are arguments about a comparator in the same service or same source arguments. The SDA 1975 is likely to be relevant where there are arguments about whether terms are contractual or not, for example in relation to discretionary bonuses. The identification of a comparator is likely to be central to the pleaded claim so that the claimant must consider very carefully whether a range of comparators will be provided or whether further information is required from the respondent to properly identify the comparators. If too many comparators are pleaded this may undermine the credibility of the claim or lead to the risk that a comparator with the lower level of earnings is used by the Tribunal (see Chapter 5).

18.18 The grounds of resistance will need to consider whether there are any jurisdictional issues if the claimant has not lodged a proper grievance or whether there are any limitation points. The respondent will need to plead that there is a genuine material factor (GMF) defence though there is nothing in the rules which provide that it needs to particularise the GMF at this stage.

CASE MANAGEMENT

18.19 Schedule 1, rule 10 of the Employment Tribunals (Constitution and Rules of Procedure) Regulations 2004, SI 2004/1861 provides for a general power to manage proceedings on the part of the Tribunal:

> '(1) Subject to the following rules, the chairman may at any time either on the application of a party or on his own initiative make an order in relation to any matter which appears to him to be appropriate. Such orders may be any of those

listed in paragraph (2) or such other orders as he thinks fit. Subject to the following rules, orders may be issued as a result of a chairman considering the papers before him in the absence of the parties, or at a hearing (see regulation 2 for the definition of "hearing").

(2) Examples of orders which may be made under paragraph (1) are orders—

(a)   as to the manner in which the proceedings are to be conducted, including any time limit to be observed;

(b)   that a party provide additional information;

(c)   requiring the attendance of any person in Great Britain either to give evidence or to produce documents or information;

(d)   requiring any person in Great Britain to disclose documents or information to a party to allow a party to inspect such material as might be ordered by a County Court (or in Scotland, by a sheriff);

(e)   extending any time limit, whether or not expired (subject to rules 4(4), 11(2), 25(5), 30(5), 33(1), 35(1), 38(7) and 42(5) of this Schedule, and to rule 3(4) of Schedule 2);

(f)   requiring the provision of written answers to questions put by the tribunal or chairman;

(g)   that, subject to rule 22(8), a short conciliation period be extended into a standard conciliation period;

(h)   staying (in Scotland, sisting) the whole or part of any proceedings;

(i)   that part of the proceedings be dealt with separately;

(j)   that different claims be considered together;

(k)   that any person who the chairman or tribunal considers may be liable for the remedy claimed should be made a respondent in the proceedings;

(l)   dismissing the claim against a respondent who is no longer directly interested in the claim;

(m)   postponing or adjourning any hearing;

(n)   varying or revoking other orders;

(o)   giving notice to the parties of a pre-hearing review or the Hearing;

(p)   giving notice under rule 19;

(q)   giving leave to amend a claim or response;

(r)   that any person who the chairman or tribunal considers has an interest in the outcome of the proceedings may be joined as a party to the proceedings;

(s)   that a witness statement be prepared or exchanged; or

(t)   as to the use of experts or interpreters in the proceedings.

(3) An order may specify the time at or within which and the place at which any act is required to be done. An order may also impose conditions and it shall inform the parties of the potential consequences of non-compliance set out in rule 13.

(4) When a requirement has been imposed under paragraph (1) the person subject to the requirement may make an application under rule 11 (applications in proceedings) for the order to be varied or revoked.

(5) An order described in . . . paragraph (2)(d) which requires a person other than a party to grant disclosure or inspection of material may be made only when the disclosure sought is necessary in order to dispose fairly of the claim or to save expense.

(6) Any order containing a requirement described in either sub-paragraph (2)(c) or (d) shall state that under section 7(4) of the Employment Tribunals Act, any person who without reasonable excuse fails to comply with the requirement shall be liable on summary conviction to a fine, and the document shall also state the amount of the maximum fine.

(7) An order as described in paragraph (2)(j) may be made only if all relevant parties have been given notice that such an order may be made and they have been given the opportunity to make oral or written representations as to why such an order should or should not be made.

(8) Any order made under this rule shall be recorded in writing and signed by the chairman and the Secretary shall inform all parties to the proceedings of any order made as soon as is reasonably practicable.'

FURTHER PARTICULARS

18.20   The powers under Rules 10(2)(b) and (f) are likely to be of importance in equal pay cases where the information is in the knowledge of the employer. This is particularly so in identifying the comparators and obtaining information about the make up of the workforce and pay and other financial details.

18.21   However, where the claimant has not even identified the comparator it may not be appropriate for the respondent to answer information about the GMF defence. In *Amey Services Ltd v Cardigan, City of Edinburgh Council v Marr* [2008] IRLR 279 the Vice President of Employment Tribunals (Scotland) made standard orders for the production of documents and the provision of written answers. The respondents received the standard orders which included the following questions:

'(a)   Is it the [employer's] position that if there is found to be a difference in pay between the claimant and any of her male comparators that this difference is genuinely due to a material factor which is not the difference of sex?

(b)   If so, what is this difference and why would it justify any difference in pay which is found to exist?'

The respondents argued that it should not have to answer these questions until a relevant comparator had been identified. The EAT revoked the order. The Tribunal had ignored certain fundamental principles of equal pay claims. It is for the claimant to identify her chosen comparator and to show that the job was of like work, work rated as equivalent or work of equal value. Once this has been done the burden passes to the respondent to advance a defence under the EqPA 1970, s 1(3). The claimants had not identified her comparators. Furthermore, the Tribunal had overlooked the point that, as a matter of principle, the employer could not be asked to address the s 1(3) defence until a comparator and disparity in pay had been shown. It was only when the nature of the case was known that the employer could be expected to address the s 1(3) issues.

18.22 In *Byrne v The Financial Times Ltd* [1991] IRLR 417, by voluntary disclosure, the employers provided detailed information about the salary history of comparators. However, the claimants sought by way of further and better particulars a breakdown of the difference between their salaries and those of their comparators and an allocation of a specific sum or a specific fraction of that difference to a particular fact in the work record or history of each comparator. The Tribunal refused the request in accordance with the views expressed by the EAT in *Enderby v Frenchay Health Authority* [1991] IRLR 44: 'the pay of the woman and the pay of the comparator have got to be looked at as one sum and that it is not permissible to split them'. The EAT upheld the Tribunal's decision stating that, in the case of an employers' defence under s 1(3), where there was a single or obvious relationship between a factor and an amount, that could be pleaded. However, in reality, it was often impossible to attribute a particular percentage or amount to a specific part of the variation. Those bargaining on each side may themselves give different importance to different factors when fixing a wage. Therefore, to require the particulars sought by the appellants could prove an impossibility; in which case, if the particulars were ordered, there was the risk that the notices of appearance could be struck out. Further, the refusal as a matter of discretion was within the powers given to the Tribunal, within guiding legal principles, and could not be held to be perverse. General principles affecting the ordering of further and better particulars include that the parties should not be taken by surprise at the last minute; that particulars should only be ordered when necessary in order to do justice in the case or to prevent adjournment; that the order should not be oppressive; that particulars are for the purposes of identifying the issues, not for the production of the evidence.

DISCLOSURE

18.23 The Tribunal has the same power to order disclosure as the county court under the Civil Procedure Rules (CPR) Part 31. In equal value cases there is specific provision under Sch 6 which has already been considered in Chapter 9. Rule 10(2)(d) provides for disclosure whilst 10(5) provides that disclosure will only be ordered when the disclosure sought is necessary in order to dispose fairly of the claim or to save expense. In *Leverton v Clywd County Council* [1985] IRLR 197 the EAT stated that a claimant cannot launch an action without any evidence and then rely upon discovery to ferret around in the employer's documents and contracts and make out some sort of case which until discovery did not even prima facie exist. The claimant had made out a prima facie case of disparity between nursery nurses and clerical staff so that an order for disclosure was appropriate of job descriptions of male clerical workers employed by the employer in grades 2, 3 and 4 of the local government clerical scale, notwithstanding that she had not named her comparators and that only 10% of the relevant clerical staff were men. Hutchison J stated that:

'... on the face of it, the applicant has a *prima facie* case of disparity, she has therefore grounds for launching this application, and when requested to give, as she was requested to give, the names of comparators, it was, in our judgment, entirely legitimate for her to say "Well, I need discovery in order to get the relevant names".'

In *Baxter v Middlesbrough Borough Council* UKEAT/0282/08 the EAT held that documents which were produced during a 2004 evaluation exercise were subject to litigation privilege and, in a second judgment, that the privilege had not been waived.

18.24 It should also be noted that, under the Trade Union and Labour Relations (Consolidation) Act 1992, s 181 employers have a duty to disclose information to recognised trade unions without which the union representatives would be impeded to a material extent in carrying on collective bargaining and which it would be good industrial relations practice to disclose. The ACAS Code of Practice on Disclosure of Information to Trade Unions for Collective Bargaining Purposes 2003, para 11 refers to disclosure of:

'*Pay and benefits*: principles and structure of payment systems; job evaluation systems and grading criteria; earnings and hours analysed according to work-group, grade, plant, sex, out-workers and home-workers, department or division, giving, where appropriate, distributions and make-up of pay showing any additions to basic rate or salary; total pay bill; details of fringe benefits and non-wage labour costs.'

A reference could be made to the Central Arbitration Committee if the employer refused to give disclosure.

PERIOD OF RECOVERY

18.25 The original 2-year limitation period in relation to arrears was found in *Levez v TH Jennings (Harlow Pools) Ltd* (Case C-326/96) [1999] IRLR 36 and confirmed in *Preston v Wolverhampton Healthcare NHS* [2000] IRLR 506 to be incompatible with Community law so that EqPA 1970 was amended.

18.26 EqPA 1970, s 2(5) provides that a woman shall not be entitled, to be awarded any payment by way of arrears of remuneration or damages:

'(a) in proceedings in England and Wales, in respect of a time earlier than the arrears date (determined in accordance with section 2ZB), and
(b) in proceedings in Scotland, in respect of a time before the period determined in accordance with section 2ZC below.'

Section 2ZB provides that, in a standard case, damages may be awarded falling 6 years before the day on which the proceedings were instituted whilst under s 2ZC the period is 5 years in Scotland. There is provision relating to concealment and disability with similar wording to s 2ZA above.

18.27 Where the claim is based on a job evaluation scheme (JES) this does not give a right to go back beyond the date of the JES, so that some other basis for a claim would be necessary (like work or equal value prior to the JES): *Bainbridge v Redcar & Cleveland Borough Council* [2007] IRLR 494.

18.28 There is no limit to access to a pension scheme other than the date of the *Defrenne* judgment in 1976 and, in the case of level of benefits, to the date of the *Barber* decision in 1990 (see Chapter 13).

REMEDIES

18.29 The claimant is likely to seek a declaration and the imposition of the equality clause. A declaration may be of efficacy where the proceedings are representative or test claimants have been nominated. Compensation will also be awarded for the losses that have been suffered, based upon pension losses or other money related claims such as the value of a company car or the differences in remuneration between the claimant and comparator. As noted, the right to equal pay does not give a right to more pay than the comparator or proportionate equal pay. Damages for injury to feelings is not recoverable as damages for non-economic loss cannot be recovered under EqPA 1970 (*Degnan v Redcar and Cleveland BC* [2005] IRLR 504). Interest would be awarded under the Employment Tribunals (Interest on Awards in Discrimination Cases) Regulations 1996, SI 1996/2803 as set out in *Redcar and Cleveland BC v Degnan* [2005] IRLR 179. Where the loss extends over a period, the calculation of interest should start at the beginning of the period, and be taken up to the date of calculation. That period should then be halved and interest at the full rate applied to half of the period

Appendix 1

THE QUESTIONNAIRE

SCHEDULE 1

Article 2

The Equal Pay Act 1970 s. 7B(2)(a)

Question Form (for complainant)

To . . . . (name of the person to be questioned (the respondent))

of . . . . *(address)*

1   I . . . . *(name of complainant)*

of . . . . *(address)*

believe, for the following reasons, that I may not have received equal pay in accordance with the Equal Pay Act 1970. *(Give a short summary of the reason(s) that cause you to believe that you may not have received equal pay).*

2

(a)   I am claiming equal pay with the following comparator(s) . . . . (Give the names or, if not known, the job titles, of the person or persons with whom equal pay is being claimed.)

(b)   Do you agree that I have received less pay than my comparator(s)?

(c)   If you agree that I have received less pay, please explain the reasons for this difference.

(d)   If you do not agree that I have received less pay, please explain why you disagree.

3   The Equal Pay Act requires equal pay between men and women where they are employed on equal work, which comprises like work, work rated as equivalent, or work of equal value.

(a)   Do you agree that my work is equal to that of my comparator(s)?

(b)   If you do not think that I am doing equal work, please give your reasons.

4   (Any other relevant questions you may want to ask.)

Any other relevant questions you may want to ask

The EOC (now the Equality and Human Rights Commission 'EHRC') comment on this part of the questionnaire at www.equalityhumanrights.com/en/foradvisers/EocLaw/EocLawSco/GuidesandLegislation/StepbysteppproceduralguidesStepbystepguideWorkofequalvalue/Pages/Takinganequalvalueclaimusingthequestionnaireprocedure.aspx but it is probably easier to go on the website of the EHRC rather than type in the above.

"'Any other relevant questions you may want to ask":

This provides you with an opportunity to discover:

1. Why your employer has decided to pay you at the rate you receive.
2. The name of a suitable comparator or comparators. If you do not know of a suitable comparator, you can ask for the identity of workers of the opposite sex doing similar jobs to you or work of equal value, including their relevant salary details and information about their jobs.
3. How your employer's pay systems operate in relation to your salary and those of your comparators.
4. General statistical evidence about the workforce – this information is useful to establish whether your employer's pay systems disadvantage workers of the same sex as you by comparison with the effect on workers of the opposite sex. If so, this is potential indirect discrimination. Where statistics show potential indirect discrimination, an employer cannot defend the difference in pay unless the employer can objectively justify the reason for maintaining the factor which is causing the difference in pay. (See the Guidance Notes to the questionnaire form at part 4, paragraph 4 "*The employer's defence*".)

Standard questions for Question 4

- Please provide full details of the duties (eg Job description and person specification) of my post and the post(s) of my comparator(s) .... [Name your comparator(s)]. Please provide a copy of the job description and a person specification for each.
- Please state whether you consider that there are any significant differences between my duties and those of my comparator(s) and, if so, give details including how often they occur in practice
- Do these differences in duties account for the whole of the difference in pay or only part of it? If only part, please indicate what proportion of the difference in pay is accounted for by these duties and explain any other factors which account for the difference in pay.
- Please provide full details of the basic pay, pay benefits (eg company car, private health insurance, occupational pension) and any other terms and conditions of the posts held by myself and my comparator(s) .... [name your comparator(s)].
- Please provide details of the method of determining the value of jobs relative to each other (eg grading, job evaluation) within the organisation.

- Please provide full details of how individual pay is determined within the organisation.
- Please provide details of how pay is reviewed annually and how pay rises are awarded within the organisation.
- Please provide details of how the relative value of my job and my comparator(s) has been determined.
- Please provide details of the starting salary of my self and my comparator and explain how these starting salaries were determined.
- Please specify the reason(s) for the difference in our starting salary and other terms and conditions
- What evidence do you have that these reason(s) were the cause of the pay difference?
- What evidence do you now have that the reason(s) remains the cause of the pay difference?
- Please give salary details for myself and my comparator for each subsequent year.
- Please provide a breakdown by sex, length of service, whether working full or part-time, job title and salary of all staff within the company employed as (i) name your job title (ii) the job title of your comparator(s) (if it is a different title from yours).
- Please provide details (including dates) of any warnings, verbal or written, about my performance, conduct or attendance at work.
- Does the company/organisation have an equal opportunities policy? If yes, please provide a copy of the policy and any supporting documentation.
- What steps have been taken by the company/organisation to implement the Code of Practice on Equal Pay of the former EOC (now EHRC)?
- What steps have been taken by the company/organisation to ensure that pay rates and other contractual terms and conditions do not, either directly or indirectly, conflict with equal pay law?
- What steps have been taken by the company/organisation to implement the EOC's (now the EHRC) Code of Practice on the Elimination of Discrimination on the Grounds of Sex in Employment?

You may wish to ask further questions relevant to the factor which you believe may have caused the difference in pay. If your employer has informed you that the difference in pay is due to market forces, red circling, skills and qualifications, experience, length of service or seniority, or if there is a job evaluation scheme operating within the company, we suggest some additional questions below.

Market Forces – Sample questions for the Questionnaire

- On what objective evidence do you base your claim that a skills shortage in my comparators area of work is the reason for the whole of the difference in our pay?
- Please provide details and/or documentation of the objective evidence on which you base your claim that it was difficult to recruit and retain skilled staff in this area.
- Please provide details and/or documentation of any research that has been carried out by yourselves in respect of "market rates" for (name your job) and my comparators job.

Red Circling – Sample questions for the Questionnaire

Please explain why my comparator has been "red-circled".

- How long has my comparator been "red-circled", and what steps have been, and are being, taken to phase his salary into line with those of the same grade?
- Please list all "red-circle" staff within the company, specifying in each case:
  o   Post
  o   Age
  o   Gender
  o   Length of service
  o   Qualifications and experience
  o   Salary
  o   Reasons for "red-circling".

Skills and qualifications, experience, length of service and seniority – Sample questions for the Questionnaire

- Please explain precisely how my comparator's skills, qualification and/or experience enable him to perform the job better than me.
- Please provide evidence (e g performance appraisal documents) showing that the performance of my comparator has been better than mine.
- As a consequence of me not possessing qualification or not having been in the job as long as my comparator please specify which tasks have: a) not been allocated to me, b) been undertaken by my comparator that could not be undertaken by me.
- Please explain precisely how skills, qualifications, experience and seniority are taken into account when determining rates of pay. Please provide copies of any company polices on the application of these criteria.
- The question of whether a material factor is a defence to a claim raises complex legal arguments and you will find further information about this in the EOC (now the EHRC) publication Sex Equality and Equal Pay for Work of Equal Value.

Job Evaluation – Sample questions for the Questionnaire

- Please provide details of any Job Evaluation Scheme operating within the company including:
  o   When the scheme was introduced
  o   What type of scheme was chosen and why it was chosen
  o   The composition of the Job Evaluation Panel
  o   What training, including equal opportunities training, was provided for members of the panel?
  o   The job factors and weightings used to assess jobs
  o   Full list of benchmark jobs and the range of jobs covered by the scheme
  o   How the scheme is maintained and reviewed.
- Please provide details of the outcome of the evaluation as it relates to my post and the post of my comparator(s).
- Please provide details of any formal appeals procedure following evaluation, and explain what steps have been taken to inform staff of this procedure.

- Please provide details of appeal(s) against the rating of my job under the Job Evaluation Scheme.
- Please provide a breakdown by gender and job title of those jobs placed in bands/grades under the Job Evaluation Scheme.'

5   Please send your reply to the following address if different from my home address above..

. . . .
. . . . *(address)*

. . . . *(signature of complainant)*

. . . . *(date)*

By virtue of section 7B of the Act, this questionnaire and any reply are (subject to the provisions of the section) admissible in proceedings under the Act and a tribunal may draw any such inference as is just and equitable from a failure without reasonable excuse to reply within 8 weeks or from an evasive or equivocal reply, including an inference that the person questioned has discriminated unlawfully.

SCHEDULE 2

Article 2

THE EQUAL PAY ACT 1970 S 7B(2)(B)

REPLY FORM (FOR RESPONDENT)

REPLY FORM (FOR RESPONDENT)

To . . . . (name of questioner (the complainant))

of . . . . (address)

1   I . . . . *(name of respondent)*

    of . . . . *(address)*

acknowledge receipt of the questionnaire signed by you and dated . . . .. *(date)* which was served on me on . . . .. *(date)*.

2   Set out below are the complainant's questions and my response to them.

    (a)   Do you agree that the complainant has not received equal pay in accordance with the Equal Pay Act 1970? . . .. (yes/no*). *(If you do not agree with the complainant's statement, you should explain why you disagree.)*

    (b)   Do you agree that the complainant has received less pay than his or her comparator(s)? . . .. (yes/no*). *(If you agree, you should explain the reasons for any difference in pay. If you do not agree, you should explain why you disagree.)*

(c)   Do you agree that the complainant is doing work equal to that of his or her comparator(s)? . . . (yes/no*). *(If you do not agree, you should explain why you disagree.)*

(d)   *(Replies to the questions in paragraph 4 of the questionnaire.)*

3   I have deleted (in whole or in part) the paragraphs numbered . . ... above, since I am (unable/unwilling*) to reply to the corresponding questions of the questionnaire (. . ... *(Give question numbers from questionnaire))* for the following reasons . . . . *(Give reasons)*.

. . . . *(signature of respondent)*

. . . . *(date)*

(*) delete as appropriate

Appendix 2

CARRYING OUT A JES: THE FIVE STAGE PROCESS RECOMMENDED BY THE EQUAL OPPORTUNITIES COMMISSION (NOW THE COMMISSION FOR EQUALITY AND HUMAN RIGHTS, KNOWN AS THE EQUALITY AND HUMAN RIGHTS COMMISSION 'THE EHRC')

STEP 1: DECIDING THE SCOPE OF THE REVIEW AND IDENTIFYING THE INFORMATION REQUIRED

What will be the scope of the review?	*The review watch points*
The equal pay review kit deals with the gap between men's pay and women's pay, but you may also want to look at ethnicity, disability and age. Before deciding to do so it can be helpful to consider the quality of the information available about the ethnicity, disability status and age of the workforce and whether this is adequate for the purposes of carrying out a wider review.	An equal pay review is concerned with an important, but narrow, aspect of sex discrimination in employment: the pay of women compared to men doing equal work (or vice versa). It does not deal with comparisons on the grounds ethnicity, disability, or age, but as a matter of good practice, employers may also want to look at these. Organisations that are obliged by the Race Relations (Amendment) Act 2000 to adopt a Race Equality Plan should ensure that the review deals with any gaps between men's and women's pay and between the pay of different ethnic groups. Organisations that use the Local Government Equality Standard will find that the kit helps them work through the Standard. In scoping the review it may be helpful to bear in mind the principle of transparency. Carrying out an equal pay review will help to ensure employees understand how their pay is made up.
The Employer needs to decide which employees are going to be included.	It is advisable to include all those employees who are in the same employment. For practical reasons the Employer may decide to carry out the review in stages, but the Employer needs to be aware that this increases the risk of an equal pay claim being made. *Scoping the review watch point* Deciding to exclude certain groups of employees will result in only a partial exercise and will increase the risk of an equal pay claim being taken.
Who should be involved?	In larger organisations an equal pay review can be a substantial exercise. The Employer may need to set up a project team.

• The project team	It is also advisable to agree on a timetable and set targets for progress.
	An equal pay review requires different types of input from people with different perspectives. The Employer will need knowledge and understanding of the pay and grading arrangements; of any job evaluation schemes; of the payroll and personnel systems and of how to get information from these. It is also useful to have some insight into how all of these have developed over time. Sensitivity to equality issues such as men and women being segregated into different types of work is also helpful.
• The workforce	The Employer needs to consider when to involve trade unions or other employee representatives. Involving the workforce is important for several reasons:
	• Employees and their representatives may be able to contribute valuable information, which managers could be unaware of, about the operation of the existing system and the likely effect of a new one.
	• Time, trouble and expense can be saved, especially by reducing the risk of any disagreement at a later stage, particularly if the outcome of the review is likely to affect existing pay differentials.
	• Employees will have more opportunity to understand the new system and the reasons for any changes. This will help to ensure that pay systems are transparent and easy to understand.
	In organisations where an independent trade union is recognised, the employer is required to disclose to that union any information necessary for collective bargaining, and this is likely to include information about pay systems.

• Experts	The Employer may also wish to consider whether to bring in expertise from outside of the organisation. The Advisory, Conciliation and Arbitration Service (ACAS), the employment relations experts, offer practical, independent and impartial help to help bring pay systems up to date.
What information will be needed?	Employers will need to collect and compare two broad types of information about each employee included in the review:
	• All the various elements of their pay.
	• The personal characteristics of each employee, ie whether male or female; what qualifications they have; their grade or pay band, what hours they work and when they work these; their length of service and so on.
	The information required will vary depending upon the type of organisation and on the particular pay and grading system.
	A full specification is given in Guidance Note 2: Data required for pay reviews.
	Information watch point
	If the Employer has difficulty in getting the necessary information together then this may be an indication that the pay systems do not meet the requirement for transparency.

STEP 2: DETERMINING WHERE MEN AND WOMEN ARE DOING EQUAL WORK

The Employer will need to carry out one or more of the following checks: Like work; Work rated as equivalent; Work of equal value.	These checks determine where men and women are doing equal work. This is the foundation of an equal pay review.
Step 2 Check 1: Like work	Like work watch points

Like work is where men and women are doing work which is the same or broadly similar	
Men and women are likely to be doing like work where they have the same job title, or where, even if their job titles differ, they do the same, or broadly similar work.	Job titles can be misleading. The Employer needs to look at what the employees actually do. Minor differences can be ignored.
Step 2 Check 2: Work rated as equivalent	Work rated as equivalent watch points
Work rated as equivalent is where men and women have had their jobs rated as equivalent under an analytical job evaluation scheme.	Employers who use analytical job evaluation schemes need to check that their scheme has been designed and implemented in such a way that it does not discriminate on grounds of sex. Further guidance will be found in Guidance Note 4: Job evaluation schemes free of sex bias. Employers who use bought in job evaluation schemes should ask their supplier if the scheme meets this standard.
Men and women are likely to be doing work rated as equivalent where they have similar, but not necessarily the same, job evaluation scores and are in the same grade.	Look carefully at jobs just above and below grade boundaries as these could easily be regarded as rated as equivalent, even though they are in different grades.
Step 2 Check 3: Equal value	Equal value watch points

Work of equal value is work that is different but which is of equal value in terms of the demands of the job. Demands mean the skills, knowledge mental and physical effort and responsibilities that the job requires.	The most reliable way of assessing whether jobs are of equal value is to use an analytical job evaluation scheme specifically designed and introduced to take account of equal value considerations and of the types of jobs being done by the workforce. Ideally the scheme should cover all employees. Employers who do not use analytical job evaluation need to find an alternative means of checking whether men and women are doing work of equal value. It is important to recognise that these alternative estimates of equal value are not as reliable as analytical job evaluation, and that the organisation is therefore still vulnerable to equal pay claims.
Which checks apply to the organisation?	Organisations with no job evaluation scheme should check: • Like work • Equal value Organisations with one or more job evaluation schemes should check: • Whether the scheme has been designed with equal value in mind. Further guidance is contained in Guidance note 5: Assessing Equal Value. • Like work • Work rated as equivalent • Equal value Organisations with a single job evaluation scheme covering all employees should check: • Whether the scheme has been designed with equal value in mind • Work rated as equivalent • Like work

STEP 3: COLLECTING AND COMPARING PAY DATA TO IDENTIFY ANY SIGNIFICANT EQUAL PAY GAPS

Once the Employer has determined where women and men are doing equal work, the Employer needs to collect and compare pay information to identify any significant gaps between men's pay and women's pay. This is done by: 1. Calculating average basic pay and total average earnings. 2. Comparing access to and amounts received of each element of pay.	Unless there is a genuine reason for the difference in pay, that has nothing to do with the sex of the jobholder, women and men doing equal work are entitled to equal pay.
1: Calculating and comparing average basic pay and average total earnings.	Comparing pay watch points
To ensure comparisons are consistent, when calculating average basic pay and average total earnings for men and women separately, the Employer should do so either on an hourly basis or on a full-time salary basis (grossing up, or down, for those who work fewer, or more, hours – excluding overtime – per week than the norm).	Averages are a useful step in identifying gaps between men's and women's pay, but averages can conceal important differences between individuals.

The Employer should review the pay comparisons to establish any gender pay gaps, and decide if any pay gaps are significant and need further investigation.	As a general guide, any differences of 5% or more, or patterns of differences of 3% or more will require exploration and explanation.
	If any of the checks reveal either:
	• Significant differences between the basic pay or total earnings of men and women performing equal work (differences of 5% or more), or
	• Patterns of basic pay difference, e g women consistently earning less than men for equal work at most, or all, grades or levels in the organisation (differences of 3% or more) then further investigation is needed.
	Further guidance will be given in Guidance Note 3: Statistical analyses, which describes some different types of statistical analyses that might be appropriate to the pay data.
	It is advisable to record all the significant or patterned pay differences that have been identified. Step 4 explores the reasons for those differences and whether they can be explained on grounds other than sex.
	There is no legal guidance on what constitutes a significant difference but techniques of statistical analysis suggest that a 5% or greater difference can be regarded as significant, wherever it occurs. A pattern of differences of 3% or more should also merit further investigation.
2: Comparing access to and amounts received of each element of pay for men and women doing equal work.	If the Step 3 analysis has shown significant gaps between the pay of men and women doing equal work then it will be necessary to work through Step 4.

For each element of pay received by men or women doing equal work employers should calculate: 1. The proportion of men and women who receive this element. 2. The average amount of each pay element received by men and women. This analysis will show: • If men and women have differential access to the various pay elements. • If men and women receive unequal pay in respect of any of the pay elements.	If the analysis does not show significant gaps, it is still good practice to examine the payment system in detail. Further guidance will be given in the checklists in Guidance Note 6: Reviewing the payment systems, policies and practices.

STEP 4: ESTABLISHING THE CAUSES OF ANY SIGNIFICANT PAY GAPS AND ASSESSING THE JUSTIFICATIONS FOR THEM

1. Find out which aspects of the pay system are contributing to the gaps between men's and women's pay and why.	Once this has been done you will be able to decide whether a particular pay policy, practice or pay element is discriminatory and whether the resultant pay gaps need to be closed. The process will also help build an Equal Pay Action Plan.
2. Find out if there is a genuine reason for the difference in pay that has nothing to do with the sex of the jobholder.	
What should be checked	These need to be checked from a variety of standpoints: design; implementation; impact. It is how pay policies and practices actually affect pay that matters not the intention behind them.
All aspects of the pay system, policies, practices and pay elements.	Guidance Note 6: Reviewing the Employer's payment systems, policies and practices will contain a series of checklists to help do this
	The Employer should check the pay policies and practices that determine basic pay and influence all the elements of pay that make up total earnings. Examples might be starting pay, pay progression, performance pay, rules on eligibility for allowance, levels of allowances paid and so on. The Employer should also check their impact on the various elements of pay: basic pay, bonuses, shift pay, allowances and so on.
Assessing the reasons	*Assessing the reasons watch point*

Once it has been established where gaps between men's and women's pay are occurring, the Employer needs to assess whether the reasons for them are satisfactory.	The question of what amounts to a satisfactory explanation of the pay gap is a complex area dependent on the detailed and individual circumstances of each organisation, as well as on equal pay case law. If there is any doubt, the Employer should seek legal advice.

The next step
The Employer can now decide whether:
• the pay policies and practices are operating free of sex bias
• the pay policies and practices are causing sex based pay inequalities and need changing
• there is a need to close any pay gaps.

STEP 5: DEVELOPING AN EQUAL PAY ACTION PLAN OR REVIEWING AND MONITORING

1. Developing an Equal Pay Action Plan is for organisations with gaps between men's and women's pay for which there is no satisfactory explanation. 2. Reviewing and monitoring is for organisations with no gaps between men's and women's pay.	What happens next depends upon whether any gaps between men's and women's pay were found for which there was no satisfactory explanation.

Developing an Equal Pay Action Plan	
The plan should include arrangements to: 1. Provide equal pay.	If there are gaps between men's and women's pay for which there is no genuine reason employers will need to provide equal pay for current and future employees.

2. Change the pay policies and practices that contribute to unequal pay.	There is no legal guidance on what amounts to a reasonable period of time within which to phase in equal pay, yet for practical reasons it may not be possible to introduce equal pay for equal work immediately. Employers need to be aware that in the interim they are vulnerable to equal pay claims. The action plan should make clear what timescale the organisation has in mind, and how it is going to compensate employees who may be entitled to equal pay. The organisation should stick to the timescale set out in the action plan. In working out the timing the Employer will need to consider the impact on employee relations. The Employer may need to manage factors such as costs and the possible dissatisfaction of employees who perceive a loss of status, or the erosion of differentials whilst equal pay is being provided.
3. Introduce an Equal Pay Policy.	It can be helpful to produce a policy that commits the organisation to providing equal pay with clear accountabilities, regular monitoring and adequate resources for Equal Pay Reviews.
4. Introduce ongoing monitoring of pay outcomes by gender.	There is a need to decide how the Employer is going to involve employees in the ongoing equal pay review process. Pay systems need to be reviewed regularly, to check existing and, in particular, any proposed changes to pay systems before they are implemented. Guidance Note 6 will provide advice on what to monitor. The Employer may also wish to examine other employment practices identified during the review. These might include gender segregation by job type and seniority, approaches to training and development.

Reviewing and Monitoring

Carrying out 3 and 4, as set out above, will help ensure the pay system is, and remains, free from sex bias.

Appendix 3

JOB EVALUATION CHECKLIST

JOB EVALUATION CHECKLIST
Formulating a Job Evaluation Scheme
• Is the scheme analytical?
• Is the scheme appropriate to the jobs it will cover?
• If any groups of workers are excluded from the scheme are there clear justifiable reasons for the exclusion?
• Is there a non-gendered use of generic/bench mark jobs?
• Is the steering committee representative of the jobs covered by the scheme and are they trained in job evaluation and avoiding sex bias?
• Is the chair impartial and does he/she have a good knowledge of equality issues?
• Are there any trade union representatives on the steering committee?
• If a proprietary scheme is to be used does the company have equal opportunities guidelines?
Job Descriptions
• Are the job descriptions written to an agreed format?
o   Are they assessed to a common standard?
o   Are they consistent, realistic and objective?
o   Does the format reflect the factor plan?
o   Are trained job analysts involved?
o   Are the job titles gender neutral?
o   Is the sex of the job holder concealed?
o   Are the job holders involved in writing their own job description?

o Has guidance been provided on the completion of job descriptions?
• Are guidance notes provided?
o Do they contain a comprehensive list of elements in the jobs to be assessed?
• Are the people responsible for collating the job descriptions trained in equal opportunities?
Scheme Awareness
• Are people covered by the scheme aware of its purpose?
• Are staff kept well informed of the progress of the scheme?
Factors
• Are the factor definitions and levels exact and detailed descriptions provided for each factor?
• Do the factors cover *all* important job demands?
• Is there any double counting?
• Do the factors operate fairly?
• Are the numbers of factor levels between the factors even and are they realistic?
• Does any variation between the points reflect real increases in demand?
Weighting
• Is the weighting system suitable for the jobs being covered?
• Does the weighting represent the correct factors for the organisation?
• Is there a rationale for the weightings?
• Does the weighting explicitly or implicitly perpetuate existing hierarchy?
• Do any high or low weights affect predominantly men or women?
Appeals
• Is there a recognised appeals procedure?
o Do staff have a clear understanding of how the appeal procedure can be used?

• Is there an appeals panel?
o   Are they representative of the workforce?
o   Are they trained in job evaluation and sex discrimination?
• Is there equal access to the procedure?
• Are appeal results monitored for gender bias?
Maintaining and Monitoring a Job Evaluation Scheme
• Has future responsibility for the scheme been clearly allocated?
• Are changes in regradings and the grading structure consistent and non-discriminatory?
• Are comprehensive records kept?
• Are the outcomes of the job evaluation checked for sex bias?
• Are existing schemes reviewed to ensure discrimination has not crept in?
• Are statistics recorded on pay broken down by gender?
• Is the collated information checked regularly?
Scheme Impact
• What is the impact of the scheme on women and men?
o   How many women have moved up and down the grades?
o   How many men have moved up and down the grades?
Pay and Benefits
• Have grade boundaries been drawn without bias?
• Do any special payments reward demands already built into the scheme?
• Is any pay protection (red-circling) free of sex bias?
• Are there justifiable reasons for any inconsistency in the relation of pay and benefits to the job evaluation results?

Appendix 4

JES CHECKLISTS: ENSURING A JES SCHEME COMPLIES WITH THE EQUAL PAY ACT 1970

Ensuring that a job evaluation scheme does not discriminate on grounds of sex involves examining every aspect of the scheme from design through implementation to monitoring the outcomes. Working through the checklists will help you ensure that any job evaluation scheme you use is free from sex bias. If you use more than one job evaluation scheme you will need to answer the questions in the checklists in respect of each of the schemes.

If you do not know the answers to some of the questions in the checklists then you may need to seek information from people involved at the time that decisions were taken, e g earlier generations of job evaluation panel members or long-standing trade union reps. You may also need to contact the consultants who designed and helped to implement the scheme. If you find you have large number of unanswered questions, then it may well be that your scheme would not stand up to scrutiny.

CHECKLIST A: BACKGROUND INFORMATION

A.1 Is the scheme 'In house' or 'Off the peg'?

If the scheme was either developed in-house or modified from the framework provided by an external supplier you should be able to use the questions given here to test whether the scheme is non-discriminatory. If it was bought 'off the shelf' you will need to assure yourself that the supplier has reviewed the principles and practices of their scheme in accordance with the guidance given here. You will also need to check out the way in which you are implementing the scheme.

A.2 When was the scheme introduced?

The older a scheme is, the more likely it is to have been developed without reference to the need to avoid gender bias. If your answers to the questions given here suggest that your scheme might not stand up to scrutiny, then you will need to decide whether a major overhaul will put things right, or whether it would be better to introduce a new scheme.

See *O'Brien v Simchem* [1980] IRLR 373, HL.

A.3 When was the scheme last reviewed?

Job evaluation schemes should be periodically reviewed to ensure that they remain free from sex bias.

A.4 Does the scheme cover all employees?

Excluding groups of jobs from a job evaluation scheme may perpetuate sex bias, especially if the groups excluded are composed predominantly of employees of one sex. Discrimination in the grading and pay of the jobs of female employees often occurs or is perpetuated by their separation into a different grading structure based on a different job evaluation scheme, or no job evaluation scheme at all. Incorporating female jobs within the same non-discriminatory job evaluation scheme as the male jobs will help you to achieve equal pay for equal work. You should only exclude groups of employees from a scheme if you have justifiable and non-discriminatory reasons for doing so. Employers and trade unions should appreciate that problems can be created if bargaining units are used as the sole basis for the scope of jobs to be covered, since this can often be discriminatory. Claims for equal pay for work of equal value can be brought where separate schemes or collective bargaining arrangements are used to justify differences in pay between the sexes, or where members of one sex are left out of a job evaluation scheme.

A. 5 Do your employees understand how the scheme works?

If your pay system, or any part of it, is characterised by a total lack of transparency, then the burden of proof is on you as the employer to show that the pay practice is not discriminatory. In respect of job evaluation, 'transparent' means that information about the design and implementation of the scheme should be available to employees in a readily understandable form.

A. 6 Is the scheme computerised?

Increasingly, the process of job evaluation is being computerised so that, for example, information on jobs is inputted onto computers in the form of answers to pre-formulated questions and a score for the job is then given. Schemes that are computerised are often quicker to implement and they are not inherently discriminatory. However, any computerised system will reflect the nature of the information it analyses. Therefore, it is important to ensure that your computerised scheme gathers comprehensive information about jobs and is based on factors that are non-discriminatory. At the benchmarking stage, you should evaluate the benchmark jobs using both the computerised format and written job descriptions or completed job questionnaires. A comparison of the two exercises should then be undertaken to check for sex bias.

CHECKLIST B: THE DESIGN OF THE SCHEME

B.1 Is the scheme analytical?

A job evaluation scheme must be analytical for it to be accepted by the courts as an appropriate method for determining whether jobs are, or are not, equivalent. You as the employer (rather than the supplier or consultant) must show that the scheme is analytical.

B.2 Does the scheme's factor plan fairly measure all significant features of all the jobs it covers?

A job evaluation scheme must be based on factors that fairly value all the main demands of the jobs covered by the scheme, irrespective of whether men or women perform them. Factors that tend to favour workers of one sex (e g physical effort) can be included, as long as the scheme also includes factors that tend to favour the other sex (e g manual dexterity). However, the point here is that the factors should reflect the fair/real value of the job rather than being a balancing act, and therefore only relevant factors should be included.

To check whether a scheme factor plan fairly measures all significant demands of jobs either:

- check the scheme factors against a list of frequently overlooked factors and a list of factors that favour typically male or female jobs; or

- analyse job information (job descriptions, person specifications) from a sample of typically male and female jobs, listing the main job features and compare them with the scheme factors. If there are job features not covered by the factors, you should consider whether these factors are more common in jobs typically carried out by one sex or the other.

If the scheme factors favour predominantly one sex, then this may indicate that factors favouring the other sex have been omitted (see Section Three: 3.14 – 3.19).

B.3 Do the factor levels in the job evaluation scheme reflect measurable steps in demand within the jobs covered by the scheme?

Factor levels should reflect significant and measurable differences in levels of demand, which are appropriately reflected in the scoring/weighting systems.

B.4 Is the rationale for the scheme's scoring and weighting system documented?

A weighting and scoring system should not introduce bias towards predominantly male or female jobs. You can check this by comparing the rank order resulting from simply adding up raw scores (1 point per level per factor) with that resulting from applying the scheme's weighting and scoring systems. If the differences in position in the two rank orders affect jobs of predominantly one sex, then this indicates the introduction of bias through the weighting and/or scoring system. Any use of 'felt fair' ranking as a basis for generating weighing should be carefully checked for bias, as it may tend to perpetuate any discriminatory features in the existing hierarchy.

CHECKLIST C: THE IMPLEMENTATION OF THE SCHEME

C.1 When jobs are evaluated or re-evaluated, do you involve jobholders in completing a Job Questionnaire or an equivalent job information document?

Jobholders know more about the demands of their jobs than anyone else, although they may need help in explaining them. Completion of Job Questionnaires by line managers or human resource staff, without jobholder involvement, can result in job demands being omitted or understated (see Section Three: 3.8 – 3.12).

C.2 Do you use trained Job Analysts to assist jobholders to complete Job Questionnaires or equivalent job information documents?

It is good job evaluation practice to use trained Job Analysts to assist jobholders to provide the information required by the scheme and to a consistently high standard, as this helps to prevent inconsistent and potentially biased evaluations.

C.3 Have the Job Analysts been trained in equality issues and the avoidance of sex bias?

Job Analysts should understand how sex bias can occur in the information collection process and be trained to avoid it.

C.4 Does the Job Questionnaire or equivalent job information document follow the job evaluation scheme factor plan? That is, does it use all of the same headings?

Job information documents, which follow the job evaluation scheme factors, are easier to evaluate and help avoid evaluators making assumptions about job demands, which can result in them being omitted or undervalued in the evaluation process.

C.5 Are jobs evaluated or re-evaluated by a job evaluation panel or committee?

Evaluation by only one or two people (eg line manager, personnel officer) can result in biased outcomes. This risk is reduced through evaluation by a panel with broad knowledge of jobs across the organisation.

C.6 Are job evaluation panel members representative of the main areas of work and gender composition of the workgroups being evaluated?

The more representative the evaluators are the greater should be their combined understanding of job demands across the workgroup.

C.7 Are panel members trained in equality issues and the avoidance of sex bias?

Training in the avoidance of sex bias in the evaluation process helps to prevent it occurring and to ensure that the exercise is seen as fair.

C.8 Are evaluation rationales or records, including the reason for each factor assessment, maintained for each job evaluated or re-evaluated?

It is good job evaluation practice to maintain detailed evaluation records, for a number of reasons. Records:

- allow evaluators to check back on their decision-making process and thus help ensure consistent evaluations;

- allow the reasons for evaluations to be explained to jobholders, for example, those considering appealing;

- provide information to appeal panel members on what information was taken into account in the initial evaluation;

- provide contemporary evidence for any evaluations that may subsequently be subject to legal challenge.

C.9 Has the impact of evaluations, re-evaluations and appeals on male and female dominated jobs been monitored?

You can monitor the impact by comparing the rank order implicit in the pre-evaluation pay structure with that resulting from the evaluation exercise (and any subsequent re-evaluations and appeals) and identifying the gender dominance, if any, of jobs that have moved up or down the rank order. If the pre-evaluation pay structure was biased against 'female' job characteristics, then upward moves would be disproportionately among female dominated jobs. Otherwise, one would expect moves to be roughly proportionate to the gender composition of the workforce.

C.10 Have all distinct jobs within the relevant employee group been analysed and evaluated?

In legal terms, jobs that have not been analysed and evaluated fall outside the scope of the job evaluation study. So a jobholder whose job has not been analysed and evaluated (or whose job has changed to the extent that the original evaluation no longer applies) could take an equal pay claim and the job evaluation scheme would not provide you with a defence.

CHECKLIST D: FOR ORGANISATIONS WITH MORE THAN ONE JOB EVALUATION SCHEME

D.1 Are all of your employees covered by one of the job evaluation schemes in use in your organisation?

Employees outside the scope of a job evaluation scheme can make an equal pay claim comparing their work with that of employees within the scope of the scheme. It is also possible for a jobholder in one scheme to claim equal pay with a jobholder in a different job evaluation scheme. Where claims such as these are made, the job evaluation scheme(s) do not provide you with a defence.

D.2 Have you made any comparisons between the demands (and pay) of jobs covered by different job evaluation schemes?

You can do this in either of two ways:

1.   By evaluating a small number of jobs from scheme A, which are closest in nature to jobs in scheme B, using both schemes; and vice versa; then comparing the results and relative pay levels.

2.   By undertaking 'equal value' checks (see EOC Equal Pay Kit Guidance Note 5: estimating equal value) on a sample of predominantly male and female jobs from each scheme, to test for vulnerability to equal pay claims.

If you have answered 'No' to any of the above Checklist questions, then your organisation's job evaluation system(s) could be vulnerable to challenge. The higher your number of 'No' responses, the greater the risk.

Appendix 5

ASSESSING EQUAL VALUE

Women. Men. Different. Equal.
Equal Opportunities Commission

Guidance Notes for the Equal Pay Review Kit

5: Assessing equal value

Introduction

This guidance note is designed to be used in conjunction with the **EOC's Equal Pay Review Model.** It describes some options for estimating equal value in the absence of a single job evaluation scheme covering all the employees in your review. It supports **Step 2** of the Model.

Whilst every effort has been made to ensure that the advice given here is accurate, only the Courts or Tribunals can give authoritative interpretations of the law.

The most reliable and objective approach to determining equal value is to use a single job evaluation scheme designed and implemented to take account of equal value considerations and your specific job population. Such a system will assess the demands of jobs under headings such as effort, skill, decision and responsibility.

Those organisations which do operate a single job evaluation system covering all employees, can rely on their 'work rated as equivalent' checks, perhaps supported by selected 'like work' checks. They will also need to undertake an equality review of the design and implementation of the job evaluation scheme – see **Guidance note 4: Job evaluation schemes free of sex bias.**

Those organisations, which do not operate a single job evaluation scheme covering all employees, should seriously consider introducing such a scheme.

Where it is judged impractical to introduce a single job evaluation scheme, you will need to estimate equal value between jobs not covered by the same job evaluation scheme. This could vary from a small number of, for example, senior managers not covered by an existing scheme, to all employees where there is no job evaluation at all.

A number of possible methods for estimating equal value are offered below. It should be noted, however, that none will be an acceptable alternative for a rigorous job evaluation-based approach to assessing equal value.

To help identify sample jobs for any of these methods for estimating equal value:

- you may first find it helpful to set out your pay structures or pay rates on a chart (see example below);
- choose jobs which are predominantly performed by either men or women rather than mixed gender jobs;
- identify likely vulnerabilities – jobs performed mainly by women (or men), which you suspect may be under (or over) valued, compared to those performed mainly by employees of the opposite gender.

1

PAYMENT STRUCTURE

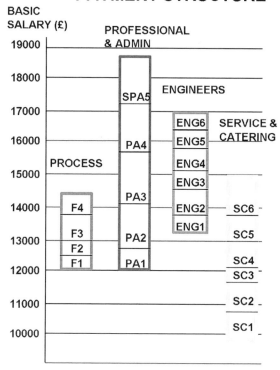

BASIC SALARY (£)

PROFESSIONAL & ADMIN

PROCESS

ENGINEERS

SERVICE & CATERING

19000

18000

17000

16000

15000

14000

13000

12000

11000

10000

SPA5

PA4

PA3

PA2

PA1

F4

F3
F2
F1

ENG6
ENG5
ENG4
ENG3
ENG2
ENG1

SC6
SC5
SC4
SC3
SC2
SC1

2

Possible methods for estimating equal value include:

a) If you use some job evaluation

EQUAL VALUE CHECK 1. For organisations with two or more job evaluation schemes covering between them all or nearly all employees.

In order to establish equal value across the schemes, use the more/most generic job evaluation scheme to evaluate a sample of jobs covered by the other scheme(s). You can cross-check the relative results, by using one or more of the other schemes.

So, if in the pay structure example above, there are three separate job evaluation schemes covering the process, professional and administrative, and service and catering groups, it would be possible to use, say, the professional and administrative job evaluation scheme to evaluate a sample of jobs from each of the process and service and catering groups. The results could be checked by evaluating the sample jobs and selected jobs from the professional and administrative structure on, for instance, the service and catering job evaluation scheme.

EQUAL VALUE CHECK 2. For organisations with a number of separate grading (and pay) structures, at least one of which is based on job evaluation.

In order to establish equal value across grading structures, you can use your job evaluation scheme to evaluate a number of jobs outside its normal remit. You may need to adapt the scheme to accommodate your sample jobs (e.g. by adding levels to the top or bottom for some factors, or adding factors to take account of the demands of the broader job population).

In the above example, you could use the professional and administrative job evaluation scheme to evaluate a sample of male dominated engineering jobs. If only the process grading structure was job evaluation based, then it would still be possible to use that scheme to evaluate a sample of jobs from each of the other three groups. In this case, it might be necessary to add levels to existing factors to accommodate, for instance, higher levels of responsibility for supervision/management of other employees, or to include a factor to measure financial or budgetary responsibilities.

b) If you have no job evaluation

EQUAL VALUE CHECK 3. For organisations with a single grading or banding structure based on a single set of criteria.

Estimate equal value by using your grades based on job profiles or a classification system.

Note:

- This method assumes that your grading criteria (profiles, grading definitions, classification system) are non-discriminatory. You will need to check this later, possibly by applying the relevant questions from the job evaluation Checklist – see Guidance Note 4

- This method is only appropriate where there is only one set of grading criteria. If you have different criteria for different job groups (e.g. for legal staff or research staff, distinct from the criteria for professional and administrative staff), even within the same grading/pay structure, then you will need to adopt an alternative method from those below.

EQUAL VALUE CHECK 4. For organisations with no formal grading structure, or more than one formal structure.

Estimate equal value by using levels in a competence framework (either NVQ/SVQ or an in-house system). If you do not have a formal competence framework, you can still estimate equal value by aligning your sample of jobs by broad NVQ/SVQ skill level, as defined in the chart at the end of this Guidance Note.

So, in the pay structure example above, if NVQ training and assessment systems have been introduced for process and engineering staff, it would be possible to compare the pay of jobs in the two groups at NVQ levels 1, 2, 3 and so on. Even if NVQs have not yet been introduced for the professional and administrative and service and catering groups, it would still be possible to use the chart to identify jobs at each level and to compare them with jobs in those groups which do use NVQs.

EQUAL VALUE CHECK 5. For organisations with no job evaluation, but with clear job families or other occupational group hierarchies.

Estimate equal value by matching those in equivalent positions in different job families or occupational hierarchies. For example, you could use categories, such as senior managers, department managers, team leaders, specialists with equivalent qualification levels, process workers, and clerks. Make sure your categories are not gender specific.

So, in the pay structure example above, you could use this method to estimate equal value between the engineering and professional and administrative groups by comparing the jobs of, for instance,

- The basic professional level from the engineers, and accountants (or solicitors or surveyors) from the professional and administrative group;

- The senior professional level of the same job groups;

- The section or department managers for the engineers, on the one hand, and accountants or surveyors, on the other.

4

EQUAL VALUE CHECK 6. For any organisations for which none of the previous checks are appropriate.

Identify a number of male and female employees' jobs within your organisation for equal value 'spot checks'. The jobs where you suspect possible equal value vulnerabilities, those performed by large numbers of men and women, those performed by low paid workers, etc. Then apply an equal value 'spot check' to estimate whether the jobs are equal in value. The equal value 'spot check' should involve a systematic assessment of the demands of the jobs under headings such as effort, skill, decision, and responsibility.

So, in the pay structure example above, if process grade F1 is male dominated and service and catering grade SC1 is female dominated, then sample jobs could be selected from each group. Or, if service and catering grade SC4, includes qualified cooks, who are mainly women, and Engineering grade 2 includes male dominated craft jobs, then jobs from each could be selected for 'spot checks'.

Skills and knowledge framework[1]

The definitions provide a general guide and are not intended to be prescriptive.

- Levels
- Definitions
- Jobs at each level of skill and knowledge

Foundation skill and knowledge (NVQ Level 1)
The job involves the application of knowledge in the performance of a range of varied work activities, most of which may be routine and predictable.

Intermediate skill and knowledge (NVQ Level 2)
The job involves the application of knowledge in a significant range of varied work activities, performed in a variety of contexts. Some of these activities are complex or non-routine and there is some individual responsibility or autonomy. Collaboration with others, perhaps through membership of a work group or team, may often be a requirement.

Advanced skill and knowledge (NVQ Level 3)
The job involves the application of knowledge in a broad range of varied work activities performed in a wide variety of contexts, most of which are complex and non-routine. There is considerable responsibility and autonomy and control or guidance of others is often required.

Higher skill and knowledge (NVQ Level 4)
The job involves the application of knowledge in a broad range of complex, technical or professional work activities performed in a variety of contexts and with a substantial degree of personal responsibility and autonomy. Responsibility for the work of others and the allocation of resources is often present.

---

[1] This framework is based on the framework used for National Vocational Qualifications.

5

Appendix 6

EMPLOYMENT DATA NEEDED FOR EQUAL PAY REVIEWS

Copyright of the former EOC (now the Commission for Equality and Human Rights, known as the Equality and Human Rights Commission 'the EHRC'). Reproduced by kind permission of the Equality and Human Rights Commission.

Steps 2 and **3** of the **EOC's (now EHRC) Equal Pay Review Model** ask you to identify equal work and calculate the average basic pay and total earnings of men and women who are doing equal work. For these steps you will need data for each employee covering both; a) job and personal characteristics, and b) pay:

(A) JOB AND PERSONAL CHARACTERISTICS

Data	Comments
Gender, full or part-time	You may wish to broaden your review to include other aspects of diversity such as ethnicity, disability, age.
For like work: Job title	Bear in mind that job titles are not necessarily reliable indicators of job content.
For work rated as equivalent (if you use job evaluation) Job evaluation score and/or job grade or pay band or pay zone for the job	You need these if you use job evaluation to allocate jobs to job grades, pay bands, or pay zones.
To indicate which work may be of equal value	What you need here will depend on which **equal value checks** you carry out. (See **Guidance Note 5: Assessing equal value**)
Job evaluation score	Job evaluation scores needed for equal value checks 1 and 2.
Job grade or band	Job grades or bands needed for equal value check 3.

| Skill/competence level or profile | Skill/competence levels or profiles needed for equal value check 4. |
| Job family level or position, generic job type | Job family level or positions, or generic job types needed for equal value check 5. |

(B) PAY INFORMATION FOR EMPLOYEES COVERED BY THE REVIEW

Data	Comments
Basic pay	Basic pay is the pay received by an employee for doing the job before any additional pay elements are added on.
Standard or normal hours of work	The hours for which basic pay is set. You need to identify part-time employees separately.
Total earnings	Total earnings = basic pay plus any additional pay arising from any other pay elements. Because total earnings include variable pay elements they should be calculated over an appropriate time period, such as the last year or year to date.
Additional hours worked	Hours additional to standard or normal hours, but worked in the same time period as that used to calculate total earnings. They are required to calculate hourly total earnings.
Department or other location indicator	This will depend on how you propose to analyse the data, e g by department, location, business unit.

Step 3 of the Equal Pay Review Model also asks you to compare access to and amounts received of each element of pay in addition to basic pay. So, as well as the data outlined above you will also need the additional data listed below for the employees covered by your review. where it applies in your organisation.

In addition, for Step 4 of the Equal Pay Review Model you are likely to need data on length of service and 'starting' salary, so these too are listed on the following pages.

If the analysis of basic pay, total earnings or individual elements of pay by gender reveals equal pay gaps of 5% or more, or there is a pattern of gender pay differences of 3% or more, then further analyses (outlined in Step 4 of the EOC's Equal Pay Review Model) are necessary.

Data	Comments
Length of service	
In job/grade/band or equal work category In the organisation	Length of service in job/grade is preferable but if this is not available length of service in the organisation may be helpful.
Starting salary*	
On joining organisation At recruitment or promotion or assimilation into current job/grade/band/equal work category	
Performance pay (if applicable)*	
Performance assessment Performance pay	You will need data on performance assessments and payments paid over an appropriate recent time period.
Competence pay (if applicable)*	
Competence, experience or skills rating received Competence, experience or skill payments	You will need data on competence, experience or skills assessments and payments over an appropriate recent time period.
Working pattern payments pay (if applicable)*	
May include: shift pay; pay for unsocial hours, being on-call, standby or similar; overtime or other working pattern payments.	You will need data on working pattern payments paid over an appropriate recent time period.
Bonus pay (if applicable)*	

Include any bonuses received	You will need data on bonus payments paid over an appropriate recent time period.
Other payments and allowances (if applicable)*	
May include items such as allowances for working conditions; attendance; responsibility.	You will need data on all other payments and allowances paid over an appropriate recent time period.
All other benefits/elements of pay (if applicable)*	
Include all other items such as: holiday entitlement; pensions; company cars; loans.	You will need data on eligibility for and receipt of these benefits/pay elements over an appropriate recent time period.

*Note: The model recommends monitoring all these elements of pay (plus basic pay and total earnings) by gender for equal work on a regular basis, particularly where they are significant components of pay in your organisation. The EOC has also produced a series of guidance notes on issues such as starting pay, bonus pay and performance pay. These explain how discrimination in pay can arise and what you can do to tackle it.

How much of the data listed above you need to collect will depend upon your payment system, eg whether you provide performance pay or not, rather than on the size of your organisation. In practice smaller organisations may have simpler payment systems which will reduce the range of data to be collected.

Whatever approach to data collection you adopt, you may find it useful to set up a standard equal pay report facility or create an ongoing equal pay database. This will allow you to regularly carry out checks on equal pay, and will make the ongoing monitoring recommended in the **EOC's Equal Pay Review Model** easier to achieve.

Appendix 7

FREQUENTLY OVERLOOKED JOB CHARACTERISTICS

Skills
• Operating and maintaining different types of office, manufacturing, treatment/diagnosis or monitoring equipment.
• Manual dexterity required for giving injections, typing or graphic arts.
• Writing correspondence for others, minute taking, proof reading and editing other's work.
• Establishing and maintaining manual and automated filing systems or records management and disposal.
• Training and orientating new staff.
• Dispensing medication to patients.
• Deciding the content and format or reports and presentations.
Physical and Emotional Demands
• Adjusting to rapid changes in office or plant technology.
• Concentrating for long periods (eg on computers or manufacturing equipment).
• Performing complex sequences of hand-eye co-ordination in industrial jobs.
• Providing a service to several people or departments while working under a number of simultaneous deadlines.
• Frequent bending or lifting.
• Providing caring and emotional support to individuals (eg children and people in institutions).
• Dealing with upset, injured, irate or irrational people.
Responsibility
• Acting on behalf of absent supervisors.

• Representing the organisation through communications with clients and the public.
• Supervising staff.
• Shouldering consequences of errors to the organisation.
• Preventing possible damage to equipment.
• Co-ordination of schedules for a number of people.
• Developing work schedules.
Working Conditions
• Stress from noise in open spaces, crowded conditions and production of noise.
• Exposure to disease.
• Cleaning offices, stores, machinery or hospital wards.
• Long periods of travel and/or isolation.
• Stress from dealing with complaints.

Appendix 8

GUIDANCE NOTES 3: STATISTICAL ANALYSES

Women. Men. Different. Equal.
Equal Opportunities Commission

Guidance Notes for the Equal Pay Review Kit

3: Statistical analyses

Introduction

This guidance note is designed to be used in conjunction with the **EOC's Equal Pay Review Model.** It describes some different types of statistical analysis that might be appropriate to your pay data.[1] These range from relatively simple averages to more sophisticated analyses using scatter graphs and lines of best fit. You will need to decide what is appropriate and practicable in your organisation.

The analyses include the initial comparison of average pay and earnings for men and women doing equal work (**Step 3** of the **EOC's Equal Pay Review Model**). They also include examples of initial, but more focussed, analysis you might undertake in order to explore the reasons for possible equal pay gaps, or as a result of discovering such gaps from your Step 3 pay and earnings comparisons. You will have drawn up the full data specification for your organisation using **Guidance Note 2: Data required for pay reviews.**

Whilst the advice given here relates to equal pay reviews that compare the pay of women and men you can also use these techniques to look at other aspects of diversity, such as ethnicity, disability, age, seniority, working pattern. If your analyses show that there is a tendency for people from one group to be favoured over another, you will then be able to find out why this happening.

Mean

In order provide an overview of the difference in pay it is useful to calculate an average. The 'mean' is the most common form of average, and is calculated by summing individual salaries and dividing by the number of employees. However, you should bear in mind that a mean is a blunt instrument. Means are unduly influenced by extreme values and in certain circumstances can become unrepresentative.

Some suggested pay analyses using means:

- Mean salary by gender for each equal work comparison
- Mean total earnings by gender for each equal work comparison
- Mean salary of men and women on entry to a grade/band or job
- Mean salary of men and women on promotion to a grade/band or job
- Mean salary of men and women on assimilation to a grade/band or job
- Mean amount of performance pay awarded for each equal work comparison
- Mean amount of bonus/overtime pay/other pay elements or benefit actually received for each equal work comparison

---

[1] The guidance given here draws heavily upon material included in the Cabinet Office guidance to departments and agencies on conducting equal pay reviews.

1

- Mean amount of incremental pay increases by men and women by grade or job

Some questions to consider:

- Are the mean salaries/amount of other pay elements received by men and women equal for each equal work comparison?
- Are the mean salaries received by men and women on promotion, on entry, and on assimilation equal?
- Are the mean amount of pay awards received by men and women equal?

Given the limitations in using an average to compare differences in salaries/benefits, it is often more useful to examine the distribution of salaries etc. The remainder of this guidance note outlines some useful techniques for doing this.

Frequency Tables

Frequency tables illustrate how many people fit into each category. They can be used to tabulate categorical data (such as gender and grade) and continuous data (such as basic salary). They can be used to look at the spread of people in your organisation by grade/band or by equal work category and this can help you decide at what level further analyses should be undertaken. A frequency count alone is not always a very good summary of the data. To compare two groups of people you should convert the counts of employees into percentages, see the example below.

Example – frequency table of employees by grade

Grade	Department 1		Department 2	
	Men	Women	Men	Women
1	257	135	1,425	562
2	554	272	3,763	1,851
3	323	252	2,209	1,672
4	289	324	1,356	1,500
5	86	134	384	656
6	130	142	473	837

Percentage: Grade	Department 1		Department 2	
	Men	Women	Men	Women
1	15.7	10.7	14.8	7.9
2	33.8	21.6	39.2	26.2
3	19.7	20.0	23.0	23.6
4	17.6	25.7	14.1	21.2
5	5.2	10.6	4.0	9.3
6	7.9	11.3	4.9	11.8
Total	100	100	100	100

In the example above Department 2 shows how a frequency table can highlight the fact that there are large numbers of employees in each grade and that it may therefore be more meaningful to split the data into smaller groups.

2

Suggested analyses using frequency tables:

- Numbers and percentage distribution of employees by gender and grade;
- Number and percentage distribution of salary bands by gender and grade;
- Number and percentage distribution of performance/competence payments by grade and gender;
- Proportion of men and women progressing through pay bands;
- Number and percentage of employees receiving certain bonuses/benefits/allowances/overtime by gender and grade or pay band;
- Number and percentage of employees affected by pay protection/red-circling by gender and grade or pay band;

Some questions to consider:

- Is the distribution of salaries for men and women similar?
- Are there staff with particularly high or low salaries? If so, do you know why?
- Is the distribution of performance payments for men and women in each grade or pay band similar?
- Is the proportion of men and women receiving certain bonuses/benefits/allowances/overtime similar?

Median, percentiles and measures of spread

Another technique to summarise data is to calculate the median, quartiles and percentiles.

When you calculate the median, you find the number that splits your data into two equal parts. Half the cases have values smaller than the median and the other half have values larger than the median. The median is often used instead of the mean to describe average salaries because it is not influenced by extreme values. One of the key differences between the mean and the median values is that any outliers influence the mean much more than the median.

You can also compute values that summarise your data in more detail. These are called percentiles and they represent the percentage of cases with values below and after them. Twenty-five per cent of the cases have values smaller than the 25th percentile, and seventy-five per cent of cases have values larger than the 25th percentile. The median is also called the 50th percentile.

There are a number of ways to calculate percentiles (of, for example, salaries) using IT packages:

- You can rank your employees in order of salary. From this you can identify the salary of people at specific points in the ordered salaries.
- Many computer packages will have an automatic function to calculate quartiles/percentiles.

Calculating a measure of spread is useful so that you can see how much the data varies within each group, for example the range of salaries will provide an indication of how widely salaries are spread. The interquartile range is the distance between the 75th and 25th percentile values.

Suggested analyses using medians, percentiles and measures of spread

The analyses suggested in the paragraphs on the mean will be applicable here.

Scatter plots/scatter graphs and best-fit lines

A scatter plot (or scatter graph) is a tool that enables you to look at the relationship between a pair of variables; for example, basic salary and length of service in grade/pay band. A scatter plot is simple to understand but conveys much information about the data. For example, when examining the relationship between basic salary and length of time in grade/pay band you will want to know if it is similar for different groups of employees. A scatter plot can identify each point with a marker that indicates what group it is in.

A scatter plot is useful to identify those employees who have unusual salaries within a job or grade. A scatter plot instantly gives an idea of where individuals or groups of individuals have unusual salaries. Where the graph shows that salaries are inconsistent, it might be necessary to undertake further research into any special factors or considerations that might apply.

To give more meaning to the scatter plot, a line of best fit can be added to the graph. A best-fit line (sometimes called a regression line) is a straight line that best summarises all the cases. Computer packages often enable you add the line of best fit.

Suggested analyses using scatter plots and lines of best fit:

- Scatter plot of basic salary by length of time in grade, separately for each grade or pay band or equal work group; separately for certain job types;
- Scatter plot of gross salary by length of time in grade/band equal work group: separately for each grade or pay band or equal work group; separately for certain job types.

4

An example scatter plot is given below.

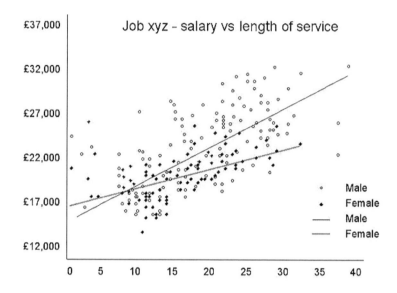

Some questions to consider:

- How widely are the points scattered for a given length of time in grade or pay band? Do you know why the points are scattered widely?
- Are there individuals or groups of individuals with unusually high or low salaries for their length of time in grade/band? What do you know about these individuals?

The analyses described above can be carried out in any organisation, including small organisations. They also have the advantage of producing results that can easily be shared with managers who make decisions that affect pay.

The analyses can be carried out in most spreadsheet packages, such as MS Excel. Whatever approach to analysing the data you adopt, you may find it useful to set up a standard equal pay report facility or create an ongoing equal pay database. This will allow you to regularly carry out checks on equal pay, and will make the ongoing monitoring recommended in the Model easier to achieve.

Appendix 9

EOC CODE OF PRACTICE ON EQUAL PAY (NOW THE COMMISSION FOR EQUALITY AND HUMAN RIGHTS, KNOWN AS THE EQUALITY AND HUMAN RIGHTS COMMISSION 'THE EHRC')

Code of Practice on Equal Pay

Women. Men. Different. Equal.
Equal Opportunities Commission

CONTENTS

2 Code of Practice on Equal Pay

INTRODUCTION

1. The Equal Pay Act gives women (or men) a right to equal pay for equal work. An employer can only pay a man more than a woman for doing equal work if there is a genuine and material reason for doing so which is not related to sex. The Equal Opportunities Commission (EOC) has issued this revised Code of Practice on Equal Pay in order to provide practical guidance on how to ensure pay is determined without sex discrimination. The revised Code (the Code) is aimed at employers, but employees and their representatives or advisers – for example, from a trade union, or Citizens Advice Bureau, may also find it useful.[1]

2. The Act applies to both men and women but to avoid repetition the Code is written as though the claimant is a woman comparing her work and pay with those of a man. The Equal Pay Act specifically deals with the pay of women compared to men, (or vice versa), and not to comparisons between people of the same sex.

3. The Code is admissible in evidence in any proceedings under the Sex Discrimination Act 1975 or the Equal Pay Act 1970 (each as amended), before the Employment Tribunal. This means that, while the Code is not binding, the Employment Tribunal may take into account an employer's failure to act on its provisions.

4. Despite the fact that it is over 30 years since the Equal Pay Act became law, women working full-time earn on average 81 per cent of the hourly earnings of male full-time employees.[2] Part-time working further accentuates the gender pay gap with women working part-time earning on average only 41% of the hourly earnings of male full-time employees. Both the Government and the EOC regard this as unacceptable. By helping employers to check the pay gap in their organisation and by encouraging good equal pay practice, this Code reinforces the Government's commitment to closing the gap between men's and women's pay.

5. Depending on the particular circumstances a number of other pieces of legislation can give rise to claims related to pay discrimination. They include the Race Relations Act, the Disability Discrimination Act, the Pensions Act 1995, the Part-Time (Prevention of Less Favourable Treatment) Regulations 2000 and the Fixed-Term Employees (Prevention of Less Favourable Treatment) Regulations 2002. A female part-time cleaner, for example, could claim equal pay under the Equal Pay Act with a male part-time cleaner, but she could also claim under the Part-Time Workers Regulations, that she was being treated less favourably than a female full-time cleaner. These other pieces of legislation are dealt with in Annex A, but employers should be aware of the need to pay particular attention to the situation in respect of part-time, black and minority ethnic employees and employees with a disability.

6. It is in everyone's interest to avoid litigation, and the Code recommends equal pay reviews as the best means of ensuring that a pay system delivers equal pay. Employers can avoid equal pay claims by regularly reviewing and monitoring their pay practices, in consultation with their workforce. Consultation is likely to increase understanding and acceptance of any changes required. Involving recognised trade unions or other employee representatives also helps to ensure that pay systems meet the legal requirement for transparency.

1 For ease of communication the word 'employee' is used throughout this document, but it is not used as a legal term. 'Employee' should be read as referring to all people who work in your organisation.
2 *New Earnings Survey 2002*, Office for National Statistics.

7. The Code includes, as good equal pay practice, a summary of EOC guidance on how to carry out an equal pay review. The full guidance is in the EOC's Equal Pay Review Kit.[3] The EOC has also produced a separate kit for smaller organisations without specialist personnel expertise.[4] Both are available on the EOC website www.eoc.org.uk or from the EOC Helpline 0845 601 5901.

8. Whilst every effort has been made to ensure that the explanations given in the Code are accurate, only the Courts or Tribunals can give authoritative interpretations of the law.

3 The EOC Equal Pay Review Kit.
4 EOC Equal Pay, Fair Pay: a guide to effective pay practices in small businesses.

4   Code of Practice on Equal Pay

SECTION ONE: Equal pay legislation

The Treaty of Rome and the Equal Pay Directive

9. The principle that a woman is entitled to equal pay for equal work is set out in European Union and British legislation.[5] The British Courts take into account the decisions of the European Court of Justice in interpreting the Equal Pay Act and the Sex Discrimination Act. A woman bringing an equal pay claim will usually do so under the domestic British legislation, but in some circumstances she can claim under European law.

10. Article 141 of the Treaty of Amsterdam (previously Article 119 of the Treaty of Rome) requires Member States to ensure that the principle of equal pay for male and female workers for equal work or work of equal value is applied. The Equal Pay Directive[6] explains the practical application of the principle of equal pay, namely the elimination of sex discrimination in pay systems. European law defines pay as:

> *'The ordinary basic or minimum wage or salary and any other consideration, whether in cash or kind, which the worker receives directly or indirectly, in respect of his employer or employment.'*

Pensions are treated as pay.

The Equal Pay Act 1970

11. The Equal Pay Act 1970, as amended, entitles a woman doing equal work with a man in the same employment to equality in pay and terms and conditions. The meaning of 'same employment' is considered in paragraph 21. The Act does so by giving her the right to equality in the terms of her contract of employment. The man with whom she is claiming equal pay is known as her comparator. Equal work is work that is the same or broadly similar, work that has been rated as equivalent, or work that is of equal value (see paragraphs 27-32).

12. Claims for equal pay are taken through the Employment Tribunal. If a woman succeeds in a claim:
- Her pay, including any occupational pension rights, must be raised to that of her male comparator
- Any beneficial term in the man's contract but not in hers must be inserted into her contract
- Any term in her contract that is less favourable than the same term in the man's contract must be made as good as it is in his
- Compensation consisting of arrears of pay (if the claim is about pay) and/or damages (if the complaint is about some other contractual term).

13. The woman can compare any term in her contract with the equivalent term in her comparator's contract. This means that each element of the pay package has to be considered separately and it is not sufficient to compare total pay. For example, a woman can claim equal pay with a male comparator who earns a higher rate of basic pay than she does, even if other elements of her pay package are more favourable than his.

14. Once a woman establishes that she and her comparator are doing equal work it is up to her employer to show that the explanation for the pay difference is genuinely due to a 'material factor' that is not tainted by sex discrimination. This defence is known as the 'genuine material factor' defence. In practice, an employer may identify more than one factor. For example, an employer may argue that the man is paid more because he is better qualified than the woman *and* because it is difficult to recruit people with his particular skills.

---

5 This Code applies to Great Britain. Northern Ireland has its own equivalent equal pay and sex discrimination legislation and Equality Commission
6 European Council Directive 75/117/EEC.

The Sex Discrimination Act 1975
15. The Equal Pay Act applies to pay or benefits provided under the contract of employment. The Sex Discrimination Act 1975, as amended, complements the Equal Pay Act. It covers non-contractual issues such as recruitment, training, promotion, dismissal and the allocation of benefits, for example, flexible working arrangements or access to a workplace nursery.

16. The Sex Discrimination Act also covers non-contractual pay matters, such as promotion and discretionary bonuses. Decisions about performance markings in a performance-related pay scheme are aspects of treatment which could be challenged under the Sex Discrimination Act if discriminatory. By contrast, where those decisions result in different levels of pay, that difference and the terms of the scheme could be challenged under the Equal Pay Act. This means that if a woman wishes to make a claim in respect of non-contractual or discretionary payments her claim will be made under the Sex Discrimination Act.[7] If there is any doubt as to which Act a payment falls under, legal advice should be sought.

Protection against victimisation
17. The Sex Discrimination Act also protects employees from being victimised for making a complaint (unless this is both untrue and made in bad faith) about equal pay or sex discrimination, or for giving evidence about such a complaint. Victimisation because a woman intends to bring a claim is also unlawful. The 'complaint' does not have to be by way of filing a claim with the Employment Tribunal, but includes any discussion or correspondence about the matter between the woman and her employer. The protection against victimisation also includes not only the woman bringing the claim, but also anyone who assists her, for example, her comparator and any trade union or employee representatives.

The scope of the Equal Pay Act

Employers
18. The Equal Pay Act applies to all employers irrespective of their size and whether they are in the public or the private sector.

Employees
19. The Equal Pay Act applies to:
- All employees (including apprentices and those working from home), whether on full-time, part-time, casual or temporary contracts, regardless of length of service
- Other workers (e.g. self employed) whose contracts require personal performance of the work
- Employment carried out for a British employer unless the employee works wholly outside Great Britain[8]
- Employment carried out on British registered ships or UK registered aircraft operated by someone based in Great Britain unless the employee works wholly outside Great Britain.

20. The Equal Pay Act also applies to Armed Services personnel, but there is a requirement to first make a complaint to an officer under the relevant service redress procedures and submit a complaint to the Defence Council under those procedures before presenting a claim to the Employment Tribunal.[9]

---

7 Also, if a woman considers that a term in a collective agreement, or an employer's rule, provides for the doing of an unlawful discriminatory act, and that the term or rule may at some time have effect in relation to her, she can challenge that term or rule under the Sex Discrimination Act 1986 as amended by section 32 of the Trade Union Reform and Employment Rights Act 1993.
8 Great Britain includes such of the territorial waters of the UK as are adjacent to Great Britain and certain areas designated in relation to employment in the offshore oil and gas industry.
9 S7A (5) of the Equal Pay Act read with the Service Redress Procedures.

6   Code of Practice on Equal Pay

Same employment
21. A woman can claim equal pay with a man working:
- For the same employer at the same workplace
- For the same employer but at a different workplace where common terms and conditions apply, for example at another branch of a store
- For an associated employer; for example, at her employer's parent company
- European law also allows a comparison to be made between employees who do not work for the same employer, but who are *'in the same establishment or service'*. As there is no clear definition of *'in the same establishment or service'* this is an area of law on which specific legal advice should be sought. However, European law as it currently stands suggests a comparison can only be made where the differences in pay are attributable to a 'common source' and there is a single body, responsible for and capable of remedying the pay inequality, for example where pay differences arise from a sector-wide collective agreement or from legislation.

The pay package
22. The Equal Pay Act covers all aspects of the pay and benefits package, including:
- Basic pay
- Non-discretionary bonuses
- Overtime rates and allowances
- Performance related benefits
- Severance and redundancy pay
- Access to pension schemes
- Benefits under pension schemes
- Hours of work
- Company cars
- Sick pay
- Fringe benefits such as travel allowances.

Comparators
23. A woman can claim equal pay for equal work with a man, or men, in the same employment. It is for the woman to select the man or men with whom she wishes to be compared, and her employer cannot interfere with her choice of comparator(s). She can claim equal pay with more than one comparator, but to avoid repetition the Code (and the law) is written as though there is only one comparator.

24. The comparator can be:
- Someone with whom she is working at the present time, subject to the usual time limits (see paragraphs 47-48)
- Her predecessor, however long ago he did the job, or her successor.

25. The comparator does not have to give his consent to being named. If the woman's equal pay claim is successful, the result will be that her pay is raised to the same level as his. There will not be any reduction in the comparator's pay and benefits.

26. There are a number of ways in which a woman may be able to select a comparator. These include:
- Her own knowledge and experience
- The internal grievance procedure (see paragraph 36)
- The Equal Pay Questionnaire (see paragraph 37)
- Discovery (asking for documents through the Employment Tribunal). Once a woman has filed her claim with the Employment Tribunal, provided that she has shown that her contractual terms are less favourable than those of male colleagues, she can apply for discovery to enable her to name appropriate comparators.

Equal pay for equal work
27. The comparator may be doing the *same* job as the woman, or he may be doing a *different* job. She can claim equal pay for equal work with a comparator doing work that is:
- The *same*, or broadly similar (known as like work)
- *Different*, but which is rated under the same job evaluation scheme as equivalent to hers (known as work rated as equivalent)
- *Different*, but of equal value in terms of demands such as effort, skill and decision-making (known as work of equal value).

Like work
28. Like work means the woman and her comparator are doing the same or broadly similar work. Job titles could be different, yet the work being done could be broadly similar - the nature of the work actually being done needs to be considered. Where differences exist the Employment Tribunal will look at the nature and extent of the differences, how frequently they occur, and whether they are of practical importance in relation to the terms and conditions of the job.

> Like work comparisons that have succeeded, in the particular circumstances of the case, include:
> - Male and female cleaners doing 'wet' and 'dry' cleaning in different locations on the same site
> - A woman cook preparing lunches for directors and a male chef cooking breakfast, lunch and tea for employees.

Work rated as equivalent
29. Work rated as equivalent means that the jobs being done by the woman and her comparator have been assessed under the same job evaluation scheme as being equivalent, that is, they have been assessed as having the same number of points, or as falling within the same job evaluation grade.

> Work rated as equivalent comparisons that have succeeded in the particular circumstances of the case, include:
> - Where a woman and a man had been placed in the same job evaluation grade, but the employer had refused to pay the woman (who had been evaluated as having fewer points) the rate for the grade.

8   Code of Practice on Equal Pay

Work of equal value

30. Work of equal value means that the jobs done by the woman and her comparator are different, but can be regarded as being of equal value or worth. This can be measured by comparing the jobs under headings such as effort, skill and decision-making.

31. Comparing jobs on the basis of equal value means jobs that are entirely different in their nature can be used as the basis for equal pay claims. Job comparisons can be made both within a particular pay/grading structure and between different structures or departments, for example, in a printing firm, between a bindery and a press room. Equal value is likely to be relevant where men and women are in the same employment but do different types of work.

> Equal value comparisons that have succeeded in the particular circumstances of the case, include:
> - Cooks and carpenters
> - Speech therapists and clinical psychologists
> - Kitchen assistants and refuse workers.

32. A woman can claim equal pay under more than one heading. For example, a woman working as an administrator in a garage could claim 'like work' with a male administrator working alongside her and 'equal value' with a mechanic.

Pregnant women and women on maternity leave

33. During the period of Ordinary Maternity Leave a woman's contract remains in place and all of her contractual terms and conditions must continue, with the exception of her normal pay (i.e. wages or salary).[10] The position with regard to bonuses, occupational pension rights, and the provision of maternity benefits over and above those required by the statutory scheme is unclear, and specific legal advice will be needed.

34. When a woman is on Additional Maternity Leave[11], even though her contract remains in place, her contractual terms cease to apply, except for some limited exceptions not relevant to pay. However, her entitlement to paid leave under the Working Time Regulations continues to accrue, and in some circumstances it may be unlawful under either the Equal Pay Act or the Sex Discrimination Act to treat a woman on maternity leave differently from other workers, e.g. by failing to pay her a bonus. The situation will vary according to the facts and again, this is an area where detailed legal advice should be sought.

35. Pay increases continue to accrue while a woman is on maternity leave and she is entitled to the benefit of any pay increases that she would have received had she been at work.[12]

---

10 Under the Employment Rights Act 1996, and the Maternity and Parental Leave Regulations 1999, as amended by the Maternity and Parental Leave (Amendment) Regulations 2002, Ordinary Maternity Leave is 26 weeks for all mothers whose expected week of childbirth is after 6 April 2003.
11 Under the Employment Rights Act 1996, as amended by the Employment Relations Act 1999, women who have at least 26 weeks service at the beginning of the 14th week before the expected week of childbirth are entitled to 26 weeks Additional Maternity Leave starting after their Ordinary Maternity Leave.
12 Gillespie & others v Northern Health and Social Services Board (1996 ECI).

Raising the matter with the employer

Using the grievance procedure

36. Before making a complaint to the Employment Tribunal, a woman should try to resolve the issue of equal pay by mutual agreement with her employer, perhaps through the employer's own grievance procedure. Employers and employees can also seek advice from an Acas conciliator. Acas can be contacted at www.acas.org.uk. However, the time limit for making a complaint to the Employment Tribunal will still apply and will not be extended to take account of the time taken to complete the grievance procedure.[13] Although there is no legal requirement to do so it is good practice for the employer, the employee, and/or her union representative, to keep records of any meetings.

The Equal Pay Questionnaire

37. A woman is entitled to write to her employer asking for information that will help her establish whether she has received equal pay and if not, what the reasons for the pay difference are. There is a standard questionnaire form which can be used to do this. The focus of the questionnaire is on establishing whether she is receiving less favourable pay and contractual terms and conditions than a colleague or colleagues of the opposite sex, and whether the employer agrees that she and her comparator are doing 'equal work'. The woman can send the questionnaire to her employer either before she files her claim with the Employment Tribunal or within 21 days of doing so. Copies of the questionnaire can be obtained from the Women and Equality Unit website www.womenandequalityunit.gov.uk.

38. If the woman takes a case to the Employment Tribunal, the information provided by her employer should enable her to present her claim in the most effective way and the proceedings should be simpler because the key facts will have been identified in advance. If her employer fails, without reasonable excuse, to reply within 8 weeks, or responds with an evasive or equivocal reply, the Employment Tribunal may take this into account at the hearing. The Employment Tribunal may then draw an inference unfavourable to the employer, for example, that the employer has no genuine reason for the difference in pay.

Responding to requests from an employee for information

Transparency

39. The European Court of Justice has held that pay systems must be transparent. Transparency means that pay and benefit systems should be capable of being understood by everyone (employers, employees and their trade unions). Employees should be able to understand how each element of their pay packet contributes to total earnings in a pay period. Where the pay structure is not transparent, and a woman is able to show some indication of sex discrimination, the burden of proof switches to the employer who then has to demonstrate that the pay system does not discriminate.

40. It is advisable for an employer to keep records that will allow him or her to explain why he or she did something, showing clearly what factors he or she relied on at the time that the decision on pay was made. Employers should be aware that employees may bring complaints or make enquiries about pay decisions which were taken many years previously, since when the person who took the decision may have left the organisation. For this reason it is advisable for employers to keep records that may, in the future, help them to explain why pay decisions were made.

---

13 A woman will be obliged to use the grievance procedure once the relevant provisions of the Employment Act 2002 have come into effect in October 2004. Time limits will be amended to allow the grievance procedure to be used.

41. Bearing in mind the guidance given in the preceding paragraphs, when responding either to a grievance or to the questionnaire employers need to:
- Decide whether or not they agree that the woman is doing equal work
- Consider the reasons for any difference in pay
- If they do not agree that the woman's work is equal to that of her comparator, they should explain in what way the work is not equal
- Explain the reasons for any difference in pay.

Further guidance is given in the notes accompanying the questionnaire.

Confidentiality
42. The principle of transparency set out above does not mean that an individual has the automatic right to know what another individual earns. The principle of transparency means that a woman has the right to know how the calculations are made, not the content of the calculation. It is necessary to balance the ideal of transparency with the rights of individual privacy. The equal pay questionnaire cannot be used to require an employer to disclose confidential information, unless the Employment Tribunal orders the employer to do so. A woman can use the questionnaire to request key information and it is likely that in many cases an employer will be able to answer detailed questions in general terms, while still preserving the anonymity and confidentiality of employees.

The Data Protection Act
43. Much of the information requested will not be confidential but some information, such as the exact details of a comparator's pay package, may be confidential to that person. Personal data is protected by the Data Protection Act 1998 and can only be disclosed in accordance with data protection principles. Pay records will usually be personal data covered by the Data Protection Act. Moreover, other issues such as ethnic origin and medical details are sensitive personal data to which particular safeguards apply. The disclosure of confidential information in the employment context is also protected by the implied duty of trust and confidence owed by an employer to an employee.

44. The EOC has produced a guidance note that explains an employer's legal obligations when responding to an equal pay questionnaire or to a request for information during the course of tribunal proceedings.[14] However, this is a developing area of law and, if in doubt, an employer should seek specific advice from the Information Commissioner www.informationcommissioner.gov.uk and/or take legal advice.

Disclosure of information to trade unions or employee representatives
45. Under the Trade Union and Labour Relations (Consolidation) Act 1992 an employer is under a duty, on request, to disclose to a recognised trade union, information to enable constructive collective bargaining. Information about pay and terms and conditions of employment usually comes within the duty to disclose, but it is important to note that the duty applies only to information for collective bargaining.

46. It also represents good practice for employers who do not recognise trade unions to communicate regularly with their workforce and, where appropriate, their representatives.

---

14 EOC practical tips: responding to an equal pay questionnaire and requests for information during tribunal proceedings in accordance with Data Protection Act principles.

Bringing an equal pay claim

The time limits for applying to an Employment Tribunal

47. If a woman wishes to lodge a claim with the Employment Tribunal she must do so within the prescribed time limits. It is her responsibility to ensure that she does so. The woman bringing the claim and her representatives should be alert to the importance of lodging the equal pay claim with the Employment Tribunal within the time limits. Using the internal grievance procedure does not extend the time limits set for lodging a claim, nor does serving the questionnaire.[15]

48. The Equal Pay Act and the Sex Discrimination Act have different time limits.
   - Claims under the Equal Pay Act can be taken at any time up to six months after leaving the employment with the employer (as opposed to leaving the particular post about which the equal pay claim is made, but remaining in the same employment). This time limit also applies to equal pay claims taken where a stable relationship with an employer has come to an end. The time limit can be extended only where the employer deliberately conceals the existence of pay inequality from the complainant, or the complainant is a minor or of unsound mind [16]
   - In contracting out situations the time limit runs from the date of the contracting out in respect of periods of service up to that date
   - Claims under the Sex Discrimination Act can be taken within three months of the alleged act of discrimination, subject to the tribunal's discretion to extend the time limit where it is just and equitable to do so
   - Because of the requirement on Armed Services personnel to use the relevant Service Redress Procedure referred to in paragraph 20 different rules apply. In the case of the Equal Pay Act, the time limit is nine months from the end of the period of service, and in the case of the Sex Discrimination Act, the time limit is six months from the date of the act complained of. The time limits can be extended only as described above.

The burden of proof

49. The woman bringing an equal pay claim has to show the Employment Tribunal that on the face of it she is receiving less pay than a man in the same employment who is doing equal work. Her employer must then either accept her claim or prove to the Employment Tribunal that the difference in pay was for a genuine and material reason, which was not the difference of sex.

The Employment Tribunal procedure

50. The fact that a woman is paid less than a man doing equal work does not necessarily mean that she is suffering sex discrimination in pay. In making a decision about a case the Employment Tribunal has to assess the evidence about:
   - The work done by the woman and her comparator
   - The value placed on the work (sometimes with the advice of an Independent Expert), in terms of the demands of the jobs
   - The pay of the woman and her comparator and how it is arrived at
   - The reasons for the difference in pay.

51. In *like work* and *work rated as equivalent* claims the procedure is the same as in any other employment case. There are special tribunal procedures for *work of equal value* claims.[17]

---

15 See footnote 13.
16 The Equal Pay Act 1970 (Amendment) Regulations 2003 (SI 2003/1656).
17 These are to be found in the Employment Tribunals (Constitution and Rules of Procedure) Regulations 2001 (SI 2001/1171) and the Employment Tribunals (Constitution and Rules of Procedure) (Scotland) Regulations 2001 (SI 2001/1170) and S 2A of the Equal Pay Act itself.

12   Code of Practice on Equal Pay

Assessing equal value
52. The concept of equal pay for work of equal value means that a woman can claim equal pay with a man doing a completely different job. In comparing such jobs the Employment Tribunal will apply techniques akin to analytical job evaluation, whereby the demands on the jobholders and the skills required of them are assessed using objective criteria. The Employment Tribunal may also appoint an Independent Expert to assess the value of the jobs. The Employment Tribunal-appointed Independent Expert may make a detailed study of an employer's pay system and the employer would be expected to co-operate with any such exercise.

53. Employers should be aware that they, and the woman bringing the claim, might also appoint someone with equal pay expertise to act as an expert on their behalf. It is important when dealing with experts to be clear who is the Independent Expert appointed by the Employment Tribunal and who is acting for the parties to the claim.

The employer's defence
54. The possible defences against an equal pay claim are as follows:
- The woman and the man are not doing equal work
- For equal value claims only - the jobs being done by the woman and the man have been evaluated and rated differently under an analytical job evaluation scheme that is free of sex bias. An analytical job evaluation scheme evaluates jobs according to the demands made on the jobholders. A non-analytical job evaluation scheme does not provide a defence to a claim
- The difference in pay is genuinely due to a material factor, which is not the difference of sex.

The job evaluation defence
55. Where employers use analytical job evaluation schemes they need to check that the scheme has been designed and implemented in such a way that it does not discriminate on grounds of sex. An analytical evaluation discriminates on the grounds of sex where values have been attributed to the different demands against which it has measured the jobs, and these values cannot be justified irrespective of the sex of the person on whom these demands are made.

56. A job evaluation scheme will be discriminatory if it fails to include, or properly take into account, a factor, or job demand, that is an important element in the woman's job (e.g. caring demands in a job involving looking after elderly people), or if it gives an unjustifiably heavy weighting to factors that are more typical of the man's job (e.g. the physical demands of being employed as a gardener).

57. A woman may also challenge a job evaluation scheme on the basis that instead of a factor, say, 'mental concentration' (in her job) being awarded fewer points than 'physical effort' (in her comparator's job), it should have received the same or more points. Similarly, she may argue that 'physical effort' (in his job) has been overrated compared with the skill her job requires for 'manual dexterity'. Even where she has received the same or more points than a man for a particular factor, she may still argue that the demands of her job under this factor have been underrated, that is, that the difference in points under the factor should have been bigger.

58. Employers also need to check the outcomes of the job evaluation for sex bias. This means checking what impact the scheme has had on women and men, that is, how many women and how many men have moved up or down the grades? Any ensuing pay protection (red-circling) should also be free of sex bias and should be phased out as soon as is practicable.[18]

18 The EOC Equal Pay Review Kit Guidance Note 4: Job Evaluation Schemes Free of Sex Bias.

59. The EOC has produced a guidance note recommending that matters, such as the following, should be considered as a matter of good practice.[19] In order to check that a scheme is non-discriminatory, an employer needs to look at matters such as:

- Whether statistics recorded on pay are broken down by gender
- Whether the scheme is appropriate to the jobs it will cover
- If a proprietary scheme is used does the supplier have equal opportunities guidelines?
- If any groups of workers are excluded from the scheme, are there clear and justifiable reasons for their exclusion?
- Is the composition of the job evaluation panel/steering committee representative of the jobs covered by the scheme and are the members trained in job evaluation and avoiding sex bias?
- Are the job descriptions written to an agreed format and assessed to a common standard? Are trained job analysts used and have the jobholders been involved in writing their own job descriptions?
- Where the scheme uses generic/bench mark jobs are these free from sex bias?
- Are the factor definitions and levels exact and are detailed descriptions provided for each factor? Do the factors cover all the important job demands?

If a job evaluation scheme is to remain free of sex bias it should be monitored. The employer (and not the job evaluation supplier or consultant) will need to show that the scheme is non-discriminatory.

The 'genuine material factor defence' - testing for sex discrimination
60. The Employment Tribunal tests for sex discrimination by first establishing a difference in pay or terms between the woman bringing the claim and a man doing equal work, and then asking whether the difference is due to discrimination or some other factor that does not amount to sex discrimination. This means that an employer can pay a man more than a woman for doing equal work, but only if the reason for doing so – the factor which the employer regards as the reason for the difference in pay – is not related to the sex of the jobholders.

61. The employer will have to show that the factor, or factors, on which he or she relies is free from both direct and indirect sex discrimination:

- Direct sex discrimination occurs when the difference in pay or terms is directly related to the difference of sex
- Indirect sex discrimination arises when the pay difference is due to a provision, criterion or practice which:
  - Applies to both men and women, but
  - Adversely affects a considerably larger proportion of women than men, and
  - Is not objectively justified irrespective of the sex of the jobholders.

62. Whether a defence succeeds or fails will always depend on the circumstances of the case and there is no such thing as an automatic or blanket defence. The defences that are likely to succeed include allowances such as London weighting and night-shift payments. Factors such as different market rates of pay for different specialisms or different levels of skills and experience have been successful in some cases but not in others.

---

19 The EOC Equal Pay Review Kit Guidance Note 4: Job Evaluation Schemes Free of Sex Bias.

63. The factor put forward to explain the difference in pay has to be significant; it has to be the real reason for the difference and it must not be connected with the sex of the people doing the job. For example, if the employer considers that the reason for paying the comparator more than the woman bringing the claim is that people will not do the work for the lower rate of pay, then the employer would have to bring evidence of actual difficulties in recruiting and retaining people to do the job being done by the male comparator.

64. Where a woman is claiming equal pay on the basis that the two jobs are work of equal value, indirect discrimination may arise where one of the jobs is done by a much higher proportion of women than the other job. The onus lies on the employee to provide evidence of significant disparate impact.[20]

65. In such a case, if the Employment Tribunal accepts that the jobs are of equal value, the employer will need to provide objective justification for the pay difference between the two kinds of job. This is a higher standard of justification than that of the material factor defence.

66. The employer must show that:
- The purpose of the provision or practice is to meet a real business need
- The provision or practice is appropriate and necessary as a means of meeting that need.

An example of objective justification is:

- A pay system that makes an additional payment to employees working unsocial hours, in which most of the employees getting the bonus are men. Here the employer would have to show that:
  - There is a real business need to create a system to encourage a particular group of employees to work unsociable hours, and
  - The additional payments meet that need, and
  - The payments are an effective way of meeting that need, and do not go beyond what is necessary to achieve it (i.e. without the payment, the extra work would not be done, and the payment is only made when the workers actually do the work).

Awards of equal pay

67. If the woman succeeds in her claim she is entitled to:
- An order from the Employment Tribunal declaring her rights
- Equalisation of contractual terms for the future (if she is still in employment)
- Compensation consisting of arrears of pay (if the claim is about pay) and/or damages (if the complaint is about some other contractual term).

Back pay can be awarded up to a maximum of six years (five years in Scotland) from the date that proceedings were filed with the Employment Tribunal.[21] In addition, the Employment Tribunal may award interest on the award of compensation. With up to six year's worth of back pay being awarded, the interest element of any award is likely to be considerable.

---

20 The advice given here is based on Nelson v Carillion Services Ltd, Court of Appeal decision 15 April 2003. Specific legal advice should be sought.
21 Special rules apply where the woman is under a disability or the employer has concealed a breach of the Equal Pay Act.

SECTION TWO: Good equal pay practice

Introduction

68. The loss to women arising out of the gender pay gap is well documented, but organisations also lose out by failing to properly reward the range of skills and experience that women bring to the workforce. The most commonly recognised risk of failing to ensure that pay is determined without sex discrimination is equal pay cases being taken against the organisation. The direct costs of a claim can include not only any eventual equal pay award to the woman bringing the claim (see paragraph 67) but also the costs of time spent at a hearing, and the costs of legal representation. The indirect costs are harder to quantify, but include lower productivity on the part of those employees who consider that they are not getting equal pay and on the part of managers whose time is taken up in dealing with the claim.

69. Tackling the gender pay gap reduces the risk of litigation. It can also increase efficiency by attracting the best employees, reducing staff turnover, increasing commitment, and reducing absenteeism. Pay is one of the key factors affecting motivation and relationships at work. It is therefore important to develop pay arrangements that are right for the organisation and that reward employees fairly. Providing equal pay for equal work is central to the concept of rewarding people fairly for what they do.

The essential features of an equal pay review

70. Employers are responsible for providing equal pay and for ensuring that pay systems are transparent. Pay arrangements are frequently complicated and the features that can give rise to sex discrimination are not always obvious. A structured pay system is more likely to provide equal pay and is easier to check than a system that relies primarily on managerial discretion. Acas, the employment relations' experts, provide basic advice on the various different types of pay systems and on job evaluation.

71. The advice given in paragraphs 39-46 on striking a balance between transparency and confidentiality are also relevant to equal pay reviews. The EOC has produced a guidance note that explains an employer's legal obligations when carrying out an equal pay review.[22]

72. While employers are not required, by law, to carry out an equal pay review, this Code recommends equal pay reviews as the most appropriate method of ensuring that a pay system delivers equal pay free from sex bias. Whatever kind of equal pay review process is used, it should include:

- Comparing the pay of men and women doing equal work. Here employers need to check for one or more of the following: like work; work rated as equivalent; work of equal value. *These checks are the foundation of an equal pay review*
- Identifying any equal pay gaps
- Eliminating those pay gaps that cannot satisfactorily be explained on grounds other than sex.

These features are the same whatever the size of the organisation and they are essential. A pay review process that does not include these features cannot claim to be an equal pay review. Moreover, an equal pay review is not simply a data collection exercise. It entails a commitment to put right any sex based pay inequalities and this means that the review must have the involvement and support of managers with the authority to deliver the necessary changes.

---

22 EOC practical tips: conducting an equal pay review in accordance with Data Protection Act principles.

73. The validity of the review and success of subsequent action taken will be enhanced if the pay system is understood and accepted by the managers who operate the system, by the employees and by their unions. Employers should therefore aim to secure the involvement of employees and, where possible, trade union representatives, when carrying out an equal pay review.

Voluntary equal pay reviews

A model for carrying out an equal pay review
74. The EOC recommends a five-step equal pay review model:

STEP 1: Deciding the scope of the review and identifying the data required

STEP 2: Determining where men and women are doing equal work

STEP 3: Collecting pay data to identify equal pay gaps

STEP 4: Establishing the causes of any significant pay gaps and assessing the reasons for these

STEP 5: Developing an equal pay action plan and/or reviewing and monitoring.

The EOC Equal Pay Review Kit sets out the detail of the model recommended here and provides supporting guidance notes.

STEP 1: Deciding the scope of the review and identifying the data required

75. In scoping the review employers need to decide:
- Which employees are going to be included? It is advisable to include all employees who are deemed to be in the same establishment or service (see paragraph 21)
- What information will be needed? Employers will need to collect and compare broad types of information about:
  - All the various elements of pay, including pensions and other benefits
  - The personal characteristics of each employee, that is, gender; full-time or part-time; qualifications relevant to the job; hours worked and when and where they work these; length of service; role and time in grade and performance related pay ratings[23]
  - It is particularly important to ensure that information is collected about part-time employees.

The information will vary depending upon the type of organisation, its pay policies and practices and the scope of the review.
- Who should be involved in carrying out the review? An equal pay review requires different types of input from people with different perspectives. There will be a need for knowledge and understanding of the pay and grading arrangements; of any job evaluation schemes; and of the payroll and human resource systems. It can also be helpful to have someone with an understanding of equality issues, particularly the effects of indirect discrimination in pay systems
- When to involve the workforce? Employers need to consider when to involve the trade unions or other employee representatives
- Whether expert advice is needed? Employers may also wish to consider whether to bring in outside expertise. Acas can provide practical, independent and impartial advice on the employee relations aspects of equal pay reviews.

---

23 The EOC Equal Pay Review Kit Guidance Note 2: Data collection provides detailed guidance on the information required to carry out an equal pay review.

The scope of the Equal Pay Review[24]
In nearly three quarters of organisations, the review applied (or applies) to the whole workforce. In over half of all the cases it involved an examination of a job evaluation system to ensure that it was free of sex bias. Moreover, just under half of organisations had extended the review beyond pay and gender, to include other processes such as recruitment and selection; two-fifths had covered pay differences by ethnicity; more than a third had covered age and nearly a third had covered disability.

The scope of the Equal Pay Review

	Percentage of organisations covering
Whole workforce	73
Examination of job evaluation system	55
Other HR processes	49
Pay differences by ethnic origin	40
Pay differences by age	36
Pay differences by disability	31
N = number of organisations	67

Include ethnicity and disability in the review
76. This Code is concerned with an important, but narrow, aspect of sex discrimination in employment – the pay of women compared to men doing equal work, (or vice versa). It does not deal with comparisons on the grounds of ethnicity or disability. However, as a matter of good practice employers may also want to look at ethnicity and disability, or age. Before deciding to do so it may be helpful to consider the quality of the information available to the employer, and whether it is adequate for the purposes of carrying out a wider review. To ensure the relevant provisions of race and disability legislation are taken into account, it would be appropriate to seek advice from the Commission for Racial Equality and/or the Disability Rights Commission.

77. Public Sector organisations obliged by the Race Relations (Amendment) Act 2000 to adopt an Equality Scheme should ensure that their pay review deals with any pay gaps between workers from different ethnic groups as well as the gaps between men's and women's pay. Here too, advice can be obtained from the Commission for Racial Equality.

24 Case study taken from *Monitoring Progress Towards Pay Equality*, Neathey, Dench & Thornson, Institute for Employment Studies, EOC 2003.

STEP 2: Determining where men and women are doing equal work

78. In Step 2 employers need to do one or more of the following checks:
- Like work
- Work rated as equivalent
- Work of equal value.

These checks determine where men and women are doing equal work. They are the foundation of an equal pay review.

> Example[25] – determining where men and women are doing equal work
> Human Resources and the unions met to agree which areas to examine. According to the HR manager, 'we already had an idea of where the discrepancies were'. Data collection was on the basis of figures from: the personnel database, the pay database, the performance pay database and the starters and leavers database. A small local consultancy had helped to introduce a new job evaluation scheme; however, the basis for making equal work comparisons was predominantly by existing grade. The organisation looked at global differences, differences by grade and differences by components of pay (basic pay, overtime and allowances).

79. Employers who do not have analytical job evaluation schemes designed with equal value in mind will need to find an alternative means of estimating whether men and women are doing equal work. The EOC Equal Pay Review Kit includes suggestions as to how this can be done.[26] Employers who do use analytical job evaluation schemes need to check that their scheme has been designed and implemented in such a way and at all times so as not to discriminate on grounds of sex.[27]

STEP 3: Collecting pay data to identify equal pay gaps

80. In Step 3 employers need to collect and compare pay information for men and women doing equal work by:
- Calculating average basic pay and total earnings
- Comparing access to and amounts received of each element of the pay package.

To ensure comparisons are consistent, when calculating average basic pay and average total earnings for men and women separately, employers should do this either on an hourly basis or on a full-time salary basis (grossing up or down for those who work fewer, or more, hours – excluding overtime - per week than the norm).

81. Employers then need to review the pay comparisons to identify any gender pay gaps and decide if any are significant enough to warrant further investigation. It is advisable to record all the significant or patterned pay gaps that have been identified.

> Example[28] – data collection and analysis
> The organisation had a well-established process for undertaking equal pay audits. Data were brought together and presented in tabular form by the data analysis section of the human resources department. The data were then reviewed, analysed and commented on by the head of employee relations, who shared the data with trade union representatives. Union and management worked together to develop action points arising from the data.

25 Case study taken from *Monitoring Progress Towards Pay Equality*, Neathey, Dench & Thomson, Institute for Employment Studies, EOC 2003.
26 The EOC Equal Pay Review Kit Guidance Note 5: Assessing Equal Value.
27 The EOC Equal Pay Review Kit Guidance Note 4: Job Evaluation Schemes Free of Sex Bias.
28 Case study taken from *Monitoring Progress Towards Pay Equality*, Neathey, Dench & Thomson, Institute for Employment Studies, EOC 2003.

STEP 4: Establishing the causes of any significant pay gaps and assessing the reasons for these

82. In Step 4 employers need to:
- Find out if there is a genuine and material reason for the difference in pay that has nothing to do with the sex of the jobholders
- Examine their pay systems to find out which pay policies and practices are contributing to any gender pay gaps.

Example[29] – finding out which policies and practices are contributing to the gender pay gap
The review showed a 23 per cent gap in the average basic pay of men and women across the organisation. In grades with a large enough number of staff to make a comparison, 50 per cent had variances of five per cent or greater in favour of either men or women. Starting pay was not found to be an issue, nor was performance pay. The key factor in grade inequalities was identified as long pay ranges and the impact of past restructuring. There was a body of staff (largely male), who had reached the upper quartile of their current pay range prior to the most recent restructuring. However, new appointees, who were increasingly female, and those who had taken career breaks, had little chance of progressing to this level.

The other area of concern identified by the review was premium payments for working unsocial hours. These were paid at the rate of 20 per cent of basic salary to some grades. However, in 1998 these payments were restricted to existing staff. The period since 1998 had seen an increase in the number of female recruits into what were traditionally male areas. Due to the change in the rules they were not eligible for the premium payments. The result was that overall in the eligible grades, men received on average two and a half times the amount of earnings from premium pay that women received.

---

83. Pay systems vary considerably. Pay systems that group jobs into pay grades or bands have traditionally treated jobs in the same grade or band as being of broadly equal value, either because they have been evaluated with similar scores under a job evaluation scheme, or because they are simply regarded as equivalent. However, recent years have seen a trend towards structures with fewer, broader grades or bands and greater use of performance pay and market factors. A single broad band or grade may contain jobs or roles of significantly different value because it encompasses a wide range of job evaluation scores. This, coupled with a wider use of other determinants of pay and more complex methods of pay progression, means that it is important for employers to check all aspects of the pay system from a variety of standpoints: design, implementation, and impact on men and women.[30]

---

29 Case study taken from *Monitoring Progress Towards Pay Equality*, Neathey, Dench & Thomson, Institute for Employment Studies, EOC 2003.
30 The EOC Equal Pay Review Kit Guidance Note 6: Reviewing your payment systems, policies and practices.

20   Code of Practice on Equal Pay

STEP 5: Developing an equal pay action plan and/or reviewing and monitoring

84. Where the reason for the pay difference is connected with sex, employers will need to provide equal pay for current and future employees.

85. Employers who find no gaps between men's and women's pay, or who find gaps for which there are genuinely non-discriminatory reasons, should nevertheless keep their pay systems under review by introducing regular monitoring undertaken jointly with trade unions. This will ensure that the pay system remains free of sex bias.

Example[31] – developing an action plan
Following the review, an Action Plan looking at internal processes was developed. This is ongoing and is reviewed through partnership processes. The aim is to integrate equal pay issues into employee relations' work.

Early action has been in relation to internal recruitment processes. This included looking at whether people were encouraged (or not) to apply for particular jobs. This lack of recognition of potential opportunities was closing off progression routes to some groups, and impacting on the organisational gender pay gap. The organisation also found that it had a body of staff (mainly women) that did not seek promotion. A challenge for the organisation was to encourage more women to aim for promotion, especially once they had fewer family responsibilities.

The remuneration manager anticipated that the gender pay gap in the main staff would fall from the 13 per cent identified in the pay review to under five per cent over the following five years. A recent repeat of the review had already shown a fall, however, the decline in the gap might not always be maintained. This is because the company's pay system is highly market sensitive and a tightening of the labour market in areas in which men are in the majority (such as Information Technology) would have a negative impact on the downward trend.

---

31 Case study taken from *Monitoring Progress Towards Pay Equality*, Neathey, Dench & Thomson, Institute for Employment Studies, EOC 2003.

SECTION THREE: An equal pay policy

The organisation's intentions in respect of equal pay

86. It is good equal pay practice to provide employees with a clear statement of the organisation's intentions in respect of equal pay. Evidence of an equal pay policy may assist an employer's defence against an equal pay claim

87. It is recommended that an equal pay policy should:
- Commit the organisation to carry out an equal pay review and to monitor pay regularly in partnership with trade union/employee representatives
- Set objectives
- Identify the action to be taken
- Implement that action in a planned programme in partnership with the workforce
- Assign responsibility and accountability for the policy to a senior manager
- Commit the organisation to set aside the resources necessary to achieve equal pay.

88. Everyone involved in setting the pay of staff should be committed to and, if possible, trained in the identification of sex discrimination in the pay process.

A model equal pay policy

We are committed to the principle of equal pay for all our employees. We aim to eliminate any sex bias in our pay systems.

We understand that equal pay between men and women is a legal right under both domestic and European law.

It is in the interest of the organisation to ensure that we have a fair and just pay system. It is important that employees have confidence in the process of eliminating sex bias and we are therefore committed to working in partnership with the recognised trade unions. As good business practice we are committed to working with trade union/employee representatives to take action to ensure that we provide equal pay.

We believe that in eliminating sex bias in our pay system we are sending a positive message to our staff and customers. It makes good business sense to have a fair, transparent reward system and it helps us to control costs. We recognise that avoiding unfair discrimination will improve morale and enhance efficiency.

Our objectives are to:
- Eliminate any unfair, unjust or unlawful practices that impact on pay
- Take appropriate remedial action.

We will:
- Implement an equal pay review in line with EOC guidance for all current staff and starting pay for new staff (including those on maternity leave, career breaks, or non-standard contracts)
- Plan and implement actions in partnership with trade union/employee representatives
- Provide training and guidance for those involved in determining pay
- Inform employees of how these practices work and how their own pay is determined
- Respond to grievances on equal pay as a priority
- In conjunction with trade union/employee representatives, monitor pay statistics annually.

Annex A

Other legislation that may impact on pay

The Race Relations Act 1976 & the Race Relations (Amendment) Act 2000 require employers not to discriminate on grounds of race or ethnicity. This means that a black or minority ethnic employee could bring a discrimination claim seeking the same rate of pay as a white colleague in the same circumstances, who is either of the same or the opposite sex. The Race Relations (Amendment) Act 2000 imposes a duty on public bodies to promote race equality. The Commission for Racial Equality can provide advice on specific issues relating to race or ethnicity.

The Transfer of Undertakings (Protection of Employment) Regulations 1981 protects the rights of workers in the event of a relevant transfer of an undertaking to a new employer. All contracts of employment and employment relationships automatically transfer to the new employer at the date of transfer. The Regulations prohibit changes in contract terms connected with a relevant transfer. (At present, terms relating to pensions do not transfer (except for some enhanced redundancy rights). The Government is consulting on this and may introduce a requirement that a transferee provides an equivalent pension to that provided by the transferor).

The Pregnant Workers Directive 1992 states that all women are entitled to a minimum of 14 weeks maternity leave. However, United Kingdom law provides for more than this. (See under Employment Rights Act 1996, as amended by the Employment Relations Act 1999 and the Maternity and Parental Leave (Amendment) Regulations 2002).

The Trade Union Labour Relations (Consolidation) Act 1992 and the Acas codes of practice on the disclosure of information and on disciplinary practice set out the regulations on the sharing of information for the purposes of collective bargaining between the employer and recognised trade unions.

The Disability Discrimination Act 1995 requires an employer with 15 or more employees not to discriminate against disabled employees. Discrimination, which includes discrimination in relation to pay, means, without justification, treating a person less favourably for a reason related to his disability or failing to make a reasonable adjustment to a physical feature of premises or to working arrangements, which place the disabled employee at a substantial disadvantage.

Currently, the Disability Discrimination Act does not, in certain circumstances, make unlawful differences in pay linked to performance (cf. the Disability Discrimination (Employment) Regulations 1996, Reg 3). However, legislation being implemented from 1 October 2004 will end both that limitation and the exemption of smaller employers. Also from 1 October 2004, direct discrimination, for example actions based purely on prejudice against disabled people, will no longer be capable of justification, and nor will a failure to make reasonable adjustments. The Disability Rights Commission can provide advice on specific issues relating to disability.

The Pensions Act 1995 provides for equal treatment in occupational pension schemes. It does so by incorporating an equal treatment rule into every occupational pension scheme. The Occupational Pension Schemes (Equal Treatment) Regulations 1995 set out the procedural rules for enforcing any rights under the equal treatment rule. The Regulations adopt the procedural structures contained in the Equal Pay Act, with some modifications, such as removing the power to grant compensation for breach of the equal treatment rule.

The Employment Rights Act 1996 requires employers to issue a written statement of terms and conditions of employment. The Act also provides the framework for maternity rights the detail of which is set out in the Maternity and Parental Leave Regulations 1999 (see next page).

The Data Protection Act 1998 does not list pay as sensitive information although it is personal data. Information about ethnic origin and medical data is listed as sensitive. The DPA does allow information about ethnic origin to be processed *'if it is necessary for the purpose of identifying or keeping under review the existence or absence of equality of opportunity of treatment between persons of different racial or ethnic origins, with a view to enabling such equality to be promoted or maintained, and is carried out with appropriate safeguards for the rights and freedoms of the data subjects'* (Sched.3 paragraph 9 of the DPA).

The Working Time Regulations 1998 set a maximum limit on how many hours people can work and provides a statutory entitlement to 20 days paid holiday per annum.

The National Minimum Wage Act 1998 and the National Minimum Wage Regulations 1999 set minimum hourly wage for all workers aged 18 and over. There is a separate lower rate for workers under the age of 18.

The Maternity and Parental Leave Regulations 1999, as amended by the Maternity and Parental Leave (Amendment) Regulations 2002, provide for Ordinary Maternity Leave of 26 weeks for all mothers whose expected week of childbirth is after 6 April 2003, and Additional Maternity Leave of a further 26 weeks for employees with sufficient length of service.

The Part-Time (Prevention of Less Favourable Treatment) Regulations 2000 give part-time male and female workers a right not to be treated less favourably than full-time workers unless any difference in treatment can be objectively justified. The regulations apply to all aspects of pay and conditions of employment (contractual and non-contractual) and will usually require that the part-time worker should be paid and receive other benefits on a pro-rata basis.

The part-timer can make comparison with a full-timer of the same sex, but otherwise, the range of comparators is more restricted than under the Equal Pay Act. Although the regulations apply to both employees and workers, a part-time worker has to name a full-time worker (not a full-time employee) as a comparator. Likewise, a part-time employee has to name a full-time employee (not a full-time worker) as

comparator. In either case, the comparator has to be doing the same or broadly similar work, so there is no scope for an 'equal value' claim under the regulations.

There is also no scope for a part-timer to name a comparator working for a different employer (even an associated employer) and there are restrictions on naming a comparator based at a different site even if they are working for the same employer. Where a full-time worker or employee becomes part-time the appropriate comparison is with their own previous full-time terms and conditions.

The Fixed-Term Employees (Prevention of Less Favourable Treatment) Regulations 2002 give fixed-term employees the right to the same pay and terms and conditions of employment as permanent employees on broadly similar work, unless their less favourable treatment can be objectively justified. An employee can make a comparison with employees of the same sex, but the range of comparators is more restrictive than under the Equal Pay Act, for example, a fixed-term employee cannot select a predecessor as a comparator, nor can she/he make a comparison with someone working for an associated employer. The Fixed-term Employees Regulations do not apply to agency workers or apprentices.

The Regulations adopt a 'package approach', whereby an employer can justify the difference in treatment by showing that the value of the fixed-term employee's package of terms and conditions is at least equal to that of the permanent employee. This approach is not permissible under the Equal Pay Act.

The Employment Act 2002 empowers the Secretary of State to make regulations to enable workers on short term contracts to enjoy the rights and benefits of permanent workers, including pay. From October 2004 the Act will make it compulsory for employers and employees to use a three-stage grievance procedure. This should assist internal resolution of disputes. The Act also introduces the equal pay questionnaire procedure and improves maternity rights.

24   Code of Practice on Equal Pay

Annex B

Useful addresses

www.acas.org.uk
The Acas site contains basic guidance on pay systems and texts of leaflets which can be printed. Some publications can be ordered on-line.

www.cipd.co.uk
The site of the Chartered Institute of Personnel and Development.

www.cre.gov.uk
The site of the Commission for Racial Equality.

www.informationcommissioner.gov.uk
The site of the Office of the Information Commission.

www.drc-gb.org
The site of the Disability Rights Commission.

www.dti.gov.uk
The DTI site contains publications, fact sheets on employment rights and employment legislation.

www.eoc.org.uk
The site of the Equal Opportunities Commission (EOC). It contains basic guidance for employers on how to put equality into practice and texts of leaflets which can be printed. Some publications can be ordered on-line.

Equal Opportunities Commission Helpline
0845 601 5901(Calls charged at local rates)
Interpreting service available for callers to the Helpline
Typetalk service available on
18001 0845 601 5901

Great Britain
Arndale House, Arndale Centre,
Manchester M4 3EQ
email: info@eoc.org.uk

36 Broadway, London SW1H 0BH
email: media@eoc.org.uk
tel: 0207 222 1110
media enquiries only: 0207 222 0004

Scotland
St Stephens House,
279 Bath Street, Glasgow G2 4JL
email: scotland@eoc.org.uk

Wales
Windsor House, Windsor Lane,
Cardiff CF10 3GE
email: wales@eoc.org.uk

www.eordirect.com
The site of Equal Opportunities Review, which has an extensive database of articles on equal pay. Users can search the cases database for tribunal and court decisions.

www.incomesdata.co.uk
The site of Incomes Data Services, the independent organisation providing information on pay, pensions and employment.

www.irsemploymentreview.com
The site of Industrial Relations Services, the independent organisation providing information on pay, pensions and employment.

www.link-hrsystems.co.uk
Through Link's partnership with TMS Equality and Diversity Consultants, the Link Equal Pay Reviewer software forms a foundation for organisations to undertake a review. Following the EOC guidelines, it assists in the collation of data with easy-to-use tools for importing data from HR systems.

www.opportunitynow.org.uk
The site of Opportunity Now giving up to date information on the Equal Pay Forum.

www.e-reward.co.uk
The site offers advice, analysis and research on all aspects of compensation and benefits.

www.womenandequalityunit.gov.uk
The site of the DTI's Women and Equality Unit contains information on equal pay issues. This includes the text of the Government's guide to the Equal Pay Act and the equal pay questionnaire.

Women. Men. Different. Equal.
Equal Opportunities Commission

© EOC December 2003
ISBN 1 84206 094 5

INDEX

References are to paragraph numbers.